Poverty and Morality
Religious and Secular Perspectives

This multiauthored book explores how many influential ethical traditions – secular and religious, Western and non-Western – wrestle
with the moral dimensions of poverty and the needs of the poor.
These traditions include Buddhism, Christianity, Confucianism,
Hinduism, Islam, and Judaism, among the religious perspectives;
classical liberalism, feminism, liberal egalitarianism, and Marxism,
among the secular; and natural law, which might be claimed by both.
The basic questions addressed by each of these traditions are linked
to several overarching themes: what poverty is, the particular vul-
nerabilities of high-risk groups, responsibility for the occurrence
of poverty, preferred remedies, how responsibility for its alleviation is distributed, and priorities in the delivery of assistance. These
essays are preceded by a background chapter on the types, scope,
and causes of poverty in the modern world and some contemporary
strategies for eliminating it. The volume concludes with Michael
Walzer's broadly conceived commentary, which provides a direct
comparison of the presented views and makes suggestions for further study and policy.

William A. Galston is a Senior Fellow at the Brookings Institution.
He has also taught at the University of Maryland, College Park,
and served as deputy assistant to President Clinton and executive
director of the National Commission on Civic Renewal. His books
include *Liberal Pluralism: The Implications of Value Pluralism
for Political Theory and Practice* (Cambridge, 2002) and *Liberal
Purposes: Goods, Virtues, and Diversity in the Liberal State*
(Cambridge, 1991).

Peter H. Hoffenberg is associate professor of history at the
University of Hawai'i, Manoa, where his courses include Comparative Economic History and the History of Economic Thought. He
is the author of *An Empire on Display: English, Australian, and
Indian Exhibitions from the Crystal Palace to the Great War* (2001)
and numerous articles and book chapters. He is currently writing a
book about the British Empire and poverty.

The Ethikon Series in Comparative Ethics

Editorial Board
Carole Pateman, *Series Editor*
Robert P. George   Sohail H. Hashmi   Will Kymlicka
David Miller   Philip Valera   Michael Walzer

The Ethikon Series publishes comparative studies on ethical issues of current importance. By bringing together scholars representing a diversity of moral viewpoints to focus on common aspects of its topics, the series aims to broaden the scope of ethical discourse and to identify commonalities and differences among influential moral traditions.

TITLES IN THE SERIES

Brian Barry and Robert E. Goodin, eds., *Free Movement: Ethical Issues in the Transnational Migration of People and Money*

Chris Brown, ed., *Political Restructuring in Europe: Ethical Perspectives*

Terry Nardin, ed., *The Ethics of War and Peace: Religious and Secular Perspectives*

David R. Mapel and Terry Nardin, eds., *International Society: Diverse Ethical Perspectives*

David Miller and Sohail H. Hashmi, eds., *Boundaries and Justice: Diverse Ethical Perspectives*

Simone Chambers and Will Kymlicka, eds., *Alternative Conceptions of Civil Society*

Nancy L. Rosenblum and Robert Post, eds., *Civil Society and Government*

Sohail H. Hashmi, ed., Foreword by Jack Miles, *Islamic Political Ethics: Civil Society, Pluralism, and Conflict*

Richard Madsen and Tracy B. Strong, eds., *The Many and the One: Ethical Pluralism in the Modern World*

Margaret Moore and Allen Buchanan, eds., *States, Nations, and Borders: The Ethics of Making Boundaries*

Sohail H. Hashmi and Steven P. Lee, eds., *Ethics and Weapons of Mass Destruction: Religious and Secular Perspectives*

Michael Walzer, ed., *Law, Politics, and Morality in Judaism*

William M. Sullivan and Will Kymlicka, eds., *The Globalization of Ethics: Religious and Secular Perspectives*

Daniel A. Bell, ed., *Confucian Political Ethics*

John Coleman, S.J., ed., *Christian Political Ethics*

William A. Galston and Peter H. Hoffenberg, eds., *Poverty and Morality: Religious and Secular Perspectives*

Poverty and Morality

Religious and Secular Perspectives

Edited by

WILLIAM A. GALSTON

The Brookings Institution

PETER H. HOFFENBERG

University of Hawai'i, Manoa

CAMBRIDGE UNIVERSITY PRESS
Cambridge, New York, Melbourne, Madrid, Cape Town,
Singapore, São Paulo, Delhi, Tokyo, Mexico City

Cambridge University Press
32 Avenue of the Americas, New York, NY 10013-2473, USA

www.cambridge.org
Information on this title: www.cambridge.org/9780521127349

© The Ethikon Institute 2010

First published 2010
Reprinted 2011

A catalog record for this publication is available from the British Library.

Library of Congress Cataloging in Publication Data

Poverty and morality : religious and secular perspectives / edited by
William A. Galston, Peter H. Hoffenberg.
    p. cm. – (The Ethikon series in comparative ethics)
Includes bibliographical references and index.
ISBN 978-0-521-76374-5 (hardback) – ISBN 978-0-521-12734-9 (pbk.)
1. Poverty – Moral and ethical aspects. 2. Poverty – Religious aspects.
I. Galston, William A. (William Arthur), 1946– II. Hoffenberg, Peter H., 1960–
BJ53.P68   2010
170.86′942–dc22   2010030599

ISBN 978-0-521-76374-5 Hardback
ISBN 978-0-521-12734-9 Paperback

Contents

x   *Contents*

Contributors

SAKIKO FUKUDA-PARR is a professor in the New School University's Graduate Program in International Affairs. A development economist, she was formerly a research Fellow at Harvard University's Kennedy School of Government. Between 1995 and 2004, she was director and lead author of the *Annual Human Development Reports* of the United Nations Development Programme. She is currently writing a book on the Millennium Development Goals and shifts in international development agendas and norms. She is founding editor of the *Journal of Human Development* and serves on the editorial board of *Feminist Economics*.

WILLIAM A. GALSTON is a senior Fellow at the Brookings Institution, where he holds the Ezra Zilkha Chair in Governance Studies. He was formerly a professor in the School of Public Affairs and director of the Institute for Philosophy and Public Policy at the University of Maryland, College Park, and deputy assistant to President Clinton for domestic policy. He has also served as executive director of the National Commission on Civic Renewal. His books include *Liberal Pluralism: The Implications of Value Pluralism for Political Theory and Practice; Liberal Purposes: Goods, Virtues, and Diversity in the Liberal State;* and *Public Matters: Politics, Policy, and Religion in the 21st Century.* He is also the author of numerous articles on political philosophy, public policy, and American politics.

SOHAIL H. HASHMI is associate professor of international relations at Mount Holyoke College and serves on the editorial board of the Ethikon Series in Comparative Ethics. He is coeditor of *Boundaries and Justice* (with David Miller) and *Ethics and Weapons of Mass Destruction* (with Steven Lee). He is currently writing a book analyzing the contemporary Islamic discourse on the rise of international law. He is also developing a book on Islamic conceptions of distributive justice.

NANCY J. HIRSCHMANN is the R. Jean Brownlee Professor of Political Science at the University of Pennsylvania. She is the author of *Gender, Class, and Freedom in Modern Political Theory; The Subject of Liberty: Toward a Feminist Theory of Freedom*, for which she received the American Political Science Association's 2004 Victoria Schuck Award for Best Book on Women and Politics; and *Rethinking Obligation: A Feminist Method for Political Theory*. She has also edited books on welfare, conceptual analysis, and John Locke and published articles in many books and journals on a wide range of topics, including household production, domestic violence, Islamic veiling, gender in the canon, and disability.

PETER H. HOFFENBERG is associate professor of history at the University of Hawai'i, Manoa, where he recently began a long-term study of poverty and the British Empire. He also teaches courses on British, British Empire, world, comparative imperial, and comparative economic histories. He is the author of *An Empire on Display: English, Australian, and Indian Exhibitions from the Crystal Palace to the Great War*. He has also published articles and book chapters on exhibitions, Indian art, travel, and landscape, most generally concerning nineteenth-century England, Australia, and India.

ANDREW LEVINE is currently a senior scholar at the Institute for Policy Studies and research professor in philosophy at the University of Maryland, College Park. He has written extensively on recent liberal theory and on historical figures including Marx, Rousseau, Locke, and Mill. Recent books include *Political Keywords; The American Ideology; Engaging Political Philosophy: Hobbes to Rawls*; and *A Future for Marxism? Althusser, the Analytical Turn, and the Revival of Socialist Theory*.

DAVID R. LOY is Besl Family Chair Professor of Ethics/Religion and Society at Xavier University in Cincinnati. He is the author of *Nonduality: A Study in Comparative Philosophy; Lack and Transcendence; A Buddhist History of the West: Studies in Lack; The Great Awakening: A Buddhist Social Theory; Money, Sex, War, Karma: Notes for a Buddhist Revolution*; and the forthcoming *Awareness Bound and Unbound*. He is a longtime Zen student and a *sensei* (teacher) in the Sanbo Kyodan tradition.

DARREL MOELLENDORF is professor of philosophy and director of the Institute for Ethics and Public Affairs at San Diego State University. He is the author of *Cosmopolitan Justice* and *Global Inequality Matters*; coeditor of *Global Justice: Seminal Essays, Current Debates in Global Justice,* and *Jurisprudence;* and the author of numerous scholarly articles and book chapters. From 1996 to 2002 he was a member of the philosophy department at the University of the Witwatersrand (Johannesburg, South Africa). In 2008–9 he was a member of the School of Social Sciences at the Institute for Advanced Study, Princeton, pursuing research on morality and climate change.

PETER NOSCO is professor of Asian studies at the University of British Columbia. A specialist in the intellectual and social history of early modern

Japan, he is the author of *Remembering Paradise: Nativism and Nostalgia in 18th Century Japan*; the editor of *Confucianism and Tokugawa Culture* and *Japanese Identity: Cultural Analyses*; and translator of Ihara Saikaku's *Some Final Words of Advice*. He has also been a guest editor of the *Japanese Journal of Religious Studies* (most recently for a special issue on Christians in Japan) and *Philosophy: East and West*. He is currently working on a study of the emergence of individuality in early modern Japan.

TOM G. PALMER is vice president for international programs at the Cato Institute, director of the Center for Promotion of Human Rights, a senior Fellow of the Institute, and director of Cato University, the Institute's educational arm. He has published chapters in several books as well as reviews and articles on politics and morality in many scholarly journals, including the *Harvard Journal of Law and Public Policy, Ethics, Critical Review*, and *Constitutional Political Economy*. He has also published in *Slate*, the *Wall Street Journal*, the *New York Times*, the *Washington Post*, and the *Spectator* of London.

STEPHEN J. POPE is professor of theological ethics at Boston College. He is the author of *Human Evolution and Christian Ethics* and the editor of *The Ethics of St. Thomas Aquinas* and *Solidarity and Hope: Jon Sobrino's Challenge to Christian Theology*. He is also the author of "Justice and Peace: Reintegration and Reconciliation of Returning Displaced Persons in Post-Conflict Situations," in *Refugee Rights: Ethics, Advocacy, and Africa*, ed. David Hollenbach, S.J. He is a member of the Society of Christian Ethics and the Catholic Theological Society of America.

ARVIND SHARMA is the Birks Professor of Comparative Religion at McGill University. He was also the convenor of the Global Congress on World Religions after September 11, which met in Montreal from September 11–15, 2006. He has published more than fifty books and numerous articles in the fields of comparative religion, Hinduism, Indian philosophy and ethics, and the role of women in religion. His most noteworthy publications include *Hinduism and Human Rights; The Hindu Gita: Ancient and Classical Interpretations of the Bhagavadgita; The Study of Hinduism;* and *A Guide to Hindu Spirituality*.

KENT A. VAN TIL is a visiting professor at Kuyper College, Grand Rapids, Michigan. His special area of focus is morality and economics. He is the author of *Less Than Two Dollars a Day: A Christian View of Poverty and the Free Market*. In addition, he has published a number of articles, including "A Biblical/Theological Case for Basic Sustenance for All" in the *Journal of Markets and Morality*; "Just Deserts: Beyond the Free Market" in the *Christian Century*; "Covenant, Community, and the Common Good: An Interpretation of Christian Ethics" in *Covenant Free Encyclopedia*; and "Subsidiarity and

Sphere-Sovereignty" in *Theological Studies*. He is currently working on an introductory text on Christian ethics.

MICHAEL WALZER is professor emeritus of social science at the Institute for Advanced Study, Princeton. His most recent book is *Thinking Politically*. He is also the author of *The Revolution of the Saints, Just and Unjust Wars, Spheres of Justice*, and *On Toleration*; coeditor of *The Jewish Political Tradition*, a four-volume set of texts and commentaries dealing with all aspects of Jewish political experience from biblical times to the present; a coeditor of *Dissent*; a contributing editor of the *New Republic*; and a member of the editorial board of the Ethikon Series in Comparative Ethics.

NOAM ZOHAR is associate professor in Jewish philosophy, director of the graduate program in bioethics, and chair of the general philosophy department at Bar-Ilan University. He teaches Rabbinics, philosophy of Halakhah, and moral and political philosophy. His recent books include *Quality of Life in Jewish Bioethics* and *Secrets of the Rabbinic Workshop: Redaction as a Key to Meaning* (in Hebrew). He is joint editor (with Michael Walzer and Menachem Lorberbaum) of *The Jewish Political Tradition*. He is also senior research Fellow at the Shalom Hartman Institute in Jerusalem and has been a faculty Fellow at Harvard University's Center for Ethics and a member of the school of social science at the Institute for Advanced Study, Princeton (2003–4).

Acknowledgments

This book is the result of a project in comparative ethics organized by the Ethikon Institute in collaboration with the Dominican Lay Scholars Community and the Shalom Hartman Institute of Jerusalem. The trustees of the Ethikon Institute join with Philip Valera, president, and Carole Pateman, series editor, in thanking all who contributed to the success of this project.

We are especially indebted to the Sidney Stern Memorial Trust and the Skirball Institute on American Values for their enabling financial support.

Special thanks are due to Marvin Hoffenberg for providing the idea for the project and to William A. Galston and Peter H. Hoffenberg for taking on the challenging task of editing this book. We are also grateful to Sohail H. Hashmi and Andrea Reynolds for their expert assistance in preparing the manuscript for publication and to Beatrice Rehl, our editor at Cambridge University Press, for her encouragement, valuable guidance, and support.

The Ethikon Institute

The Ethikon Institute, a nonprofit organization, is concerned with the social implications of ethical pluralism. Its dialogue-publication projects are designed to explore a diversity of moral outlooks, secular and religious, and to clarify areas of consensus and divergence among them. By encouraging a systematic exchange of ideas, the Institute aims to advance the prospects for agreement and to facilitate the peaceful accommodation of irreducible differences. The Ethikon Institute takes no position on issues that may divide its participants, serving not as an arbiter but as a neutral forum for the cooperative exploration of diverse and sometimes opposing views.

The Dominican Lay Scholars Community

The Dominican Lay Scholars Community is an ecumenical organization that promotes both interreligious contact and carefully structured dialogue between religious scholars and professional scholars in other intellectual disciplines. Among its other objectives, the DLSC encourages a systematic and impartial search for common intellectual ground among secular and religious outlooks on a wide range of important issues.

The Shalom Hartman Institute

The Shalom Hartman Institute is a research and leadership training institute whose mission is to revitalize Judaism, strengthen Jewish identity, and foster religious pluralism by providing scholars, rabbis, educators, and lay leaders of all denominations with tools to address the central challenges facing Judaism.

I

Introduction

William A. Galston and Peter H. Hoffenberg

"The poor are always with us" – at all times, in every society. Nonetheless, societies have responded differently to the enduring questions such privation raises: who is poor, why are some poor while others are not, and what (if anything) should be done about their condition?

In keeping with the Ethikon Institute's mission of addressing significant global public policy questions in its Series in Comparative Ethics, this volume explores how great moral traditions, secular and religious, Western and non-Western, wrestle with basic questions about poverty and the poor. These traditions include Buddhism, Christianity, Confucianism, Hinduism, Islam, and Judaism among the religious perspectives; classical liberalism, feminism, liberal egalitarianism, and Marxism among the secular; and natural law, which might be claimed by both.

Contributors to this volume were asked to discuss how their particular traditions deal with questions clustered around overarching themes.[1] What is poverty? Who are the poor? Is poverty a matter only of material conditions?[2] Are some people poor because of their own choices? Is poverty a deserved (if unintended) consequence of individuals' behavior? Are some individuals and groups more vulnerable and thus more likely to become impoverished? Is it the responsibility of the nonpoor to reduce – or, if possible, eliminate – poverty? Or should they eschew direct intervention on the grounds that such action might not alleviate poverty but rather worsen it or exacerbate other social problems? To what extent is the alleviation – or abolition – of poverty a feasible option? Which measures are likely to be most effective and ethically appropriate? Should these measures be undertaken by the government,

---

[1] The complete list of "topic-related questions" for the authors includes the definitions of poverty, identification of high-risk groups, role of volition, goals of poverty-related ideas and programs, remedies, scope and priorities, and responsibility and conditionality.

[2] World Bank South Asia recently estimated that about 1.1 billion people in South Asia live on less than two dollars per day; 700 million in India live on less than that; and 300 million people in India live on less than one dollar per day.

individuals, or voluntary organizations – or some combination? Who should receive assistance? And what are the limits to individual and communal obligations?

It should come as no surprise that the great religious and philosophical traditions respond to these questions in highly diverse ways. Not only do they offer different answers to the core questions poverty raises; they arrive at those answers in different ways. The moral and ethical authority might lie in sacred texts, bodies of law – witness the Jewish halakhic-based and Muslim *shari'a*-based responses to poverty and the poor – or the philosophy of leading thinkers.[3] Does one refer to the writings of John Locke, John Stuart Mill, and John Rawls when considering what to do about poverty and the poor, or to the Hebrew Bible and the Talmud, the New Testament and the Qur'an? The essays in this volume prompt us to wonder whether we are compelled to choose between secular and religious approaches to poverty.

Indeed, these approaches share an important characteristic: most were developed in circumstances in which individuals, households, and local communities took principal responsibility for identifying the poor and alleviating their plight. This raises a practical question: how, if at all, do these approaches apply in modern conditions, when the definition of poverty reflects economic theory and data and its rectification often falls to national and international institutions? To illuminate (though not to answer) this question, the volume begins with a background essay on "Global Poverty and Unequal Development: Contemporary Trends and Issues." Authored by Sakiko Fukuda-Parr, director and lead author of the *Annual Human Development Reports* of the United Nations Development Programme, this essay provides the quantitative global picture of the poor and poverty and also outlines thinking among key economists and policy makers concerning the types, scope, and causes of poverty and its remedies in the modern world.

As Fukuda-Parr notes, recent history offers examples of both success and failure. For example, economic growth in China and India has significantly reduced income-based poverty in those polities. By contrast, income-based poverty in other parts of South Asia and nearly all of sub-Saharan Africa has proved less tractable. Such uneven development can also be seen in the disproportionate number of women and children all around the world living and dying in poverty.

On the conceptual level, there remain disagreements about the precise working definition of poverty, a debate often focusing on whether a specific income level defines poverty, whether it is better viewed in relative terms, or perhaps in noneconomic terms such as social exclusion or deprivation of

---

[3] Jill Jacobs, "Toward a Halakhic Definition of Poverty," *Conservative Judaism* 57, no. 1 (Fall 2004): 3–20; and Adam Sabra, *Poverty and Charity in Medieval Islam: Mamluk Egypt, 1250–1517*, Cambridge Studies in Islamic Civilization (Cambridge: Cambridge University Press, 2000).

capabilities.[4] (The work of Amartya Sen, a Nobel laureate in economics, is of particular importance in this debate; his contributions to the questions of poverty and the poor inform several of the following essays, most significantly the ones on feminism and liberal egalitarianism.)[5] Not surprisingly, differing definitions of poverty often result in further disagreements about whether progress is being made in the war against poverty and, if so, where and at what cost.

There are also major disagreements about the relationships among growth, prosperity, equality, and poverty.[6] Many scholars argue that efforts by institutions and governments to fight poverty through policies of income redistribution and employment protection end up reducing economic efficiency, growth, and wealth, thereby increasing poverty. Perhaps economic growth and direct measures to enforce equality are not compatible; but what about economic growth and poverty reduction, a query pondered in the classical and egalitarian liberal traditions? What should be the balance between promoting economic growth and attacking poverty, notably when growth exacerbates inequality (as has often been the case in recent decades)? Would it be more efficient and equitable to practice trickle-down or percolate-up growth policies?[7] Those are not new queries. After all, Adam Smith and his colleagues in the Scottish Enlightenment investigated strategies for generating

---

[4] Helpful consideration and comparison of different definitions of poverty are included in Dag Ehrenpreis, ed., *Poverty in Focus: What Is Poverty? Concepts and Measures* (Brasilia: International Poverty Centre, United Nations Development Programme, 2006); Frances Stewart, Ruhi Saith, and Barbara Harriss-White, eds., *Defining Poverty in the Developing World* (New York: Palgrave, 2007), esp. Stewart, Saith, and Caterina Ruggeri Laderchi, "Introduction: Four Approaches to Defining and Measuring Poverty," 1–35; and Paul Spicker, *The Idea of Poverty* (London: Policy Press, 2007).

[5] Among other works, see "Poverty as Capability Deprivation," *Development as Freedom* (New York: Anchor Books, 1999), 86–110.

[6] The classic post-1945 analysis of comparative national economic growth remains Simon Kuznets, *Modern Economic Growth: Rate, Structure and Spread* (New Haven: Yale University Press, 1966). More recently, the various relationships among inequality, growth, wealth, and poverty are discussed in Benjamin M. Friedman, *The Moral Consequences of Economic Growth* (New York: Knopf, 2005); Liah Greenfeld, *The Spirit of Capitalism: Nationalism and Economic Growth* (Cambridge, MA: Harvard University Press, 2002); Fred Hirsch, *Social Limits to Growth* (Cambridge, MA: Harvard University Press, 1978); Jonas Pontusson, *Inequality and Prosperity: Social Europe vs. Liberal America* (Ithaca, NY: Cornell University Press, 2005); Theo S. Eicher and Stephen J. Turnovsky, eds., *Inequality and Growth: Theory and Policy Implications* (Cambridge, MA: MIT Press, 2007); Paul Johnson, "The Welfare State, Income and Living Standards," in *The Cambridge Economic History of Modern Britain*, vol. 3: *Structural Change and Growth, 1939–2000*, ed. Roderick Floud and Paul Johnson (Cambridge: Cambridge University Press, 2004), 213–37; and Laura de Dominicis, Raymond J. G. M. Florax, and Henri L. F. de Groot, "A Meta-Analysis on the Relationship between Income Inequality and Economic Growth," *Scottish Journal of Political Economy* 55, no. 5 (November 2008): 654–82.

[7] Santonu Basu and Shushanta Mallick, "When Does Growth Trickle Down to the Poor? The Indian Case," *Cambridge Journal of Economics* 32, no. 3 (May 2008): 461–77.

wealth, enhancing liberty, and reducing "pauperism" while trying to solve the riddle of "why some nations are so rich and some so poor."[8] Economists and others attempt to understand the possible connections between international trade and finance on one hand and poverty and inequality on the other. Do global institutions such as the World Bank, movements such as the liberalization of international trade, and overseas policies including foreign aid affect the poor and poverty itself?[9] If so, what are the effects of such globalization, or economic integration, on the poor and poverty, within and among nations?[10] Might globalization benefit the poor and

[8] Istvan Hont, "The 'Rich Country–Poor Country' Debate in Scottish Classical Political Economy," in *Wealth and Virtue: The Shaping of Political Economy in the Scottish Enlightenment*, ed. Hont and Michael Ignatieff (Cambridge: Cambridge University Press, 1983), 271–315; and David S. Landes, *The Wealth and Poverty of Nations: Why Some Are So Rich and Some So Poor* (New York: W. W. Norton, 1998). Scholarship on the early political economists' views and policies regarding "pauperism" includes Mary Poovey, *A History of the Modern Fact: Problems of Knowledge in the Sciences of Wealth and Society* (Chicago: University of Chicago Press, 1998); Donald Winch, *Riches and Poverty: An Intellectual History of Political Economy in Britain, 1750–1834* (Cambridge: Cambridge University Press, 1996); and D. P. O'Brien, "3. Pauperism," in O'Brien, *The Classical Economists Revisited* (Princeton, NJ: Princeton University Press, 2004), 337–39.

[9] The relationships among trade, finance, and poverty as interconnected global phenomena are the subject of a recent explosion of policy studies and publications. The main contours and points of disagreement if not outright opposition on such issues can be discerned by comparing Joseph E. Stiglitz, *Globalization and Its Discontents* (New York: W. W. Norton, 2002), and Deepak Lal, *Reviving the Invisible Hand: The Case for Classical Liberalism in the Twenty-first Century* (Princeton, NJ: Princeton University Press, 2006). For discussion of trade liberalization and other international measures, including the importance of a case-by-case approach, and their consequences for both growth and poverty, see Richard Kneller, C. W. Morgan, and Sunti Kanchanahatakij, "Trade Liberalisation and Economic Growth," *World Economy* 31, no. 6 (June 2008): 701–19; Stijn Claessens, Geoffrey R. D. Underhill, and Xiaoke Zhang, "The Political Economy of Basle II: The Costs for Poor Countries," *World Economy* 31, no. 3 (March 2008): 313–44; and Bernard M. Hoekman and Marcelo Olarreaga, *Global Trade and Poor Nations: The Poverty Impacts and Policy Implications of Liberalization* (Washington, DC: Brookings Institution Press, 2007). Among the economic, political, and to a degree moral connections considered is that between poverty and foreign aid. What are the effects on the poor and poorer nations of the international system of foreign aid? Might the efficiency and impact of foreign aid as a tool to fight poverty be improved? What should be the focus of foreign aid if the goal is poverty reduction? These are among the topics discussed in William Easterly, *The White Man's Burden: Why the West's Efforts to Aid the Rest Have Done so Much Ill and So Little Good* (New York: Penguin Books, 2006), and Easterly, *Reinventing Foreign Aid* (Cambridge, MA: MIT Press, 2008). Some scholars ask the fundamental question of whether aid itself is the most sensible approach to poverty reduction. Among examples of such considerations is John Weiss, "The Aid Paradigm for Poverty Reduction: Does It Make Sense?" *Development Policy Review* 26, no. 4 (July 2008): 407–26.

[10] The impact of global economic integration on poverty within and between nations is considered in Dani Rodrik, *One Economics, Many Recipes: Globalization, Institutions, and Economic Growth* (Princeton, NJ: Princeton University Press, 2007); M. Shahid Alam, *Poverty from the Wealth of Nations: Integration and Polarization in the Global Economy since 1760* (New York: Palgrave, 2000); and Ann Harrison, ed., *Globalization and*

help reduce poverty, as some contend?[11] Or does economic integration across borders increase poverty and inequality? Might the causes of success and failure in countries such as Bangladesh and the Ivory Coast be found in matters of local culture, including religion? Does poverty reflect domestic political institutions or geographic circumstances, and how should such specifics shape poverty-fighting policies? Do these more local factors interact with international institutions and actions to relieve or rather perpetuate poverty? As Fukuda-Parr's overview reveals, these and other queries remain controversial among both experts and the general public.

These contemporary issues challenge the great religious and philosophical traditions without undermining their relevance. Some – the Catholic natural law tradition, for example – have spent much of the past century rethinking the relationship between the basic premises of their creed and the distinctive features of modern economies, and their teachings have proved widely influential. Others, such as Islam, have been integrated into the legal architecture of modern nations-states. Scholars studying Asian nations have probed the influence of historic traditions such as Buddhism and Confucianism on the organization of their economies. And, of course, philosophical traditions such as the variants of liberalism have developed with modern economies and political institutions steadily in view.

"Poverty is a hydra," Kent van Til proclaims in his chapter on "Poverty and Morality in Christianity." That is not a minority view. Reflections on the

Poverty: National Bureau of Economic Research Conference Report (Chicago: University of Chicago Press, 2007). Daniel Cohen changes the nature of the discussion by contending that the poorer nations neither gain from nor are exploited by globalization. Rather, they are forgotten, ignored, and excluded, thus essentially victims of the unbridgeable gap between economic expectations and resources. See *Globalization and Its Enemies* (Cambridge, MA: MIT Press, 2007). The vast contemporary literature on the relationship between public policy and global poverty more often than not places the problems in the historical and current frameworks of "The West and the Rest." Such works include Easterly, *The White Man's Burden*; Paul Collier, *The Bottom Billion: Why the Poorest Countries Are Failing and What Can Be Done about It* (New York: Oxford University Press, 2007); and Landes, *The Wealth and Poverty of Nations*. China's economic growth and political grasp, not to mention appetite for natural resources, have now placed it alongside "the West" as a source of foreign aid and investment.

[11] Among the most controversial and influential "neoliberal" supporters of globalization's antipoverty consequences is Jagdish Bhagwati, the prominent South Asian economist. He claims that multinationals "can have a potentially major role to play in the alleviation of poverty" – as long as "their adverse effects can be removed by appropriate domestic policies." See "Why Multinationals Help Reduce Poverty," *World Economy* 30, no. 2 (February 2007): 211–28; *In Defense of Globalization* (New York: Oxford University Press, 2004); and *Free Trade Today* (Princeton, NJ: Princeton University Press, 2004). Bhagwati has most recently argued that international trade can address questions of growth and poverty if it is without what he terms "termites," or preferential agreements, which, in fact, create unfair and unfree trade. Please see *Termites in the Trading System* (New York: Oxford University Press, 2008).

poor and poverty typically reveal the ways in which various strands of human thought and behavior – material, ethnic, and intangible – are interwoven.[12] The famous "Adam Smith Problem" – the seeming contradiction between the *Theory of Moral Sentiments* and the *Wealth of Nations* – is in essence the same as a query raised by Max Weber more than a century later and renewed by this volume's contributors: what is the relationship in human nature and society between the pursuit of material self-interest and the moral connections binding members of the social order – in ethical terms, between virtue and greed, cooperation and competition?

One group of scholars has recently argued that exchange itself makes us more virtuous, thereby combining the moral and material objectives of modern society and economy.[13] That is not the conclusion reached by most of the traditions represented in this volume. The contributors do consider, however, the way their particular tradition theorizes the relationship between morality and the market. Much is at stake in naming and describing this "hydra," not the very least what Barrington Moore Jr. has called "the moral aspects of economic growth."[14]

Among the foundational issues with which the contributors grapple are conceptions of self and society, human nature and the good life. David Loy's "The Karma of Poverty: A Buddhist Perspective" suggests how Buddhist societies and practicing Buddhists turn to "four noble truths" to define, address, and endure poverty. Texts and principles guide responses to poverty and the poor, including the ways in which impoverishment is considered a cause of *dukkha*, or ill-being, suffering, and delusions. Buddhism offers a way of thinking about poverty and wealth that challenges most "Western" approaches. Negotiating the tensions between spirituality and materialism, that tradition recognizes that extreme impoverishment makes it difficult to follow the intended spiritual path and that wealth can be used properly. That claim is consistent with Buddhism's critique of consumerism and materialism, and of the values often accompanying the pursuit of wealth and higher standards of living. Unlike most of the traditions considered in this volume, Buddhism

---

[12] Robert C. Lieberman, *Shaping Race Policy: The United States in Comparative Perspective* (Princeton, NJ: Princeton University Press, 2007).

[13] Paul J. Zak, ed., *Moral Markets: The Critical Role of Values in the Economy* (Princeton, NJ: Princeton University Press, 2008). Also see, Daniel Friedman, *Morals and Markets: An Evolutionary Account of the Modern World* (New York: Palgrave Macmillan, 2008).

[14] Barrington Moore Jr., *Moral Aspects of Economic Growth, and Other Essays* (Ithaca, NY: Cornell University Press, 1998). Among the other essays in this collection, "Principles of Inequality" pursues the historical reasons for the failure of egalitarian projects, most notably in the modern compulsion for social coordination and the division of labor. One could contrast Moore's fatalism about the pursuit of equality with W. G. Runciman's more optimistic challenge for governments, such as Great Britain's and other Western ones, to at the very least reduce the probability that children born into poverty become impoverished parents themselves. See "Commentary: Always with Us? Why There Does Not Have to Be an Underclass," *Times Literary Supplement*, December 11, 1998, 13–16.

offers a fundamental rethinking of the self and of the individual's relationships with others as a guide to the right pursuit and use of material wealth. (Darrell Moellendorf does point out some of the ethical considerations in egalitarian liberalism concerning equality, rights, and distributive justice that might prompt a reconsideration of the unchecked pursuit of wealth.)

One might readily add to the list of foundational issues how the traditions define one's moral obligation to individuals and groups, whether others are considered to be "one of us," and whether membership is defined according to religious, civic, household, ethnic, or other criteria. Do particular traditions make room for obligations to nonmembers, to "strangers"? Do certain societies and their leading moral traditions make distinctions among those who are poor, focusing on women and children, for example, or those who are thought to be deserving? The sociology inherent in each moral tradition sheds light on such matters. In the case of Hinduism, for example, Arvind Sharma argues that distinctions among castes helps explain that tradition's historical and contemporary responses to poverty in India.

The idea of differentiating among those recognized as poor is an old one. During the medieval period in Europe, distinctions were made between the "shamefaced poor" and others, thus between those who deserved charity and those who did not.[15] The distinction between the deserving and the undeserving poor, allegedly rendered obsolete in the West by the rise of the welfare state, has witnessed a revival during the past generation. Today, we often distinguish between the working poor and others.

Such distinctions are connected to larger issues. Have some subordinate groups been understood as inferior, hence undeserving, or as unfairly vulnerable, hence deserving? For example, when did the category of "child poverty" arise, and why does it denote such a compelling problem? Is it a common concern among various societies, cultures, and ethical traditions? Do some traditions differentiate child poverty from other kinds because of an ethically grounded understanding of how children should be treated? Peter Nosco's discussion of Confucianism's emphasis on households and Nancy J. Hirschmann's exploration of feminist understandings of motherhood both shed light on the familial relationships that shape poverty.

The link between gender and poverty is at the heart of Hirschmann's chapter, "Poverty and Morality: A Feminist Perspective," in which she considers the reasons for the disproportionate number of women living in poverty, and the structural and cultural chains that often prevent women from escaping those conditions.[16] The debate in the West about the "feminization of poverty"

---

[15] Bronislaw Geremek, *Poverty: A History* (Malden, MA: Blackwell, 1997).

[16] For example, women tend to endure longer periods of unemployment, or longer periods between jobs. A recent analysis of "durations of unemployment" in China suggests that women are just as serious about getting a new job but that their efforts are obstructed by gender-based obstacles, such as lack of access to social networks, unfair treatment with respect to mandatory retirement, and unequal entitlement or access to reemployment

has non-Western correlates. The chapters on Buddhism and Islam also consider the ways by which gender and poverty intersect. The Buddhist approach
is not without its own internal dilemmas – for example, the contrast between
the high social status of monks who achieve *karma* and the low social status
of women who do not. The public problem of female prostitution in Buddhist
societies is one of the more extreme examples of this tension.

Another threshold issue is whether a tradition views poverty as a moral
and ethical challenge that must be publicly acknowledged and addressed.
John Stuart Mill wrote in the 1830s that the modern age, or "civilization," is
marked – and marred – by its determination to place whatever we find ugly
and disturbing far away and beyond sight. We build prisons not only to incar-
cerate criminals but also to hide them (the English once dispatched them to
the Antipodes); we place the insane in asylums; and we move to avoid living near or even interacting with the poor.[17] Acting against poverty requires
Western traditions to reconsider the moral and philosophical premises underlying these practices of separation. Should the poor share the public space
with the nonpoor? Do they have a right to be visible and audible, regardless of
the discomfort the better-off members of society may feel?

If the poor are experienced as threatening and thought of as unlike others, how can the more fortunate be motivated to take care of "the needs of
strangers"?[18] In light of the natural law tradition, for example, Stephen Pope
asks whether a society can be considered decent if it fails to address the needs
of the homeless, a group pushed to the margins. Can one make a greater leap
and cease thinking of the poor as strangers at all? Some of the traditions discussed in this volume, including Christianity, move us in this direction, setting
up a tension between communal ties and universal obligations.

The possibility that moral claims for assistance rest not on community
membership but rather on universal human ties raises a question about the
relationship between poverty and democracy. Most of the authors address
democracy as an ethical ideal and practice. To see why, we may turn to some
radical groups in seventeenth-century England that argued that the poor man
has as much rightful power and authority as the rich man. The poor were thus
part of the people or the commonwealth.[19] As the Leveller Colonel Thomas

services. See Fenglian Du and Xiao-yuan Dong, "Why Do Women Have Longer Durations
of Unemployment Than Men in Post-Restructuring China?" *Cambridge Journal of
Economics* 33, no. 2 (October 2008): 233–52.
[17] John Stuart Mill, "Civilization," in *Mill's Essays on Literature and Society*, ed. J. B.
Schneewind (New York: Collier Books, 1965), 148–82. The essay was originally published
in the April 1836 issue of the *London and Westminster Review*.
[18] Michael Ignatieff, *The Needs of Strangers* (New York: Picador Books, 1984).
[19] Christopher Hill, "The Poor and the People in Seventeenth Century England," in *History
from Below: Studies in Popular Protest and Popular Ideology*, ed. Frederick Krantz (New
York: Blackwell, 1988), 29–52; and David Wootton, "The Levellers," in *Democracy: The
Unfinished Journey, 508 B.C. to A.D. 1993*, ed. John Dunn (New York: Oxford University
Press, 1993), 71–89.

Rainsborough boldly proclaimed in 1647, "For really, I think that the Poorest he that is in England hath a life to live, as the greatest he."[20]

Those making such claims about the lives of the poor are what we may call normative democrats – which is not to say that, in practice, democratic publics will always choose to assist their poor, let alone the poor living outside their borders.

Indeed, the record of democracies in combating poverty and address-ing the needs of the poor is decidedly mixed. Many claim that democratic societies do more to improve the welfare of the poor, or at the very least, as Sen argues, avoid catastrophes such as famines, in contrast to undemocratic regimes. While some claims about the superiority of democratic governance in avoiding economic disaster and deprivation are empirically sound, others stand on shakier foundations.[21]

Among the moral dilemmas democracies face is the problem of inherited wealth. Can democratic societies eliminate or significantly reduce poverty without reshaping the intergenerational transmission of resources? As sev-eral of this volume's authors emphasize, this is not only an economic question but also an ethical one. Can democratic governments limit inheritance rights in the name of fighting poverty, for example, and argue that individual and familial rights to property can be compromised for the greater social good of sharing that property within the larger community?[22] In a number of tradi-tions, secular and religious, the answer to this question is affirmative, and the "larger community" is defined as including all human beings, wherever they may reside.

The essays in this volume invite – perhaps compel – readers to grapple with a number of painful and often-overlooked issues. Among them is violence – specifically, the moral and ethical relationship between violence and poverty. In what ways are coercion and violence, such as rape and war, connected to poverty? Some argue that individuals and groups are poor because they suffer systematic and structural violence. Are the poor not only more vulnerable to violence but also less likely to recover from it? If so, poverty may be at once a

---

[20] For an accessible transcript of the debate, see "The Putney Debates (the Second Day, 29 October 1647) in the Clarke Manuscripts," in *The Levellers in the English Revolution*, ed. G. E. Aylmer, Documents of Revolution, series ed. Heinz Lubasz (Ithaca, NY: Cornell University Press, 1975), 97–130.

[21] Is it true that nondemocracies treat their poor worse than democracies do? A recent study reveals that democratic countries spend more money than authoritarian ones on education and health but that the benefits of such expenses are more often than not enjoyed dispro-portionately by the nonpoor, the middle- and upper-income groups. Also, democracy has little if any effect on infant and child mortality rates among the poor. See Michael Ross, "Is Democracy Good for the Poor?" *American Journal of Political Science* 50, no. 4 (October 2006): 860–74.

[22] Those and complementary questions about inheritance law in France, Germany, and the United States are addressed in Jens Beckert, *Inherited Wealth*, trans. Thomas Dunlap (Princeton, NJ: Princeton University Press, 2007).

cause *and* a result of violence. From a different but connected point of view, many contend that poverty morally justifies acts of violence to overcome the condition of impoverishment and perhaps achieve equality, or a lessening of inequality. There is a hint of that "just war" on the part of the poor in Pope's discussion of Bartolome de las Casas and his moral defense of Amerindians in the face of the brutal sixteenth-century conquest of the Americas.[23]

The essays on Buddhism, feminism, and Marxism also refer in various ways to the importance of violence in understanding poverty and the poor. The introductory discussion of current economic studies concerns violence, including war and rape, as a cause of poverty or, at the very least, an obstacle to overcoming it. Violence directed against individuals, groups, and their property is also connected to questions of personal and public security. It is widely recognized that poverty is both a cause of insecurity and a consequence of such insecurity, most notably in the cases of weak states and civil wars.[24]

Mancur Olson once asked, "Why is the 'right' to protection from poverty or low income less amenable to solution by legal or constitutional fiat than some other problems?"[25] Many traditions have indeed offered laws and policies to do just that. Sometimes the proposed solution has included the right to a living or "basic" wage.[26] Other efforts in this direction have focused not on income

---

[23] See Bartolome de las Casas, *The Devastation of the Indies: A Brief Account*, trans. Herma Briffaul, ed. Bill M. Donovan (1522; Baltimore: Johns Hopkins University Press, 1992).

[24] Lael Brainhard and Derek Chollet, eds., *Too Poor for Peace? Global Poverty, Conflict and Security in the 21st Century* (Washington, DC: Brookings Institution Press, 2007). For a provocative analysis of the relationship between economic development and violence, see Amy Chua, *World on Fire: How Exporting Free Market Democracy Breeds Ethnic Hatred and Global Instability* (New York: Doubleday, 2004). Closely connected to questions of economic and security policies is that of food supply and pricing, the convergence of issues sometimes referred to as "food security." For a discussion of how international economic institutions and their policies affect food and poverty, see John Madeley, *Hungry for Trade: How the Poor Pay for Free Trade* (Halifax: Fernwood Publishing, 2000).

[25] Mancur Olson, "A Less Ideological Way of Deciding How Much Should Be Given to the Poor," *Daedalus* 112, no. 4 (Fall 1983): 217–36.

[26] Carole Pateman, for example, has argued that a "basic income" policy would be a more efficient and just way not only to confront poverty but also to fulfil ideals of democratic citizenship. Others have pointed out that the inability to secure a regular living wage makes men and women – particularly women – vulnerable to health and security problems. The lack of that wage might not be the immediate cause of poverty, but it is a proximate or only slightly removed cause. A guaranteed income was proposed in recent American history as an alternative to welfare payments and considered by various presidential advisors, elected officials, and economists as a way to ensure basic economic security. In addition to considerable political opposition, recommendations for a guaranteed income in various different forms also confronted some of the cultural and ethical dilemmas in the distinction between the "deserving" and "undeserving" poor and in the discussion of whether such a policy would be a question of charity or of justice. For further discussion, see Brian Steensland, *The Failed Welfare Revolution: America's Struggle over Guaranteed Income Policy* (Princeton, NJ: Princeton University Press, 2007).

but rather on the right to socioeconomic goods such as basic shelter and food, health care, employment, and a decent burial – that is, on a purportedly fundamental right not to live and die without essential resources, opportunities, and capabilities. Within some traditions, such social and economic rights are considered less important than or even as threats to legal, civil, and political rights. This is one of the great dividing lines among traditions, such as classical and egalitarian liberalism, that otherwise have much in common.

It is often assumed that if something is a right, the government has an obligation to enforce it. Some traditions that care deeply about poverty believe that governmental responses are misguided and that its alleviation is best done through the voluntary organizations or civil society. This is the approach Tom Palmer urges in his chapter on the classical liberal tradition. Other traditions argue that communal and governmental actions are required as well. According to Noam Zohar, the legal and sacred texts of Judaism command public, official responses to poverty. Buddhism can also prompt social engagement and state action to alleviate poverty. Peter Nosco reminds us that Confucianism morally empowers leaders to take measures to alleviate famine and other crises.

There are fascinating cases in history – such as the Confucian-based response to Chinese famines – in which the poor assumed significant roles as agents rather than subjects. Those are moments of discovery and rediscovery of the poor, stretching from late republican Rome through medieval Islamic and Jewish societies to the Great Depression of the 1930s, and up through today's American cities and South Asian countryside.[27] In each case poverty was considered significant enough to warrant public attention and action, for a variety of reasons. Those might include the poor as a threat to political and social order, as potential sources of communal strength if more generously treated and fully included, or as the recipients of charitable acts in keeping with their society's particular ethical, moral, or religious tradition.

---

[27] Margaret Atkins and Robin Osborne, eds., *Poverty in the Roman World* (Cambridge: Cambridge University Press, 2006); Michael Bonner, Mine Ener, and Amy Singer, eds., *Poverty and Charity in Middle Eastern Contexts*, SUNY Series in the Social and Economic History of the Middle East (Albany: State University of New York Press, 2003); Sabra, *Poverty and Charity in Medieval Islam*; Mark R. Cohen, *Poverty and Charity in the Jewish Community of Medieval Egypt* (Princeton, NJ: Princeton University Press, 2005); Cohen, *The Voice of the Poor in the Middle Ages: An Anthology of Documents from the Cairo Geniza* (Princeton, NJ: Princeton University Press, 2005); David L. Carlton and Peter A. Coclanis, eds., *Confronting Southern Poverty in the Great Depression: "The Report on Economic Conditions of the South" with Related Documents* (New York: Bedford/St. Martin's, 1996); George Orwell, *The Road to Wigan Pier* (1937; San Diego, CA: Harcourt, 1958); Ira N. Gang, Kunal Sen, and Myeong-Su Yun, "Poverty in Rural India: Caste and Tribe," *Review of Income and Wealth* 54, no. 1 (March 2008): 50–70; and Ruhi Saith and Abhilasha Sharma, "Poverty in India: A Comparison of Different Approaches," in Stewart, Saith, and Harriss-White, *Defining Poverty in the Developing World*, 114–59.

The tradition-based chapters provide specific examples of historical and contemporary antipoverty measures legitimized by their connections to Buddhism and Islam, for example, or to classical liberalism and natural law. More often than not, these traditions buttressed private, neighborly, familial, and clerical responses; only more recently have these responses tended to be governmental. Welfare and charity are old; the welfare state and social justice are not.[28]

Pious endowments or *waqfs* played a vital role in providing food, education, and medical care to the poor in Mamluk Cairo, or medieval Egypt, and religious practices and ideas continued to help guide the definition of and responses to the poor as Egypt became more secular and nationalist during the nineteenth and twentieth centuries.[29] Poor relief as a form of "tradition"-authorized charity was common throughout the Levant during the medieval period, in Muslim, Christian, and Jewish communities. Complexities arise when modern states seek to enlist these older traditions in the cause of public antipoverty policies. That is of particular interest to the authors of chapters on Islam, Confucianism, Hinduism, and Buddhism when they come to consider government responses to poverty in the name of their respective traditions.

Across the oceans in Europe and the Americas before the welfare state or formal welfare programs as we know them, there was direct outdoor relief, or charity.[30] Fears of radicalism, "masterless men," and vagrancy converged to forge policies directed at the poor, perhaps more so than poverty itself, and a policy tradition that evolved into the more famous Victorian workhouses, health reforms for urban slums, and, by the 1950s, the "cradle-to-grave" welfare state and society, originally outlined in "The Beveridge Report" of 1942.[31] One can chart in the British Isles and throughout the British Empire

---

[28] For the origins, history, and reconfiguring of the welfare state and the welfare system as we have come to understand them, see E. P. Hennock, *The Origin of the Welfare State in England and Germany, 1850–1914: Social Policies Compared* (Cambridge: Cambridge University Press, 2007); Gosta Esping-Andersen, *The Three Worlds of Welfare Capitalism* (Princeton, NJ: Princeton University Press, 1990); Esping-Andersen, "After the Golden Age? Welfare State Dilemmas in a Global Economy," in Esping-Andersen, *Welfare States in Transition: National Adaptations in Global Economies* (London: Sage, 1996), 1–31; and Jochen Clasen, *Reforming European Welfare States: Germany and the United Kingdom Compared* (New York: Oxford University Press, 2005).

[29] Sabra, *Poverty and Charity in Medieval Islam*, and Mine Ener, *Managing Egypt's Poor and the Politics of Benevolence, 1800–1952* (Princeton, NJ: Princeton University Press, 2003).

[30] For example, please see Seth Rockman, *Welfare Reform in the Early Republic: A Brief History with Documents* (Boston: Bedford/St. Martin's, 2003); and Geremek, *Poverty: A History*.

[31] For the history of the English Poor Laws, see Anthony Brundage, *The English Poor Laws, 1700–1930* (New York: Palgrave, 2002); Lynn Hollen Lees, *The Solidarities of Strangers: The English Poor Laws, 1700–1948* (Cambridge: Cambridge University Press, 1998); Paul Slack, *The English Poor Law, 1531–1782*, New Studies in Economic and Social History (Cambridge: Cambridge University Press, 1995); and Paul A. Fideler,

the interconnected histories of poor relief and the welfare state, Christianity and liberal philosophy.

Transnational and multicultural debates about poverty and the poor are increasingly common, suggesting that men and women are eager for at least some shared global understanding. That elusive consensus might result from the hegemony of a particular universalist tradition, from some overlapping consensus among traditions, from the creation of a new syncretic tradition out of the plurality of current understandings, or from the response of a unitary ethical tradition to local traditions and circumstances. For example, the ethical and moral tradition upon which Nigerians draw to define and confront poverty might very well combine wider Islamic principles with indigenous ones from villages and tribes.[32] David Loy's discussion of Buddhism's contributions to antipoverty measures as part of a "Buddhist economics" in South and Southeast Asia points to that creative hybridity of traditions. Sohail H. Hashmi's discussion of Islamic-inspired approaches to poverty – "Islamic economics" – helps us better understand that tradition's significance to antipoverty and other social service measures undertaken and experienced by Muslim communities, whether they are living in Islamic polities or as minorities within non-Islamic ones.

The following essays addressing questions about poverty and the poor within specific ethical traditions articulate ethical or normative theories rather than empirical claims. Such claims are often made regularly about household and national incomes, among other criteria, within and across eras and borders. They are made in a variety of scholarly and popular media and publications.[33] On the other hand, comparative theorizing about the poor and poverty has only rarely been attempted. As noted in each of the tradition-focused essays, specific traditions might have a long history of contemplating

Social Welfare in Pre-industrial England: The Old Poor Law Tradition, Social History in Perspective (New York: Palgrave Macmillan, 2006).

[32] For discussion of the historical and contemporary relationships in Africa between Islam, poverty, and charity, see John Iliffe, *The African Poor: A History* (Cambridge: Cambridge University Press, 1992).

[33] Recent comparative empirical studies of global welfare, poverty, and inequality include Carola Gruen and Stephen Klasen, "Growth, Inequality, and Welfare: Comparisons across Space and Time," *Oxford Economic Papers* 60 (April 2008): 212–36, and Branko Milanovic, *Worlds Apart: Measuring International and Global Inequality* (Princeton, NJ: Princeton University Press, 2007). Those and other comparative studies reveal a variety of results. For example, the coexistence of social progress and social inequalities is considered in Danny Dorling, "A Century of Progress? Inequalities in British Society, 1901–2000," in *Geographies of British Modernity: Space and Society in the Twentieth Century*, ed. David Gilbert, David Matless, and Brian Short (Malden, MA: Blackwell, 2003), 31–53. Additionally, such studies point to the difficulty in agreeing upon a definition of poverty across time and space and finding "regular, comparable" data, as discussed in David Stifel, "Tracking Poverty over Time in the Absence of Comparable Consumption Data," *World Bank Economic Review* 21, no. 2 (March 2007): 317–41.

within their own finite ethical world the question of the poor, but rather rare on the part of adherents or scholars is the systematic and comprehensive attempt to compare such contemplations among the traditions.

The essays thus provide readers with the opportunity to make such comparisons between and among those secular and religious traditions, as well as to make comparisons within what are never truly homogeneous and unchanging systems of ethical thought, texts, and behavior. As the authors recognize and address, each tradition has its own internal diversity and sometimes incongruities, if not perhaps contradictions, when thinking about and encouraging behavior regarding poverty. Additionally, as Andrew Levine importantly remarks in his essay on Marxism, some traditions – Marxism among them – address the question of poverty only generally and indirectly as part of a larger philosophical, if not ethical, approach, rather than doing so specifically and directly, as Christianity and Judaism, among others, do.[34] They are all fluid traditions to a great degree in terms of their chronological development, geopolitical contexts, and contacts with other traditions. This exercise in comparative ethics thus crosses space and time, both within and between the specific traditions, providing a sense of the contemporary status and the historical development of ethical and moral approaches to poverty and the poor.

Addressing poverty across – not just within – national boundaries requires a better understanding of the variegated intellectual and religious traditions that have shaped our global civilization. In a modest and tentative way, the essays in this volume can help build that understanding and, in so doing, contribute to the alleviation of deprivation and want, wherever it may exist. The volume ends with Michael Walzer's broadly conceived commentary, which provides the most direct comparison of the various traditions and reminds readers of the foundational issues raised by the decision to identify poverty and the poor as subjects worthy of reflection and action.

[34] One could argue that philosophical and ethical distinctions about issues such as poverty and distributive justice were subsumed in Marxism under the major consideration of private property and that the replacement of private by public ownership replaces their centrality found in liberal discussions of seemingly similar matters. Please see Xiaoping Wei, "From Principle to Context: Marx versus Nozick and Rawls on Distributive Justice," *Rethinking Marxism* 20, no. 3 (July 2008): 472–86.

Global Poverty and Unequal Development

Contemporary Trends and Issues

Sakiko Fukuda-Parr

Questions about global poverty and inequality inspire some of the most contentious debates not only among academics but also among politicians and the public at large. People look to data on poverty and inequality as they might a stock market index to gauge how the world is doing. Are things on the right track? Is enough being done? In this age of globalization, the question is inevitably about whether "globalization" brings prosperity and, if so, is it prosperity for just a few or is it widely shared. Is it just material prosperity or a more meaningful set of life choices for people?

The aim of this introductory chapter is to assess recent empirical trends on poverty and inequality, with a focus on human well-being rather than on income alone as a measure of well-being. It argues that the past decade was one of unprecedented progress for some but stagnation and reversal for others and that there is a growing gap among developing countries as well as among all countries of the world.

Concept of Poverty in Development Economics

Over the years, economists and social scientists have defined poverty in different ways, and these definitions have been a significant part of the policy debates about methodologies for measurement. The conventional approach in both developed and developing countries had been the income and consumption (or "monetary") perspective, focusing on lack of income and material resources as the defining characteristic of poverty.[1] The main method for measuring poverty was the "headcount" – an estimate of the proportion of a

---

The data used in this paper were the latest available as of February 2008. They therefore do not reflect changes in PPPs published by the World Bank in July 2008. Research assistance from Andy Thornton is gratefully acknowledged.

[1] See, for example, the work of B. S. Rowntree, *Poverty, A Study of Town Life* (London: Macmillan, 1902).

population with an income of less than a "poverty line." This line was drawn at a level considered to be the minimum necessary to meet basic needs, especially food, however these needs are defined.

Human-Centered Approaches

Although the literature on poverty dates back to the 1950s, it was in the 1990s that a number of new nonincome perspectives became more widely discussed and used. This was a time of increased policy attention to poverty in both developed and developing countries, perhaps in response to controversies over the spread of neoliberalism and economic reform programs that were pursued in almost all countries of the world. In this context, the limitations of the income approach became evident; it fails to capture the complex realities of poverty as a lived experience and neglects the nonincome, social, and political factors that explain, shape, or drive poverty trends. Important approaches that emerged at that time and that are now used widely include the participatory, social exclusion, and capability (and human development) approaches,[2] as well as the related basic needs and human rights approaches.

The *participatory approach* pioneered by Robert Chambers[3] and further developed by Narayan and others in the landmark publication *Voices of the Poor*[4] emphasizes the contextual nature of poverty. Poverty is not a single, homogeneous phenomenon and takes a particular form depending on the context; people themselves define poverty differently and use different criteria to identify households and individuals as poor. Participatory Poverty Assessment, a methodology for assessing the extent of poverty and identifying poor people on the basis of what the people themselves said, contrasts with surveys based on objectively observed indicators.[5]

The *social exclusion approach* focuses on exclusion from participation in society in important areas, such as employment and education. The European Union[6] and the International Labour Organization (ILO) played leading roles in developing this concept, perhaps a result of the challenges that European policy makers faced as they began to reform social welfare policies. They

[2] For an excellent review of these approaches, see Caterina Ruggeri Laderchi, Ruth Saith, and Frances Stewart, "Does It Matter That We Do Not Agree on the Definition of Poverty? A Comparison of 4 Approaches," *Oxford Development Studies* 31, no. 3 (September 2003): 36–54.

[3] Robert Chambers, *Whose Reality Counts? Putting the First Last* (London: Intermediate Technology Publications, 1997).

[4] Deepa Narayan and B. Patel, *Voices of the Poor: Can Anyone Hear Us?* (New York: Oxford University Press, 2000).

[5] Robert Chambers, "The Origins and Practice of PRA," *World Development* 22, no. 7 (1994): 953–69.

[6] European Foundation for the Improvement of Living and Working Conditions, *Public Welfare Services and Social Exclusion: The Development of Consumer Oriented Initiatives in the European Union* (Dublin: The Foundation, 1995).

recognized that people who have adequate incomes can nonetheless still be marginalized and excluded from opportunities in many areas of life such as employment. Conventional policy approaches to providing income support alone were not sufficient to address exclusion. Different types of analysis and data were needed to formulate new policy approaches.

A third concept that became widespread is the *capability and human development approach* promoted by Amartya Sen[7] and others, notably the United Nations Development Programme (UNDP) through its *Human Development Reports (HDRs)*.[8] Sen and the *HDRs* argued that development is about the expansion of choices and capabilities that people can have to lead lives they value. Thus, the focus of poverty should not be on incomes but on capabilities and should be measured accordingly.

In this perspective, poverty is defined as the failure to achieve some minimally required or basic capabilities for a tolerable life, such as being well nourished and avoiding preventable morbidity. In the 1997 edition, the *HDR* introduced the term "human poverty" to distinguish it from "income poverty"[9] and developed the Human Poverty Index (HPI), a multidimensional nonincome-based measure of poverty that incorporates indicators for nutrition, access to water, illiteracy, and likelihood of dying before age forty.[10]

The capability approach is related to the *basic needs approach*, but there are important differences, and the two concepts should not be conflated, as is often the case. The basic needs approach emerged in the 1970s and 1980s, before Sen's ideas on capabilities became influential in the development field, and was pioneered by Paul Streeten, Mahbub ul Haq, Javed Burki, and Frances Stewart[11] working from the World Bank. They argued that development should be evaluated by how well people's basic needs are met. Like the capability approach, this approach focuses on the lives of people and uses many of the same indicators to assess progress, such as education, access to water, and basic health services. But this approach is not conceptually framed in a particular theory of human welfare. On the other hand, Sen's capability

[7] Amartya Sen, *Resources, Values and Development* (Oxford: Blackwell, 1984); *Development as Freedom* (Oxford: Oxford University Press, 1999); "Development as Capability Expansion," *Journal of Development Planning* 19 (1989): 41–58, reprinted in *Readings in Human Development*, ed. S. Fukuda-Parr and A. K. Shiva Kumar (New Delhi: Oxford University Press), 3–16.

[8] United Nations Development Programme (UNDP), *Human Development Report, 1990* (New York: Oxford University Press, 1990), and subsequent annual editions.

[9] UNDP, *Human Development Report, 1997* (New York: Oxford University Press, 1997).

[10] First introduced in UNDP, *Human Development Report, 1996*, and refined in 1997. See UNDP, *Human Development Report, 1997*. The HPI was developed by Sen and Anand as explained in Sakiko Fukuda-Parr, "The Human Development Paradigm, Operationalizing Sen's Ideas on Capabilities," in *Feminist Economics*, special issue on Sen and Gender, 9, nos. 2–3 (2007): 301–17.

[11] See, for example, Paul Streeten et al., *First Things First, Meeting Basic Human Needs in Developing Countries* (New York: Oxford University Press, 1982).

approach offers a consistent set of critiques on the limitations of utilitarianism.[12] The capability approach rejects the commodity basis for assessing human well-being and focuses on the individual's agency. The capability approach to poverty reduction would emphasize the role of people in improving their own lives and changing public policy and social institutions – a point that can easily be neglected in the basic needs approach.

The capability approach is also very close to the *human rights approach*, which emerged in the late 1990s and has become increasingly widely adopted by development agencies and nongovernmental organizations (NGOs).[13] This approach sees the realization of all human rights (economic, social, cultural, political, and civil) as the purpose of development. Key features of the human rights approach include nondiscrimination and equality, empowerment of poor people, accountability of the state and other powerful actors such as corporations, and implementation of national and international human rights instruments.[14] Government policies – such as expanding access to basic schooling – are matters of obligations to secure a right rather than charitable acts to achieve an aspiration. There is a substantial equivalence between poverty as failure to achieve basic capabilities and failures to fulfill basic human rights because the basic capabilities and basic human rights in question overlap.[15] More fundamentally, the two approaches share a common motivation: commitment to expanding human freedom and dignity as the basic objective of development.[16] They both assign high priority to equity and empowerment in policy agendas.

Today, there is no consensus on the definition and measurement of poverty, but there is at least a broad recognition that the income perspective is too narrow to capture the complexity of poverty as a life experience of people. The three nonincome approaches differ in the units of analysis and focus of concern. Each one of the approaches has its own limitations for analysis and policy design, such as measurability and quantification, universal applicability and comparability, whether progress can be subjectively or objectively measured, and the time horizon.[17]

---

[12] Amartya Sen and B. Williams, *Utilitarianism and Beyond* (Cambridge: Cambridge University Press, 1982).

[13] Sakiko Fukuda-Parr, "Human Rights and Development," in *Social Welfare, Moral Philosophy and Development: Essays in Honour of Amartya Sen's Seventy-fifth Birthday*, ed. Kaushik Basu and Ravi Kanbur (Oxford: Oxford University Press, 2008).

[14] P. Hunt, M. Nowak, and S. Osmani, *Human Rights and Poverty Reduction: A Conceptual Framework* (Geneva: Office of the United Nations High Commissioner for Human Rights, 2004), http://ohchr.org/english/issues/povertyguidelines.htm.

[15] Ibid. Hunt, Nowak, and Osmani also argue that the range of capabilities and human rights in question are those that are constrained by availability of resources.

[16] Amartya Sen, "Elements of a Theory of Human Rights," *Philosophy and Public Affairs* 34, no. 4 (2004): 315–56; UNDP, *Human Development Report, 2000* (New York: Oxford University Press, 2000).

[17] See Ruggeri Laderchi, Saith, and Stewart, "Does It Matter That We Do Not Agree on the Definition of Poverty?" for a full review of approaches to definition and measurement of poverty.

Implications for Policy Agendas

Each of these different conceptual approaches to poverty has important policy implications and leads to divergent priorities. As Ruggeri Laderchi, Saith, and Stewart point out,[18] the income perspective focuses on expanding economic output and therefore improving efficiency as a primary means to combating poverty, whereas the basic needs perspective draws attention to the broad range of obstacles that prevent people from achieving basic capabilities, including the provision of public goods. The social exclusion perspective focuses on the social processes that exclude.

Both the participation and capability approaches emphasize the importance of human agency – what poor people can do themselves – and of empowerment as both an end and a strategy for poverty reduction. These perspectives recognize the significance of economic growth but also emphasize the need to address institutionalized discriminatory processes that are the root causes of poverty. Indeed, it is interesting that the World Bank's most recent flagship publication on poverty, *World Development Report, 2000/2001*[19] concludes that employment that generates growth and expansion of social services is not enough to reduce poverty; people are poor because they are powerless and lack access to opportunities. This implies paying attention to political and institutional processes in poverty reduction strategies and to the importance of empowerment. It emphasizes strategies to expand peoples' assets through access to resources such as credit, schooling, or community wood lots.[20] But these material assets are not enough; people also need the political freedom to hold authorities to account and to have a say in decisions that affect their lives. However, it should be remembered that today's consensus on the multidimensional nature of poverty and on policy approaches such as the Millennium Development Goals (MDGs) presents a minimum agenda more consistent with the basic needs approach than the capability approach.

Another dimension of human well-being that recently began to be explicitly recognized is security, an issue that is explored in the three country studies covered in this report. Studies by social scientists such as Moser have drawn attention to the impact of violence and poverty,[21] and violence against women both in domestic and in public contexts has become a focus of feminist movements. The concept of "human security" emerged as an important

---

[18] Ibid.
[19] World Bank, *World Development Report, 2000/2001: Attacking Poverty* (Oxford: Oxford University Press, 2000), http://web.worldbank.org/WBSITE/EXTERNAL/TOPICS/EXTPOVERTY/0,,contentMDK:20194762~pagePK:148956~piPK:216618~theSitePK:336992,00.html.
[20] Caroline Moser, *Reducing Global Poverty, A Case for Asset Accumulation* (Washington, DC: Brookings Institution, 2007).
[21] Ibid.

part of global debates on poverty and development cooperation.[22] This broad concept covers both freedom from physical violence (such as torture or murder) and freedom from economic insecurity (such as sudden loss of a job).[23] It is important for conceptual and policy debates on poverty, as it brings in two new elements to the debate: vulnerability to downside risks that could arise from causes as diverse as war to earthquakes to global financial instability; and vulnerability to physical harm from such causes as war and social conflict.

While there is not much disagreement over the idea that poverty is more than lack of income and is multidimensional, many economists continue to use the income poverty framework. This is because they would argue that economic growth is the primary means to reduce poverty and that there is strong correlation between income poverty and nonincome human deprivations. Moreover, while the evolution of the World Bank's *World Development Reports* (*WDRs*) and the poverty reduction strategy (PRS) concept reflects a significant conceptual shift in the organization, this shift is not always reflected in implementation. Common comments in many evaluations of the PRS are that the policy framework is not much different from the policy framework papers that formed the basis of structural adjustment programs, that participation is not seriously implemented, and that the growth strategy is not pro-poor.

Measurement Approaches

To understand how the world is faring we must look beyond economic growth alone to indicators that capture important human outcomes and that reflect capabilities more directly. Despite the consensus on the concept of poverty as multidimensional deprivation, the development and spread of human-centered measurement approaches have lagged. The recent consensus on the MDGs as global policy priorities has drawn greater attention to the nonincome measures. Still, money metrics – particularly the one-dollar-a-day threshold – have dominated international monitoring of global poverty and its analysis and policy prescriptions. Almost all the empirical studies on global inequality focus on income measures.

Many argue that income measures should dominate because they are an important means to meeting basic needs, satisfying human rights, and achieving basic capabilities.[24] They would further argue that incomes correlate with

---

[22] For example, security is one of the three pillars of the agenda proposed by the *World Development Report, 2000/01*; human security is the centerpiece of Japan's development cooperation policy.

[23] See UNDP, *Human Development Report, 1994* (New York: Oxford University Press, 1994). This report played a critical role in the emergence of this concept and provided a definition. Commission on Human Security, *Human Security Now* (New York, 2003).

[24] See Kate Raworth and David Stewart, "Critiques of the Human Development Index: A Review," in *Readings in Human Development*, ed. Sakiko Fukuda-Parr and A. K. Shiva Kumar (New Delhi: Oxford University Press, 2003).

human outcomes in such areas as longevity, literacy, and school enrollment. But there is no perfect relationship between income and these human outcomes.[25] Countries such as Pakistan and Vietnam have similar levels of GDP per capita but have stark differences in life expectancy. Korea and the United States have the same levels of life expectancy, but Korea has less than half the income of the United States. It is true that there is an overall correlation between per capita income and such human outcome measures as life expectancy or mean years of schooling when taking account of data for the entire world. However, this covers countries whose incomes range from about $1,500, the average income of the least developed countries (LDCs), to $33,800, the average income of high income OECD countries. If this group is subdivided into lower-, middle-, and high-income countries, the correlation weakens, and for low income countries it disappears altogether.

Another argument for the income measures involves data availability and the ease with which they can be used to aggregate, disaggregate, and analyze. However, it should not be forgotten that data sets on income and income inequalities are far from satisfactory for reasons of both availability and the measurement tools being used. The one-dollar-a-day poverty measure, for example, is available for 51 out of more than 100 developing countries only, and global aggregates must rely on estimates. Critics have also argued that the methodology for setting the global poverty line at one dollar a day is arbitrary and that the purchasing power parity (PPP) used to convert currencies is unreliable.[26] Although data on indicators such as life expectancy and child mortality have numerous weaknesses, their coverage is better and relies less on estimates.

The strength of monetary indicators is that they provide a convenient summary number that can be easily aggregated and compared across time and groupings. In contrast, measures aiming to capture human poverty are too complex and involve too many dimensions.[27] This line of thinking motivated Mahbub ul Haq to launch the composite measure of human development – the Human Development Index (HDI).[28] Furthermore, because different

[25] Data can be found in the World Bank's *World Development Indicators* (Washington, DC: World Bank, annual publication) or UNDP's *Human Development Reports* (New York: Oxford University Press, annual publication).

[26] For example Sanjay Reddy and Thomas Pogge, "How Not to Count the Poor," Working paper, 2006, posted on SSRN Web site: http://papers.ssrn.com/sol3/papers.cfm?abstract_id=893159).

[27] Capabilities are in fact difficult to measure because they refer to what an individual can do rather than what an individual actually does (functionings). Most attempts at measuring capabilities – including the HDI – in fact measure functioning.

[28] HDI did indeed prove itself to be a highly effective tool for drawing attention to policy priorities for human development. Amartya Sen, "A Decade of Human Development," *Journal of Human Development* 1, no. 1 (2000): 17–23, explains how he initially opposed the creation of an index to measure human development (or capability expansion) on the grounds that the concept was too complex to be measured. Haq persistently argued that

capabilities are important for different people and societies at different times, a question arises as to which ones should be used in tracking global poverty and inequality?[29] However, such concerns can be overcome as demonstrated in the widespread use of the Human Development Index (HDI), annually published in the *HDRs*. A multidimensional human poverty measure – the Human Poverty Index (HPI) – uses the same concept and methodology to measure deprivation in the same dimensions of human development.

Trends in Global Poverty, 1990–2005

According to data from the World Bank and the United Nations, the global GDP expanded from $49 trillion to $61 trillion over the past fifteen years (1990–2005). How have poor people fared in this period? Tables 2.1–2.5 outline some of the key indicators. Development over the past fifteen years was the best of years and the worst of years. Some regions and countries saw unprecedented progress, while others stagnated or reversed. Within regions and countries, opportunities for jobs, better health, new knowledge, free cultural expression, and participation in decision making and many other important choices in life expanded for some, but for others meeting basic needs continued to be a struggle. What is most striking is the extent of the stagnation and reversals, signaling a human development crisis not seen in previous decades. These issues are often obscured in many debates that focus on the positive global trends rather than on the failing countries and on successes of countries measured by national averages that hide failing regions and groups within countries.

Declines in Global Poverty
The magnitude of global poverty is huge and daunting but has declined substantially since 1990:[30]

An estimated 986 million people (18.4 percent of developing world population), live on less than one dollar a day, down from 1,247 million (28.7 percent) in 1990 (Tables 2.1 and 2.2; Figure 2.1a).

only a measure "as vulgar as the GDP" would persuade "busy policymakers" of the urgent priority to take action on human priorities.

[29] Such concerns dominated the debates that led to the development of the Human Development Index (HDI), as Amartya Sen's (ibid.) own account makes clear.

[30] Data in this section are drawn from World Bank, *World Development Indicators, 2007* (Washington, DC: World Bank, 2007); UN, *The Millennium Development Goals Report, 2007* (New York: United Nations, 2007); and UNDP, *Human Development Report, 2007* (New York: Oxford University Press, 2007), unless otherwise noted. They report the latest data available from harmonized international series. Latest data refer to either 2004 or 2005, whichever is the later year available. Data cover developing countries that include all countries except the United States, Canada, Japan, Western Europe, Australia, New Zealand – or "high income OECD member countries."

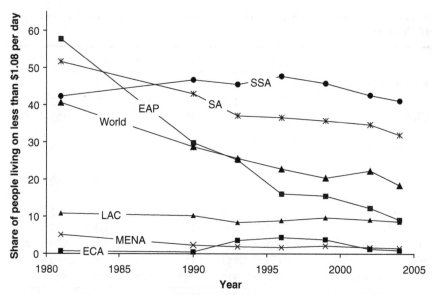

FIGURE 2.1A. Number of people living on less than $1.08 (constant PPP US$): Regional trends. EAP = East Asia and Pacific; ECA = Europe and Central Asia; LAC = Latin America and the Caribbean; MENA = Middle East and North Africa; SA = South Asia; SSA = sub-Saharan Africa. *Source*: World Bank, *World Development Indicators, 2007.*

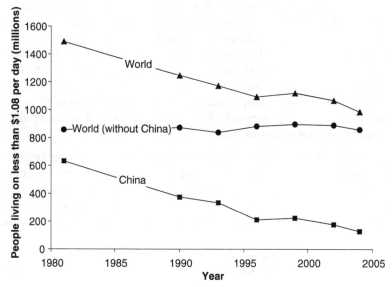

FIGURE 2.1B. China driving decline in world poverty, 1980–2005 (people living on less than $1.08 per day, constant PPP US$). *Source*: World Bank, *World Development Indicators, 2007.*

TABLE 2.1. *Number of People Living on Less Than $1.08 per Day, 1980–2004 (PPP constant in millions)*

	1981	1990	1993	1996	1999	2002	2004
East Asia and the Pacific	796	476	420	279	277	227	169
China	632	374	334	211	223	177	128
Europe and Central Asia	3	2	17	21	18	6	4
Latin America and the Caribbean	39	45	39	43	49	48	47
Middle East and North Africa	9	5	5	4	6	5	4
South Asia	473	479	440	459	475	485	462
Sub-Saharan Africa	168	240	252	286	296	296	298
World	1,489	1,247	1,172	1,093	1,120	1,067	986
World (without China)	857	873	838	882	897	890	858

Source: World Bank, *World Development Indicators, 2007.*

The proportion of children younger than five who are underweight declined from 33 to 27 percent of the age group.

Seventy-two million primary school age children – 57 percent of whom are girls – are still out of school and 15 percent of those enrolled do not complete primary education.[31] But net primary enrollment rose from 80 to 88 percent (Figure 2.2). Some one billion adults are illiterate, though literacy rates increased from 68 to 79 percent (Figure 2.3).[32]

Ten million children die annually before reaching their fifth birthday, mostly from preventable causes. For those younger than five, mortality rates improved from 106 to 83 deaths per 1,000 live births (Figure 2.4), and life expectancy at birth increased from 65 to 68 (Figure 2.5).

An estimated 1.5 billion people do not have access to clean water and 2.6 billion to improved sanitation.[33]

The gains recorded are historically unprecedented, continuing the twentieth-century progress that has achieved more in removing poverty than during any other historical era.[34] Many success stories – agricultural productivity doubled in Malawi in 2006–7 in response to a voucher program for fertilizers and seeds; dramatic increases in primary school enrollment resulted from

[31] UN, *The Millennium Development Goals Report, 2007.*
[32] Data refer to 1985–94 and 1995–2005. Source: UNDP, *Human Development Report, 2007.*
[33] UN, *The Millennium Development Goals Report, 2007.*
[34] UNDP, *Human Development Report, 1997.*

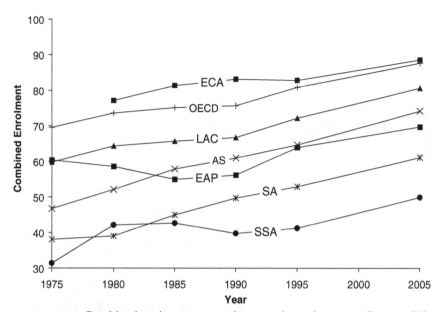

FIGURE 2.2. Combined primary, secondary, and tertiary enrollment (%). AS = Arab states; EAP = East Asia and Pacific; ECA = Europe and Central Asia; LAC = Latin America and the Caribbean; SA = South Asia; SSA = sub-Saharan Africa. *Source*: UNDP, *Human Development Report, 2007.*

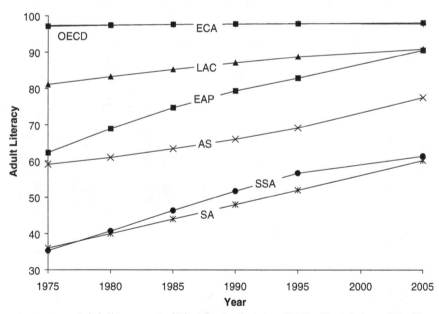

FIGURE 2.3. Adult literacy rate (%). AS= Arab states; EAP = East Asia and Pacific; ECA = Europe and Central Asia; LAC = Latin America and the Caribbean; SA = South Asia; SSA = sub-Saharan Africa. *Source*: UNDP, *Human Development Report, 2007.*

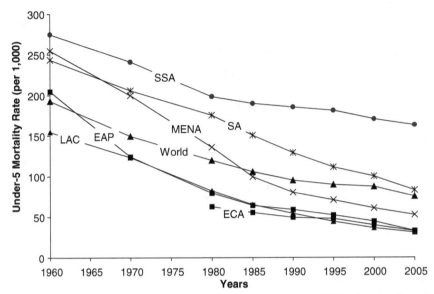

FIGURE 2.4. Mortality rate for those younger than five years. EAP = East Asia and Pacific; ECA = Europe and Central Asia; LAC = Latin America and the Caribbean; MENA = Middle East and North Africa; SA = South Asia; SSA = sub-Saharan Africa. *Source*: World Bank, *World Development Indicators, 2007.*

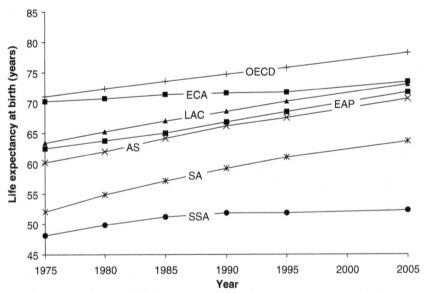

FIGURE 2.5. Life expectancy at birth. AS= Arab states; EAP = East Asia and Pacific; ECA = Europe and Central Asia; LAC = Latin America and the Caribbean; SA = South Asia; SSA = sub-Saharan Africa. *Source*: UNDP, *Human Development Report, 2007.*

removal of school fees in Kenya, Tanzania, Uganda, and elsewhere, among many other examples throughout the world – demonstrate the possibilities of achieving rapid improvements. The longer term trends from the 1970s or 1980s show a steady progress in reducing income deficiencies and human poverty (Figures 2.1–2.5).

In a historical perspective of human progress, these recent gains over a few decades are equivalent to gains that took hundreds of years to achieve in earlier centuries.[35] Yet it is far from adequate judged against the commitments made in the Millennium Declaration, adopted at the UN 2000 General Assembly, in which governments of every country committed to do their utmost to end global poverty as a major objective for the new century along with securing peace, democracy, and human rights. They set specific goals with quantitative measurements, to be achieved by 2015. A year later, these were further elaborated in a follow-up implementation document that came to be known as the Millennium Development Goals. They encompass eight goals measured by eighteen targets for improving income wealth, primary education, child and maternal health, HIV/AIDS prevention, gender equality, the environment, and a global partnership for development. At current rates of progress, only one of the eight goals – the MDG1 measured by halving the proportion of people living on less than one dollar a day[36] – would be met by the target date of 2015.[37] Moreover, progress with this target is being driven by China, India, and a few other countries of Asia that have been making huge strides in reducing income poverty as a result of high economic growth. If only China was taken out of the global aggregates, the trend would be diminished (see Figure 2.1b). In fact, the number of people in extreme income poverty would be rising.

Trends in hunger and nutrition graphically illustrate just how slow the rate of progress has been. The proportion of malnourished people fell from 21 percent in 1991 to 18 percent in 1999,[38] but with population growth, this represents a decline of only 39 million out of around 800 million people – at this pace it would be close to 150 years until hunger were eradicated.[39] The consequences of hunger are particularly dire for children – more than fifteen thousand children die every day as a result of malnutrition, and many more suffer impaired mental development. At current rates of progress, about 1 billion children will be growing up by 2020 with impaired mental development.[40]

[35] See Angus Maddison, *Contours of the World Economy, 1–2030 A.D.: Essays in Macroeconomic History* (Oxford: Oxford University Press, 2010).
[36] MDG1 is measured by three targets (income poverty, hunger, and employment). At current trends, only the income poverty target would be met.
[37] UN, *The Millennium Development Goals Report, 2007*.
[38] Food and Agriculture Organization of the United Nations (FAO), *The State of Food Insecurity in the World* (Rome: FAO, 2002).
[39] UNDP, *Human Development Report, 2003* (New York: Oxford University Press, 2003).
[40] UN Millennium Project Task Force on Hunger, *Halving Global Hunger: It Can Be Done* (London: Earthscan, 2005).

28 *Sakiko Fukuda-Parr*

TABLE 2.2. *Proportion of People Living on Less Than $1.08 per Day, 1981–2004 (PPP constant)*

Region	1981	1990	1993	1996	1999	2002	2004
East Asia and the Pacific	57.7	29.8	25.2	16.1	15.5	12.3	9.1
Europe and Central Asia	0.7	0.5	3.6	4.4	3.8	1.3	0.9
Latin America and the Caribbean	10.8	10.2	8.4	8.9	9.7	9.1	8.6
Middle East and North Africa	5.1	2.3	1.9	1.7	2.1	1.7	1.5
South Asia	51.6	43.0	37.1	36.6	35.8	34.7	31.9
Sub-Saharan Africa	42.3	46.7	45.5	47.7	45.8	42.6	41.1
World	40.6	28.7	25.6	22.8	20.4	22.3	18.4

Source: World Bank, *World Development Indicators, 2007.*

Uneven Progress among Regions and Countries

As Figures 2.1–2.5 graphically show, behind the global averages lie vast disparities between regions. The contrasts are particularly striking in the reduction of income poverty; the dramatic decline in East Asia and the Pacific stands out against the stagnation in all other regions. In fact, there are nearly twice as many people living in extreme poverty in sub-Saharan Africa today (2004) as there were in 1981 (Table 2.1), and the decline as a proportion of population was only 1.2 percentage points during this period (Table 2.2).

In East Asia and the Pacific, the proportion of those hungry has fallen dramatically, from 16 to 10 percent. But in the world's hunger hot spots there has been little overall change; in South Asia one in four people is still malnourished, and in sub-Saharan Africa as many as one in three still goes hungry.[41] In fact, in twenty-one countries the number of undernourished people actually increased over the 1990s.[42] And of the thirty-three countries with data, ten have experienced reversals.[43]

All of the world's regions have experienced improvements in primary school enrollment. East Asia and the Pacific, Eastern Europe and the Commonwealth of Independent States (CIS), and Latin America and the Caribbean are converging toward achieving universal primary education. South Asia is further behind, but the number of children enrolled has increased to 87 percent, catching up with other regions that are in the 90–95 percent range. In sub-Saharan Africa, however, enrollment remains at 72 percent despite recent increases. Enrolling in primary school is only the first step; it is increasingly evident that

[41] FAO, *The State of Food Insecurity.*
[42] UNDP, *Human Development Report, 2003.*
[43] World Bank, *World Development Indicators, 2003* (Washington, DC: World Bank 2003).

lagging completion is the major challenge. In South Asia completion rates are around 82 percent, and in Africa little more than half of children who start primary school will be there at the end.[44] Combined with low enrollments, this means that only one in three children in sub-Saharan Africa is currently completing primary education in the region.[45]

Progress in reducing child mortality has also been uneven, with some regions progressing much faster than others. Again the hot spots are South Asia and sub-Saharan Africa. While the mortality rate for those younger than five declined in South Asia, from 12.5 percent to around 8 percent, it is still 16 percent in sub-Saharan Africa despite recent gains (Figure 2.4). Thirteen countries have a greater proportion of children dying in 2006 than in 1990. All but one is in sub-Saharan Africa, particularly in countries struggling to deal with the HIV/AIDS pandemic.[46]

Much is known about reducing child mortality, and a key factor in countries that have succeeded has been successful immunization programs. After impressive increases in the 1970s and 1980s, however, there have been reductions since the 1990s in some developing regions, most noticeably in sub-Saharan Africa and East Asia. Immunization, however, is far from enough. Of the countries performing best and worst in reducing deaths in children under five the immunization rates are similar – it is inaction against the ravages of HIV/AIDS that is currently proving to be a child's worst enemy. In four of the five countries with the greatest increases in child mortality, HIV/AIDS prevalence among children mirrors the increases in child deaths.[47]

Although life-spans improved steadily in all regions of the world from the 1960s to the 1980s (Figure 2.4) and the trend continues on average for all regions, many countries saw these gains wiped out in the 1990s with the devastation of HIV/AIDS. For example, life expectancy at birth dropped dramatically in sub-Saharan Africa so that today the gap between this region and high-income OECD countries increased from twenty-four years twenty years ago to thirty-three years today.[48] Similarly, life expectancy dropped in Russia by eleven years (seventy to fifty-nine years) from the mid-1980s to 2004.[49]

Among the 6.5 billion people living in the world today, by far the largest concentration of those living in poverty can be found in Asia; for example, 631 million or 64 percent of the 1 billion income-poor peoples reside in this region (Figure 2.1b). This is partly because of the size of this region's population,

[44] UN Millennium Project Task Force on Education, *Toward Universal Primary Education: Investments, Incentives, and Institutions* (London: Earthscan, 2005).
[45] Sakiko Fukuda-Parr and David Stewart, "Unequal Development in the 1990s: Gaps in Human Capabilities," in *Debates on the Measurement of Global Poverty*, ed. Sudhir Anand, Paul Segal, and Joseph E. Stiglitz (New York: Oxford University Press, 2010).
[46] UNICEF, *State of the World's Children 2008*, http://www.unicef.org/sowc08/.
[47] World Bank, *World Development Indicators, 2003*.
[48] UNDP, *Human Development Report, 2005* (New York: Oxford University Press, 2006).
[49] Ibid.

which, at 4 billion, dwarfs the rest of the world, but also because poverty rates are high in South Asia. Poverty rates are low and getting rapidly lower in East Asia. But South Asia's income poverty rate is 31 percent, and the region also has high rates of child mortality for those younger than five, illiteracy, low school enrollment, limited access to clean water, and particularly high rates of undernutrition. For example, in India about half the children under five are underweight for age (47 percent) or less than average height for age (51 percent), while 30 percent have low birth weights. These numbers stand out in comparison to countries with similar levels of overall development as measured by the HDI, such as Botswana, Morocco, or South Africa, and similar levels of income such as Honduras and Egypt.

Nonetheless, the greatest challenge among the regions is in sub-Saharan Africa where income and human poverty rates are the highest and where progress has been slow if not stagnant. Over the past fifteen years, while there was a decline in income poverty when measured as a percentage of the population, the total numbers increased as the rate of progress was not adequate to keep up with population growth (Table 2.2, Figure 2.1) and is projected to increase further into the next decade.[50] Under-five mortality rates dropped from 185 to 166 per 1,000 live births, but further progress is needed to achieve the target of two-thirds' reduction by 2015. As the UN notes,[51] maternal health is a global scandal; a woman in Africa today has a 1 in 16 chance of dying due to complications of pregnancy and childbirth during her lifetime, while the risk for women in developed countries is 1 in 3,800.[52] The proportion of underweight children declined only from 33 to 29 percent since 1990, barely a 10 percent decline against the target of 50 percent.[53] In these and in many other areas, livelihoods are fragile for people in Africa, and the challenges are huge.

In Latin America and the Caribbean and in the Middle East and North Africa, progress is not as rapid as in East Asia, and large challenges remain. But from the perspective of the international community, these countries are not the priority because national governments in these regions should have the domestic resources and institutional capacity to address the obstacles. In contrast, most countries of sub-Saharan Africa are in the low-income category and do not have adequate resources to expand investments in social infrastructure necessary to accelerate improvements in many of the areas. They are thus a priority for international concern.

The declines of the 1990s are particularly apparent in the Human Development Index (HDI). The index usually moves steadily upward – though usually slowly because two of its key components, literacy and school

---

[50] World Bank, *World Development Indicators, 2007.*
[51] UN, *The Millennium Development Goals Report, 2007.*
[52] Ibid.
[53] Ibid.

enrollment rates, take time to change. So when the HDI falls, it indicates a crisis, with nations depleting their basis for development – people, their real wealth. After a steady increase since the mid-1970s, there has been a deceleration in HDI progress. The slowdown, particularly in the late 1980s and first half of the 1990s, was led by countries in Central and Eastern Europe and the CIS. Many of these countries had already started on a downward spiral in the mid-1980s, but between 1990 and 1995 the HDI declined on average in the region. In sub-Saharan Africa overall growth in the HDI merely slowed, but some countries suffered terrible declines.[54] According to the *Human Development Report, 2003*, the HDI declined in twenty-one countries in the 1990s. This unfortunate trend does not appear to have reversed in the first years of the new millennium – between 2000 and 2005 the HDI declined in fourteen countries.[55] This is a new phenomenon as only four countries saw their HDIs fall in the 1980s. Much of the decline since 1990 can be traced to the spread of HIV/AIDS, which lowered life expectancies, and to a collapse in incomes, particularly in the CIS.

Seldom if ever is income poverty reduced in a stagnant economy, and the regions growing fastest economically are also the ones that have reduced income poverty most. But the link between economic growth and income poverty reduction is far from automatic, as successive UNDP *HDRs* have emphasized. In Indonesia, Poland, and Sri Lanka poverty rose in the 1990s despite economic growth.[56] For most regions, economic growth has been far from impressive, and only East Asia grew faster than the OECD countries. In fact, over the period 1990–2003, out of 177 countries, 76 averaged annual growth of 2 percent or more.[57] Among the rest, 41 countries saw average incomes fall, including 18 in Sub-Saharan Africa.[58] Of that region's 44 countries, only 11 achieved annual growth of 2 percent or more.[59]

Countries Face Different Challenges
The *Human Development Report, 2003* identified 59 countries (out of 147 with data) in which income and human poverty rates across several dimensions are highest and recent progress slow, or in reversal. Though concentrated in sub-Saharan Africa, they also include 4 countries from East Asia and the Pacific, 6 from the Arab states, 5 from Central and Eastern Europe and the CIS, 4 from Latin America and the Caribbean, and 2 from South Asia. In an effort to analyze obstacles facing these countries, the report identified some common characteristics among these 59 countries in their geography, population,

---

[54] Fukuda-Parr and Stewart, "Unequal Development in the 1990s."
[55] UNDP, *Human Development Report, 2007*.
[56] Fukuda-Parr and Stewart, "Unequal Development in the 1990s."
[57] UNDP, *Human Development Report, 2007*.
[58] Ibid.
[59] Ibid.

and economic structure. Many are landlocked or have a large portion of their populations living far from a coast. Most (54 out of 59) are small – only 5 contain more than 40 million people. Being far from world markets and having a small economy could be important factors in the current economic environment of global market integration, posing an obstacle to diversifying exports and reducing dependence on primary commodities to less volatile sectors with more value added. Indeed, in 21 of 26 countries with data, primary commodities make up more than two-thirds of their exports.

Small size and geographic location as well as dependence on primary commodities are major factors behind poor economic performance.[60] Analysis of 84 countries between 1980 and 1998 found that inland countries (more than 75 percent of the population living at least 100 kilometers from the coast) fared consistently worse in economic growth than coastal countries. Small countries (with populations less than 40 million) that also had inland populations did particularly badly; of 53 countries with these characteristics, only 24 had positive growth rates, and the average per capita growth rate for the group as a whole was –0.2 percent unlike other categories that all registered positive growth rates. On export patterns, transition economies[61] and fuel exporters experienced highly negative growth rates in the 1980 to 1998 period (–1.7% and –1.5 percent, respectively) as did nonfuel commodity exporters (–0.1 percent). Of the 61 countries in this last category, only 29 countries had a positive growth performance. This contrasts starkly with manufacturing exporters, where 23 out of 24 countries experienced positive average annual growth rates with an overall average of 2.7 percent per capita.[62]

Economic stagnation is an important factor but is only one of the obstacles to poverty reduction. For many countries, the spread of HIV/AIDS has led to many setbacks. Dramatic declines in life-spans wiped out decades of gains in some of the most affected countries. The repercussions go beyond death and ill health to economic and social stresses. Yet another is violent conflict, which not only is a source of death and injury, loss of livelihood, and social breakdown but is also intricately intertwined with the challenges of poverty. The World Bank focuses on "fragile states" – defined as "countries with particularly weak governance, institutions and capacity" – as countries where the prospects for meeting the MDGs are least likely.[63]

More research is needed on the factors that lie behind the reversals in important indicators of human well-being such as education, nutrition, and survival to determine if these were due to economic stagnation or to other factors.

---

[60] Ibid.
[61] Transition from centrally planned to market economic systems.
[62] UNDP, *Human Development Report, 2003*.
[63] World Bank, *Global Monitoring Report, 2007* (Washington, DC: World Bank, 2007).

Trends in Global Inequalities

The previous sections focused on poverty, not on inequality. While poverty is about deprivation, inequality is about distribution. Moreover, as Amartya Sen pointed out more than two decades ago, income and material means are not an adequate measure of inequality any more than poverty if we are concerned with differences in human well-being. However, the recent literature on empirical trends in inequality across countries focuses almost exclusively on the distribution of income. The divergent trends in poverty reduction, economic growth, and human development would imply growing gaps between the rich and prospering countries and regions (OECD countries, East Asia) and the poor and stagnating countries and regions (sub-Saharan Africa and others, least developed countries and others). However, this is not the only aspect of inequality or the only way that inequality can be measured.

Empirical trends in inequality can be analyzed at three levels: first, within countries; second, between countries; and third, across people in the world.

Inequalities within Countries

A country doing well to reduce poverty through growth and development may not be doing well to reduce inequality. Growth and development generally reduce poverty – although the relationship is not automatic – but as the benefits are not equally shared, inequality may increase.[64] For example, while China as a whole has forged ahead, this has occurred mostly in the coastal provinces. Whereas Shanghai has a life expectancy and income similar to Portugal, many inland provinces have fared much worse; Huizhou has an income per capita little more than $1,000 (U.S. PPP), more comparable to Tajikistan.[65]

The problem is widespread. Growing evidence suggests that within-country inequality is on the rise, measured as gaps between the very rich and very poor. The UN (2007) shows the share of national consumption of the poorest quintile shrinking between 1990 and 2004 in developing countries as a whole, from 4.6 to 3.9 percent, a trend that is particularly marked in Eastern Asia (7.3 to 4.5 percent) and in the former Soviet Union (7.9 to 6.2 percent). Averages for countries of Latin America and the Caribbean, sub-Saharan Africa, Southeast Asia, and North Africa show no or negligible change.

A recent study of income distribution that looks at country-level data shows that between 1980 and the mid-1990s income inequalities increased in forty-three of seventy-three countries with complete and comparable data; in only

[64] There is intense debate and a large literature on this relationship.
[65] UNDP, *Human Development Report, 2003.*

TABLE 2.3. *Child Mortality Rates: Inequalities within Countries vs. Changes in National Averages, 1980s and 1990s, Selected Countries*

	Relative Gap (between Rich and Poor)		
	Narrowing	Constant	Widening
Average level			
Improving	Guatemala	Egypt	Bangladesh
		Mali	Bolivia
		Morocco	Brazil
		Peru	Colombia
		Senegal	Dominican Rep.
			Ghana
			Indonesia
			Uganda
Constant	Togo	Burkina Faso	Philippines
	Zambia	Cameroon	Tanzania
		Niger	
Worsening		Kenya	Kazakhstan
			Zimbabwe

Source: Alberto Minujin and Enrique Delamonica. "Equality Matters for a World Fit for Children: Lessons from the 90s." UNICEF Staff Working Papers, Division of Policy and Planning Series No. 3 (New York, 2003).

six of the thirty-three developing countries with data was there a significant reduction in income inequality measured by the Gini coefficient.[66] Another study on child mortality shows that of fourteen countries with data where child mortality is improving at the national level, in eight the gaps between rich and poor in terms of child mortality are increasing, in five inequality remains stable, and in only one are child mortality rates between rich and poor narrowing (Table 2.3).[67]

Women throughout the world play critical roles in development, because their contributions have an impact on households, communities, and national economies. Yet some two-thirds of the world's 781 million illiterates are women,[68] women still earn only 75 percent as much as men on average,[69] and around the world at least one woman in every three has been beaten, coerced

[66] Giovanni Andrea Cornia with Sampsa Kiiski, "Trends in Income Distribution in the Post-World War II Period Evidence and Interpretation," World Institute for Development Economics Research, Discussion paper 2001/89 (Helsinki).

[67] Alberto Minujin and Enrique Delamonica, "Equality Matters for a World Fit for Children: Lessons from the 90's," UNICEF Staff Working Papers, Division of Policy and Planning Series, No. 3 (New York, 2003).

[68] UNESCO, *Education for All: Global Monitoring Report, 2007* (Paris: UNESCO Publishing, 2007).

[69] UN Millennium Task Force Report, *Taking Action: Achieving Gender Equality and Empowering Women* (London: Earthscan, 2005).

into sex, or otherwise abused.[70] It is estimated that there are as many as 100 million women 'missing' – or not born or dying prematurely – as a result of infanticide, neglect, and sex-selective abortions.[71] Gender gaps have narrowed in several important areas of life such as education. Disparities are now small in some areas such as primary and secondary schooling where girls' enrollment is now 94 percent of boys'. But gaps remain in other areas of life. For example, the average global level of women's participation in nonagricultural employment is still only 39 percent, rising slowly from 36 percent, and of women's representation in parliament is still only 17 percent.[72]

Inequality across Countries
Empirical trends in world income distribution began to receive increasing attention in public policy debates since the 1990s and consequently in research agendas. Since then, inequality has been one of the most hotly contested issues among economists. A recent review of this literature concludes that "there is no simple answer to the question of whether or not the world is becoming more unequal. If a variety of methods are employed and compared, a complex answer emerges, showing that inequality is both declining in some ways and increasing in others."[73] Seemingly contradictory conclusions emerge from studies that rely on different methodologies on inequality within or between countries, whether the local currencies are converted by PPP or market exchange rate, which data sources are used, and how inequality is defined and calculated. In particular, while studies using measurement of gaps in the incomes of the poorest and richest groups consistently indicate growing inequality, studies of the distribution using measures such as the Gini coefficient lead to different conclusions.

Comparing average GDP per capita across the regions of the world, Sutcliffe[74] shows disparity since 1990 between rich countries of the North and the rest of the world, at about 15 percent, whereas from 1950 up to the 1980s there was a general widening disparity from 20 to 15 percent. However, while China and the rest of Asia as a whole have been catching up since the 1980s, the distance from the North's income level has risen for other regions. Wade makes the same calculation using World Bank rather than OECD data and arrives at the same conclusion on the general trend.[75]

---

[70] Ibid.
[71] Sen was the first to estimate the extent of discrimination against women that is reflected in population sex ratios in India and to explain the higher populations of males by gender-biased abortions, infanticide, and neglect.
[72] The average of all countries. Proportion in the lower house of parliament where there are two houses.
[73] Bob Sutcliffe, "A Converging or Diverging World?" DESA Working Paper No. 2 (New York, 2005).
[74] Ibid.
[75] Robert Hunter Wade, "Is Globalization Reducing Poverty and Inequality?" *World Development* 32, no. 4 (2004): 567–89.

Using the Gini coefficient, Sutcliffe shows an improvement in world income distribution since 1980, following a rise up to 1980, regardless of which of the three data sets is used. However, if China is taken out of these calculations, inequality would be rising.

Income Inequality between Persons within the World
Several studies have attempted to measure inequality among persons. These calculations use models of global income distribution and draw on different methodologies and data sources. Milanovic shows sharply rising inequality between 1988 and 1993, with the Gini coefficient estimated at 0.63 and 0.66.[76] On the other hand, studies by Sala-i-Martin[77] and Sutcliffe[78] and Dikhanov[79] show a reduction in inequality from 1980 through 1990 to 2000. However, while Milanovic uses household consumption data and an estimate of income from public services that are important for poor people,[80] the other studies use national income data. The Milanovic methodology is based on a more adequate measure of resources available to people and households.[81]

As several authors have emphasized,[82] there is little disagreement about the magnitude of inequality, whatever data sets and methods are used, and whatever the conclusions about trends. The estimated Gini coefficients are consistently very high and prompt debate about what level is acceptable in a human community. The *Human Development Report, 2002* captures this conclusion as "global inequality – grotesque levels, ambiguous trends." World income distribution is more unequal than the distribution in any given country.[83] Moreover, given the divergent growth trends in the world's regions and countries, there is increasing polarization between the world's rich and poor. The share of global income of the richest quintile is now estimated at three-quarters, and that of the poorest quintile is a mere 1.5 percent.[84] As the *Human Development Report, 2005* notes, "In 1990, the average American

[76] Branko Milanovic, *Worlds Apart: Measuring International and Global Inequality* (Princeton, NJ: Princeton University Press, 2005).
[77] Xavier Sala-i-Martin, "The World Distribution of Income (Estimated from Individual Country Distributions)," NBER Working Paper No. 8933 (Cambridge, MA: National Bureau of Economic Research, 2002), http://www.nber.org/papers/w8933.
[78] Bob Sutcliffe, "A More or Less Unequal World?" *Indicators: The Journal of Social Health* 2, no. 3 (Summer 2003): 24–70.
[79] Yuri Dikhanov, "Trends in Global Income Distribution, 1970–2015," background paper for UNDP, *Human Development Report, 2005,* http://hdr.undp.org/en/reports/global/hdr2005/papers/.
[80] Milanovic, *Worlds Apart.*
[81] Sutcliffe, "A More or Less Unequal World?"
[82] Ibid.; UNDP, *Human Development Report, 2006.*
[83] UNDP, *Human Development Report, 2005.*
[84] Dikhanov, "Trends in Global Income Distribution, 1970–2015."

TABLE 2.4. *How Many Times More Likely a Child Is to Die before His Fifth Birthday Than in a High-Income OECD Country*

	1990	2001
Arab states	9.4	11.0
East Asia and the Pacific	6.0	6.5
Latin America and the Caribbean	5.5	5.2
South Asia	13.1	14.7
Sub-Saharan Africa	18.8	26.3
Central and Eastern Europe and the CIS	3.9	5.5

Source: Sakiko Fukuda-Parr and David Stewart, "Unequal Development in the 1990s: Growing Gaps in Human Capabilities," in Sudhir Anand, Paul Segal, and Joseph Stiglitz, eds., *Debates on the Measurement of Global Poverty* (New York: Oxford University Press, 2010). Calculations based on World Bank, *World Development Indicators, 2003*, CD-ROM (Washington, DC).

was 38 times richer than the average Tanzanian. Today, the average American is 61 times richer."[85]

Inequality in Human Development and Human Capabilities

It is difficult to capture inequality in human development and capabilities in a way that is adequate to reflect the breadth and complexity of opportunities that people value. But we can rely on a few leading indicators of choices that are fundamentally and universally important for people around the world. The *Human Development Report, 2005* states that "there is no more powerful – or disturbing – indicator of capability deprivation than child mortality."[86] The gaps in child mortality between rich and poor countries have unambiguously widened. In the early 1990s children under five were nineteen times more likely to die in sub-Saharan Africa than in rich countries – and today, twenty-six times more likely (Table 2.4). Among all developing regions, only Latin America and the Caribbean saw no worsening in the past decade relative to rich countries, with children still about five times more likely to die before their fifth birthday.[87] Sub-Saharan Africa now accounts for 44 percent of the 10 million child deaths, though only 22 percent of live births.[88]

Another disturbing trend is widening gaps in education after primary levels in an increasingly knowledge-driven world economy. Although primary

[85] UNDP, *Human Development Report, 2005*, 37.
[86] Ibid., 24.
[87] Fukuda-Parr and Stewart, "Unequal Development in the 1990s."
[88] UNDP, *Human Development Report, 2006*.

school enrollment gaps are closing, gaps in total years of schooling are widening.[89] Quality issues add to the disparity.[90]

Global Solidarity and the International Policy Agenda

Global Consensus on Inclusive Globalization
The twenty-first century opened with the adoption of the Millennium Declaration, a stronger statement of global solidarity to fight poverty than any previous global document. The largest gathering ever of heads of state and governments – 147 in total – made explicit commitments to address not only national but global poverty:

We recognize that, in addition to our separate responsibilities to our individual societies, we have a collective responsibility to uphold the principles of human dignity, equality and equity at the global level. As leaders we have a duty therefore to all the world's people, especially the most vulnerable and, in particular the children of the world, to whom the future belongs.[91]

The 1990s into the mid-2000's was a period of prosperity during which most rich countries enjoyed an economic boom and when much of Southeast and South Asia registered major gains in poverty reduction. In China alone, those in extreme poverty declined by nearly 200 million people, adding to the decline of 260 million in the 1980s. Life-spans increased by five years in East Asia. Yet another trend of this period was stagnation and unprecedented reversals, signaling a decade of development crisis.

As the process of market integration – globalization – proceeded and accelerated in the 1990s, driven by economic liberalization and new information and transport technologies, it also became increasingly clear that the prosperity and dynamism of this new era was not being widely shared. As the trends documented in this chapter make apparent, many countries and groups within countries were marginalized from the global economy. The consensus that emerged from the end of the 1990s and into the twenty-first century was the need to make globalization more inclusive.

This led to the Millennium Declaration, which set the ending of poverty as its overall objective and not only outlined broad aspirations but defined specific goals with quantitative, time-bound targets. This consensus on poverty, with explicit emphasis on the human dimensions such as education and health, is new. In earlier decades, poverty did not always feature so prominently and consistently on international development agendas that prioritized issues such as economic reforms, economic growth, and industrialization. These

[89] Ibid.
[90] Ibid.
[91] UN Millennium Declaration, 2000, United Nations, Resolutions adopted by the General Assembly, General Assembly 55/2. A/RES/55/2, p.1.

new goals were also unique in having included goals for stronger efforts by rich countries in development aid, debt relief, trade reform, and technology transfer. They reflect a normative framework of global solidarity and responsibility of people across national borders as reflected in the statement quoted here. These commitments to global solidarity were reinforced at the Doha meeting of the World Trade Organization (WTO) in 2001, in the Monterrey Conference on Financing for Development in 2002, at the Johannesburg Conference on Sustainable Development in 2002, and in the UN Summit of 2005. Poverty, with Africa as a priority concern, has been a major theme of each of the G-8 summit meetings since 2000. The Gleneagles Summit of 2005 in particular set out an ambitious agenda for action. These commitments were part of a broader policy framework for global cooperation that recognized the mutual responsibilities of developing countries and of the donor countries to undertake policy change and increase their respective efforts for poverty reduction.[92]

Policies

Although there may be consensus on ending poverty as a priority objective, there is much controversy over how to achieve it. There is a lively controversy among economists on explaining why globalization has not been more inclusive, and why some countries have succeeded so much more than others. Are countries to be blamed for the way they have managed their economies, with ill-designed economic policies and weak institutions? Or are some countries stagnating because of inadequate savings and capital inflows, especially infusion of development aid? Or is the unfavorable global economic environment for developing countries the result of trade rules that are pitched against developing countries, the unsustainable debt owed to multilateral financial institutions, barriers to global technology, and instability in global financial systems?

While the dominant view of the international community, led by the World Bank and International Monetary Fund (IMF), focuses on the need for domestic policy reform – especially macroeconomic policies and market liberalization – and strengthening economic governance, many economists challenge this agenda. It is outside the scope of this chapter to review these debates and the literature on these policy issues. Nonetheless, a review of the more influential books that have shaped this discussion can highlight some of the policy debates.

In the *End of Poverty*, Jeffrey Sachs argues that poor countries are stuck in a "poverty trap" created by certain structural conditions and obstacles that

---

[92] This framework was formalized in the Monterrey Consensus and is complemented by the commitments by donors in the OECD Development Assistance Committee to principles for improved quality and quantity of aid.

they face.[93] In addition to the disadvantages of geography and historical trade patterns, poverty itself is a trap that leaves people unable to save and invest and too unhealthy to be productive. These countries therefore need massive injections of capital and technological solutions for social and economic investment to pull themselves out of the trap. He argues for application of available technology and massive infusions of capital, from development aid, to increase investments in communities and countries.

Nobel laureate Joseph Stiglitz does not argue against policy reform agendas but argues in *Globalization and Its Discontents* that these policy prescriptions are too often prescribed by the IMF and World Bank and required by the WTO trade agreements in a "one size fits all" approach, without taking account of different prevailing conditions. Trade and capital market opening, for example, should be carried out at different paces. In *Making Globalization Work*, he points out that the multilateral trade rules negotiated under the WTO, for example, are pitted against the developing countries.[94] In *Bad Samaritans: The Myth of Free Trade and the Secret History of Capitalism* and *Kicking Away the Ladder*, Ha-Joon Chang goes further to argue that the policy agenda promoted as the key to growth was in fact not one that led to the development of Western Europe and the United States.[95] Many of the policies and institutions that are considered to be critical to successful global market integration, such as trade openness or strong intellectual property rights, were adopted by the United States and European countries only after they industrialized.

While these books are concerned with failures of economic growth and management, another important policy debate is focused on people's lives. Antiglobalization movements argue that globalization not only has benefited few but is socially destructive; corporate investments in export-processing zones exploit female labor, use child labor, and put in place a "rush to bottom" where countries lower labor and environmental standards to attract investors. Investments in oil, mining, and logging destroy the environment and livelihoods of communities, especially of indigenous people, most notably sustainable livelihoods through natural resource exploitation.

Jagdish Baghwati, a leading economist well known for his positions promoting free trade, addresses these issues in *In Defense of Globalization* and argues that globalization not only is not socially benign but in fact is socially beneficial.[96] For example, child labor has been a pervasive problem

---

[93] Jeffrey Sachs, *End of Poverty* (New York: Penguin Books, 2005).

[94] Joseph Stiglitz, *Globalization and Its Discontents* (New York: Norton, 2003) and *Making Globalization Work* (New York: Norton, 2006).

[95] Ha-Joon Chang, *Bad Samaritans: The Myth of Free Trade and the Secret History of Capitalism* (London: Bloomsbury Press, 2002) and *Kicking Away the Ladder: Development Strategy in Historical Perspective* (London: Anthem Press, 2002).

[96] Jagdish Bhagwati, *In Defense of Globalization* (New York: Oxford University Press, 2004).

in developing countries, but it did not appear as a result of corporate investments and is more likely to disappear with investments that expand job opportunities and family incomes and introduce higher wages and labor standards. He recognizes that, during the time it takes for such benefits to be realized, people may suffer. A rich array of publications, such as UNDP's *Human Development Reports*, and the World Bank's *World Development Reports*, aims to develop policy alternatives that would effectively address the social costs and promote economic growth.

A particularly influential publication has been Amartya Sen's *Development as Freedom* that provides an important countercurrent to the economy-centered debates by shifting the unit of analysis from countries to individuals and from economies and incomes to capabilities and thus to human freedom.[97] The UNDP *Human Development Reports* – to which Sen contributed in shaping the conceptual frameworks based on his capability approach – takes these ideas further by identifying annually the key policy obstacles and solutions that lie with both national policy and international policy not only in areas of economic policy but also in social policy and governance.[98] They emphasize development as essentially a process of creating an enabling environment – economic, social, political, cultural, and institutional – for people to exercise their own capabilities and choices.

Concluding Remarks

An important achievement of the past decade has been the consensus achieved by the international community on eradicating extreme poverty as a global priority for the twenty-first century. But there is no political consensus on inequality as a problem; there is no Millennium Development Goal to reduce inequality between and within countries. For long, economists have argued that growth in inequality was an inevitable part of development and economic transformation. Kuznets argued that, in the initial stage of development and industrialization, societies would become more unequal while inequality would decline as societies became "developed" and became mature economies. Today, the Kuznets curve theory is largely discounted. The recent literature on the relationship between inequality and economic growth is inclusive, while newer studies focus on inequality as a major obstacle to growth that explains the poor performance of economies in Latin America.[99] Decreasing inequality, it is then argued, is important not only for moral reasons but as

[97] Amartya Sen, *Development as Freedom* (New York: Oxford University Press, 1999).
[98] See Sakiko Fukuda-Parr, "The Human Development Paradigm: Operationalizing Sen's Ideas on Capabilities," *Feminist Economics* 9, nos. 2–3 (2003): 301–17, for an account of the role that Sen and Sen's ideas played in shaping the Human Development Reports.
[99] David de Ferranti, Guillermo Perry, Francisco Ferreira, and Michael Walton, *Inequality in Latin America: Breaking with History*, Latin America and Caribbean Series (Washington, DC: World Bank, 2004).

a means to growth and prosperity of all. Such arguments appeal not only to moral concerns but to the self-interest of the rich.

The unprecedented commitments made at the start of this century to increase efforts to eradicate poverty stand in stark contrast to the slow progress evident earlier and the lack of action taken then to deliver on the promises made. Of the concrete commitments made – increased development aid, debt relief, reforms in trade agreements, and access to technology – progress is visible only on debt. Donors have committed nearly $60 billion to two multilateral debt relief programs that have in turn provided debt relief to some thirty countries.[100] Debt service payments fell by about 2 percent of GDP from 1999 to 2005. For developing countries as a whole, debt service payments have steadily decreased as a proportion of export revenues since 1999.[101] In areas other than debt relief, there has been no significant policy shift. On development aid, many donor countries had begun to increase their aid budgets from 2000, thanks particularly to vigorous lobbying by development ministers and civil society pressure groups. Moreover, the donor community as a whole committed to an increase by $50 billion between 2004 and 2010 at the 2005 G-8 and Millennium+5 summits. According to the OECD,[102] Official Development Assistance (ODA) had increased from 2001 but started to decline in 2006. However, according to its analysis, much of the increase since 2004 reflected higher levels of debt relief grants, especially $3.3 billion for Iraq and $9.4 billion for Nigeria. Aid to Africa increased sharply, and even without counting debt forgiveness, aid increased by 13 percent. Aid budgets of most of the donor countries fall far short of the UN commitment of 0.7 percent of gross national income with the notable exceptions of Denmark, Luxembourg, the Netherlands, Norway, and Sweden.

Trade negotiations are at the heart of the challenge of inclusive globalization that can spread the benefits of expanding markets to all countries and all people. While the 2001 WTO meeting agreement at Doha agreed to complete by 2007 a series of WTO negotiations focusing on improving conditions for developing countries, there has been little progress on any of the key issues while WTO talks have remained moribund. Moreover, the liberalization of trade in clothing and textiles with the expiration in 2005 of the Agreement of Textiles and Clothing not only created important opportunities for some countries but also undermined emerging manufacturing sectors in many countries, including several of the least developed countries in Africa.[103]

The academic controversies raging today over whether globalization is making the world more unequal and the poor poorer indicate little more than the fact that conclusions depend on how the questions are asked and which

---

[100]   Highly Indebted Poor Country (HIPC) Initiative and the Multilateral Debt Relief
        Initiative (MDRI) provide debt relief to eligible countries meeting specified criteria.
[101]   UN, *The Millennium Development Goals Report, 2007.*
[102]   *OECD Journal on Development*, Development Cooperation Report, 2007 (Paris).
[103]   UN, *The Millennium Development Goals Report, 2007.*

data series are used. These controversies dominate research debates but indicate little more than how economists and statisticians can find many answers to the same questions. These debates mask two more fundamental issues: the growing disparities in human lives rather than in economic performance; and the grotesque levels of poverty and inequality rather than of change in recent years.

Indeed, the key characteristics of global poverty are unambiguously clear. First, the size of global poverty is massive – however it is measured – and unacceptable in today's world of great wealth and technological advancement. Second, even if the trends are ambiguous, the level of inequality is grotesque. Third, the pace of progress in reducing poverty is too slow and concentrated in a few countries and regions within countries, as evidenced by the fact that most regions and countries are not on track to meeting the MDGs. Fourth, the world is increasingly polarized between those countries and people for whom globalization is expanding opportunities and those who are marginalized.

3

The Karma of Poverty

A Buddhist Perspective

David R. Loy

Religious traditions are often conflicted about poverty. Poverty is bad because deprivation involves suffering. Yet the salvation religions offer is not material wealth, and certain types of poverty can even be beneficial in reducing distractions that otherwise interfere with the spiritual life.

Perhaps this tension was easier to live with in premodern cultures, where (what we now consider) poverty was common, if not the norm, and options were more limited. Modern developed (or "economized") societies offer the possibility of a more secular and materialistic salvation from life's ills. Whether this deliverance actually delivers us, we now have the economic and technological resources to liberate all human beings from extreme deprivation, if we care to do so. Should that be a collective priority? Can it be done in ways that remain sensitive to other religious hesitations about wealth and do not convert whole societies to consumerism and "moneytheism"?[1]

Buddhism offers a particularly clear example of this tension. Buddhist societies make a strong distinction between the laity and a monastic *sangha* composed of mendicants (today mostly male). *Bhikkhu* monks, who engage in no productive work, are expected to live very simply with almost no personal possessions except three robes and an alms bowl. At the same time, however, the Buddhist tradition does not encourage laypeople to be poor – on the contrary, some surplus is needed to support the *sangha*.

There are obvious parallels with certain forms of Christian monasticism. In some other ways, however, Buddhism provides a revealing contrast to the Abrahamic religions (Judaism, Christianity, Islam). Consider, for example, the "moral imperative" to relieve extreme poverty. In the Abrahamic faiths, morality is the central theme and obligation, for it is the main way that

---

[1] Elsewhere I have argued that consumer capitalism is the most successful missionary religion that the world has ever known. See "The Religion of the Market," *Journal of the American Academy of Religion* 65, no. 2 (Summer 1997): 275–90.

divinity and humanity communicate; God instructs us how to live and what will happen to us if we do not live that way. This world is the place where good and evil contend with each other, both in history and within ourselves. For Buddhism, however, morality plays a subordinate role in the spiritual path that leads to liberation, because the primary struggle is between ignorance and wisdom. The fundamental ignorance that causes us to suffer is unawareness of the "emptiness" of the self, for we need to realize our nonduality with the world.

This difference is worth noticing because it has consequences for how we respond to poverty. The Abrahamic response is part of its larger concern with justice, including social justice – concepts lacking in traditional Buddhism. For Buddhism, poverty is bad because it causes *dukkha* (ill-being or suffering in the broadest sense), but *dukkha* is also cognitive: a function of our delusions, including our delusive ways of thinking about poverty and wealth. Any understanding of the Buddhist perspective on poverty must be sensitive to both dimensions of this issue.

Buddhism originated in northeast India sometime during the sixth century BCE, as one of several religious responses to caste-based Brahmanism. The *sangha* that Shakyamuni, the historical Buddha, established was egalitarian, open to any caste (precedence within the order was determined by when one joined) and even to women (but see the subsequent discussion).

Buddhism was the first of the three big missionary religions and, like Christianity and Islam, owed much of its success to the fact that it became the religion of an empire. The Mauryan empire of Ashoka united most of India in the third century BCE and helped Buddhism spread to Ceylon and much of Southeast Asia. By the time the Christian era began, Buddhism had begun to split into the Theravada, which still thrives in Sri Lanka and Southeast Asia, and the Mahayana, found in Central and East Asia. Today, both types of Buddhism have become popular outside of Asia – in fact, Buddhism has become the most popular non-Abrahamic tradition in the West.

Theravada bases itself upon the Pali Canon, the oldest Buddhist scriptures, which were preserved orally for more than three centuries before being written down. These texts include the *suttas* (Sanskrit, *sutras*) that purportedly preserve the original words of Shakyamuni. The Mahayana has its own *sutras*, which also claim to be words of the Buddha, but these later texts add little of significance to what the Pali Canon says about poverty, and what follows refers mainly to the early scriptures and a few of their commentaries.

The Buddha often summarized his teachings into four noble truths: *dukkha*, its cause, its end, and its cure. He was sometimes called a great physician, because this logic is similar to how medicine approaches physical disease. What does this understanding of *dukkha*, and how to end it, imply about poverty and how to end it?

What Is Poverty?

According to the traditional story, Shakyamuni Buddha renounced a privileged life of wealth and pleasure for the arduous life of a poor, mendicant forest dweller, yet his ascetic practices did not produce the enlightenment he sought. He eventually discovered a "middle way" that focuses on calming and understanding the mind, which can liberate us from our usual preoccupation with trying to satisfy our cravings. Contrary to the stereotype of Buddhism as a world-denying religion, this goal does not involve transcending this world in order to experience some other reality. Rather, it is better understood as *awakening* to the true nature of this world, including the true nature of oneself. "The Buddha" literally means "the awakened one."

These concerns are reflected in the Buddhist attitude toward wealth and poverty. In the words of Sizemore and Swearer, "a non-attached orientation toward life does not require a flat renunciation of all material possessions. Rather, it specifies an attitude to be cultivated and expressed in whatever material condition one finds oneself. To be non-attached is to possess and use material things but not to be possessed or used by them."[2] The main issue is not how poor or wealthy we are, but how we respond to our situation, for "the greatest wealth is contentment."[3] In the Samyutta Nikaya, Shakyamuni warned repeatedly against a life devoted to acquiring wealth: "Few are those people in the world who, when they obtain superior possessions, do not become intoxicated and negligent, yield to greed for sensual pleasures, and mistreat other beings."[4] Instead, the Buddha praised those who renounce attachment to material things in favor of a life devoted wholeheartedly to the path of liberation, by joining the *sangha*.

A world in which envy (*issa*) and miserliness (*macchariya*) predominate cannot be considered one in which poverty has been eliminated. This follows from the second noble truth of the Buddha: the cause of *dukkha* is *tanha*, "craving." When human beings gain an intense acquisitive drive for some object, that object becomes a cause of suffering. Such objects are compared to the flame of a torch carried against the wind or to a burning pit of embers: they involve much anxiety but very little satisfaction.

Nevertheless, this does not mean that wealth is in itself an obstacle to following the spiritual path. As a worldview and way of life that advocates eliminating *dukkha*, Buddhism cannot value poverty that is a source of *dukkha*. In the Anguttara Nikaya, the Buddha says that for a person who enjoys sense pleasures, poverty (Pali, *daliddiya*) is miserable, because it leads to borrowing

---

[2] Russell F. Sizemore and Donald K. Swearer, eds., *Ethics, Wealth and Salvation: A Study in Buddhist Social Ethics* (Columbia: University of South Carolina, 1990), 2.

[3] Dhammapada, verse 204, in *The Dhammapada*, trans. Eknath Easwaran, 2nd ed. (Tomales, CA: Nilgiri Press, 2007).

[4] Samyutta Nikaya, Kosalasamyutta Sutta, in *The Connected Discourses of the Buddha*, trans. Bhikkhu Bodhi (Boston: Wisdom Publications, 2000), 169.

and increasing debts and thus ever-increasing suffering. *Daliddiya* is lacking the basic material requirements for leading a decent life free from hunger, exposure, and disease. Buddhism recognizes the importance of such minimum material needs even in the case of those who aspire to its spiritual goal, and in fact the basic needs of a monk or nun provide a useful benchmark for measuring that level of subsistence below which human beings should not be allowed to fall. The four requisites of a Buddhist renunciant are food sufficient to alleviate hunger and maintain one's health, clothing sufficient to be socially decent and to protect the body, shelter sufficient for serious engagement with cultivating the mind, and health care sufficient to cure and prevent physical illness. People who voluntarily renounce worldly possessions and pleasures in favor of a life of such minimal needs are viewed as belonging to the community of "noble ones" (*ariyapuggala*).

Extreme poverty makes it more difficult to follow the spiritual path. According to one incident in the Pali Canon, the Buddha could see (with his special powers) that a poor man who lived in the village of Alavi was ripe to realize the first level of enlightenment, so he traveled there to give a discourse. But that very morning the man was busy hunting for his lost ox, while the others were enjoying their alms food. When he finally returned, he was tired and hungry, so the Buddha told the donors to offer food to him as well and waited for him to eat. Only after that did the Buddha expound the Dharma, and the man was awakened. The *bhikkhus* were surprised the Buddha had waited until the man was fed, and on the way back to their monastery he responded: "Bhikkhus! You do not understand that I came all this way because I knew that he was in a fitting condition to take in the Dharma. If he were feeling very hungry, the pangs of hunger might have prevented him from taking in the Dharma fully. That man had been out looking for his ox the whole morning, and was very tired and also very hungry. After all, there is no ailment which is so difficult to bear as hunger."[5]

The five precepts commonly followed (or at least accepted) by all Buddhists are to avoid harming living beings, taking what is not given, improper sexual behavior, false speech, and intoxicants that encourage heedlessness. These mention nothing about abstaining from riches or property, although the precepts do have implications for how one should pursue them and make use of them. Properly acquired wealth is seen as a sign of virtue and, properly used, can be a boon for everyone, because wealth creates opportunities to benefit people and – just as important in Buddhism – to cultivate one's own nonattachment by developing generosity. In one *sutta*, the Buddha speaks of the four kinds of happiness (*sukha*) attained by householders: possessing enough

---

[5] This story is from the Annataraupasakavatthu in the Sukhavagga of the Dhammapadatthakatha, vol. III 261f, cited in http://departments.colgate.edu/greatreligions/pages/buddhanet/genbuddhism/dv/poverty.txt (accessed August 12, 2008).

material resources, enjoying those resources, sharing them with relations and friends, and being free from debt.

On another occasion, the Buddha was told about a rich old miser who had recently died without an heir to his huge fortune. In response, the Buddha contrasted the unused wealth of such a miser with that of a wise man who uses his riches to support family, servants, employees, and religious mendicants. The miser's money "is like a forest pool, clear, cool and fresh, with good approaches and shady setting, but located in a forest of ogres. No one can drink, bathe in or make use of that water." The wise man's wealth "is like a forest pool not far from a village or town, with cool, clear, fresh water, good approaches and shady setting. People can freely drink of that water, carry it away, bathe in it, or use it as they please."[6]

According to another metaphor of the Buddha, some people are like the completely blind because they do not have the vision to improve their material circumstances or the vision to lead a morally elevated life. Others are like the one-eyed because, although they have the vision to improve their material conditions, they do not have the vision to live a morally elevated life; the third and best class of people have the vision to improve both.

Thus, what is blameworthy is to earn wealth improperly, to become attached to it and not to spend it for the well-being of everyone, and to squander it foolishly or use it to cause suffering to others. "Wealth destroys the foolish, though not those who search for the goal."[7] Wealth can be beneficial, and destitution is certainly *dukkha*, but when evaluating the quality of someone's life it is not enough to measure the material conditions. Monastic *bhikkhu* are expected to live very simply; this points to the balance that Buddhism recommends for laypeople.

The Problem of Karma

The Buddhist *sangha* offered an egalitarian alternative to the Hindu Brahmanical caste system. In the Agganna Sutta, the Buddha redefines what it means to be a member of the highest (priestly) caste: one's actions, not one's birth, determine whether someone is a Brahmin.[8] This *sutta* concludes with a myth that explains, in effect, how the social order is a human construct and that all people are equal in origin. From the beginning, then, Buddhism questioned social hierarchies. In terms of the basic Buddha nature and the ability to awaken to it, there are no significant differences among caste, class, race, or nationality. Historically, however, the doctrines of karma and rebirth have served to complicate this issue. Consider, for example, the role of gender.

---

[6] Samyutta Nikaya, Kosalasamyutta Sutta, 182–83.
[7] Dhammapada, verse 355.
[8] Digha Nikaya, sutta 27, in *The Long Discourses of the Buddha*, trans. Maurice Walshe (Boston: Wisdom Publications, 1995), 413–14.

Brahmanism emphasized the inferiority of women. As later codified in the Manusmrti, women were fettered to men for life: first as obedient daughters, then as subservient wives, and finally as aging mothers dependent on sons. A wife's main duty was to produce sons. Although early Buddhism did not completely escape this misogyny, the Buddha's main teaching to householders was revolutionary in this context. In the Sigalovada Sutta, he instructs a husband to minister to his wife in five ways: by being courteous to her, not despising her, being faithful to her, giving her authority, and providing her with ornaments. From the other side, a wife should also show her compassion in five ways: by performing her work well, being hospitable to relations and attendants, being faithful, protecting what he brings home, and being skilled in discharging her duties.[9] Although such injunctions may seem unremarkable today, understanding the marital relationship to be reciprocal, with both sides having rights and responsibilities, was a momentous step in Iron Age India.

But what about the spiritual potential of women? When a delegation of women asked for an order of *bhikkhuni* nuns to be established, the Buddha initially refused, but when his attendant Ananda asked him if women were equal to men in their capacity for enlightenment, he admitted that they were as capable of following the contemplative life and achieving its goals. He then yielded to their request, although with special conditions, eight additional rules of conduct, that made nuns forever subordinate to the monks. (Unsurprisingly, internal textual evidence strongly suggests that those rules were added to the text later.)[10]

The *bhikkhuni* – the first order of female monastics in history – thrived at first, although their contributions to the tradition have been neglected by the male monastics who compiled its history. But once the Buddha passed away, patriarchy began to reassert itself, and their situation deteriorated.

In Theravada countries, the *bhikkhuni* order declined and eventually disappeared. In Thailand today, women renunciants called *mae chi* have shaven heads and white robes but no official status and are not respected as *bhikkhu* monks are; most of them live in temples where they are treated as servants, often cleaning for the *bhikkhu* and eating their leftover alms food. In Tibetan Buddhism, nuns are allowed to take only novice vows, not full ordination; their monasteries are poorer than monks', and they also receive a poorer education. The situation of Buddhist laywomen is more complicated, but in general Asian Buddhist societies remain quite patriarchal today.

There is a Buddhist explanation for the inferior status of women: those unfortunate enough to be born as women are reaping the fruits of their inferior karma.

---

[9] Digha Nikaya, sutta 31, in *The Long Discourses*, 467.
[10] The founding of the *bhikkhuni* order is recounted in the Cullavagga, the fifth book of the Theravada Vinaya, which is part of the Pali Canon.

Ouyporn Khuankaew, a Thai social worker who counsels abused women, describes the problem well:

In Buddhist societies where women are not allowed to be fully ordained as monks, women are often told by monks that having been born a woman is a result of bad karma. In order to remedy this problem, the only thing that women can do is to accumulate a lot of merit in this life, so that in their next life they will be born a man, and then they can become a monk if they choose to. This way of thinking makes women feel inferior and that they are to blame for the outcome of their lives. It makes them more willing to accept whatever gender-based violence that they experience, since it is seen as a direct result of their unlucky fate in having been born a woman.

When a woman asks for guidance from a monk when the husband is the cause of her suffering (such as instances where he has another woman, is physically or mentally abusive to her, gambles their money away, drinks alcohol, etc.), the monk's main advice is for her to be patient and compassionate. Often times, the monk will say that karma is the cause of her suffering, so she has no choice but to accept and deal with the situation, and continue to be kind to her husband so that one day the karmic force will subside and everything will be fine. We found that this kind of thinking is not only the belief of the monks themselves but that it is also prominent among the followers of Buddhism in Southeast Asia, including women.[11]

This passage shows the relationship between the subordination of women (including the violence and poverty they suffer) and the popular Buddhist understanding of karma. It also has important implications for the Thai sex industry.

Much of the problem is a sharp contrast between the high social status of monks and the inferior status of women, who often suffer from low self-esteem. Somewhat similar to the Catholic mother whose son becomes a priest, a Buddhist mother whose son becomes a *bhikkhu* gains much karmic merit (*punna*), as well as an enhanced status in society, but the *sangha* is no longer an option for their daughters, who therefore may be called upon to serve their families in other ways. Most Thai sex workers, like those in other Asian nations, work to send money to their families, which are often large and impoverished. They are trying to fulfill their sense of duty to their parents by sharing the economic burden, and sex work is much better paid than factory work. The recurring problems of rural agriculture, sometimes aggravated by father's or sons' gambling debts, not infrequently cause parents to ask a daughter to "sacrifice" for the sake of the family.[12]

One part of a solution to this situation might involve reintroducing the *bhikkhuni* sangha.[13] Although this would not resolve the economic woes of

[11] Ouyporn Khuankaew, "Buddhism and Domestic Violence," *WFB Review: Journal of the World Federation of Buddhists* 39, nos. 3–4 (July–December 2002): 23–24.
[12] Chatsumaarn Kabilsingh, *Thai Women in Buddhism* (Berkeley: Parallax Press, 1991), 78.
[13] See Tavivat Puntarigvivat, "A Thai Buddhist Perspective," in *What Men Owe to Women: Men's Voices from World Religions*, ed. John C. Raines and Daniel C. Maguire (Albany: State University of New York Press, 2001), 211–38.

rural families, it would raise the status (and therefore the self-esteem) of women, whose capacity for enlightenment is thereby acknowledged. Not only would parents also gain merit when their daughter became a nun, but respected *bhikkhuni* would be in a better position to advise other women and offer spiritual guidance.

There have been recent attempts to reintroduce the *bhikkhuni* order in Sri Lanka, Thailand, and Burma, yet they continue to be resisted by the established *bhikkhu* hierarchy. The official *sangha* authorities tend to be quite conservative regarding such social issues, while some individual monks and temples actually profit from emphasizing the inferiority of women in general and the bad karma accumulated by sex workers in particular. Women and prostitutes are encouraged to offer *dana* (money and other valuables) to the temple in order to make more merit and gain a better rebirth next time. As a result, some temples, especially in northern Thailand, have become wealthy and well adorned as an indirect result of the sex industry.[14]

It is a classic case of "blaming the victim" and wrapping the structures of exploitation in invisibility and inevitability.[15] The basic presupposition is that one's present life situation, whether wealthy or poor, enjoyable or painful, is a consequence of one's behavior in previous lifetimes. One can gain merit by reciting *suttas* and other devotions, but the main way is by making *dana* to the monks and temples.

This understanding of karma and rebirth has important implications for much more than the Thai sex industry. In addition to other types of physical and structural violence against women, including their increased vulnerability to poverty, there are other nongendered consequences regarding the rationalization of racism, economic oppression, birth disabilities, and so forth. Like the "divine right" of kings in early modern Europe, karma has been used to justify both the authority of political elites, who therefore deserve their wealth and power, and the subordination of those who have neither. It provides the perfect theodicy: there is an infallible cause-and-effect relationship between one's actions and one's fate, so there is no need to work toward social justice, because getting what you deserve is already built into the moral fabric of the cosmos.

For these reasons, karma is a critical issue for contemporary Buddhist societies. But has it been misunderstood? Is it a fatalistic doctrine or an empowering one?

According to the popular understanding, the amount of merit (in your karmic bank account) depends not only on the value of your donation but also on the spiritual status of the recipient, which is why you benefit more by

---

[14] Chatsumaarn Kabilsingh, "Prostitution and Buddhism," *WFB Review: Journal of the World Federation of Buddhists* 39, nos. 3–4 (July–December 2002): 97.

[15] See Rita Nakashima Brock and Susan Brooks Thistlewaite, *Casting Stones: Prostitution and Liberation in Asia and the United States* (Minneapolis: Fortress Press, 1996), 237.

giving food to a well-fed *bhikkhu* than to a low-status *mae chi*, much less to a starving homeless person (who is obviously experiencing the consequences of some very poor karma). Curiously, the Buddhists responsible for preserving such teachings also happen to be the ones who most benefit from them – the *bhikkhus* themselves.

Another basic teaching of Buddhism is impermanence, which in this context reminds us that Hindu and Buddhist doctrines about karma and rebirth have evolved over time. Earlier Brahmanical teachings understood karma more mechanically and ritualistically. To perform a sacrifice in the proper fashion would invariably lead to the desired consequences. If those consequences were not forthcoming, then either there had been an error in procedure or the causal effects were delayed, perhaps until your next lifetime (hence implying reincarnation). The Buddha revolutionized this ritualistic approach to getting what you want out of life into a moral principle by focusing on *cetana*, "motivations, intentions." *Cetana* is the key to understanding how he "ethicized" karma. The Dhammapada, perhaps the most popular Theravada Buddhist text, begins by emphasizing the preeminent importance of our mental attitude:

Experiences are preceded by mind, led by mind, and produced by mind. If one speaks or acts with an impure mind, suffering follows even as the cart-wheel follows the hoof of the ox.... If one speaks or acts with a pure mind, happiness follows like a shadow that never departs.[16]

To understand this innovation, it is helpful to distinguish the three aspects of a moral act: the *results* that I seek; the *rule* or *regulation* I am following (whether a moral precept or ritualistic procedure); and my mental attitude or *motivation* when I do something. By no coincidence, in modern moral philosophy there are also three main types of theories. *Consequentialist* theories such as utilitarianism focus on results, *deontological* theories focus on general principles such as the Buddhist precepts (to avoid killing, stealing, lying, improper sex, and drugs that cloud the mind), and *virtue* theories focus on one's character and motivations.

The "law" of karma and rebirth is usually understood as a way to control how the world treats us, which implies, more immediately, that we must accept our own causal responsibility for whatever is happening to us now. This misses the significance of the Buddha's reinterpretation, that karma is the key to spiritual development: *how our life situation can be transformed by transforming the motivations of our actions right now.* When we add the Buddhist teaching about *anatta*, "nonself" – in contemporary terms, the claim that the sense of self is a mental construct – karma is not something the self *has* but is what the sense of self *is*, and what the sense of self is changes according to one's conscious choices. "I" (re)construct myself by what "I" intentionally

---

[16] The Dhammapada, verses 1–2.

do, because "my" sense of self is a precipitate of habitual ways of thinking, feeling, and acting. Just as my body is composed of the food I have eaten, so my character is composed of the conscious choices I have made. "I" am constructed by my consistent, repeated mental attitudes. People are "punished" or "rewarded" not for what they have done but for what they have become, and what we intentionally do is what makes us what we are.

Buddhism attributes our *dukkha* unhappiness to the three "unwholesome roots" (*akusala-mula*) or motivations of action: greed, ill will, and delusion.[17] For better karma, these must be transformed into their more wholesome counterparts: greed into generosity, ill will into loving kindness, and the delusion of separate self into the wisdom that realizes our interdependence with others. To become a different kind of person is to experience the world in a different way. When your mind changes, the world changes, and when we respond differently to the world, the world responds differently to us.

This more naturalistic understanding of karma does not necessarily exclude other, perhaps more mysterious possibilities regarding the consequences of our motivations. In either case, however, it becomes clear that karma-as-how-to-transform-one's-life-situation-by-transforming-one's-motivations-right-now is not a fatalistic doctrine that enjoins one to yield meekly to the problematic circumstances of one's life. It becomes a more empowering religious teaching, with important implications for how we respond to poverty, whether our own or someone else's.

Goals and Priorities

How important for Buddhism is the alleviation of poverty? Is it a moral imperative that we do so, or a requirement of justice? Neither of those descriptions quite fits the Buddhist perspective. Justice is not a Buddhist concept, except in the sense that karma implies justice is built into the way the cosmos functions. If alleviating poverty is a moral imperative, who or what requires us to do so? No one is required to take the five precepts; rather, they are vows one commits oneself to follow, to train oneself in these ways, because doing so will improve one's karma and reduce one's *dukkha*. How does this individual self-project intersect with a commitment to reduce the poverty *dukkha* of others?

This brings us back to one of my introductory remarks, which contrasted the Abrahamic moral worldview with the Buddhist cognitive worldview. For Buddhism, the primary issue is a struggle not between good and evil but between ignorance and insight. The fundamental ignorance is unawareness of the "emptiness" of the self, and the fundamental insight is realizing our nonduality with the world "outside" us.

---

[17] See, for example, Anguttara Nikaya III, in *Numerical Discourses of the Buddha: An Anthology of Sutras from the Anguttara Nikaya*, trans. and ed. Nyanaponika Thera and Bhikkhu Bodhi (New York: Altamira, 1999), 49–50.

What is perhaps most distinctive about the Buddhist perspective is its emphasis on the relationship between *dukkha*, suffering, and *anatta*, the delusion of self: the sense of being a self that is separate from the world one is "in" is illusory – in fact, it is our most dangerous delusion. There is no unconditioned self within the constructed sense of self, and this is the source of our deepest anguish.

To use more modern terms, the sense of self is a psychosocial construct: *psychological* because the ego self is a product of mental conditioning, and *social* because a sense of self develops in relation with other constructed selves. According to Buddhism, there is always something uncomfortable about this construct, because there is *nothing* within or "behind" it. This means that "my" constructed sense of self is ungrounded and therefore haunted by a basic sense of unreality and insecurity.

What does this have to do with poverty? Quite a bit. It has implications for how we *think* about poverty (and wealth, its conceptual twin), and it helps us understand what *motivates* Buddhists to address others' poverty – a motivation that does not derive from justice or moral imperatives.

For Buddhism, the lack of a real self causes anxiety because we tend to view it as "something is wrong with me" or "there is something missing in my life." In effect, the sense of self is shadowed by a sense of *lack*. What is it that is lacking? How I understand that depends upon the kind of person I am and the kind of society I live in. The vague sense that something is wrong with me needs to be given more specific form if I am to be able to do something about it. Medieval Christianity provided an answer – we are *sinful* – and provided religious ways for us to atone for our sins (confession, penance, etc.). Modern secular societies do not accept anything like the concept of sin, so our sense of lack has to sneak in through the back door: today I am perhaps most likely to understand my lack as not having enough money – regardless of how much money I may already have. Money is important to us not only because we can buy almost anything with it but also because it has become accepted as a collective *reality symbol*. Because money does not really end one's deepest *dukkha* – it cannot fill up one's sense of lack – this way of understanding what ails us often becomes a trap. You are a multimillionaire but still feel as if something is wrong with your life? Obviously, you don't have enough money yet.

According to Buddhism, then, our tendency to become preoccupied with money can often be traced back to the basic ungroundedness of the self. But if a desire for wealth is in fact a symptom of something else – an attempt to fill up one's sense of lack – then one can never have enough money (or possessions, or fame, or sexual conquests, or power) because they cannot fill up the sense of lack.

I wonder if the globalization of corporate capitalism adds a collective dimension to this wealth-poverty dualism. Can the world's *poverty problem* be understood separately from its *wealth problem*? Is waging a "war on poverty" the flip side of our preoccupation with wealth creation? Perhaps this is how we rationalize a way of life obsessed with economic growth, no matter what its other costs. "Undeveloped" poor people must be miserable because that is how we would experience their circumstances. Global poverty is conceptually necessary if the rest of the world is to be commodified and monetarized. Otherwise, one cannot justify the profound social reorientation (experienced by most people as social disorganization) that is required. Traditional cultures must be redefined as obstacles to be overcome, and local elites must become dissatisfied with them, in order to create a consumerist lifestyle.

I am not making light of the situation for those whose destitution needs to be alleviated as soon as possible. The issue is whether one of the causes of poverty today is the delusions of the rich – delusions that have very concrete effects on the well-being of many people, including themselves. Perhaps we should not focus only on the poverty side of the problem; maybe, to correct the bias, we should be as concerned about the wealth side: the personal, social, and ecological costs of our collective obsession with wealth creation and perpetual economic growth. A Buddhist approach emphasizes the importance of seeing through such dualisms if our efforts to help the destitute are actually to be successful.

What motivates Buddhist efforts to relieve poverty, if not a moral imperative or a concern for social justice? This brings us back to the Buddhist solution to the *dukkha* of self.

According to the Pali Canon, Shakyamuni himself did not say much about the nature of *nirvana* except that it is the end of *dukkha*, craving, and delusion. Buddhist "awakening" obviously involves realizing something about the constructedness of the sense of self. Usually the nothingness at our core makes us so uncomfortable that we try to evade it, by identifying with something that seems to offer stability and security. We keep trying to fill up that hole, yet nothing that we can ever attain or achieve can end our sense of lack.

But what happens when we do not run away from that void at our core? Meditation is an important part of the Buddhist path because when we meditate we "let go" of the physical and mental tendencies – the habitual ways of thinking, feeling, acting and reacting – that constitute the sense of self. Insofar as these habits *are* the self, letting go of them – observing them without being motivated by them or identifying with them – is letting go of one's sense of self. Dogen, a thirteenth-century Japanese Zen master, summarized this process nicely:

To study Buddhism is to study yourself. To study yourself is to forget yourself. To forget yourself is to be enlightened by the ten thousand things [of the world]. To be enlightened by the ten thousand things is to be freed from attachment to the mind and body of one's self and of others.[18]

<hr>

[18] This is the beginning of Genjo-koan, the first fascicle of Dogen's Shobogenzo.

We are enlightened by the things of the world when we realize our nonduality with them. To awaken is to realize that the sense of separation between me "inside" and the rest of the world "outside" is a delusion – in fact, it is the basic ignorance at the root of our most troublesome *dukkha*. This does not involve getting rid of the self, because there never has been a self, but simply recognizing what has always been the case.

What does this have to do with relieving poverty? It clarifies the Buddhist motivation for addressing it. To wake up to my nonduality with the world is to realize my responsibility for the world. Why do I take care of my leg? What a question! I take care of my leg because it is (part of) my body. The same is true for my world. The Buddhist tradition emphasizes compassion as much as wisdom, because compassion is how enlightenment manifests itself in daily life.

According to the traditional stereotype, a Theravada *bhikkhu* aspires to become an *arhat*, who dwells in perfect serenity because he or she has put an end to all craving. According to Mahayana, however, the spiritual goal is to become a *bodhisattva*, who is selflessly devoted to helping all beings awaken to their true nature. This is usually understood as a sacrifice: the bodhisattva will not enter into nirvana until all others have entered nirvana. That way of expressing it misses the main point: the bodhisattva understands that he (or she) cannot be fully enlightened until everyone is, because he knows that he is not separate from them. Any sense that all my own *dukkha* can be resolved without also addressing the *dukkha* of others is a delusion.

Needless to say, this describes the ideal, not the way most people actually live in Buddhist societies, Asian or Western. Many, perhaps most Asian Buddhists are not interested in pursuing enlightenment, at least not during this lifetime, and prefer to accumulate merit for a better rebirth next time.

In pursuit of the goal of eradicating or reducing poverty, in particular, which other human goods can be licitly subordinated? The Buddhist tradition has not addressed this issue directly, as far as I know, but neither does Buddhism emphasize the economic freedom of the individual or the inviolability of property rights – two of the most important principles often cited against redistributive solutions. I would surmise that, for Buddhism, the only human good that should never be subordinated to poverty reduction is the possibility of spiritual awakening and the path that leads to such awakening. It is difficult to imagine an instance of such illicit subordination – except perhaps the forceful conversion to a new consumerist worldview. To be a Buddhist is to hope that this is not the only way to reduce poverty.

What about priorities? Should our main concern be to address the most extreme poverty, no matter where it may be and who may be afflicted, or should we rather focus on the less extreme poverty within (or near) our own communities? Again, I am not aware that Buddhists have reflected on this issue. One could draw on elements within the tradition to argue for either side. The bodhisattva vows to save all living beings, anywhere, suggesting a universalism that would want to alleviate the worst deprivation. By being so universal, however, such a concern also becomes abstract, tending to draw attention away from our immediate situation, from those we personally (and nondually) encounter in our daily lives. Perhaps the Mahayana principle of *upaya kausakya*, "skill-in-means," implies that no generally applicable, definitive answer can be given to this dilemma, for we need to be sensitive to each individual situation and decide on a case-by-case basis. The same applies to issues of short-term pain versus long-term gain, with the obvious caveat that those with the most to gain should not be inflicting the pain on others.

The Role of the State

Who or what has the greatest responsibility for alleviating poverty – and, if possible, eradicating it? The Buddhist text that has the most to say about this issue is the Lion's Roar Sutta (Cakkavatti-sihanada Sutta), which includes the lengthiest discussion of poverty anywhere in the Pali Canon. This *sutta* offers a myth that claims a causal relationship between material destitution and social deterioration and attributes responsibility for that relationship to the ruler.

The Buddha tells the story of a monarch in the distant past who at first followed the Buddhist teachings, doing as his sage advised: "Let no crime prevail in your kingdom, and to those who are in need, give property." Later, however, he began to rule according to his own ideas and did not give property to the needy, with the result that poverty became widespread. Because of poverty, one man took what was not given and was arrested; when the king asked him why, the man said he had nothing to live on. So the king gave him some property, saying that it would be enough to carry on a business and support his family.

Exactly the same thing happened to another man who stole. When other people heard about this they too decided to steal so they would be treated in a similar way. Then the penny finally dropped, and the king realized that if he continued to give property to such men, theft would continue to increase. So he decided to get tough on the next thief: "I had better make an end of him, finish him off once for all, and cut his head off." And he did.

At this point in the story, one might expect a moralistic parable about the importance of deterring crime, but it turns in exactly the opposite direction:

Hearing about this, people thought: "Now let us get sharp swords made for us, and then we can take from anybody what is not given, we will make an end of them, finish them off once and for all and cut off their heads." So, having procured some sharp swords, they launched murderous assaults on villages, towns and cities, and went in for highway robbery, killing their victims by cutting off their heads.

Thus, from the not giving of property to the needy, poverty became widespread; from the growth of poverty, the taking of what was not given increased; from the increase of theft, the use of weapons increased; from the increased use of weapons, the taking of life increased.[19] Despite its fanciful elements, this myth has some interesting implications. Poverty is presented as a root cause of immoral behavior such as theft, violence, and falsehood. The solution has nothing to do with accepting our (or others') "poverty karma." The problem begins when the king does not give property to the needy – in modern terms, when the state neglects its responsibility to maintain a minimum of what we now call distributive justice. The *sutta* argues, in effect, that social breakdown cannot be separated from broader questions about the benevolence and "distributive justice" of the social order. The solution to poverty-induced crime is not to punish severely but to enable people to provide for their basic needs.

A similar point is made in the Kutadanta Sutta, in which a counselor tells his king that there is much lawlessness and civil disorder in his kingdom, making property insecure. The king is advised to deal with this not by taxation, or by attempting to suppress it forcibly, but by improving the people's lot directly:

> Suppose Your Majesty were to think: 'I will get rid of this plague of robbers by executions and imprisonment, or by confiscation, threats and banishment,' the plague would not be properly ended.... To those in the kingdom who are engaged in cultivating crops and raising cattle, let Your Majesty distribute grain and fodder; to those in trade, give capital; to those in government service, assign proper living wages. Then these people, being intent on their own occupations, will not harm the kingdom. Your Majesty's revenues will be great, the land will be tranquil and not beset by thieves, and the people, with joy in their hearts, will play with their children, and will dwell in open houses.[20]

Both these *suttas* illustrate that *dana*, "generosity," is the most important concept in traditional Buddhist thinking about poverty and social responsibility, because it is the main way nonattachment is cultivated and demonstrated. Buddhists are called upon to show compassion to those who need our help. Those who suffer are reaping the fruit of their previous deeds, yet their lot is not understood in a punitive way. Although they may be victims of their own previous selfishness, the importance of generosity for those walking the Buddhist path does not allow us the luxury of being indifferent to their situation. We are expected, even required, to lend assistance. This appeal, however, is not to justice for a victim. Despite the prudential considerations expressed in the *sutta* – what may happen if we are not generous – it is the karma and spiritual progress of the *giver* that is the main issue. No one can evade responsibility for his or her own deeds and efforts, yet generosity is not optional: we are obligated to respond compassionately to those in need.

In the Lion's Roar Sutta, the king started the social breakdown when he did not fulfill this obligation. Does this mean that the poor are not responsible for addressing their own poverty? They have the same responsibility as the

---

[19] Digha Nikaya iii 65ff., in *The Long Discourses*, 396–405.
[20] Kutadanta Sutta, in *The Long Discourses*, 133–41.

king, and everyone else: in accordance with their own situation, they need to transform the motivations of their own deeds, from the "three poisons" of greed, ill will, and delusion to generosity, loving kindness, and the wisdom that recognizes our interdependence. Given the greater opportunities provided to the king, he will be able to be much more generous, of course, but the spiritual challenge he faces is basically the same as that of anyone else trying to follow the Buddhist path. Today that includes billionaires and national leaders.

Socially Engaged Buddhism

Whether or not Shakyamuni Buddha had a broader social vision, Buddhism as it developed historically and institutionally has had very little to say about *how* to address involuntary poverty. As we have seen, the main emphasis has been on *dana*, or generosity, which according to the karma doctrine may be even more beneficial to the donor than to the recipient. Perhaps we should not underestimate the possibilities of such an approach, especially if it accompanies a widespread realization of our interdependence and nonduality. But that caveat foregrounds the problem: most of the world is not Buddhist, and most people who consider themselves Buddhist understand karma as merit making rather than character reforming. Individual *dana* will not provide the solution to global poverty in a globalizing economic system that emphasizes competitive success.

Recently, however, a movement sometimes called *socially engaged Buddhism* is developing fresh perspectives that open up new possibilities. Perhaps the most prominent figure has been the Vietnamese *bhikkhu* and Zen master Thich Nhat Hanh, who has a wide following in the West. His work has not focused specifically on poverty, but he has reformulated and updated the traditional five precepts of early Buddhism into the fourteen precepts of engaged Buddhism. These include:

4. Do not avoid suffering or close your eyes before suffering. Do not lose awareness of the existence of suffering in the life of the world. Find ways to be with those who are suffering, including personal contact, visits, images and sounds. By such means, awaken yourself and others to the reality of suffering in the world.

5. Do not accumulate wealth while millions are hungry. Do not take as the aim of your life fame, profit, wealth, or sensual pleasure. Live simply and share time, energy, and material resources with those who are in need.

13. Possess nothing that should belong to others. Respect the property of others, but prevent others from profiting from human suffering or the suffering of other species on Earth.[21]

---

[21] Originally published in Thich Nhat Hanh, *Interbeing: Fourteen Guidelines for Engaged Buddhism* (Berkeley: Parallax Press, 1993), http://buddhism.kalachakranet.org/resources/14_precepts.html (accessed July 20, 2008).

This new version of the precepts expands the original focus considerably. Students are encouraged to become aware of poverty and to live simply in ways that do not exploit others. Again, this has great implications *personally,* but it is not clear what it means *socially* – what it implies for how we might address widespread, structural destitution. What should we be doing to prevent others from profiting from human and nonhuman suffering?

Engaged Buddhism has become a force in Thailand as well, mostly as a result of the efforts of various students of the influential reformist monk Buddhadasa Bhikkhu (1906–93). The social critic Sulak Sivaraksa, in particular, founded the International Network of Engaged Buddhists (INEB) and has initiated a number of social, humanitarian, and ecological movements, some of them addressing the relative poverty of most farmers. These include *bhikkhus* helping to establish village co-ops that buy farming necessities, such as seeds and fertilizers, and also combine crops to obtain better prices from middlemen.

By far the most innovative and successful Buddhist-inspired antipoverty project has been the Sarvodaya Shramadana movement, which provides development and conflict resolution programs to villages in Sri Lanka. Based on Buddhist and Gandhian principles, it was founded in 1958 by A. T. Ariyaratne, a Sinhalese schoolteacher. The organization claims that it is active in almost half of Sri Lanka's 38,000 villages, and that at least 11 million people have benefited from its programs.

Sarvodaya programs begin when a village invites staff members to lead a discussion on what the village needs. In a sequence of stages, staff members assist villagers in setting up a village council, then building a school and clinic, creating family programs and economic opportunities, starting a village bank, and finally offering to help other villages. In place of institutional handouts, the emphasis is very much on *self*-development; according to their famous phrase, "We build the road, and the road builds us."

Partly in response to the ethnic conflict that has plagued Sri Lanka in recent years, Sarvodaya has also sponsored large public meditations in which many thousands of Buddhists, Hindus, Muslims, and Christians meditate together to promote each other's welfare, by practicing what Buddhists call the *Brahmavihara* (Abodes of God) meditation. This type of contemplative practice is acceptable to non-Buddhists as well, and in fact all Sarvodaya programs are nonsectarian, open to members and villagers of all faiths.[22] Ironically, this attitude is itself very Buddhist: if you are a Buddhist, whether or not someone else is a Buddhist is not very important in affecting how you respond to him or her. Bodhisattvas vow to save all living beings, not only Buddhists, and for that matter not only human beings.

[22] For more on this movement, see Joana R. Macy, *Dharma and Development: Religion as Resource in the Sarvodaya Self-Help Movement* (Sterling, VA: Kumarian Press, 1991), and George D. Bond, *Buddhism at Work* (Sterling, VA: Kumarian Press, 2003).

Conclusion

The number of impoverished people in the world is increasing (partly due to population growth), and by most measures the gap between rich and poor is also increasing worldwide. What should be done about this? If poverty is an economic issue, what is the point of an essay on Buddhist perspectives?

No one knows how many Buddhists there are, but upward of 400 million is a reasonable estimate. A large majority lives in underdeveloped countries, and many are impoverished – by modern Western standards, at least. If international agencies are to help them, it may be important to understand their own cultural attitudes toward wealth and the lack of it.

This essay has focused on something else, however. Poverty is one aspect of a cluster of economic and social issues that are not culturally neutral. Absolute deprivation – insufficient food and water, clothing, shelter, and access to basic medical care – needs to be addressed wherever and whenever it occurs. Beyond that, though, agencies should be careful not to impose solutions that assume "we know what you need and what you need to do to get there."

My presentation of Buddhist perspectives has highlighted what I think Buddhism has to contribute. The Buddhist tradition is intellectually sophisticated and its different worldview may become more relevant as the globalization of corporate capitalism becomes more problematic. Its implicit critique of consumerism, in particular, challenges the values that often accompany a higher standard of living. The popular understanding of karma as merit making tends to make Buddhism into a kind of "spiritual materialism," but I have tried to demonstrate that this distorts the Buddha's own emphasis on transforming the quality of our lives by transforming our motivations.

Most important, perhaps, is the correlation Buddhism emphasizes between one's sense of being a discrete self – an individual whose ultimate well-being can be pursued separately from the well-being of others – and *dukkha*, one's basic dissatisfaction or disease. If such a self *is dukkha*, and if "awakening" involves realizing our interdependence with others, there are great implications for how we understand poverty and how to end it.

4

Poverty and Morality in Christianity

Kent A. Van Til

Christianity, with Judaism and Islam, is one of three Abrahamic faiths. Its roots and basic presuppositions derive from Judaism. The Jewish scriptures form the first or Old Testament of Christianity. The Old Testament together with the Christian New Testament forms the Christian Bible, the source of Christian revelation. Christianity's Jewish origin is significant for this study inasmuch as Christian assumptions about anthropology, cosmology, and law are derived from Judaism.

Like Jews, Christians believe that humans are created in "the image and likeness" of God (Gen. 1:27). While Christian philosophers in ages past were fond of speculating on the metaphysical possibilities of this phrase, recent Jewish and Christian scholars recognize that this text does not set forth an ontological theory. Rather, being created in God's image shows that all human persons are created in such a way that they can relate to other humans, to God, and to the physical world in love, hatred, or indifference.

Christianity also accepts the Jewish understanding of humanity's task in creation. We are to "cultivate and guard the garden" (Gen. 2:15), which has been created for our delight. We have been given authority over creation – birds, fish, animals, and land. All of creation may be used for our benefit, while recognizing that creation itself has intrinsic value. Christianity also derives its understanding of the divine person(s) and will from Judaism. While Judaism insists that "God is one," Christianity believes in a god who is three-in-one. Yet this three-in-one God maintains the characteristics of the one God of Israel. This divine Tri-unity is not the god of a particular aspect of nature, or a state of being, but a god of history. A Christian is thus not a person who lives in a particular place, or has a particular ancestry, but is one who follows this God in and through history, bearing the hope that his or her own history will end with a loving, face-to-face encounter with God.

As a God who is claimed to be "one nature yet three persons" (Nicene Creed), this God is a communal being who shares love and power among its persons. The creation of humankind is a reflection of this plurality. All humans are of one race and share the same nature.

The distinguishing factor between Christians and Jews is the person of Jesus. For Christians, he was more than a human Messiah; he was a divinely incarnated messiah, sent as God's divine Son to deliver God's people through the human nature he assumed. His deliverance entails the restoration of God's people to wholeness in their relationships to other persons, to God herself, and to the physical world. Jesus did this by taking upon himself our nature as humans and perfecting it via obedience and sacrifice. For Christians, Jesus is the model and goal for humanity.

Definitions

Within both the Hebrew Bible (Christian Old Testament) and the New Testament, the absence of material goods is the foundational meaning of poverty. Numerous Hebrew terms such as *anawim, dal, ebyon, ras*, and *misken* emphasize aspects of poverty such as humility, neediness, lowliness, thinness, and dependency. In the New Testament, the Greek term *ptochos*[1] is used for "poor" and assumes the connotations of these Old Testament terms.

To be poor in its most abstract sense is to be less than the whole, integral human self that God created and restored in Christ. The gospel of Luke in particular shows this wide angle when it ties the term "poor" to others such as "lepers, blind, lame, hungry, oppressed, deaf" (see Luke 4:18, 6:20, 7:22, 14:13, 14:21, 16:20–22). Poverty for Luke implies any characteristic that isolates a person from his or her community. All of the difficulties that Luke mentions separate people from the good and wholesome relationships that they were meant to have in God's creation. Leprosy, for example, is a contagious disease that required lepers to remove themselves from society. The leper was ritually impure, physically disabled, and socially ostracized. Luke includes such marginalized individuals in his lists of those whom Jesus came to restore. The poor, so considered, are those whose dignity as image bearers of God has been besmirched.

Jesus's Sermon on the Mount is recorded in the gospels of Matthew and Luke. Luke's gospel reads, "Blessed are the poor, for they shall inherit the Kingdom of God" (Luke 6:20), whereas Matthew's gospel reads "Blessed are the poor *in spirit* for theirs is the Kingdom of Heaven" (Matt. 5:3). It is clear that in both gospels the poor are identified with the other subjects of the beatitudes – the mournful, the meek, the pure, the persecuted, the peacemakers, and those who hunger and thirst for righteousness.[2] Poverty as lack

---

[1] Two exceptions are the use of *penes* in 2 Cor. 9:9 and Luke 21:2.

[2] Leif E. Vaage, "The Sermon on the Mount," in *God's Economy: Biblical Studies from Latin America*, ed. Ross Kinsler and Gloria Kinsler (Maryknoll, NY: Orbis, 2005), 129.

of material goods thus correlates with other conditions of lack and distress. These passages and others indicate that poverty has numerous causes and shapes. Poverty can result from spiritual oppression in which one's material goods are wrongly given over to spiritual or ecclesiastical powers. Poverty can result from laziness or foolishness. Or it can result from oppression, maldistribution, or divine punishment.

One subject that must be defined in order to understand the Christian conception of poverty is that of *property*. If poverty is a lack of goods, the way that goods become property merits attention.

For the Christian, the world is God's Creation. This means that matter is formed, shaped, and directed by a personal, divine Creator. Things are thus not merely commodities but aspects of the world that have intrinsic value in relation to the Creator. Material things are ultimately "owned" by God. Leviticus 25:23 reads, "The land must not be sold permanently, because the land is mine and you are but aliens and my tenants." Humans thus have a temporary right, rather than an absolute right, to use material things. In the Protestant tradition, Christians are thus considered "stewards" of God's property. The sixteenth-century reformer John Calvin wrote:

Let him who possesses a field, so partake of its yearly fruits, that he may not suffer the ground to be injured by his negligence; but let him endeavour to hand it down to posterity as he receive it, or even better cultivated. Let him so feed on its fruits that he neither dissipates it by luxury, nor permits to be marred or ruined by neglect. Moreover, that this economy, and this diligence, with respect to those good things, which God has given us to enjoy, may flourish among us; let every one regard himself as the steward of God in all things, which he possesses. Then he will neither conduct himself dissolutely, nor corrupt by abuse those things, which God requires to be preserved.[3]

Such a view of property contrasts with the Roman view of property in the ancient world in which Christianity developed. According to Roman law, a property owner had the right to use, enjoy, or abuse whatever he owned – *ius utendi, fruendi, abutendi*.[4] These rights applied to slaves and cattle, as well as physical property. This view of property is clearly at odds with the Jewish-Christian view of property. Historian Justo Gonzalez writes:

The Jewish understanding of property differed radically from that of Roman law. While the latter tended to be absolute, with few limitations set on it, Jewish property rights were limited by the rights of God, by the rights of the property itself, which must not be abused, and by the rights of the needy – the poor, the sojourner, the orphan, and the widow. Along these lines the commandment against stealing is to

---

3 John Calvin, *Commentary on Genesis*, trans. Rev. John King (Grand Rapids, MI: Eerdmans, 1948), 125.
4 W. W. Buckland and Peter Stein, *A Textbook of Roman Law from Augustus to Justinian* (Cambridge: Cambridge University Press, 1966), 188.

be understood, not as a safeguard for the rights of private property, but rather as a safeguard against abuse that would destroy life.[5]

Thus, the poor had a divine right to some property because God is the final owner of all, and all of creation is destined for all of God's image bearers. Saint Ambrose of Milan (d. 397) writes:

God our Lord willed that this land be the common possession of all and give its fruit to all. But greed distributed the right of possessions. Therefore, if you claim as your private property part of what was granted in common to all human beings and to all animals, it is only fair that you share some of this with the poor, so that you will not deny nourishment to those who are also partakers of your right (by which you hold this land).[6]

Ambrose, in this and other passages, is not delegitimating private property as much as he is calling into question the then current Roman understanding of property rights. Ambrose and Calvin echo the Jewish understanding of property that included an intrinsic value for the goods themselves, and a moral demand upon them in light of the needs of the poor.

High-Risk Groups

In Judaism as well as the ancient Roman Empire within which Christianity grew, women, children, and aliens had no legal standing without the intercession of an adult male patron. Thus, in Hebrew law codes, widows, orphans, and aliens were shown special concern in light of this dependent status. This special concern for the disempowered carried over into the New Testament. Echoing his own Jewish tradition, James, the brother of Jesus says, "Religion that God our Father accepts as pure and faultless is this: to look after orphans and widows in their distress and to keep oneself from being polluted by the world" (James 1:22).

In passages that appear to contradict this special concern for women and children, Pauline and Petrine traditions emphasize that women were not to have authority within the Church. In their "Haustafelen" or household codes, both Pauline and Petrine letters insist on a subservient role for women. For example, in Ephesians 5:22 Paul instructs wives to "submit to your husbands as to the Lord. For the husband is the head of the wife as Christ is the head of the church." Paul then goes on to instruct Christian children, slaves, and masters how to live as imitators of Christ in their roles. It is clear that Paul writes to those who understood the roles that women, children, and slaves played in ancient Greco-Roman society. At many points within Jewish and Christian traditions women have been viewed as inferior to men. Women have been

---

[5] Justo Gonzalez, *Faith and Wealth: A History of Early Christian Ideas on the Origin, Significance, and Use of Money* (San Francisco: Harper & Row, 1990), 22.

[6] Ambrose, *De Nabuthe Jez*, cited in Gonzalez, *Faith and Wealth*, 191.

thought of as the source of sin (Gen. 3), as less rational, and as subservient humans whose roles must be childbearing and homemaking.

While Christians today receive such writings as inspired scripture, most no longer presume the social roles that were then assumed. As Hannah Arendt shows, a division between the polis and the family, or the public and the private realm, was axiomatic throughout ancient political thought.[7] As a result women and children of antiquity were not permitted access to the economic sphere of life and were themselves considered property of the male. This cultural understanding of roles has clearly contributed to the impoverishment of women throughout Christendom. The ancient world's view of social roles has only recently been rejected. In 1891 for example, Pope Leo XIII stated that "women, like children, are dependent and in need of protection" and are "by nature bound to the home."[8]

While this view of women has been dominant, there are some elements within the Christian scriptures themselves, however, that undercut these sexist assumptions. God is presented by means of feminine metaphors such that of a nursemaid (1 Peter 2:2) or a hen (Matt. 23:37). Women were followers and disciples of Jesus who financed his ministry (Luke 8:1–3) and were the first to find the resurrected Christ (Luke 24:1–3). Women received the Holy Spirit at Pentecost where Peter pointedly quotes the prophet Joel: "I will pour out my Spirit on all people. Your sons and daughters will prophesy, even on my servants, both men and women I will pout out my spirit in those days" (Acts 2:17–18). Women in the early church were honored as equals (e.g., Acts 1:14; 16:11–16, Rom. 16:4–5, 12), serving as teachers, evangelists, prophetesses, deaconesses, and financiers, as well as prisoners and martyrs.[9] This civil and religious equality has continued in practice among some monastic Christian groups as well as later Protestants, such as the Shakers and Quakers, who practiced complete equality since the eighteenth century.

By the later twentieth century, great progress in overcoming sexism has occurred in most Christian churches. Pope John XXIII stated in 1963:

It is obvious to everyone that women are now taking a part in public life. This is happening more rapidly perhaps in nations with a Christian tradition, and more slowly, but broadly, among peoples who have inherited other traditions and cultures. Since women are becoming ever more conscious of their dignity, they will not tolerate being treated as inanimate objects or mere instruments, but claim, both in domestic and public life, the rights and duties that befit a human person.[10]

---

[7] Hannah Arendt, *The Human Condition* (Chicago: University of Chicago Press, 1958), 28.
[8] *Rerum Novarum*, par. 33, cited in Marvin Krier Mich, *Catholic Social Teaching and Movements* (Mystic, CT: Twenty-Third Publications, 1998), 348.
[9] See, for example, Mary T. Malone, *Women and Christianity*, vol. 1 (Maryknoll, NY: Orbis, 2001).
[10] *Pacem en Terris* no. 41, in David O'Brien and Thomas Shannon, *Catholic Social Thought: The Documentary Heritage* (Maryknoll, NY: Orbis, 1992).

In recent times, sexism has been decried by many Christians as a sin inasmuch as it reduces the inherent dignity that women have as God's human image.

In sum, Christianity has not spoken univocally about women. Christian teaching has long held that men and women are equally human, and equally children of God, but often qualified this equality by speaking of women's unique "role" or "nature." These roles, implicitly or explicitly, are those of bearing and caring for children and working within the home rather than outside in the workplace in which well-paying jobs can be found. Inasmuch as Christianity has limited women to these roles, it has often placed them in situations of economic dependence and its resultant poverty.

Volition

We must speak in this section of the volition of both God and humans. Remember that the Creator is the ultimate owner of all things (see Lev. 25:23) and that His or Her will is to be followed in the distribution of all goods. Viewed as such, private property is theologically understood as property that is leased from God. As such, it must be used as God, its owner, would.

The will of God was and is that all people have basic sustenance.[11] The world was created by God as a gift for all people, not as an estate for a limited number of property owners. The world belongs to God, and the fruits of the earth belong to all of God's children. God's ideal is that His children thrive as they live in love with each other, care for the earth, and live holy and just lives. If humans are to achieve any of these ends, they must have the basic material sustenance to do so. This physical sustenance is inherently "good." God declares the creation to be good in Genesis 1, and steps into history at various points to ensure that His people may have not only basic sustenance but sufficient goods to thrive. In the book of Exodus, for example, God liberates the Hebrews from their slavery and brings them into a land "flowing with milk and honey." The ultimate historical intervention, for the Christian, is the incarnation of God, as Jesus the Christ. Christ is the fullness of God and brings his followers into the Kingdom of God, which is characterized by fullness and blessing for the poor and distress and punishment for the rich and unjust. This reversal of fortunes is seen, for example, in Mary's song: "For he has filled the hungry with good things, and sent the rich away empty" (Luke 1:53–55).[12]

The life of Jesus himself is an example of this reversal. Philippians 2 says that God in Christ "emptied himself" of divine glory to become not only a

---

[11] See Kent A. Van Til, *Less than $2.00 a Day: A Christian View of World Poverty and the Free Market* (Grand Rapids, MI: Eerdmans, 2007), esp. chap. 2.

[12] See also Luke 6:20–26, 13:30, 16:19–31, 18:18–30, etc., for other passages showing this reversal of fortunes.

member of the human race but a poor, enslaved, and tortured member of it. The incarnate one was crucified – unjustly condemned and wrongfully killed. The perfect man and image bearer of God was treated with disdain and hatred by the powerful. Yet his death is not the last word for the oppressed. That word is "resurrection," and resurrection is followed by glorification and honor. The resurrection shows God's ultimate plan for the marginalized: a life of fullness with God, a life in which there will be no suffering, or sorrow or pain (Rev. 21:4). Yet, note that even the resurrected Christ still wears the wounds of his suffering on his resurrected flesh, thus maintaining his identity with the poor and oppressed (Luke 24:39).

Jesus announced that the poor would be the focus of his own ministry, using language derived from the Jewish Year of Jubilee:

The Spirit of the Lord is on me, because he has anointed me to preach good news to the poor. He has sent me to proclaim freedom for the prisoners and recovery of sight for the blind, to release the oppressed, and to proclaim the year of the Lord's favor. (Luke 4:18)

The divine intrusion of God via the incarnate Christ is the source of liberation from poverty. Jesus liberates the land and the people and frees all to live in dependence upon a gracious God. Followers of Christ must then be the means by which the goods of God's creation are distributed according to God's mandates. By distributing goods in accordance with God's will, we participate in God's holiness, justice, and providence.[13]

Each Sunday worship service is a celebration of Christ's resurrection and a call to serve. The liturgy of the church recognizes that all are needy and that all must call upon God to forgive and restore. It includes the anticipatory celebration of the feast of God. It propels Christians to do the work of God. A life that speaks of God's love and performs proper religious rituals is not a true Christian (or Jewish) life unless the ritual is lived out in deed.[14]

In Christian history, some religious orders such as the Benedictines insisted that all possessions be held in common. Following the pattern of the church in Acts 4, the Rule of Saint Benedict commands, "Above all, this evil practice

---

[13] See Albino Barrera, O.P., *God and the Evil of Scarcity: Moral Foundations of Economic Agency* (Notre Dame, IN: University of Notre Dame Press, 2005).

[14] The Hebrew prophet Isaiah, for example, speaks of the religious ritual of fasting but insists it is useless unless accompanied by service to the poor:

> Is not this the kind of fasting I have chosen:
> to loose the chains of injustice
> and untie the cords of the yoke
> to set the oppressed free and break every yoke?
> Is it not to share your food with the hungry and to provide
>   the poor wanderer with shelter
> When you see the naked to clothe him
> and not to turn away from your own flesh and blood?
>
> (Isaiah 58: 6–7)

must be uprooted and removed from the monastery. We mean that without an order from the abbot, no one may presume to give, receive or retain anything as his own."[15] This did not imply that the orders themselves were poor; indeed, the order itself might have held great possessions. Rather, the motivation for relinquishing personal possessions among the religious orders was typically to liberate themselves from the mundane pursuits that might impede spiritual growth. This liberation from the pursuit of possessions in turn freed them to serve the poor. Of them Benedict insists, "Great Care and concern are to be shown in receiving poor people and pilgrims, because in them more particularly Christ is received; our very awe of the rich guarantees them special respect."[16] Throughout the history of Christianity, some Christian groups have held goods in common and served the needs of the poor with the surplus. Many Christians today also relinquish some goods or fast in order to show solidarity with the poor.

The Bible does recognize that poverty is sometimes due to the evilness or weakness of the poor themselves. People make bad choices and must live with the results. These bad choices often bring about harm not only to one person but to other generations or to neighbors near and far. In the Hebrew wisdom writings, this person is simply a "fool," and his actions lead to his own destitution and eventual destruction.

In light of the fact that some are poor because of their own folly, many Christians have attempted to determine which poor are deserving and which are undeserving. Though this practice has a long history, it also has a long history of condemnation. John Chrysostom, the fourth-century bishop of Constantinople, has harsh words for those who wish to discern which of the poor merit the favor of the rich.

We point our finger at the idleness of the poor, and yet we ourselves often work at things that are worse than idleness.... You who often spend the day in the theatres and in merriments, you who gossip about the whole world, think that you are not idle. And then you look at someone who spends the entire day asking and begging, in tears and suffering, and you dare ask for an account![17]

Liberation theology is especially forceful in showing that poverty is a result of socioeconomic structures, rather than failings of the poor themselves. Gustavo Gutierrez writes, "The question of poverty is a question of the very meaning of life and the collective course of humanity. Poverty is the result of a system that institutionalizes privileges for some and poverty, humiliation and death for others."[18] Elsa Tamez notes that poverty strikes at both the

---

[15] *The Rule of St. Benedict*, ed. Timothy Fry, O.S.B. (Collegeville: Liturgical Press, 1981), 231.

[16] Ibid., 259.

[17] Chrysostom, *De eleem*, cited in Gonzalez, *Faith and Wealth*, 211.

[18] Gustavo Gutierrez, "The Violence of a System," in *Concilium: Christian Ethics and Economics: The North-South Conflict*, ed. Jacques Pohier and Dietmar Mieth (Edinburgh: T & T Clark, 1980), 93.

oppressed and the oppressor: "The foundation of the option for the poor is the intention to end structural sin that produces dehumanization for the poor as well as those responsible for the poverty."[19] In the vast majority of cases then, Christians see poverty as contrary to the will of God and the result of conditions and events over which the poor have little or no control.

Goals

The alleviation of poverty is a moral imperative among Christians, as God's will serves as the standard of morality. In the Hebrew scriptures, the alleviation of poverty not only was a moral imperative but took on the force of covenantal law. The conditions in the New Testament times, however, were quite different from those under the Israelite monarchs. The early Christian Church was a tiny sect in the vast Roman Empire. Early Christians were thus hardly in a position to make the alleviation of poverty a matter of law. Nevertheless, the early church felt a great moral burden to meet the needs of its own members. Historian Justo Gonzalez reports:

There is in the *Didache*[20] no indication that one should dispossess oneself of such goods for the sake of renunciation, or that one should give them to the community for the sake of a principle of shared property. The reason why one should not claim the rights of private property is the need of the other. The governing principle in giving is neither a communistic ideal nor an ascetic renunciation, but the need of the other.[21]

As the church grew and the Roman Empire fell, the church took the lead in alleviation of poverty because the institutions of the empire dissolved in the waves of barbarian invasions. It may be during this time that the distinction between civil justice and religious charity developed. Historian Samuel Fleischaker notes, "It would be closer to the truth to say that the premodern church saw assistance to the poor as an obligation of charity or mercy and not as an act of justice, not as something to which the needy had a right."[22] For the history of this distinction between justice and charity, Fleischaker suggests we turn to Cicero:

The distinction between justice and charity, or beneficence was introduced by Cicero in *De Officiis*. In his *De Officiis*, Cicero contrasts justice with beneficence, saying that justice can and should be legally required of us while beneficence should

---

[19] Elsa Tamez, "Poverty, the Poor, and the Option for the Poor," in *The Option for the Poor in Christian Theology*, ed. Daniel G. Groody (Notre Dame, IN: University of Notre Dame Press, 2007), 46.

[20] Also known as "The Doctrine of the Twelve Apostles," a series of Christian teachings from the second century CE.

[21] Gonzalez, *Faith and Wealth*, 94.

[22] Samuel Fleischaker, *A Short History of Distributive Justice* (Cambridge, MA: Harvard University Press, 2004), 49.

not be, that violations of justice inflict positive harm while failings of beneficence merely deprive people of a benefit and that duties of justice are owed to anyone, anywhere, while duties of beneficence are owed more to friends, relatives and fellow citizens than to strangers.[23]

Debate continues to this day among Christians as to whether the alleviation of poverty is a demand of justice or an option of charity. However, the distinction between justice and charity may be misplaced, inasmuch as it equates justice with civil obligation and charity with religious supererogation. For within the Christian tradition, charity as well as justice is obligatory. Charity demands justice as its basis. In the early twentieth century, Monsignor John A. Ryan takes up this issue. While he maintains that there is a distinction between justice and mercy, he urges that within Christian faith both are obligatory:

It cannot, indeed, be too strongly nor too frequently insisted that charity is not a substitute for justice; on the other hand, any solution of the social problem based solely upon conceptions of justice, and not wrought out and continued in the spirit of charity, would be cold, lifeless, and in all probability of short duration. If men endeavor to treat each other merely as equals, ignoring their relation as brothers, they cannot long maintain a pure and adequate notion of justice, nor apply the principles of justice fully and fairly to all individuals.[24]

Note how Ryan attaches the relation of citizen to that of brother. Although he seems to accept Cicero's distinction between justice and charity, he tempers it with the confession that people are not only fellow citizens but also fellow children of God, and therefore brothers and sisters to whom we are obligated to show mercy.

Contemporary liberation theology clearly takes the view that the provision of basic necessities is a requirement of justice. Gustavo Gutierrez writes:

Life, a gift from God, is also the first human right. The poverty and insignificance in which many people live violates that right. In effect, poverty means death, both physical death that is early and unjust, due to lack of the most basic necessities for life, and cultural death, as expressed in oppression and discrimination for reasons of race, culture, or gender. Theologically speaking, poverty is the negation of the significance of creation.[25]

The Christian tradition recognizes that the elimination of poverty for some may cause pain for others. Specifically, succor of the poor may result in losses for the rich. Yet, this is not necessarily a grave moral problem. The Hebrew prophet Isaiah condemned the ancient Israelites saying, "The plunder from

---

[23] Cicero, *De Officiis* I.20–59, III.21–28, cited in ibid., 20.
[24] Msgr. John A. Ryan, "The Church and the Workingman," *Catholic World* 89 (April–September 1909), cited in *On Moral Business*, ed. Max Stackhouse, Dennis McCann, and Shirley Roels (Grand Rapids, MI: Eerdmans, 1995), 299.
[25] Gustavo Gutierrez, "Memory and Prophecy," in Groody, *The Option for the Poor in Christian Theology*, 27.

the poor is in your houses" (Isa. 3:14b). The view that wealth has been taken from the poor by the rich makes the return of that wealth more a matter of restitution than theft. Saint Ambrose writes, "When you give to the poor, you give not of your own, but simply return what is his, for you have usurped that which is common and has been given for the common use of all. The land belongs to all, not to the rich; and yet those who are deprived of its use are many more than those who enjoy it."[26]

Thomas Aquinas addresses the same issue, asking:

Is it lawful to steal in case of necessity?[27]

Although theft and robbery are mortal sins, there is this qualification. In the case of need all things are common property, so that there would seem to be no sin in taking another's property, for need has made it common.... If the need be so manifest and urgent, that it is evident that the present need must be remedied by whatever means be at hand (for instance when a person is in some imminent danger, and there is no other possible remedy), then it is lawful for a man to succor his own need by means of another's property, by taking it either openly or secretly; nor is this properly speaking theft or robbery. "That which he takes for the support of his life becomes his own property by reason of that need."[28]

The Christian's goal is the elimination of need and the restoration of the poor into community. Nevertheless, Christians recognize that there will always be poor (Deut. 15:11) among them and throughout the world until the return of the Lord. Recall that poverty is a wide-ranging term in Christianity that includes not only economic but physical, psychic, and social aspects as well. Restoration of the poor thus entails recognition of the full personhood of the poor. The poor are not merely objects of our benevolent attention but human persons with their own initiatives, histories, and communities. In some cases, Christian missionaries have not respected different communities when working among the poor. Some Christian missionaries have likely created "Rice Christians" – poor people who claim that Jesus is their Savior in order to receive a handout of rice. The gospel certainly does not support this practice, but when the gospel and food come from the same person, it is hard to avoid the perception that receiving the gospel is the precondition for receiving the food.

Christian missionaries and development workers recognize that restoration may be piecemeal, and, in the ultimate sense, no one may be perfectly whole before the eschaton. Nevertheless, knowing that all our efforts fall short of the goal that only Christ can accomplish, Christians go forward with a wide variety of remedial steps. The earliest Church is one example of how this was done. This church seems to have brought all into its community, regardless of

[26] St. Ambrose, *De Nabuthe Jez*, cited in Gonzalez, *Faith and* Wealth, 191.
[27] Thomas Aquinas, *Summa Theologica* II-II, q. 66, q. 7, resp.
[28] Ibid., ad 2.

class, gender, or status. According to the Acts of the Apostles, the members of the new Christian Church lived as a Jubilee community (Acts 2:42–47).

1. They devoted themselves to the apostolic teaching.
2. They gave as they had ability to one another as each had need.
3. They shared in the Eucharist, and offered prayer for one another.
4. They performed signs and wonders of salvation.[29]

This kind of community is what is depicted in narratives about the Kingdom of God – the ultimate goal of Christianity. The picture of the kingdom is variously described as a banquet or wedding feast, a Sabbath rest, fullness, and victory over all enemies including poverty. When John the Baptist sent his disciples to ask whether Jesus is the Messiah, Jesus answered by saying: "Go tell John what you hear and see: the blind receive sight, the lame walk, those who have leprosy are cured, the deaf hear, the dead are raised, and the good news is preached to the poor" (Matt. 11:4–5). The prince of this kingdom, Jesus, demonstrated its presence by performing these deeds. The call of Christian faith entails that we also do such deeds and share the good news of restoration.

The Apocalypse of John portrays the scarcity and oppression of this age, and contrasts it with the fullness and justice of the age to come. For example, the price of grain stated in Revelation 6:5–6 places it out of reach for the poor. Products like oil and wine, however, which are not staples for the poor but market commodities, are normally priced. The evil beast takes economic power over the world, requiring that all have his mark on their right hand in order to buy and sell (Rev. 12:16–17). The demonically ruled Babylon is characterized by extravagance, self-indulgence, and disregard for the poor (Rev. 18). The New Jerusalem, on the other hand, is characterized by justice and plentitude for all. Precious gems line the streets, gates are made of pearls, and the city is made of gold. Common people walk these streets and enter these gates. The righteous from all nations are welcomed. In this city, "God will wipe away every tear from their eyes. There will be no more death or mourning or crying or pain, for the old order of things has passed away" (Rev. 21:4).[30]

The ultimate goal for the Christian is to be found acceptable by the Lord in the final Day of Judgment. Jesus says that, on that day,

The King will say to those on his right, "Come, you who are blessed by my Father; take your inheritance, the kingdom prepared for you since the creation of the world. For I was hungry and you gave me something to eat, I was thirsty and you gave me something to drink, I was a stranger and you invited me in, I needed clothes and you clothed me, I was sick and you looked after me, I was in prison and you came to

---

[29] Pablo Richard, "Now Is the Time to Proclaim the Biblical Jubilee," in Kinsler and Kinsler, *God's Economy*, 54.
[30] Cf. Nestor O. Miguez, "Economics and Abundant Life in New Testament Apocalyptisicm," in Kinsler and Kinsler, *God's Economy*, 220–40.

visit me." Then the righteous will answer him, "Lord, when did we see you hungry and feed you, or thirsty and give you something to drink? When did we see you a stranger and invite you in, or needing clothes and clothe you? When did we see you sick or in prison and go visit you?" The King will reply, "I tell you the truth, whatever you did for one of the least of these brothers of mine you did for me." (Matthew 25:34–41)

Remedies

The Christian tradition has employed a very wide range of remedies for poverty. In this section I address three concrete remedies – work, charity, and hospitality – and three remedies more related to the practice of virtue – generosity, forgiveness, and Christ-likeness.

Productive work is the primary remedy for poverty. Humans are made in the image of their Creator and are thus creative workers. We are assigned to "cultivate and care for" the world (Gen. 2:15). The world is fruitful, and its produce is ours to use. The ideal then is that our labors in creation provide each person with basic sustenance or even abundance. Poverty occurs when we cannot work, or our labor is insufficiently productive. Particularly in Protestantism, Christians have insisted on the importance of a vocation for all believers. Each person is called by God to holy service. That service may well be in construction work, education, or agriculture. All vocations are religious inasmuch as all vocations fulfill God's original mandate to till and protect the earth. All work is work for God, using the materiel that God provides. As Luther puts it, "When a man works at his trade, walks, stands, eats, drinks, sleeps, and does all kinds of work for the nourishment of his body or for the common welfare, God is pleased."[31]

Numerous Christian organizations today attempt to help the poor become employable or to help them start their own businesses.[32] In so doing, they enable the poor to fulfill their divine calling. At the same time, many within the Christian tradition insist upon a "living wage" for such laborers.[33] Prominently among these are Monsignor John A. Ryan and Pope Pius XI. In his 1931 encyclical *Quadragesimo anno*, the Pope states, "In the first place, the wage paid to the workingman must be sufficient for the support of himself and of his family."[34]

---

[31] Martin Luther, cited in Ian Hart, "The Teaching of Luther and Calvin about Ordinary Work," *Evangelical Quarterly* 67, no. 1 (1995): 36.

[32] For example, I am involved with a group called Partners Worldwide, which attempts to build the economic capacities of the poor. See www.partnersworldwide.org.

[33] This is in contrast with a "market" or "prevailing" wage, which may or may not be enough for basic sustenance.

[34] *Quadragesimo anno* no. 71, in O'Brien and Shannon, *Catholic Social Thought: The Documentary Heritage* (Maryknoll, NY: Orbis, 1992).

Nonetheless, poverty strikes at both working and nonworking poor. The traditional response of the church has been beneficence, broadly conceived. In New Testament times, Saint Paul took up offerings for the mother church in Jerusalem among the Gentile churches around the Aegean (Rom. 15:25–29, 1 Cor. 16:1–4, II Cor. 8:1–15).

Offerings were also taken for the poor within specific congregations and for the poor among other Christian congregations. By the time of Augustine, almsgiving together with prayer and fasting had become a way of atoning for small sins. But by almsgiving, the church fathers did not mean giving loose change to the occasional beggar. They meant that one ought to give from one's surplus to assuage another's need.[35] As Augustine believed, "By giving to the poor, one uses one's perishable wealth to build up an imperishable treasure in heaven."[36] The text to which Augustine refers, Matthew 6:19–20, reads: "Do not lay up for yourselves treasures on earth, where moth and rust destroy, and where thieves break in and steal. But store up for yourselves treasures in heaven, where moth and rust do not destroy, and where thieves do not break in and steal. For where your treasure is, there your heart will be also." Commenting on this passage, Calvin says:

But how shall we transmit them? Surely, by providing for the needs of the poor; whatever is paid out to them, the Lord reckons as given himself [cf. Matt. 25:40]. From this comes that notable promise: "He who gives to the poor lends to the Lord" [Prov. 19:17]. Likewise, "He who sows bountifully shall reap bountifully" [2 Cor. 9:6]. For what is devoted to our brothers out of the duty of love is deposited in the Lord's hand. He, as he is a faithful custodian, will one day repay it with plentiful interest.[37]

The New Testament church assigned care of the poor to its first officers, the deacons, insisting that this work was essential to the church's life (Acts 6:1–6). Ambrose writes, "Nothing graces the Christian soul so much as mercy; mercy as shown chiefly towards the poor, that thou mayest treat them as sharers in common with thee in the produce of nature, which brings forth the fruit of the earth for use to all."[38] Later, "Parishioners were expected, but not forced to pay tithes to the church (out of which some funds for hospitality and relief were taken), and above that to contribute to poor relief."[39]

---

[35] Gonzalez, *Faith and Wealth*, 217.
[36] Ibid.
[37] John Calvin, *Institutes of the Christian Religion*, ed. John T. McNeill, trans. Ford Lewis Battles (Philadelphia: Westminster Press, 1960), 827.
[38] Ambrose, *De Nabuthe Jez*, cited in Gonzalez, *Faith and* Wealth, 191.
[39] Brian Tierney, *Medieval Poor Law: A Sketch of Canonical Theory and Its Application in England* (Berkeley: University of California Press, 1959), 93, 97, 126, cited in Christine D. Pohl, *Making Room: Recovering Hospitality as a Christian Tradition* (Grand Rapids, MI: Eerdmans, 1999), 49.

By the mid-fourth century, the Christian community had won a reputation for its practice of *philanthropia* toward the poor and marginalized. This was so widely recognized that the "apostate" emperor Julian strongly criticized human greed among his fellow Romans as the root cause of poverty and urged that the generosity and hospitality among Hellenes be comparable to that of "the impious Galileans."[40] He writes:

> Why do we not observe that it is their benevolence to strangers, their care for the graves of the dead and the pretended holiness of their lives that have done most to increase atheism? For it is disgraceful that, when no Jew ever has to beg, and the impious Galileans [Christians] support not only their own poor but ours as well, all men see that our people lack aid from us. Teach those of the Hellenic faith to contribute to public service of this sort.[41]

Hospitality was and is practiced as a remedy for poverty. This practice follows that of Jesus's own teaching:

> When you give a luncheon or dinner, do not invite your friends, your brothers or relatives, or your rich neighbors; if you do, they may invite you back and so you will be repaid. But when you give a banquet, invite the poor, the crippled, the lame, and blind, and you will be blessed. Although they cannot repay you, you will be repaid at the resurrection of the righteous. (Luke 14:12–14)

Though the Greeks and Romans also practiced hospitality, theirs was not the same. Ancient Greek and Roman philanthropy was more a display by the wealthy than a project aimed at alleviating poverty.[42] As Christine Pohl notes, "Greek and Roman views of benevolence and hospitality stressed formal reciprocal obligations between benefactor and recipient. Because a grateful response from the beneficiary was key to the ongoing relationship, the tradition emphasized the worthiness and goodness of recipients rather than their need."[43]

Christians, on the other hand, were expected to practice hospitality without thought of recognition or reward. It was to be a welcoming, an act of grace in which the one offering hospitality accepts the poor as a member of his or her extended family. Lactantius, the Christian tutor of Constantine's son, said that "the house of a just man ought not to be open to the illustrious, but to the lowly and abject. For those illustrious and powerful men cannot be in want of anything."[44] True Christian hospitality for Lactantius and the Christian

---

[40] Brian E. Daley, "The Cappadocian Fathers and the Option for the Poor," in Groody, *The Option for the Poor in Christian Theology*, 84.

[41] Julian (The Apostate), *The Works of the Emperor Julian*, Loeb Classical Library, vol. 3, 67–71, cited in Pohl, *Making Room*, 44.

[42] Daley, "The Cappadocian Fathers and the Option for the Poor," 83.

[43] Pohl, *Making Room*, 18.

[44] Lactantius, *The Divine Institutes*, bk. 6, chap. 12, in *The Ante-Nicene Fathers*, ed. Alexander Roberts and James Donaldson (Edinburgh: T & T Clark, 1867–72), vol. 7, 176, cited in Pohl, *Making Room*, 18.

tradition must be directed toward the poor; otherwise, it would become a reciprocal exchange rather than an act of grace. Hospitality provides strangers with a sense of place and belonging. It often became a woman's virtue as it was practiced in a "woman's sphere," the home.

Less concretely, poverty is remedied by replacing the vice of greed with the virtue of generosity. During the early years of the church, only idolatry was considered a worse sin than greed. Both greed and idolatry were "an attack on God's exclusive rights to human love and devotion, trust and confidence, and service and obedience."[45] The desire for self-sufficiency, as opposed to dependence on God, is widely condemned in the Christian tradition. For example, during a time of famine, Saint Basil of Cappadocia served in what today would be called "a soup kitchen," and he condemned the greed that left many destitute:

Who then, is greedy? The one who does not remain content with self-sufficiency. Who is the one who deprives others? The one who hoards what belongs to everyone. Are you not greedy? Are you not one who deprives others? You have received these things for stewardship and have turned them into your own property! ... The bread that you hold on to belongs to the hungry; the cloak you keep locked in your storeroom belongs to the naked. You do an injury to as many people as you might have helped with all these things![46]

Gregory of Nazianzus clearly ties the idea of philanthropy to the generous, self-giving work of Christ. For Gregory of Nazianzus, *philanthropia*, the active love of our fellow men and women that is most tellingly expressed in love of the poor, is the highest of all the human virtues, "since nothing else is more proper than this to God, who will save us by the grace and philanthropy of our Lord Jesus Christ."[47]

The work of Christ is a work of forgiveness. Jesus instructs his disciples to pray "forgive us our debts, as we forgive our debtors," and this refers not only to spiritual forgiveness. The term used in Matthew 6:12 "to forgive" us our debts as we forgive our debtors

is a specific technical term used to characterize the forgiveness of debts.... It goes back to a heritage of Jewish Jubilee traditions. *Deror* is a technical term used to speak of the liberation of male and female slaves, and also of the cancellation of debts (see also Ex. 21 and Dt. 15).... That liberation is concrete and profoundly economic and social. It is part of the web of social relationships, and also the relationship of gender. The persons by whom the principles of *deror* and aphesis are reclaimed are indebted persons who have been turned into slaves or who are in the

---

45 Brian S. Rosner, *Greed as Idolatry: The Origin and Meaning of a Pauline Metaphor* (Grand Rapids, MI: Eerdmans, 2007), 173.

46 St. Basil of Caesarea, *Homilies* 6.7 (J. P. Migne, ed., *Patrologia Graeca*, 31.276C8–77A8), cited in Daley, "The Cappadocian Fathers and the Option for the Poor," 80.

47 Daley, "The Cappadocian Fathers and the Option for the Poor," 82. Daley cites from Gregory of Nazianzus, *Orations* 14.5 and 1 (A. Van Heck, ed. *Gregorii Nysseni De pauperibus amandis orationes duo* [Leiden: Brill, 1964]).

process of becoming slaves through the process of indebtedness, or through wars of conquest or occupation. What is intended is a broad liberation, encompassing both enslaved persons and debts.[48]

For the Christian, life itself is a gift, as is the renewal of life provisioned by Jesus Christ. The foundation of our faith is the fact that we have been forgiven by God for our moral failings. Forgiveness then becomes the primary action that Christians need practice toward others. It is the gift we have received, and the one that we must in turn extend.

It is not surprising then that the principal sacrament of the church is the gift of God's self via a fellowship meal. The Lord's Supper, or Eucharist, is a sacrament in all Christian traditions. Jesus was recognized for dining with outcasts and sinners. In fact one biblical exegete suggests that "Jesus was crucified because of how he ate."[49] The Eucharist is a sign of the unity of all those who share in Christ, regardless of their race, their gender, or their economic status. All are one in Christ's body. "Because there is one loaf, we who are many are one body, for we all partake of the one loaf" (1 Cor. 10:17). It is a foreshadowing of the holy meal of the kingdom in which all will eat together. Jesus says, "I confer on you a kingdom, just as my Father conferred one on me, so that you may eat and drink at my table in my kingdom and sit on thrones, judging the twelve tribes of Israel" (Luke 22:29–30). The meal is a precursor of the Messianic age, an age of fullness and justice, in which no one is hungry.

Casiano Floristan notes that the linguistic parallels derived from the Latin terms for knowing and tasting give a profound sense to the meaning of the Eucharist. "Through taste one perceives the flavor of food. Let us remember that taste (*sabor*) and knowledge (*saber*) come from the word wisdom (*sabiduria*), perceived in two ways: as food and as knowledge. The Eucharist could be called a morsel and a drink within the context of a meal. Tasting God is finding a delicious knowledge of God."[50]

Knowing God must result in doing God's will. As noted, God wills that all humans have basic sustenance. By providing sustenance for all, we participate in the work of God. As Father Albino Barrera, O.P., puts it, we become the instrumental righteousness of God. Barrera writes, "Moral life, including economic agency, is fundamentally a participation (or lack thereof) in God's righteousness. Economic life can either be an avenue for or an obstacle to faith's being in act. However, in order to serve a faith that bears abundant

---

[48] Ivoni Richter Reimer, "The Forgiveness of Debts in Matthew and Luke," in Kinsler and Kinsler, *God's Economy*, 161.

[49] Robert J. Karris, *Luke: Artist and Theologian* (New York: Paulist Press, 1985), 47, cited in Casio Floristan, "The Place of the Poor in the Eucharistic Assembly," in Groody, *The Option for the Poor in Christian Theology*, 245.

[50] Floristan, "The Place of the Poor in the Eucharistic Assembly," 240.

harvest in the here and now, economic agency has to be self-sacrificing."[51] This self-sacrifice is to be the hallmark of the Christian ethic. Jesus said, "Let any one who would follow me deny himself, take up his cross and follow me" (Matt. 8:34). Jesus denied himself the privileges of divinity, took up his cross, and carried it to the place of crucifixion (see Philippians 2, cited earlier).

Scope and Priorities

For Christians, as is the case for others, there are some people who are placed in close relational and geographic proximity to us. The scope of our responsibilities begins here. "If anyone does not provide for his relatives, and especially for his immediate family, he has denied the faith and is worse than an unbeliever" (1 Tim. 5:8). Yet the Christians' obligations are not limited by proximity. Jesus's famous parable of the Good Samaritan shows that our obligations extend even to those whom we might despise. This is how Calvin interprets this parable:

Who is our neighbor?

Now since Christ has shown in the parable of the Samaritan that the term "neighbor" includes even the most remote person [Luke 10:36] we are not expected to limit the precept of love to those in close relationships. I do not deny that the more closely a man is linked to us, the more intimate obligation we have to assist him…. This does not offend God for his providence, as it were, leads us to it. But I say: we ought to embrace the whole human race without exception in a single feeling of love; here there is no distinction between barbarian and Greek, worthy and unworthy, friend and enemy, since all should be contemplated in God, not in themselves.[52]

This runs contrary to human nature. We love our own. But the radical love of Christ compels us to act in this way. Again, Calvin's commentary is apt:

Whatever man you meet who needs your aid, you have no reason to refuse to help him. Say, "He is a stranger," but the Lord has given him a mark that ought to be familiar to you…. Say, "he is contemptible and worthless"; but the Lord shows him to be one to whom he has deigned to give the beauty of his image. Say that he does not deserve even your least effort for his sake; but the image of God, which recommends him to you is worthy of your giving yourself and all your possessions.[53]

The reason that the scope is so wide is that Jesus is present in and among the poor. Jesus was a poor man, as have been most of his followers. And in the

---

[51] Albino Barrera, *God and the Evil of Scarcity: Moral Foundations of Economic Agency* (Notre Dame, IN: University of Notre Dame Press, 2005), 127.

[52] Calvin, *Institutes*, 418.

[53] Ibid., 696.

judgment scene mentioned earlier, Jesus says, "As you have done it to the least of these my brothers, you have done it unto me."

Consider the following biblical evidence that Jesus was poor and cared for those in poverty.

- Mary speaks of herself as the humble one (Luke 1:48).
- The sacrifice Mary offered at Jesus's birth (Luke 2:24) was the offering of the poor.
- Jesus accepted help and subsidies (Luke 8:1–3).
- Jesus had no home (Luke 9:58).
- Jesus may well have carried no money (Luke 20:20–26).[54]

In addition, Jesus insisted that we honor the poor and give away possessions to serve the poor. Jesus's miracles also served the poor – he fed them, healed them, and liberated them from demonic possession. Clearly, Jesus was himself poor and showed a preference to the poor.

In light of the fact that Jesus Christ was poor, our service to the poor serves Christ. Gregory of Nazianzus (ca. 375 CE) writes:

If you believe me at all, then, servants and brothers and sisters and fellow heirs of Christ, let us take care of Christ while there is still time, let us minister to Christ's needs, let us give Christ nourishment, let us clothe Christ, let us gather Christ in, let us show Christ honor – not just at our tables, as some do, nor just with ointment, like Mary, nor just with a tomb, like Joseph of Arimathea…. But since the Lord of all things "desires mercy and not sacrifice" (Hosea 6:6), and since "a compassionate heart is worth more than tens of thousands of fat rams" (Dan. 3:40 LXX) let us give this gift to him through the needy, who today are cast down on the ground, so that when we all are released from this place they may receive us into the eternal tabernacle, in Christ himself.[55]

This tradition of service to Christ via service to the poor has continued into modern times. Archbishop Oscar Romero, who was martyred in his homeland of El Salvador in 1980, proclaimed:

I rejoice in the fact that our church is persecuted, precisely for its preferential option for the poor, and for trying to incarnate itself in the interest of the poor. How sad it would be, in a country where such horrible murders are being committed, if there were no priests among the victims! They are the testimony of a church incarnated in the problems of its people.[56]

54 Rene Kruger, "Conversion of the Pocketbook," in Kinsler and Kinsler, *God's Economy*, 178.
55 Daley, "The Cappadocian Fathers and the Option for the Poor," citing Gregory of Nazianus, *Orations*, 14, 40, 86.
56 Cited from Romero's homilies in Jon Sobrino, "The Latin American Martyrs," in Groody, *The Option for the Poor in Christian Theology*, 99.

Responsibility and Conditionality

Responsibility for the alleviation of poverty is distributed widely among individuals and institutions in Christian thought. This general rule applies: "From everyone who has been given much, much will be demanded; and from the one who has been entrusted with much, much more will be asked" (Luke 12:48b). This passage comes at the end of one of Jesus's parables in which a servant is commanded to manage the master's house while the master is away. The good servant manages wisely, but the foolish servant squanders the master's resources and is beaten for his profligacy upon his return. The parable is a reference to God, who gives responsibility to his servants while "away" from the estate. With these two texts as a foundation, it may be said that the greatest responsibility for combating poverty falls upon those who have the greatest resources to address it.

One biblical text that is commonly used to qualify this principle is that of Saint Paul in 2 Thessalonians 3:10, "For even when we were with you, we gave you this rule: 'If a man will not work, he shall not eat.'" This suggests that willingness to work is a precondition of aid. While true, it is a truth in a very limited context. The church to which Paul wrote this letter was preoccupied with the second coming of Christ – so much so that its members gave up their daily work as they waited for his imminent return. So Paul's admonition is directed specifically to those who thought that the imminent return of Christ released them from their earthly duties.

Biblical scholar Beverly Roberts Gaventa thus recommends an appropriate contextualized reading of this text:

Some will be tempted to hear the command: "Anyone unwilling to work should not eat" as an inviting slogan for a new social policy. Those who wish to render this bit of proverbial wisdom into a rule of law proscribing the care of human beings for one another need to remember that this is not the only word in the canon about how people are to be fed. It is one thing to say that idle people should get back to work, but the unmistakable message of the Bible is that humankind rightly honors its creator only when it also protects all those made and loved by that same creator.[57]

Protection and succor of the poor can be the duty of individuals, churches, or government. Poverty is a hydra. Its many heads include spiritual domination, lack of access to goods, physical or emotional weakness, and isolation from information or markets. Thus, the team that alleviates poverty must include a wide variety of players. Businesses have a primary role in generating employment that uses and rewards human creativity. Churches have a role of

---

[57] Beverly Roberts Gaventa, *First and Second Thessalonians* (Louisville: John Knox Press, 1998), 131–32.

aiding the weakest in their parishes, via a wide variety of congregational programs. Individuals are called upon to serve others face to face and by supporting their churches or Christian philanthropic organizations. Some churches
have spun off nongovernmental organizations, and other churches support
their own denominationally controlled relief and development agencies, for
example, Catholic Charities and the Lutheran World Services. At present, the
line between churches and Christian NGOs has become thin.

If, as I do, a Christian believes that all humans have a *right* to basic sustenance, the issue becomes one of civil justice, and thus entails the presence of
government as establisher and enforcer of this justice. Many churches have
teams that work on economic-justice-related issues by lobbying governments
and writing policy. Christians pursue economic justice at all governmental
levels – local, state, and federal – and international bodies such as the United
Nations. Though methods may vary, Christians are obligated to serve the
poor.

5

Classical Liberalism, Poverty, and Morality

Tom G. Palmer

"Classical liberalism" refers to that tradition of ethical, political, legal, and economic thought that places the freedom of the individual at the center of political concern and that sees that freedom as, in John Locke's language, each person's enjoyment of a *"Liberty* to dispose, and order, as he lists, his Persons, Actions, Possessions, and his whole Property, within the Allowance of those Laws under which he is; and therein not to be subject to the arbitrary Will of another, but freely follow his own."[1]

Many different streams of thought have contributed to that tradition. They have drawn on a variety of religious and philosophical ideas. Steve Scalet and David Schmidtz note that,

as the variety of classical liberalism's philosophical sources may suggest, classical liberalism is not itself a foundational philosophical theory. The heart of classical liberalism is a simple policy prescription: Nurture voluntary associations. Limit the size and, more importantly, the scope of government. So long as the state provides a basic rule of law that steers people away from destructive or parasitic ways of life

I wish to acknowledge the research assistance of my colleague Diogo Costa, editor of OrdemLivre.org, who, as a serious student of political thought, provided helpful insights, and Lech Wilkiewicz, who helped me track down a number of obscure items.

[1] John Locke, *Two Treatises of Government*, ed. Peter Laslett (Cambridge: Cambridge University Press, 1988), Second Treatise, VI, 57, 306. Note that for Locke the term "property" covers far more than the term does in contemporary English, in which it is limited to what Locke termed "estate." Locke, in contrast, refers to "Lives, Liberties, and Estates, which I call by the general name, *Property*." Ibid., Second Treatise, IX, 123, 350. Compare also James Madison, in his essay "On Property." "This term in its particular application means 'that dominion which one man claims and exercises over the external things of the world, in exclusion of every other individual.' In its larger and juster meaning, it embraces every thing to which a man may attach a value and have a right, and which leaves to every one else the like advantage." *National Gazette*, March 29, 1792, http://press-pubs.uchicago. edu/founders/documents/v1ch16s23.html.

and in the direction of productive ways of life, society runs itself. If you want people to flourish, let them run their own lives.[2]

Classical liberals, despite often vigorous disagreement among themselves over both the foundations of liberty and the proper limits on state power, have generally agreed on the thesis of the presumption of liberty; that is, that it is interference with the freedom of others that must be justified, and not their free action itself. The exercise of power requires justification; the exercise of liberty does not.[3]

Three commonly accepted core elements of classical liberal thought are:

1. A conviction, expressed in many different ways, that "individuals have rights and that there are things no person or group may do to them (without violating their rights)"[4]
2. An appreciation for the capacity for social order and harmony to emerge spontaneously, without the conscious direction of any mind or the imposition of any plan, as an unintended consequence of people interacting freely on the basis of rights (property) that are well defined, defendable, and structured by legal rules facilitating contract
3. A commitment to constitutionally limited government that is authorized to enforce the rules of just conduct but is strictly limited in its powers

Thus, the tradition of classical liberal thinking draws primarily from three disciplines – moral philosophy, social science, and political (or juridical) science, supplemented by ancillary disciplines such as psychology, history, and sociology. Each of the three elements reinforces the others to produce a coherent theory of the relationship of freedom, rights, government, and order.

Adam Smith, a doyen of the classical liberal tradition and a contributor to all three of those primary disciplines – moral philosophy (*The Theory of Moral Sentiment*), social science (*An Inquiry into the Nature and Causes of the Wealth of Nations*), and political or juridical science (*The Lectures on Jurisprudence*) – connected all three pillars in a famous statement:

Little else is requisite to carry a state to the highest degree of opulence from the lowest barbarism, but peace, easy taxes, and a tolerable administration of justice; all the rest being brought about by the natural course of things. All governments which thwart this natural course, which force things into another channel, or which endeavour to arrest the progress of society at a particular point, are unnatural, and to support themselves are obliged to be oppressive and tyrannical.[5]

2 Steven Scalet and David Schmidtz, "State, Civil Society, and Classical Liberalism," in *Civil Society and Government*, ed. Nancy L. Rosenblum and Robert C. Post (Princeton, NJ: Princeton University Press, 2002), 26.
3 See Anthony de Jasay, "Liberalism, Loose or Strict," *Independent Review* 9, no. 3 (Winter 2005): 427–32.
4 Robert Nozick, *Anarchy, State, and Utopia* (New York: Basic Books, 1974), ix.
5 Quoted by Dugald Stewart from a now lost manuscript in Stewart's "Account of the Life and Writings of Adam Smith, LLD," in Adam Smith, *Essays on Philosophical Subjects*,

Definitions

Classical liberalism has had a long engagement with the issue of poverty, partly because of its intimate association with economic science in particular and the study of spontaneous forms of social order and improvement in general. Classical liberals have insisted that the question of the "wealth of nations" comes logically before "the poverty of nations." Poverty is meaningful only in comparison to wealth, and wealth must be produced. Poverty is the natural base line against which wealth is measured; poverty is what you have if wealth is not produced. The classical liberal economist Peter Bauer of the London School of Economics famously retorted to John Kenneth Galbraith's discussion of the "causes of poverty": "Poverty has no causes. Wealth has causes." As the historians Nathan Rosenberg and L. E. Birdzell Jr. put the matter, "If we take the long view of human history and judge the economic lives of our ancestors by modern standards, it is a story of almost unrelieved wretchedness."[6] Widespread poverty is the historical norm; the wealth explosion of the past two centuries is the aberration that requires explanation.

Prosperity, as it is understood today, is a uniquely modern phenomenon. The experience of the great bulk of the human race for most of its existence, up until quite recently, has been the experience of early death, sickness, ignorance, almost unrelieved physical toil, and uncertain access to sufficient food to sustain life. The picture of the past commonly carried by so many intellectuals is deeply misleading, as it is derived almost entirely from the writings of other intellectuals, that is, from that tiny minority fortunate enough to enjoy the leisure to write about their lives. Such accounts are hardly representative of the lives of the great bulk of the human race. The difference between the material conditions of existence that characterized most of the human past and now is substantial. In the words of classical liberal economic historian Deirdre McCloskey,

The heart of the matter is twelve. Twelve is the factor by which real income per head nowadays exceeds that around 1780, in Britain and in other countries that have experienced modern economic growth.

... Most conservatively measured, the average person has about twelve times more bread, books, transport and innocent amusement than the average person had two centuries ago. No previous episode of enrichment approaches modern economic growth – not China or Egypt in their primes, not the glory of Greece or the grandeur of Rome.[7]

ed. W. P. D. Wightman and J. C. Bryce, vol. 3 of the *Glasgow Edition of the Works and Correspondence of Adam Smith* (Indianapolis: Liberty Fund, 1982), 322.
[6] Nathan Rosenberg and L. E. Birdzell Jr., *How the West Grew Rich: The Economic Transformation of the Industrial World* (New York: Basic Books, 1986), 3.
[7] Deirdre McCloskey, "1780–1860: A Survey," in *The Economic History of Britain since 1700*, vol. 1: *1700–1860*, ed. Roderick Floud and Deirdre McCloskey (Cambridge: Cambridge University Press, 2000), 242.

TABLE 5.I. *Levels of GDP Per Capita in European Colonial Powers and Former Colonies, 1500–1998 (1990 international dollars)*

	1500	1700	1820	1913	1950	1998
Britain	762	1,405	2,121	5,150	6,907	18,714
France	727	986	1,230	3,485	5,270	19,556
Italy	1,100	1,100	1,117	2,564	3,502	17,759
Netherlands	754	2,110	1,821	4,049	5,996	20,224
Portugal	632	854	963	1,244	2,069	12,929
Spain	698	900	1,063	2,255	2,397	14,227
China	600	600	600	552	439	3,117
India	550	550	533	673	619	1,746
Indonesia	565	580	612	904	840	3,070
Brazil	400	460	646	811	1,672	5,459
Mexico	425	568	759	1,732	2,365	6,655
United States	400	527	1,257	5,301	9,561	27,331
Ireland	526	715	880	2,736	3,446	18,183

Source: A. Maddison, *The World Economy*, vol. 1: *A Millennial Perspective*, and vol. 2: *Historical Statistics* (Paris: OECD, 2006), 92.

It is only the past few hundred years that have witnessed an explosion of productive energy, as shown by the enormous changes in per capita income from 1500 to 1998 (Table 5.I). The data are more striking when looked at graphically from the year 1 to the present (Figure 5.I).

The sudden and sustained rise in income from the takeoff period around the middle of the eighteenth century (for Western Europe and North America, a century or more later for others) is unprecedented in all of human history. It is the sudden shift from a nearly horizontal line to a nearly vertical line that demands explanation.

The data can be disaggregated to show the rise of income through life expectancy, infant mortality rates, literacy, and other forms of wealth; the conditions of most previous generations of humans – as judged by the standards of the present – are no less than horrifying. The focus of classical liberal historical, economic, and legal research has been on explaining the causes of that great change, and the general consensus has been that the key change was the growth of institutions conducive to the production of wealth.

The classical liberal insistence that the explanation of wealth production – of what made possible the sudden trend upward in Figure 5.I – is primary is not merely because of the suddenness of the change but also for reasons of conceptual clarity. Poverty is what results if wealth production does not take place, whereas wealth is not what results if poverty production does not take place.

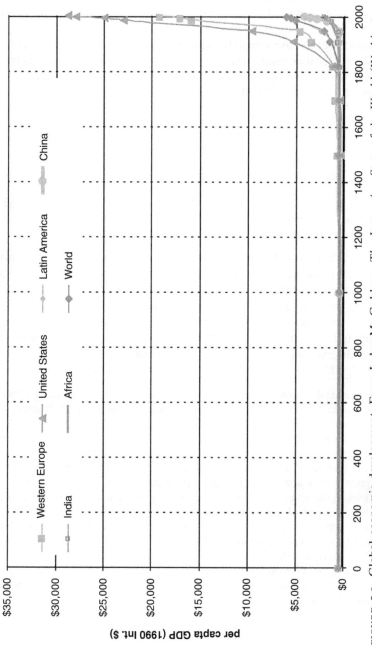

FIGURE 5.1. Global economic development. From Indur M. Goklany, *The Improving State of the World* (Washington, DC: Cato Institute, 2007), 43.

88   *Tom G. Palmer*

The suddenness of the wealth explosion shown in Figure 5.1 is the reason that the dominant narrative in the classical liberal tradition has been one of prosperity defined against a norm of widespread poverty, not in terms of relative well-being.

Classical liberals have sought to explain the presence of wealth rather than taking as the fundamental puzzle its absence. The idea of a "vicious circle of poverty" as an explanation for the absence of wealth was criticized by the development economist P. T. Bauer:

> To have money is the result of economic achievement, not its precondition. That this is so is plain from the very existence of developed countries, all of which originally must have been underdeveloped and yet progressed without external donations. The world was not created in two parts, one with ready-made infrastructure and stock of capital, and the other without such facilities. Moreover, many poor countries progressed rapidly in the hundred years or so before the emergence of modern development economics and the canvassing of the vicious circle. Indeed, if the notion of the vicious circle of poverty were valid, mankind would still be living in the Old Stone Age.[8]

Humans – all but a few of them, at least – have escaped the Stone Age. In those countries that saw increases in per capita income, the effect was especially significant for the poor, whose status and even definition changed dramatically. As Carlo Cipolla noted of the impact of the "Industrial Revolution," it is undeniable that one of the main characteristics of preindustrial Europe, as of all traditional agricultural societies, was a striking contrast between the abject misery of the mass and the affluence and magnificence of a limited number of very rich.[9] "The poor" referred to people on the verge of starvation:

> Most people lived at a subsistence level. They had no savings and no social security to help them in case of distress. If they remained without work, their only hope of survival was charity. We look in vain in the language of the time for the term *unemployed*. The unemployed were confused with the poor, the poor were identified with the beggar, and the confusion of the terms reflected the grim reality of the times. In a year of bad harvest or of economic stagnation, the number of destitute people grew conspicuously. The people of preindustrial age were inured to drastic fluctuations in the number of the poor. Especially in the cities the number of the poor soared in years of famine because starving peasants fled the depleted countryside and swarmed to the urban centers, where charity was more easily available and hopefully the houses of the wealthy had food in storage. Tadino reported that in Milan (Italy) during the famine of 1629 in a few months the number of the poor grew from 3,554 to 9,715. Gascon found that in Lyon (France) "in normal years the poor represented 6 to 8 percent of the population; in the years of famine their number grew up to 15 or 20 percent."

---

[8] Peter Bauer, *From Subsistence to Exchange* (Princeton, NJ: Princeton University Press, 2000), 6.
[9] Carlo Cipolla, *Before the Industrial Revolution: European Society and Economy, 1000–1700* (New York: W. W. Norton, 1980), 9–10.

The fundamental characteristic of the poor was that they had no independent income. If they managed to survive, it was because income was voluntarily transferred to them through charity.[10]

The great growth of industry made the poor – in the form of large numbers of urban workers – visible to literate urban dwellers in a way that they had not been before. But no longer were they swarming masses of starving peasants hoping for alms. Their status was decidedly different. As F. A. Hayek and others have noted, the increases in population made possible by industrialism did not arise from an increase in birth rates but from a drop in death rates, notably premature death. "If we ask," Hayek wrote, "what men most owe to the moral practices of those called capitalists the answer is: their very lives. Socialist accounts that ascribe the existence of the proletariat to an exploitation of groups formerly able to maintain themselves are entirely fictional. Most individuals who now make up the proletariat could not have existed before others provided them with means to exist."[11]

Classical liberals have persistently worked to debunk the false image of the past – common to socialists and conservatives alike, in which happy peasants gamboled on the village green, life was tranquil and unstressed, and each peasant family enjoyed a snug little cottage.[12] The common yearning for a

---

[10] Ibid., 18–19. Economic historian Robert William Fogel has placed great stress on the role of access to nutrition in eliminating beggary:

> The relatively generous poverty program developed in Britain during the second half of the eighteenth century, and the bitter attacks on that program by Malthus and others, have given the unwarranted impression that government transfers played a major role in the secular decline in beggary and homelessness. Despite the relative generosity of English poor relief between 1750 and 1834, beggary and homelessness fluctuated between 10 and 20 percent. Despite the substantial reduction in the proportion of national income transferred to the poor as a result of the poor laws of 1834 and later years, homelessness declined sharply during the late nineteenth and early twentieth centuries. The fact is that government transfers were incapable of solving the problems of beggary and homelessness during the eighteenth and much of the nineteenth centuries, because the root cause of the problems was chronic malnutrition. Even during the most generous phase of the relief program, the bottom fifth of the English population was so severely malnourished that it lacked the energy for adequate levels of work. At the end of the eighteenth century British agriculture, even when supplemented by imports, was simply not productive enough to provide more than 80 percent of the potential labor force with enough calories to sustain regular manual labor. It was the huge increases in English productivity during the later part of the nineteenth and the early twentieth centuries that made it possible to feed even the poor at relatively high caloric levels. Begging and homelessness were reduced to exceedingly low levels, by nineteenth century standards, only when the bottom fifth of the population acquired enough calories to permit regular work.

Robert William Fogel, *The Escape from Hunger and Premature Death, 1700–2100: Europe, America, and the Third World* (Cambridge: Cambridge University Press, 2004).

[11] F. A. Hayek, *The Fatal Conceit: The Errors of Socialism* (Chicago: University of Chicago Press, 1988), 130–31.

[12] The classic refutation can be found in Thomas Babington Macaulay's January 1830 review of Robert Southey's 1829 Tory attack on industrialism, *Sir Thomas More; or, Colloquies*

past "golden age," a yearning that is still with us ("Ah, for the 1950s, when everyone ..."), was elegantly described and dismissed by the classical liberal historian Thomas Babington Macaulay in the mid-nineteenth century:

It is now the fashion to place the golden Age of England in times when noblemen were destitute of comforts the want of which would be intolerable to a modern foot-man, when farmers and shopkeepers breakfasted on loaves the sight of which would raise a riot in a modern workhouse, when to have a clean shirt once a week was a privilege reserved for the higher class of gentry.

The way of life of Macaulay's generation would today be considered unbear-able by even the poorest among us, as Macaulay presciently recognized:

We too shall, in our turn, be outstripped, and in our turn be envied. It may well be, in the twentieth century, that ... numerous comforts and luxuries which are now unknown, or confined to a few, may be within the reach of every diligent and thrifty workingman. And yet it may then be the mode to assert that the increase of wealth and progress of science have benefited the few at the expense of the many.[13]

As Macaulay understood, there is no naturally discernible dividing line between "poverty" and "wealth." The poor of today enjoy amenities unavail-able to the wealthy of the past, even the relatively recent past. (If anyone doubts that, he or she should compare the experience of dentistry among the super wealthy fifty years ago with that of the poor in advanced countries today; who could doubt that the wealthy of the past would have given their eye teeth, so to speak, to enjoy the anesthesia and modern dental techniques available to even the poorest in industrial countries today.)

    Despite the attention to absolute definitions of wealth and poverty, com-parative approaches have not been lacking in the classical liberal tradi-tion. The Abbé de Condillac, in an influential work published in the same year as Smith's *The Wealth of Nations*, distinguished between mere lack of wealth and poverty, for "there is only poverty where essential needs are not met, and it is not being poor to lack a type of wealth of which one has

---

on the Progress and Prospects of Society, in "Southey's Colloquies," in Macaulay, *Critical and Historical Essays*, vol. 2 (New York: Dutton, 1967), 187–224. See also for a summary T. S. Ashton, *The Industrial Revolution: 1760–1830* (Oxford: Oxford University Press, 1997).

13 Thomas Babington Macaulay, *The History of England from the Accession of James II* (Philadelphia: E. H. Butler, 1849), 291–92. As Macaulay noted in his "Southey's Colloquies," "If we were to prophesy that in the year 1930 a population of fifty millions, better fed, clad, and lodged than the English of our time, will cover these islands, that Sussex and Huntingdonshire will be wealthier than the wealthiest parts of the West Riding of Yorkshire now are, that cultivation, rich as that of a flower-garden, will be carried up to the very tops of Ben Nevis and Helvellyn, that machines constructed on principles yet undiscovered will be in every house, that there will be no highways but railroads, no ravel-ling but by steam, that our debt, vast as it seems to us, will appear to our great-grandchil-dren a trifling encumbrance, which might easily be paid off in a year or two, many people would think us insane" (p. 223).

not acquired a need, and which one does not even know."[14] The progress of the arts and sciences and the creation of ever greater wealth generates new needs, the satisfaction of which entails new forms of consumption, an insight that Condillac deployed against those who argued that only agriculture produced wealth:

Thus it is that all, farmers, merchants, artisans, come together to increase the mass of wealth.

If one compares the state of deprivation our tribe is in, when, without artisans, without merchants, it is confined to goods of prime need, with the state of plenty in which it finds itself, when, through the hard work of artisans and merchants, it enjoys goods of secondary need, that is, of a host of things that habit turns into needs for it; one will understand that the work of artisans and merchants is as much a source of wealth for it as the very work of the farmers.

Indeed, if on the one hand we have seen that the land is the source of products, and hence of wealth, we see on the other hand that industry gives value to a number of products, which otherwise would have none. It is therefore proved that in the final analysis industry is also a source of wealth.[15]

Adam Smith added an additional element. Poverty consists not only in the consciousness of unmet needs but also in the comparison of one's status with that of others in a way that causes shame. Shame is a defining feature of what is a "necessity," that is, something without which one would be accounted poor:

By necessaries I understand, not only the commodities which are indispensably necessary for the support of life, but whatever the custom of the country renders it indecent for creditable people, even of the lowest order, to be without. A linen shirt, for example, is, strictly speaking, not a necessary of life. The Greeks and Romans lived, I suppose, very comfortably, though they had no linen. But in the present times, through the greater part of Europe, a creditable day-labourer would be ashamed to appear in publick without a linen shirt, the want of which would be supposed to denote that disgraceful degree of poverty, which, it is presumed, no body can well fall into without extreme bad conduct. Custom, in the same manner, has rendered leather shoes a necessary of life in England. The poorest creditable person of either sex would be ashamed to appear in publick without them. In Scotland, custom has rendered them a necessary of life to the lowest order of men; but not to the same order of women, who may, without any discredit, walk about bare-footed. In France, they are necessaries neither to men nor to women; the lowest rank of both sexes appearing there publickly, without any discredit, sometimes in wooden shoes, and sometimes bare-footed. Under necessaries therefore, I comprehend, not only those things which nature, but those things which the established rules of decency have rendered necessary to the lowest rank of people. All other things, I call luxuries; without meaning by this appellation, to throw the smallest degree of reproach upon the temperate use of them. Beer and ale, for example, in Great Britain, and

[14] Étienne Bonnot, Abbé de Condillac, *Commerce and Government Considered in Their Mutual Relationship*, trans. Shelagh Eltis (Cheltenham: Edward Elgar, 1997), 103.
[15] Ibid., 105.

wine, even in the wine countries, I call luxuries. A man of any rank may, without any reproach, abstain totally from tasting such liquors. Nature does not render them necessary for the support of life; and custom no where renders it indecent to live without them.[16]

Under both absolute and comparative conceptions, wealth and poverty are moving standards. An accumulation of assets that may qualify one as wealthy in one year may, in a wealthier succeeding year, qualify one as poor, and a wealthy person in one society may be poor in another.

Consistent with their focus on wealth as the phenomenon to be explained, then, classical liberals addressed themselves assiduously to the analysis of why some fare better or worse than others. Smith's book was famously called, not merely *The Wealth of Nations*, but *An Inquiry into the Nature and Causes of the Wealth of Nations*. Each term is important to understanding his enterprise. Most prior writers had identified the wealth of a nation (its nature) with the wealth of the ruling elite. In contrast, Smith began his work by identifying the nature of a nation's wealth, not with its military power or the gold and silver in the king's treasury, but with the annual produce of the combined labor power of the nation, divided by the number of consumers, a conception that persists in the modern notion of per capita gross domestic product.[17]

The wealth of a nation is to be measured, then, not by the power of its rulers or the bullion in the state treasury, but by the access to wealth on the part of any randomly chosen member of it. The primary causes or determinants of wealth are the institutions that create incentives for wealth production. Poverty, then, as measured against a background of wealth, represents a failure to create (or hold on to) wealth, and the causes of such failure are those institutions or practices that create *dis*incentives for wealth production and/or incentives for predatory transfers that directly impoverish some for the benefit of others. One may deserve one's poverty if one refuses to take advantage of one's opportunities and prefers indolence to work, but it would be hard (and illiberal) to argue that one deserves the institutions that are imposed on one, that a slave deserves to be enslaved, that a serf deserves to be a serf, or that a hard-working farmer or factory worker deserves to be excluded from selling her products to voluntary purchasers or procure at less cost the necessities of life by protectionism.

If opportunities, understood as freedoms to engage in voluntary activities to create wealth, are unequally distributed, it is likely that that will entail an

[16] Adam Smith, *An Inquiry into the Nature and Causes of the Wealth of Nations*, vol. 2, ed. R. H. Campbell and A. S. Skinner (Indianapolis: Liberty Fund, 1981), 869–70.
[17] "According therefore, as this produce, or what is purchased with it, bears a greater or smaller proportion to the number of those who are to consume it, the nation will be better or worse supplied with all the necessaries and conveniencies for which it has occasion." Adam Smith, *An Inquiry into the Nature and Causes of the Wealth of Nations*, vol. 1, ed. R. H. Campbell and A. S. Skinner (Indianapolis: Liberty Fund, 1981), 10.

unequal distribution of wealth, not because a sum of "socially created" wealth has been divided unfairly, but because the opportunities to produce wealth have been withheld from some, who as a consequence are able to produce less. Classical liberals have emphasized that every act of production is itself an act of distribution. If freedom to produce is unequal, holdings of wealth will also be unequal. For example, recipients of state grants of monopoly can charge higher prices in the absence of competition and reap monopoly rents as a consequence, a process (now known as rent seeking) that both transfers wealth from one party to another and, in the process, diminishes the aggregate of wealth produced, as resources are diverted to rent seeking itself and away from production of value, thus making the society as a whole less wealthy than it would have been in the absence of rent-seeking behavior.[18]

If some have the power to force others to produce not for their own benefit but for the benefit of the powerful, they will transfer wealth from the coerced to those who coerce, sometimes at a great net loss in productivity. Slavery, serfdom, conscription, and other forms of forced labor transfer wealth from some to others. Theft and other forms of involuntary transfers confiscate from some what they have produced, generally to the benefit of the confiscators.[19] Restrictions on some from competing with others generate rents to those with monopolistic powers, at the expense of their customers and potential competitors. A society in which some are forbidden by force of law from owning land, entering certain trades, or purchasing commodities at freely negotiated prices would likely see a difference in per capita income between those groups that suffered from legal disabilities and those that did not. Examples from history abound.[20]

Vulnerability to Poverty

Vulnerability to poverty is seen by classical liberals as substantially dependent on institutional settings. When there are rewards to violence or procurement of political power and force, the violent and the politically ambitious will benefit by snatching from the industrious the wealth they have produced, impoverishing the industrious and diminishing incentives for further production

[18] See Gordon Tullock, "The Welfare Costs of Tariffs, Monopolies, and Theft," *Western Economic Journal* 5, no. 3 (June 1967): 224–32, and Anne Krueger, "The Political Economy of the Rent-Seeking Society," *American Economic Review* 64, no. 3 (June 1974): 291–303.

[19] For a detailed description of the most egregious example of the twentieth century, see Götz Aly, *Hitler's Beneficiaries: Plunder, Racial War, and the Nazi Welfare State* (New York: Metropolitan Books, 2005).

[20] The origins and functioning of the apartheid system as such an example is explained by the classical liberal economist W. H. Hutt, *The Economics of the Colour Bar* (London: Andre Deutsch, 1964). White-dominated trade unions succeeded in imposing restrictions on the abilities of blacks to create wealth, thus eliminating them as competitors and reaping special rents (pp. 58–81). See also Ralph Horwitz, *The Political Economy of South Africa* (New York: Frederick A. Praeger Publishers, 1967).

of wealth, to the relative impoverishment of all. The history of civilization is seen by classical liberals as a history of limitations on power and violence, achieved by a variety of means.[21]

In legal orders characterized by well-defined, legally secure, and transferrable property rights, with strong limitations on predatory behavior, poverty tends to be transformed from the dividing line between survival and starvation and becomes a matter of relative affluence, with the lesser affluence of the poor largely a matter of inability or unwillingness to produce wealth or to save, rather than to squander, what one has acquired. Thus, "character" (also known as possession of the virtues)[22] is a factor, as the industrious and the thrifty are in such legal orders unlikely to experience poverty, reckoned in either absolute or relative terms.

Classical liberals have frequently argued that in relatively free and prosperous societies, the best predictors of relative poverty tend to be the degree to which one is a recipient of state assistance, which, they have argued, tends to foster the vices of indolence and irresponsibility. The classic example was the working of the "Poor Laws" in relatively prosperous England, and especially the "Speenhamland System" of "outdoor relief" that subsidized the working poor.[23] As Alexis de Tocqueville argued in his *Memoir on Pauperism*, written after a tour of England, the availability of "legal charity" in wealthy countries such as Britain, before the reform of the "Poor Laws," was itself a cause of poverty, for it had, he argued, created a permanent class of paupers. His investigation was aimed at resolving an apparent paradox: "The countries appearing to be most impoverished are those which in reality account for the fewest indigents, and among the people most admired for their opulence, one part of the population is obliged to live on the gifts of the other in order to live."[24]

---

[21] Taming violence as a means to create incentives for savings, investment, and productivity is the theme of Robert H. Bates's *Prosperity and Violence: The Political Economy of Development* (New York: W. W. Norton, 2001).

[22] For a treatment of the virtues of liberalism, see Deirdre N. McCloskey, *The Bourgeois Virtues: Ethics for an Age of Commerce* (Chicago: University of Chicago Press, 2006). See also Thomas L. Haskell, "Capitalism and the Origins of the Humanitarian Sensibility," parts I and II, *American Historical Review* 90, no. 2 (April 1985): 339–61 and no. 3 (June 1985): 547–66.

[23] "After 1795 many parishes in the South, following the policy of the magistrates of Speenhamland, began to give outdoor relief according to a scale based on the price of bread and the size of the family. There was nothing to object to in this: it was only sensible and humane to see that the income of the poor did not fall below the minimum of subsistence. But many of the authorities, confusing the problem of the wage-earner with that of the pauper, undertook to make up from the rates the amount by which the wages of the labourer fell short of their standard. A grant of relief that varies inversely with earnings is the worst form of subsidy, since it destroys the incentive for the worker to demand, or the employer to offer, higher wages." Ashton, *The Industrial Revolution*, 89.

[24] Alexis de Tocqueville, *Memoir on Pauperism* (Chicago: Ivan R. Dee, 1997), 37.

As Tocqueville concluded from his investigation, "Any measure that establishes legal charity on a permanent basis and gives it an administrative form thereby creates an idle and lazy class, living at the expense of the industrial and working class."[25] In addition to creating incentives for some to become dependent on others, the Poor Laws created incentives for the industrious to attempt to control the movement of the recipients of "outdoor relief," lest newcomers become burdens to ratepayers. According to Tocqueville,

Legal charity affects the pauper's freedom as much as his morality. This is easily proved. When local governments are rigorously obligated to aid the indigent, they necessarily owe relief only to the poor who reside in their jurisdiction. This is the only fair way of equalizing the public burden which results from the law, and of proportioning it to the means of those who must bear it. Since individual charity is almost unknown in a country of organized public charity, anyone whose misfortunes or vices have made him incapable of earning a living is condemned, under pain of death, to remain in the place of his birth. If he leaves, he moves through enemy territory. The private interest within the parish, infinitely more active and powerful than the best organized national police could be, notes his arrival, dogs his every step, and, if he wants to establish a new residence, informs the public authority who takes him to the boundary line. Through their Poor Laws, the English have immobilized a sixth of their population. They have bound it to the earth like the medieval peasantry. Then, man was forced against his will to stay on the land where he was born. Legal charity keeps him from even wishing to move.[26]

A similar dynamic of controls set in motion by welfare statism has been invoked by classical liberals to explain the profoundly illiberal policies of restrictions on freedom of movement across international borders, as immigrants are often seen by the inhabitants of welfare states as parasites who threaten to consume the wealth of the locals, rather than as potential producers of wealth who come for mutual benefit.[27] (The socialist writers Richard A. Cloward and Frances Fox Piven have diagnosed the origins and functions of modern welfare states in ways that echo classical liberal critiques.)[28]

---

[25] Ibid., 58. Tocqueville clearly distinguished "voluntary charity" from "legal charity" and endorsed the former as establishing a "moral tie" "between those two classes whose interests and passions so often conspire to separate them from each other, and although divided by circumstances they are willingly reconciled. This is not the case with legal charity. The latter allows the alms to persist but removes its morality. The law strips the man of wealth of a part of his surplus without consulting him, and he sees the poor man only as a greedy stranger invited by the legislator to share his wealth" (p. 60).

[26] Ibid., 62–63.

[27] See, for example, the treatment in Jason L. Riley, *Let Them In: The Case for Open Borders* (New York: Gotham Books, 2008), esp. 91–125. As Riley concludes, "If conservatives are worried about too many snouts at the trough – and if they're remotely interested in any sort of ideological consistency – they should be working to restrict welfare payments, not immigrants" (p. 125).

[28] See especially Richard A. Cloward and Frances Fox Piven, *The Politics of Turmoil: Poverty, Race, and the Urban Crisis* (New York: Vintage Books, 1972) and *Regulating the Poor: The Functions of Public Welfare* (New York: Pantheon Books, 1971).

Institutionalization of the Political and
Economic Means to Wealth Acquisition

Classical liberal theorists played a central role in formulating and popular-
izing the idea that a major – indeed, the most important – factor of production is neither land, nor labor, nor capital, but the institutional framework
that facilitates voluntary cooperation for mutual benefit. Wealth production
is a result of institutional changes that create incentives for productivity and
mutual gains resulting from trade. As Benjamin Friedman notes, "This bold
new concept had strong moral content. For the first time people saw the possibility of acquiring wealth in a way that need not be inherently exploitive. At
the individual level, the idea of voluntary exchange was that in any transaction both parties expected to come out ahead. But the same point applied
even more strikingly at the level of the entire society. The route to national
wealth was commerce, not conquest."[29] Following on that insight, classical
liberals have distinguished two means of acquiring wealth: the "economic
means" of production and exchange and the "political means" of deploying
force.[30] Herbert Spencer distinguished between two ideal types of society, the
"militant" and the "industrial," the former characterized by command and
hierarchy and the latter by cooperation and contract.[31]

As special privileges in law will generate differences in wealth and income,
classical liberals devoted enormous efforts to identifying and eliminating
those special privileges that harmed some to the benefit of others.[32] Thus,
classical liberals have campaigned vigorously against guild privileges that
restricted entrance to trades; racial, ethnic, religious, and gender barriers
to ownership of property or entry to trades; protectionist barriers to cheap
imports, which raise prices to consumers to benefit small minorities of domestic producers; and a wide array of obstacles to the efforts of people to improve
their situations. Legal equality, freedom of trade, and careers open to talent
were watchwords of classical liberal theorists of social progress.[33]

[29] Benjamin M. Friedman, *The Moral Consequences of Economic Growth* (New York: Alfred
A. Knopf, 2005), 39.
[30] See, for example, Franz Oppenheimer, *The State* (Indianapolis: Bobbs-Merrill, 1914).
"There are two fundamentally opposed means whereby man, requiring sustenance, is
impelled to obtain the necessary means for satisfying his desires. These are work and robbery, one's own labor and the forcible appropriation of the labor of others" (p. 24). The
former Oppenheimer labeled the "economic means" and the latter the "political means."
See also Vilfredo Pareto, *Sociological Writings*, ed. S. E. Finer (Totowa, NJ: Rowman and
Littlefield, 1976), especially the discussions of "spoliation."
[31] See, for example, Herbert Spencer, *Structure, Function and Evolution*, ed. Stanislav
Andreski (New York: Charles Scribner's Sons, 1971), 153–65.
[32] See, in the context of state-imposed disadvantages on the basis of race, Walter Williams,
The State against Blacks (New York: McGraw-Hill, 1982).
[33] Henry Sumner Maine described "the movement of the progressive societies" from inherited relations, based on family membership to personal liberty and civil society as "a movement from Status to Contract." Henry Sumner Maine, *Ancient Law* (New Brunswick,
NJ: Transaction, 2003), 170.

Classical liberals prided themselves on the results of their efforts. As the classical liberal journalist E. L. Godkin noted in the pages of the *Nation* in 1900, "To the principles and precepts of Liberalism the prodigious material progress of the age was largely due. Freed from the vexatious meddling of governments, men devoted themselves to their natural task, the bettering of their condition, with the wonderful results which surround us."[34]

Wealth and Inequality

Just as classical liberals do not see poverty as "the cause" of poverty (in the "vicious circle of poverty" argument criticized by P. T. Bauer), they do not see the existence of wealth as the cause of poverty, as it is by some socialists, who argue that not giving a poor person goods and services is the "cause" of that person's poverty.[35] Voluntarily acquired wealth is, in fact, a cause of the

---

[34] E. L. Godkin, "The Eclipse of Liberalism," *Nation*, August 9, 1900. He continued in a very pessimistic vein, "But it now seems that its material comfort has blinded the eyes of the present generation to the cause which made it possible. In the politics of the world, Liberalism is a declining, almost a defunct force. The condition of the Liberal party in England is indeed parlous. There is actually talk of organizing a Liberal-Imperialist party; a combination of repugnant tendencies and theories as impossible as that of fire and water. On the other hand, there is a faction of so-called Liberals who so little understand their traditions as to make common cause with the Socialists. Only a remnant, old men for the most part, still uphold the Liberal doctrine, and when they are gone, it will have no champions." The essay is a dire prediction of the racism, imperialism, socialism, and war that Godkin believed would follow the rejection of the classical liberal doctrines of natural rights, limited government, and free trade. Most strikingly, he notes, "We hear no more of natural rights, but of inferior races, whose part it is to submit to the government of those whom God has made their superiors. The old fallacy of divine right has once more asserted its ruinous power, and before it is again repudiated there must be international struggles on a terrific scale." A more chilling prediction of the course of the twentieth century was never written.

[35] See G. A. Cohen, "Incentives, Inequality, and Community," in *The Tanner Lectures on Human Values*, vol. 13, ed. B. Peterson (Salt Lake City: University of Utah Press, 1992), 263–329, and Philip Green, *The Pursuit of Inequality* (New York: Pantheon Books, 1981). Some figures associated with classical liberalism have at times asserted a similar claim, with regard to initial appropriations. Thus, the free-trade advocate Henry George argued that "the persistence of poverty amid advancing wealth" was because "with increase in productive power, rent tends to even greater increase, thus producing a constant tendency to the forcing down of wages.... Land being necessary to labor, and being reduced to private ownership, every increase in the productive power of labor but increases rent the price that labor must pay for the opportunity to utilize its powers; and thus all the advantages gained by the march of progress go to the owners of land, and wages do not increase." Henry George, *Progress and Poverty* (New York: Modern Library, n.d.). Hillel Steiner, in *An Essay on Rights* (Oxford: Blackwell, 1994), without endorsing the account of poverty given by George, accepts George's account of the legitimacy of ownership of land and other "initially unowned things," to which "each is entitled to an equal portion," and derives a theory of just redistributions from the "fund" "on which under-appropriators have just claims" (p. 268). Steiner calls for global redistribution on the grounds that "each person's original right to an equal portion of initially 'unowned things' amounts to a right to an equal share of their value" (p. 271). He identifies his overall system, including

wealth of others, not of their poverty. "Say's Law," according to which "it is production which opens a demand for products," postulated that the wealth of one person, group, or nation was to the benefit of those who traded with them.[36]

What could an active manufacturer, or an intelligent merchant, do in a small deserted and semi-barbarous town in a remote corner of Poland or Westphalia? Though in no fear of a competitor, he could sell but little, because little was produced; whilst at Paris, Amsterdam, or London, in spite of the competition of a hundred dealers in his own line, he might do business on the largest scale. The reason is obvious: he is surrounded with people who produce largely in an infinity of ways, and who make purchases, each with his respective products, that is to say, with the money arising from the sale of what he may have produced.[37]

The focus of classical liberals has been, not on the intentions or motivations of various parties in society, but on the institutions that structure interaction. Institutions create incentives and incentives shape behavior. As Douglass North puts it, "Institutions provide the incentive structure of an economy; as that structure evolves, it shapes the direction of economic change towards growth, stagnation, or decline."[38]

Classical liberal theorists stress that outcomes are not in general subject to choice; at best, one can choose one process over another, not one outcome over

the redistribution, with "classical laissez faire liberalism of the natural rights-based kind" (p. 282). Very few classical liberals have taken that approach, and it is not widely accepted for a number of reasons, including the problems of disentangling "rent" from "improvements," the compatibility of such redistributive states with the rule of law, and the counterintuitive conclusion that perhaps poor people who have appropriated but failed to improve naturally occurring resources (say, people in relatively resource-rich Congo) would owe the rest of the world for excluding others from such rich, but underdeveloped, natural resources.

[36] Jean-Baptiste Say, *A Treatise on Political Economy* (New York: Augustus M. Kelley, 1971), 133.

[37] Ibid., 137. See also Jean-Baptiste Say, *Letters to Mr. Malthus* (London: Sherwood, Neely, and Jones, 1821), 3–4: "Let us only look back two hundred years, and suppose that a trader had carried a rich cargo to the places where New York and Philadelphia now stand; could he have sold it? Let us suppose even, that he had succeeded in founding there an agricultural or manufacturing establishment; could he have there sold a single article of his produce? No, undoubtedly. He must have consumed them himself. Why do we now see the contrary? Why is the merchandize carried to, or made at Philadelphia or New York, sure to be sold at the current price? It seems to me evident that it is because the cultivators, the traders, and now even the manufacturers of New York, Philadelphia, and the adjacent provinces, create, or send there, some productions, by means of which they purchase what is brought to them from other quarters." The implications for the classical liberal theory of international relations are obvious and seriously undercut the arguments of advocates of protectionism, as also of imperialist mercantilism.

[38] Douglass C. North, "Institutions," *Journal of Economic Perspectives* 5, no. 1 (Winter 1991): 97. See also Douglass C. North, *Structure and Change in Economic History* (New York: W. W. Norton, 1981), 201–2: "Institutions are a set of rules, compliance procedures, and moral and ethical behavioral norms designed to constrain the behavior of individuals in the interests of maximizing the wealth or utility of principles."

another. What may seem like the choice of an outcome (e.g., higher wages) is, in fact, the choice of a process (prohibiting the creation or fulfillment of labor contracts below a certain wage). Processes do not always generate the outcomes that the choosers may have hoped for. Daniel Shapiro notes that "institutions cannot be adequately characterized by their aims."[39] Thus, classical liberals have criticized a great deal of intervention into voluntary exchange on the grounds that it does not generate the outcomes promised. Minimum wage laws, for example, do not raise wages – increasing the marginal product of labor raises wages, and that is not subject to control by legislative fiat, but such laws do increase unemployment and force people out of free markets into black markets, by forbidding those with low marginal value products (typically the low-skilled, the uneducated, and the young) from offering their services at prices that would command buyers.[40]

Societies characterized by fully equal rights and freedom will still display income inequalities, just as do unfree societies. (No social order eliminates differences of income; they usually merely disguise the inequalities, as Mancur Olson argued in his essay "The Theory of Soviet-Type Autocracies.")[41] What distinguishes free societies, classical liberals have argued, is a general circulation of elites – artistic, cultural, political, and economic. In his general study of the "circulation of elites" among different types of social orders, Vilfredo Pareto noted that, like militant societies, liberal, industrial societies are also characterized by the circulation of elites, but on the basis of entirely different processes. In a militaristic ("bellicose") society, war provides the impetus for "the ordinary soldier to become a general," but in "commercial and industrial societies," for the poorest to attain wealth requires both freedom and "commercial and industrial development of sufficient scale to make this a real possibility for an appreciable number of citizens."[42] Commercial relations based on production and voluntary exchange tend to produce systems of dynamic inequalities, rather than rigidly maintained systems of inequality; that is, persons and families rise and fall in the relative scale of wealth, as the aggregate wealth of the whole society is increasing.[43]

[39] Daniel Shapiro, *Is the Welfare State Justified?* (Cambridge: Cambridge University Press, 2007), 5. Shapiro's book is an admirable comparison of the aims of various political philosophies with evidence about the outcomes of various policies that are often associated with them. The results are often surprising. For a similar empirically based treatment, see Olaf Gersemann, *Cowboy Capitalism: European Myths and American Realities* (Washington, DC: Cato Institute, 2005). (Note: I supervised the translation and editing of the book.)

[40] "The state can legislate a minimum wage rate. It can hardly require employers to hire at that minimum wage all who were formerly employed at wages below the minimum." Milton Friedman, *Capitalism and Freedom* (Chicago: University of Chicago, 2002), 180.

[41] Mancur Olson, *Power and Prosperity* (New York: Basic Books, 2000), 111–34.

[42] Pareto, *Sociological Writings*, 162.

[43] For contemporary evidence, see W. Michael Cox and Richard Alm, *Myths of Rich and Poor* (New York: Basic Books, 1999), especially the discussion of upward mobility in incomes (pp. 69–78).

The key distinction that classical liberal sociologists and economists have drawn on in analyzing the ever-changing "distribution of wealth" in free society is that between "ownership," a legal concept, and "wealth," an economic concept. Voluntary exchange entails reallocation not only of ownership rights but of wealth as well, and not only among those who are contractual parties to the exchange. When Henry Ford bought steel, rubber, and glass from vendors and employed workers to make automobiles, he not only caused property to change hands among those involved directly in the exchange but also bid up the value of those resources, caused the value of the resources employed in making horse saddles to go down, and increased the wages of labor by increasing its marginal value product. The transfers of wealth involved were far greater than the value of the property that changed hands in the transactions. Changes in valuation determine what an asset is worth, that is, what wealth it represents for the owner, and values change regularly, as new production processes are introduced, tastes change, and so on, causing the wealth of some to rise and that of others to fall.

The market economy is thus seen to be a leveling process. In a market economy a process of redistribution of wealth is taking place all the time before which those outwardly similar processes which modern politicians are in the habit of instituting, pale into comparative insignificance, if for no other reason than that the market gives wealth to those who can hold it, while politicians give it to their constituents, who, as a rule, cannot.[44]

Classical liberals have rejected the "natural resource" theory of wealth in favor of an "industrial" approach. Wealth is not so much what we find, as what we produce. Thus, the influential classical liberal economist Jean-Baptiste Say distinguished "existing materials" (what would today be called "natural resources") from "wealth": "All that man can do is, to re-produce existing materials under another form, which may give them an utility they did not before possess, or merely enlarge one they may have before presented. So that, in fact, there is a creation, not of matter, but of utility; and this I call production of wealth."[45]

There are many societies surrounded by abundant natural resources whose populations are far, far poorer than societies with far fewer resources but governed by institutions that facilitate the creation of wealth. It is a commonplace of development economics, dating back hundreds of years, that abundant resources are not a significant determinant of wealth.[46] Classical liberalism is

[44] Ludwig Lachmann, "The Market Economy and the Distribution of Wealth," in Lachmann, *Capital, Expectations, and the Market Process* (Kansas City: Sheed Andrews and McMeel, 1977), 313.

[45] Say, *A Treatise on Political Economy*, 62.

[46] Joyce Appleby notes, in her chapter on "The Dutch as a Source of Evidence," why the relatively "resource-poor" Dutch achieved enormous levels of per capita wealth: "The Dutch had been willing to nurture this complex social organization of the market by protecting the

characterized by the belief that the production of wealth is fostered, and absolute poverty eliminated, by the legal institutions of well-defined and legally
secure rights that can be freely exchanged on the basis of a system of contract
and law, or Adam Smith's "peace, easy taxes, and a tolerable administration
of justice."[47] Moreover, freedom of production and exchange, classical liberals have maintained, undermines hierarchies, castes, and other rigid forms of
inequality.

But wealth production through free markets was never the only classical
liberal response to poverty. Such exchanges are but one element in a wider
array of cooperative activities to combat poverty.

Self-Help, Mutual Aid, Charity, and Public Assistance

Legal equality is a defining element of the classical liberal tradition, and classical liberals were pioneers in the extension of ideas of equality to both genders,
and all races, nations, and social groups. Advocacy of equal rights for women
to participate in the workplace, without gender-based job exclusion laws, and
to acquire, own, and dispose of property independently has been promoted
not only for reasons of moral consistency but to improve the lot of women and
eliminate their involuntary dependence on men. As the nineteenth-century
classical liberal abolitionist and feminist Sarah Grimké noted, "There are few
things which present greater obstacles to the improvement and elevation of
woman to her appropriate sphere of usefulness and duty, than the laws which
have been enacted to destroy her independence, and crush her individuality;
laws which, although they are framed for her government, she has had no
voice in establishing, and which rob her of some of her *essential rights.*"[48]

The freedom to exercise one's talents, classical liberals believed, would lead
to the improvement of the lot of the oppressed, of the have-nots, of the disadvantaged, of the poor. Self-help was promoted by the elimination of obstacles
to self-help and the active assertion of personal responsibility, as exemplified in the best-selling book by the Scottish classical liberal reformer Samuel
Smiles, *Self Help; With Illustrations of Conduct and Perseverance*, published
in 1859. But other means were also available. The first, which is widely associated with classical liberalism, is the advocacy of charity as a means to the
improvement of the lot of the poor. Classical liberals focused attention on
the importance of charity to assist those who had fallen on hard luck or who
needed assistance and insisted that it was the voluntary associations of society,
and not the involuntary association of the state, that best bore such responsibility. The key, in this as in other campaigns organized by classical liberals,

individual initiative on which it throve." *Economic Thought and Ideology in Seventeenth-
Century England* (Princeton, NJ: Princeton University Press, 1978), 96.
[47] Smith, *Essays on Philosophical Subjects*, 322.
[48] Sarah Grimké, "Legal Disabilities of Women," in *Freedom, Feminism, and the State*, ed.
Wendy McElroy (Oakland: Independent Institute, 1991), 107.

was to avoid conditions of permanent dependence. Thus, Bernard Bosanquet, a stalwart of the Charity Organisation Society in Great Britain, was deeply critical of the institutionalization of poverty, of seeing "the institution of 'the poor' as a class, representing, as an ethical idea in the modern mind, a permanent object of compassion and self-sacrifice. 'Poverty,' it has been said, 'has become a status.' The 'déclassés' have become a social class, with the passive social function of stimulating the goodness of others."[49] The purpose of charity was not to further dependency but to foster the ability of the recipients of charity to take care of themselves and their families. Bosanquet distinguished economic individualism (the system of free exchange) from moral individualism (selfishness) and economic socialism (statism) from moral socialism (voluntary solidarity with others), and he claimed (perhaps confusingly to contemporary ears) that "Economic Individualism would go with Moral Socialism, and Moral Individualism (or Egoism) with Economic Socialism."[50] His point was that economic socialism, based on commands and central planning, would produce selfishness, while voluntary cooperation would produce respect for others and fellow feeling. The experience of life under real existing socialism would seem to have borne out that prediction.[51] And even in the case of modern welfare states, as Norman Barry notes, "Contemporary experience indicates that, far from encouraging a communitarian and socially concerned 'self,' the institutions of the welfare state have simply reproduced the traditional *homo economicus* in a different context."[52]

After self-help, which was promoted primarily by removing obstacles to the free exercise of one's faculties, classical liberals actively promoted and took part in a variety of "friendly societies," "fraternal societies," and "mutual aid societies" that pooled both the efforts and the risks faced by persons of

[49] Bernard Bosanquet, "Institutions as Ethical Ideas," in *The Philosophical Theory of the State and Related Essays*, ed. Gerald F. Gaus and William Sweet (South Bend, IN: St. Augustine's Press, 2001), 280.

[50] Bernard Bosanquet, "The Antithesis between Individualism and Socialism," in ibid., 329. A similar argument is presented by the classical liberal political scientist Bertrand de Jouvenel in *The Ethics of Redistribution* (Indianapolis: Liberty Fund, 1990), in which he claimed that the arguments for "redistribution" rest on an untenable theory of income as a means to isolated consumer satisfaction, or "gnawing the income bone." See especially pp. 51–80.

[51] As the classical liberal Soviet dissident Vladimir Bukovsky pointed out in his memoirs, "Khrushchev wasn't very far from the truth when he said in one of his speeches: 'If people in our country would cease stealing for even a single day, communism could have been built long ago.' But the thing he failed to understand was that, without this stealing, the Soviet system wouldn't work at all. Without these rigged figures and manipulations hardly a single target would be met, and without this private, hence illegal, initiative, nothing at all would be produced in our country. All these collective and State farms that have become showplaces, without turnovers in the millions, wouldn't have survived for one minute if they hadn't been managed by clever swindlers." Bukovsky, *To Build a Cage: My Life as a Dissenter* (London: Andre Deutsch, 1978), 150–51.

[52] Norman Barry, *Welfare* (Buckingham: Open University Press, 1990), 120.

limited means. At their height, friendly societies actively involved millions of people in social movements that dwarfed the now much-better-known trade-union movements of the time. Although some of them had roots dating back even to the burial societies of ancient Rome, they flourished as never before in the eighteenth, nineteenth, and early to mid-twentieth centuries. As Otto von Gierke observed in 1868 of the "laws of fellowship," "In our century, initiative and creative power have passed back to the people: the free personal fellowship, never entirely extinguished, has been developed into a great number of different branches, and given a form capable of fitting the most varied purposes."[53]

Such fellowships not only provided insurance against illness, accident, death, and other catastrophes but also promoted good character and such virtues as civility, respect for women (male members who beat their wives were normally expelled from societies), sobriety, and charity. Through voluntary association, they went beyond the personal responsibility often associated with classical liberalism and voluntarily embraced various forms of collective responsibility, forms of interaction that are generally underappreciated parts of the classical liberal understanding of liberty and social order. David Schmidtz has argued that "it is internalized responsibility (rather than individual responsibility per se) that makes people better off. Institutions that lead people to take responsibility for themselves as a group also help to internalize responsibility, albeit in a collective form. They too can make people better off."[54] Mutual aid was historically a key element in the classical liberal approach to social order and improvement. Like marriage, such associations are seen by classical liberals not as restrictions on liberty but as exercises of them.

David Green, a classical liberal historian and political scientist who has studied extensively the history of friendly societies in the United Kingdom and Australia, has documented their rapid growth.

Membership of the friendly societies grew steadily during the eighteenth century. By 1801 an authoritative study by Sir Frederic Eden estimated that there were about 7,200 societies with around 648,000 adult male members out of a total population of about nine million. This can be compared with a figure based on the Poor Law return for 1803 when it was estimated that there were 9,672 societies with 704,350 members in England and Wales alone....

The rate of growth of the friendly societies had been accelerating. In 1877, registered membership had been 2.75 million. Ten years later it was 3.6 million, increasing at an average of 85,000 a year. In 1897 membership had reached 4.8 million,

[53] Otto von Gierke, *Community in Historical Perspective*, ed. Antony Black (Cambridge: Cambridge University Press, 1990), 205. See also Antony Black, *Guild and State* (New Brunswick, NJ: Transaction, 2003), esp. 167–83.

[54] David Schmidtz, "Taking Responsibility," in David Schmidtz and Robert E. Goodin, *Social Welfare and Individual Responsibility* (Cambridge: Cambridge University Press, 1998), 95.

having increased on average by 120,000 a year. And by 1910 the figure had reached 6.6 million, having increased at an annual average rate since 1897 of 140,000.[55]

The friendly societies represent perhaps the most poorly documented great social movement ever. They flourished in many countries as the obstacles to civil association were lowered or eliminated, and they faded away as for-profit firms competed with them by offering actuarially sound insurance policies (in fact, some friendly societies transformed themselves into insurance firms, such as the Modern Woodmen of America, Prudential Insurance, and Metropolitan Life)[56] and as the welfare state displaced them.[57] Voluntarily organized friendly societies provided mutual aid not only to skilled workers but to the unskilled and the poor.[58] In the United States, immigrant groups participated heavily in friendly societies (many older buildings in American cities bear their names, as they were originally built to house lodge meetings; few recognize the origins of those names, such as the old "OBA" building in Washington, D.C., which once stood for "Oriental Building Association"); and African Americans, who were systematically excluded from benefits and social and economic advancement by Jim Crow laws and other restrictions on association, established numerous friendly societies, many of which provided core elements of the civil rights movement, such as the United Order of Friendship and the Knights of Tabor.[59]

Working-class people themselves drew distinctions between the deserving poor and the undeserving poor. Rather than acknowledging any unconditional right to assistance, groups of the poor who pooled their resources for mutual aid distinguished between those who deserved assistance and those who did not, either because of their own unwillingness to assist others when they could or because their situation was of their own voluntary making. The editor of the *Fraternal Monitor* noted that "fraternity, like religion or a savings bank, gives most to those who put in most. And the best deposit in the bank of fraternity is heart-felt interest and support."[60]

[55] David G. Green, *Reinventing Civil Society: The Rediscovery of Welfare without Politics* (London: Institute of Economic Affairs, 1993), 32. Green points out that the numbers did not include membership in unregistered friendly societies, which were generally considered as numerous as those in registered societies (pp. 63–69).

[56] David Beito, *From Mutual Aid to the Welfare State: Fraternal Societies and Social Services, 1890–1967* (Chapel Hill: University of North Carolina Press, 2000), 24.

[57] Green makes much of the involvement of the medical profession in promoting the National Insurance Act of 1911, which substituted a monopsony controlled by doctors and their political allies for the competitive market created by multiple friendly societies of working people. See David Green, *Working Class Patients and the Medical Establishment* (New York: St. Martin's Press, 1985); the result of substituting involuntary taxes for voluntary dues as a source of payment was, as Green dryly notes, that "pay increases were far more easy to obtain than in the market" (p. 115). The other result was the waning of the friendly societies, as working people found themselves paying twice for the same access to medical services – once to a friendly society or affiliated medical institute, and again to the state.

[58] See ibid., 89–106.

[59] Beito, *From Mutual Aid to the Welfare State*, 181–203.

[60] Quoted in ibid., 57.

Classical liberal thinkers, as well as the leaders of voluntary organizations, focused on fostering the traits of character suitable for success in civil society. In Green's words, the members of friendly societies "were united not by their physical proximity but by their attachment to shared ideals. Central to the purpose of the societies was the promotion of good character, a consideration of great importance for classical-liberal thought, some of whose advocates tend to take good conduct and a desire for a better life for granted."[61] Assistance from a friendly society was, indeed, a matter of right, but not an unearned or unconditional right; the manual of the African American "Knights of Pythias" in the United States stated that the "sick among our brethren are not left to the cold hand of public charity; they are visited, and their wants provided for out of the funds they themselves have contributed to raise, and which, in time of need, they honorably claim, without the humiliation of suing parochial or individual relief – from which the freeborn mind recoils with disdain."[62]

Mutual aid allowed the poor to escape the paternal condescension that accompanied charity, which was normally associated with cases of extreme desperation. Being needy was a state that one should seek to avoid, not to embrace. John Locke, in the *First Treatise of Government*, stated:

As *Justice* gives every Man a Title to the product of his honest Industry, and the fair Acquisitions of his Ancestors descended to him; so *Charity* gives every Man a Title to so much out of another's Plenty, as will keep him from extream want, where he has no means to subsist otherwise; and a Man can no more justly make use of another's necessity, to force him to become his Vassal, by with-holding that Relief, God requires him to afford to the wants of his Brother, than he that has more strength can seize upon a weaker, master him to his Obedience, and with a Dagger at his Throat offer him Death or Slavery.[63]

The precise meaning of such a right is not easy to parse; it could mean a right to state assistance in cases of "extreme want"; it could mean a right to receipt of charity (an "imperfect right"), but not a right to seize or compel (a "perfect right"); or it could be a case against debt slavery or other forms of enslavement based on necessity.[64] It seems likely, from the context, that the claim is directed largely against the old system of debt slavery and, as Stephen Buckle notes, "Since ... the high productivity of the system of private appropriation

---

[61] Green, *Reinventing Civil Society*, 46.

[62] Quoted in Beito, *From Mutual Aid to the Welfare State*, 57–58. The concerns about the effects of the "cold hand of public charity" are echoed in the empirical studies of another classical liberal, Charles Murray, notably in his *Losing Ground: American Social Policy, 1950–1980* (New York: Basic Books, 1984), which showed a rise in dependency (latent poverty) and socially dysfunctional behavior associated with the growth of "public charity." The book had a tremendous impact on welfare policies in the United States and contributed to the "welfare reforms" of the Clinton administration.

[63] Locke, *Two Treatises of Government*, I, 42, 170.

[64] Stephen Buckle, in *Natural Law and the Theory of Property* (Oxford: Clarendon Press, 1991), 124, 159–61, parses the statement as primarily a case against debt enslavement, and rejects the interpretation of it as an imperfect right to receive charity.

keeps cases of necessity rare, and Locke restricts the operations of charity
to 'extream want' or 'pressing Wants,' where no other means of survival is
available – the right of charity does not play a major role in Locke's system of
justice. Still, it should not be overlooked, providing as it does a buffer against
extreme necessity."[65]

Charity remains closely connected with classical liberal thought, but it
was normally third in the list of methods of helping the poor, after self-help
and mutual aid. Transfer payments from taxpayers were considered the least
desirable means, to be employed only when other forms of improvement in
the lot of the poor were unavailable or inadequate. As John Stuart Mill, in his
essay on "The Claims of Labour," noted:

> To give money in alms has never been, either in this country or in most others,
> a rare virtue. Charitable institutions, and subscriptions for relief of the destitute,
> already abounded; and if new forms of suffering, or classes of sufferers previously
> overlooked, were brought to notice, nothing was more natural than to do for them
> what had already been done for others.[66]

The giving of alms was long associated with sacred obligations and, unsurprisingly, often organized by religious institutions. The giving of alms to the
needy has generally been understood in the classical liberal tradition as an
exercise of the virtues of generosity and compassion.[67] Thus, classical liberals typically recognized a moral obligation to assist those in need as a result
of misfortune and promoted a wide variety of voluntary arrangements to
provide such assistance. While voluntary action was laudatory and virtuous,
it was not properly made compulsory. A representative view can be found
in Adam Smith's *The Theory of Moral Sentiments*. Although the sentiment
of beneficence was a necessary element in virtuous activity ("No action can
properly be called virtuous which is not accompanied with the sentiment of
self-approbation"),[68] beneficence and charity were trumped by considerations
of justice: he noted that "we feel ourselves to be under a stricter obligation
to act according to justice, than agreeably to friendship, charity, or generosity: that the practice of these last mentioned virtues seems to be left in some

[65] Ibid., 160. See also David Conway, *Classical Liberalism* (London: Macmillan, 1995),
20–24.
[66] John Stuart Mill, "The Claims of Labour," in *The Collected Works of John Stuart Mill*,
vol. 4: *Essays on Economics and Society*, part I, ed. John Robson (Toronto: University of
Toronto Press, 1967), 372.
[67] In Bernard Bosanquet's words, "Morality ... consists in the social purpose working by
its own force on the individual will. Economic Socialism is an arrangement for getting
the social purpose carried out just not by its own force, but by the force of those compulsory motives or sanctions which are at the command of the public power." Bernard
Bosanquet, "The Antithesis between Individualism and Socialism" (1890), in Bosanquet,
The Philosophical Theory of the State and Related Essays, 329. See also Tibor R. Machan,
Generosity: Virtue in Civil Society (Washington, DC: Cato Institute, 1998).
[68] Adam Smith, *The Theory of Moral Sentiments* (Indianapolis: Liberty Fund, 1982), 178.

measure to our own choice, but that, somehow or other, we feel ourselves to be in a peculiar manner tied, bound, and obliged to the observation of justice."[69] According to Smith, in a passage that represented one of the central moral commitments of most later classical liberals, "We must always, however, carefully distinguish what is only blamable, or the proper object of disapprobation, from what force may be employed either to punish or to prevent."[70]

The later utilitarian argument that a redistribution of wealth from the richer to the poorer would merely take what was of little value to the former to give what was of greater value to the latter was solidly rejected by classical liberals, who saw in the idea a threat to the general rules on which free and prosperous societies rest.[71] Thus, in Smith's words, "One individual must never prefer himself so much even to any other individual, as to hurt or injure that other, in order to benefit himself, though the benefit to the one should be much greater than the hurt or injury to the other. The poor must neither defraud nor steal from the rich, though the acquisition might be much more beneficial to the one than the loss could be hurtful to the other." To do so would violate "one of those sacred rules, upon the tolerable observation of which depend the whole security and peace of human society."[72]

Bertrand de Jouvenel's *The Ethics of Redistribution*, originally given as a series of lectures in 1949 at Cambridge University, addressed directly the utilitarian arguments for redistribution. Rather than offering the "external critique" that coercively redistributive policies would violate general rules, he offered an "internal critique": a leveling of income or wealth to maximize welfare (small reductions in the welfare of the rich being much more than offset by large improvements in the welfare of the poor) would effectively eliminate the expenditures on higher culture associated with wealth, which the advocates of redistribution invariably address by calling for taxation to redirect resources toward support of cultural establishments. As de Jouvenel noted, "All advocates of extreme redistribution couple it with most generous measures of state support for the whole superstructure of cultural activities."[73] He accused them of inconsistency, for the utilitarian welfare-maximization argument for income redistribution was undercut by the redirection of wealth by the state to favored cultural institutions: "It is then an inconsistency, and a very blatant one, to intervene with state support for such cultural activities as do not find a market. Those who spontaneously correct their schemes of redistribution by schemes for such support are in fact denying that the ideal allocation of resources and activities is that which maximizes the sum of satisfactions."[74]

---

[69] Ibid., 80.

[70] Ibid.

[71] See ibid., 163: "Without this sacred regard to general rules, there is no man whose conduct can be much depended upon."

[72] Ibid., 138.

[73] De Jouvenel, *The Ethics of Redistribution*, 42.

[74] Ibid., 44.

Thus, classical liberals typically argued, such redistribution typically carried along with it oppressively paternalist features. J. S. Mill noted that the
imposition of a "moral or a legal obligation, upon the higher classes, that they
shall be answerable for the well-doing and well-being of the lower," was characteristic not of liberal societies but of illiberal societies. As he argued, "the
ideal state of society which the new philanthropists [advocates of compulsory
assistance] are contending for" was that of "The Russian boors." He continued, "There are other labourers, not merely tillers of the soil, but workers in
great establishments partaking of the nature of manufactories, for whom the
laws of our own country, even in our own time, compelled their employers to
find wholesome food, and sufficient lodging and clothing. Who were these?
The slaves on a West Indian estate."[75]

Compulsory assistance was associated in the minds of classical liberals not
only with condescension but with systems of paternalistic control and loss
of independence and liberty. The experience of the Poor Laws and the associated controls on behavior were still vivid memories for the liberals of the
nineteenth and twentieth centuries. As Mill noted, "There are governments
in Europe who look upon it as part of their duty to take care of the physical
well-being and comfort of the people.... But with paternal care is connected
paternal authority. In these states we find severe restrictions on marriage. No
one is permitted to marry, unless he satisfies the authorities that he has a
rational prospect of being able to support a family."[76]

The fear of such controls has motivated much classical liberal opposition
to, or at least uneasiness with, "welfare reform" schemes that require labor for
the state as a condition for receipt of assistance.

A major concern about compulsory redistribution that was central to the
critique of the Poor Laws and continues to this day in debates on welfare
policy and "foreign aid" is whether such state measures actually improve the
well-being of the poor, or merely make those who advocate them feel good
about themselves, as if they had discharged a moral obligation, not by helping
others but by advocating policies. For most classical liberals, consequences,
and not merely stated intentions, matter in the evaluation of policies.[77] Thus,
the question of whether state aid resting on compulsion in fact represents an
improvement for the poor has always been a central concern of classical liberals when addressing plans for redistribution. That is an empirical question

---

[75] Mill, "The Claims of Labour," 374.

[76] Ibid. Bernard Bosanquet noted the unpromising history of state provision of welfare: "It
      is often alleged that the time of the factory development a hundred years ago was a time of
      unmixed Economic Individualism. But this is not so; perhaps the worst evils of that time
      arose directly from the intentionally lax or 'socialistic' Poor Law. It was the public institu-
      tions that for the most part supplied the children who were ill-treated." Bosanquet, "The
      Antithesis between Individualism and Socialism," 330.

[77] See David Schmidtz's essay in Schmidtz and Goodin, *Social Welfare and Individual
      Responsibility*, especially the section on "Consequences Matter," 86–88.

to which classical liberal scholars have contributed a substantial body of research.[78]

The French classical liberal economist and journalist Frédéric Bastiat argued that, regardless of the intention of the legislator, the principle of compulsion was illegitimate:

I certainly do not deny that among the innumerable systems that this false principle gives rise to, a great number, the greater number even, originate from benevolent and genuine intentions. But what is vicious is the principle itself. The manifest end of each particular plan is to equalize prosperity. But the still more manifest result of the principle on which these plans are founded is to equalize poverty; nay more, the effect is to force the well-to-do families down into the ranks of the poor and to decimate the families of the poor by sickness and starvation.[79]

In listing the order of preferences among classical liberals, Wilhelm Röpke stated that "our rule and norm and our cheerfully accepted ideal should be security through individual effort and responsibility, supplemented by mutual aid."[80] Nonetheless, Röpke differed from some classical liberals in accepting state provision of a minimum of assistance:

We cannot, nowadays, do without a certain minimum of compulsory state institutions for social security. Public old-age pensions, health insurance, accident insurance, widows' benefits, unemployment relief – there must naturally be room for all these in our concept of a sound social security system in a free society, however little enthusiasm we may feel for them. It is not their principle which is in question, but their extent, organization, and spirit.[81]

Many classical liberals have thus accepted some state provision, but only with some reluctance and as the least preferred method of assistance to the poor. Milton Friedman, for example, offered two reasons to support a limited

[78] Dambisa Moyo's *Dead Aid: Why Aid Is Not Working and How There Is Another Way for Africa* (London: Allen Lane, 2009) is the most recent critique from a classical liberal perspective of foreign aid on the grounds that it fosters corruption, undermines democratic accountability, and destroys or retards economic growth and improvements in well being. Another concern has been whether such redistribution serves, on balance, to entrench political power, which is exercised by people who are decidedly not at the lower end of the economic order. Edward Tufte in his book *Political Control of the Economy* (Princeton, NJ: Princeton University Press, 1978) demonstrated how transfer payments in the United States have been manipulated to achieve electoral outcomes, notably by the administration of Richard Nixon. See especially chapter 2, "The Electoral Cycle and Economic Policy," in which he shows how transfer payments tend to peak immediately before election days: "The quickest way to produce an acceleration in real disposable income is for the government to mail more people larger checks – that is, for transfer payments to increase" (p. 29).
[79] Frederic Bastiat, "Property and Law," in *Selected Essays on Political Economy*, ed. George B. de Huszar (Irvington-on-Hudson: Foundation for Economic Education, 1995), 107–8.
[80] Wilhelm Röpke, *A Humane Economy: The Social Framework of the Free Market* (Indianapolis: Liberty Fund 1971), 177.
[81] Ibid., 175.

degree of state compulsion for purposes of assisting the poor. The first was the exercise of legal compulsion to force people to purchase annuities for their own old age because "the improvident will not suffer the consequence of their own action but will impose costs on others. We shall not, it is said, be willing to see the indigent aged suffer in dire poverty. We shall assist them by private and public charity. Hence the man who does not provide for his old age will become a public charge. Compelling him to buy an annuity is justified not for his own good but for the good of the rest of us."[82] (As he quickly noted, "The weight of this argument clearly depends on fact.") The second was the exercise of legal compulsion to force taxpayers as a class to support those who are in need, on the grounds that state coercion to provide a collective (or public) good is acceptable on liberal grounds: "It can be argued that private charity is insufficient because the benefits from it accrue to people other than those who make the gifts.... I am distressed by the sight of poverty; I am benefited by its alleviation; but I am benefited equally whether I or someone else pays for its alleviation; the benefits of other people's charity therefore partly accrue to me." Such concerns would, according to Friedman, set "a floor under the standard of life of every person in the community."[83]

F. A. Hayek also, although not an enthusiast for the welfare state, argued, on the grounds of provision of public goods, that some limited state provision of welfare was compatible with classical liberal principles: "All modern governments have made provision for the indigent, unfortunate, and disabled and have concerned themselves with questions of health and the dissemination of knowledge. There is no reason why the volume of these pure service activities should not increase with the general growth of wealth. There are common needs that can be satisfied only by collective action and which can be thus provided for without restricting individual liberty."[84]

Friedman's and Hayek's public goods argument was rejected by Robert Nozick, who offered a more consistently antistatist interpretation of classical liberalism. After a discussion of the economics and the ethics of public goods, Nozick concluded, "Since it would violate moral constraints to compel people who are entitled to their holdings to contribute against their will, proponents of such compulsion should attempt to persuade people to ignore the relatively few who don't go along with the scheme of voluntary contributions. Or, is it relatively *many* who are to be compelled to contribute, though they would not so choose, by those who don't want to feel they are 'suckers'?"[85]

The debates among classical liberals on those issues have been vigorous and have focused on a number of questions, such as how competent and

---

[82] Milton Friedman, *Capitalism and Freedom* (Chicago: University of Chicago Press, 1962), 188.

[83] Ibid., 191.

[84] F. A. Hayek, *The Constitution of Liberty* (Chicago: University of Chicago Press, 1960), 257.

[85] Nozick, *Anarchy, State, and Utopia*, 268.

trustworthy state institutions – even subject to democratic supervision – may be, whether any compulsion at all is consistent with the principles of liberalism, and whether state provision of even a "safety net" would set in motion a process of fostering dependence and displacing the network of mutual aid associations that was closely associated with classical liberalism.

The classical liberal legal theorist A. V. Dicey expressed the fear of state provision that was general among classical liberals:

> The beneficial effect of State intervention, especially in the form of legislation, is direct, immediate, and, so to speak, visible, whilst its evil effects are gradual and indirect, and lie out of sight.... few are those who realize the undeniable truth that State help kills self-help. Hence the majority of mankind must almost of necessity look with undue favour upon governmental intervention. This natural bias can be counteracted only by the existence, in a given society, as in England between 1830 and 1860, of a presumption or prejudice in favour of individual liberty – that is, of *laissez faire*. The mere decline, therefore, of faith in self-help – and that such a decline has taken place is certain – is of itself sufficient to account for the growth of legislation tending towards socialism.[86]

Herbert Spencer, toward the end of his life, saw the growth of the state provision of services and of measures to substitute coercion for voluntary action as "the New Toryism" and "the Coming Slavery."[87] Like other classical liberals toward the end of the nineteenth century, he connected the rise of nationalism, imperialism, racism, socialism, and the welfare state as outgrowths from the shared root of collectivism.[88]

The fear of state provision was not limited to Anglo-Saxons but was – and remains – a common feature of classical liberal thought. As François Guizot noted, "Nothing is more evident or sacred than the duty of the government to come to the assistance of the classes less favoured by fate, to ease their wretchedness and to assist them in their endeavour to rise toward the blessings of civilization. But to maintain that it is through the defects in the social organisation that all the misery of so many human beings originates, and to impose on the government the task of guaranteeing and distributing equally the good things of life, is to ignore absolutely the human condition, abolish the responsibility inherent in human liberty and excite bad passions through false hopes."[89] Wilhelm von Humboldt despised the Poor Laws for killing

---

[86] A. V. Dicey, *Lectures on the Relation between Law and Public Opinion in England during the Nineteenth Century* (Indianapolis: Liberty Fund, 2008), 182.

[87] Herbert Spencer, *The Man vs. the State*, in *Political Writings*, ed. John Offer (Cambridge: Cambridge University Press, 1994).

[88] See Sheri Berman, *The Primacy of Politics: Social Democracy and the Making of Europe's Twentieth Century* (Cambridge: Cambridge University Press, 2006), on the common intellectual roots of Marxism, fascism, national socialism, and social democracy.

[89] François Guizot, "Mémoires pour servir à l'histoire de mon temps," in *Western Liberalism: A History in Documents from Locke to Croce*, ed. E. K. Bramsted and K. J. Melhuish (London: Longman Group, 1978), 335–36.

charity and hardening hearts: "Does anything tend so effectually to deaden
and destroy all true sympathy – all hopeful yet modest entreaty – all trust in
man by man? Does not everyone despise the beggar, who finds it more convenient to be cared for in an almshouse than, after struggling with want, to find,
not a mere hand flinging him a pittance, but a sympathizing heart?"[90]
There remain questions of the extent of moral obligations to the poor.
Those are not easily answered from within the classical liberal tradition, for
the simple reason that classical liberal thought distinguishes – as many other
traditions do not – between those duties and obligations that are enforceable
and those that are not. A classical liberal may embrace the obligation of tith-
ing or of *zakat* but will insist that that obligation not be made compulsory;
it is an expression of one's religious and moral – not legal – obligations. The
universalist tendencies of classical liberalism have generally promoted concerns with persons per se rather than with co-religionists or co-nationals.
The responsibility of not harming others is applicable to all, regardless of
whether they are close members of one's own community or complete strangers living in a far-distant nation. As Adam Smith noted, "Mere justice is,
upon most occasions, but a negative virtue, and only hinders us from hurting
our neighbour. The man who barely abstains from violating either the person, or the estate, or the reputation of his neighbours, has surely very little
positive merit. He fulfils, however, all the rules of what is peculiarly called
justice, and does every thing which his equals can with propriety force him
to do, or which they can punish him for not doing. We may often fulfil all
the rules of justice by sitting still and doing nothing."[91] Positive obligations,
in the classical liberal view, are normally acquired on the basis of one's acts
(they are adventitious rather than connate);[92] as such, one is not born with or
assigned particular enforceable obligations to particular people on the basis
of the relative poverty of those persons. Because of their focus on eliminating
injustice, in the form of the harms visited by some on others, classical liberals
led the international movements to abolish forced labor[93] and slavery, which

[90] Wilhelm von Humboldt, *The Limits of State Action* (Cambridge: Cambridge University
Press, 1969), 40. See also the description of the opposition of German liberals to Bismarck's
modern welfare state in Ralph Raico, "Der Aufstieg des modernen Wohlfahrtsstaates
und die liberale Antwort," in Raico, *Die Partei der Freiheit: Studien zur Geschichte des
deutschen Liberalismus* (Stuttgart: Lucius & Lucius, 1999), 153–79.
[91] Smith, *The Theory of Moral Sentiments*, 82.
[92] Compare Samuel Pufendorf on "connate" and "adventitious" obligations: "Now obligation can, by reason of its origin, be divided into connate and adventitious. The former
belongs to all men immediately upon birth by virtue of the fact that they are such, fully
exerting itself as soon as they have begun to be able, on account of their age, to understand
its force and to regulate their actions through reason…. Adventitious obligations are those
voluntarily assumed by those who have already been born, or those enjoined by the command of a superior or by law." *The Political Writings of Samuel Pufendorf*, ed. Craig L.
Carr, trans. Michael J. Seidler (Oxford: Oxford University Press, 1994), 50.
[93] See, for example, the efforts by Anne Robert Jacques Turgot to eliminate forced peasant
labor (the corvée) in France, described in *The Life and Writings of Turgot*, ed. W. Walker
Stephens (New York: Burt Franklin, 1971), esp. 124–49.

movements promoted the freedom and well-being of the worst-off and most abused members of humanity. Similarly, the moral urgency of the classical liberal case for freedom of trade has focused a substantial amount of attention on the denial of opportunities for improved welfare among the people of poor nations, who are sacrificed by protectionist policies to the well-being of those much wealthier than they. Freeing the poor from coercive controls over their behavior benefits the poor, as well as all who engage in trade; classical liberals see the gains from trade as mutual. It is not a concession to others to remove restrictions on one's own ability to purchase freely. As the nineteenth-century German classical liberal economist and parliamentarian John Prince Smith argued, "The removal of import tariffs is an economic concession which we grant primarily to ourselves and not merely to foreign countries."[94]

The same logic has been applied to immigration, as classical liberals have generally promoted freedom of movement as much as they have freedom of trade.[95] As such, classical liberals have been active proponents of "globalization" through freedom of speech, trade, and travel.[96] It is ironic that socialists and welfare statists often pose as champions of the poor at the same time that they vigorously defend restrictions on migration that use barbed wire, armed patrols, and other forms of force to keep desperately poor people away from wealthy countries where they would have opportunities to improve their lot. Classical liberals have traditionally opposed such restrictions and favor

---

[94] John Prince Smith, "On the Significance of Freedom of Trade in World Politics," in Bramsted and Melhuish, *Western Liberalism*, 357. The insistence on the value of unilateral free trade by classical liberals has received greater emphasis in recent years; see Razeen Sally, *Trade Policy, New Century: The WTO, FTAs, and Asia Rising* (London: Institute of Economic Affairs, 2008).

[95] For recent works, see Philippe Legrain, *Immigrants: Your Country Needs Them* (London: Little, Brown, 2006), and Jason L. Riley, *Let Them In: The Case for Open Borders* (New York: Gotham Books, 2008).

[96] The term "globalization" has many meanings. The project of the Soviet Union, for example, entailed worldwide imposition of one-party Communist rule; that is one kind of "globalization." Even nationalist and anticosmopolitan forces promote a kind of "globalization," in the form of a global movement of competing nationalisms, an idea that contains the seeds of endless conflict. Classical liberals have promoted certain universal standards of peaceful interaction through voluntary trade, tourism, travel, migration, and exchange of ideas. The result is compatible with a wide variety of different cultural forms, although hostile to any that are imposed by force on nonconsenting parties. For classical liberal treatments of such topics, see Tom G. Palmer, *Globalization and Culture: Homogeneity, Diversity, Identity, Liberty* (Berlin: Liberales Institut, 2004), http://tomgpalmer.com/papers/liberales2.pdf, and "Globalization, Cosmopolitanism, and Personal Identity," *Etica & Politica*, no. 2 (2003), http://tomgpalmer.com/wp-content/uploads/papers/palmer-globcosmoidentity.pdf. Classical liberals have been disparaged by socialist critics as "neoliberals," a term that virtually no classical liberal has accepted, partly because the term is used to refer not only to freer trade, travel, and migration but too often very illiberal statist development programs promoted by state-backed organizations, such as the World Bank, the International Monetary Fund, and the USAID, which classical liberals have traditionally opposed.

freedom of trade, travel, and migration, which they consider a superior alternative to state redistributive programs that, they generally argue, are unsuccessful at lifting people from poverty to wealth.

Classical liberal thinkers, despite often robust disagreement among themselves, have agreed that the creation of more wealth is the solution to the alleviation of poverty and that, because outcomes are not themselves generally subject to choice, just and efficient institutions are the key to increasing wealth and diminishing poverty. Moreover, although many make room for state provision of assistance to the poor and indigent, all agree that there is a hierarchy of means for the alleviation of poverty, cascading from personal responsibility and self-help, to mutual aid, to charity, to the least preferred option, state compulsion.

6

Confucian Perspectives on Poverty and Morality

Peter Nosco

It is difficult to essentialize any tradition, but for various reasons Confucianism seems more difficult than most. For one, Confucianism lacks the kind of doctrinal statements that characterize many religious traditions, and there are no noble truths as in Buddhism or creeds as in Christianity. Over centuries, however, there did emerge a constructed lineage of authorities whose writings have attained both intellectual and official acceptance as orthodox Confucianism.

Although there is no Confucian scripture with prophetic claims, from the very start Confucianism embraced a curriculum, and it has always held learning to be a central activity. Confucius (552–479 BCE) himself stressed knowledge of the poetic, historical, and ritual tradition that was already centuries old, and in this sense "Confucianism" can be said to antedate Confucius, who spoke of himself as the transmitter of an ancient tradition rather than the inventor of a new one. Within a century or two of Confucius's death, this curriculum comprised Five Classics, works the mastery of which was deemed to be fundamental to the training of a *junzi* or gentleman.[1] In later times these works were superseded by the more familiar Four Books, which included the major canonical writings of Confucius's *Analects* and the writings of Mencius (391–308 BCE).[2]

Before Confucius, heredity was understood to be the essential qualification for rulership. Kings represented themselves as the descendants of deities or cosmic forces, and only limited claims were made regarding the moral

---

[1] The Five Classics included the Spring and Autumn Annals (Chunqiu), which recorded events from Confucius's native state of Lu from 722 to 481 BCE; the Book of Changes (Yijing), the classic divination text; the Book of Documents (Shujing), which included the pronouncements of monarchs from the earliest sage kings; the Book of Ritual (Liji), which outlined ritual for the lower aristocratic ranks; and the Book of Odes (Shijing), a collection of 305 ancient poems said to have been edited by Confucius. One finds references to a sixth classic, the Book of Music (Yuejing), which is not extant.

[2] Along with the briefer Doctrine of the Mean (Jungyung) and Great Learning (Daxue).

dimensions of authority. Confucius changed this by arguing that governing was too important to be trusted entirely to heredity and should be properly understood as the prerogative of a morally superior elite. He spoke of the ruler's responsibility to help households and the individuals within them to grow in the direction of goodness, with goodness understood not as an idealized abstraction but in the practical context of everyday associations and interactions.

Confucianism, as a doctrine that in various ways supersedes the *Analects*, has throughout its 2,500-year history been dynamic, evolving to mean quite different things at different times, and the tradition as a whole has had few authentic interpreters, other than the obvious Confucius and Mencius. During the Han dynasties (206 BCE–220 CE), the scholar-official Dong Zhongshu (179–104 BCE) refashioned Confucianism to absorb the cosmology of Yin-Yang and the Five Elements, along with associated divination practices that included the geomancy of *feng shui*.[3] This in fact was the Confucianism that initially reached Japan, where its teachings were for centuries more valued for these metaphysical accruals than for the earlier social, political, and ethical core. After the fall of the Latter (Eastern) Han Dynasty in 220 CE and the division of China into a number of warring kingdoms, Confucianism was discredited as a philosophy of governing, though at the same time its rhetorical value was prized. One studied Confucianism if one wished to be an essayist of note or to succeed in the civil service examination, but its value as a philosophy of government was devalued.

During the Southern Song (1127–1279), Confucianism again refashioned itself, this time as a response to the Buddhism that filled the spiritual vacuum created during the centuries of Confucianism's relative decline. The government of the succeeding Mongol Yüan Dynasty (1280–1368) endorsed the commentaries of the Song scholar Zhu Xi (1130–1200) and a handful of others as the official interpretations for the now all-important civil service examinations, lending them the mantle of intellectual orthodoxy. These same commentaries were soon similarly prized in both Japan and Korea, where they inspired legions of followers as well as a broad range of challenges and challengers, but throughout East Asia it was the lineage of Confucius, Mencius, Dong, and Zhu that came to be sanctioned as the orthodox transmission of the Confucian Way.

While this dynamic quality to the tradition has made it difficult to essentialize, for more than two thousand years intellectuals throughout East Asia have addressed concerns that are widely recognized as being *Confucian* in nature, and these concerns can broadly be divided into the political-social,

---

³ Yin-Yang: the doctrine that male and female complementary principles inform the universe. Five Elements (*wuxing*): the doctrine that five basic elements – water, wood, fire, earth, and metal – constitute the world and through their sequential progressions influence its activity.

the domestic-familial, and the personal-individual. Within the political-social sphere, Confucianism aspires to orderly society and good government. The social order is meant to mirror the order and balance that lie at the very heart of the cosmos, and good government is humane government, about which much of this chapter is directly concerned. For now, suffice it to say that humane government is one in which rulers treat their subjects with the same solicitous care that parents show their children.

Confucianism at the same time insists that a society's political health is contingent upon the integrity of the human relationships within it. In this sense, Confucianism is fundamentally social, imagining goodness entirely in the context of those person-to-person interactions which constitute its life-blood. Confucianism sees these relationships as mostly vertical, with clear superiors and subordinates. The superiors are typically also the benefactors and the subordinates the beneficiaries, making interactions more symbiotic than one might initially gather. That is to say, within these relationships those below owe their undivided allegiance to those above, while those above are obliged to care for their subordinates in a fundamentally parental manner, and it is through these relationships that we measure our own growth in the direction of goodness.

Confucianism imagines the state to be composed not of communities or other geographic units but rather of households. It gives priority to domestic-familial relationships, making it understandable that the primary Confucian virtue should be filial piety, which is viewed as both natural and inevitable. It is assumed that we all learn the mutual responsibilities inherent to filial piety. Initially this entails obedience and respect on the part of children, and subsequently it matures into humane care for one's own children on the part of parents. From filial piety, individuals move on to other relationships within the home, such as the one between siblings and eventually the relationship between spouses, the coordinate virtue in all these various relationships being humanity (*ren*), also translated as benevolence or goodness. Note again that Confucianism never conceives of this humanity in some abstract sense but always in the concrete form of goodness expressed through the interaction of one person with another.

The Confucian household acquires a corporate character, in the sense of a complex yet integrated body, an organic whole composed of constituent parts. To be sure, affection between parents and children is just as important to the harmonious operation of the Confucian household as is an understanding of separate functions and correct sequence, but Confucians have not traditionally conceived of the household as the kind of emotional unit that typically emerges in contemporary European and North American discussions of families. Rather, Confucians would say that the family is a kind of laboratory or training facility wherein, through these various domestic relationships, we are one and all prepared for those interactions and relationships that arise outside the home, such as those with one's neighbors, teachers, and rulers.

At the level of society and the state, Confucianism proposes to restore the idealized conditions believed to have existed at various times in the past when sage kings ruled, especially the reign of the sagely Duke of Zhou in the eleventh century BCE. Confucianism maintains that if rule was at different times in the past endowed with correctness, that is, if rulers in these halcyon days followed the ancient guidelines proscribed in the Classics for both courtly ritual and music, then Heaven blessed their realm accordingly. Most importantly, Confucianism assumes that the same sociopolitical perfection of this ancient arcadia can be resurrected in the here-and-now and that through dint of human effort one can achieve a kind of paradise on earth.

Taken to the personal-individual level, Confucianism becomes an exercise in human perfection. Confucianism proposes that we all grow in the direction of a moral absolute, with some perhaps even attaining to sagehood. Mencius once phrased this by saying (6A:7), "The sage and I are the same in kind," but despite the egalitarian implications, sagehood remained the loftiest of ideals. At any level, however, the fulfillment of our human potential for goodness can be done through the three means of self-cultivation, by which is meant the nurturing of a healthy goodness that represents humankind's birthright; learning, which can mean both classical learning and learning about oneself; and mastery of the complex ritual traditions of the past, or at least those appropriate to one's station in life. In theory, for Confucianism there is no person for whom this quest for self-perfection is not a plausible exercise.

As mentioned, a thousand years ago Confucianism in China sought to recast itself in order to recapture the hearts and minds of those Chinese who had embraced the beliefs and assumptions of Buddhism. This refashioned Confucianism of which Zhu Xi was the master craftsman is often styled Neo-Confucianism, but Neo-Confucianism added little to the discourse on poverty and morality within traditional or classical Confucianism, and so, despite its importance to the intellectual history of East Asia, it does not figure prominently in this chapter.

In more recent years, Confucianism has often been identified with authoritarian regimes in Asia, where self-styled Confucian rulers have invoked the doctrine to veil their essentially dictatorial impulses. Remarkably, after decades of vilifying Confucius and his interpreters as one of the Four Bad Olds, the government of China now champions Confucianism's concerns with social order and political stability, while on Taiwan, for much of the twentieth century Confucianism's most articulate international spokesman, many have rediscovered Confucianism's traditional rival of Daoism. None of these modern or contemporary developments figure prominently in this chapter, and I focus instead on classical Confucianism, whose ancient teachings were, as we have already seen, profoundly concerned with the human condition and its potential for amelioration.

Definitions

The classic statement of the utopian Confucian vision is found in the *Book of Rites*, one of the Five Classics, where it is said that one day after sighing deeply Confucius described that perfect age *in illo tempore* as follows:

> When the Great Way was practiced, All-under-Heaven was public-spirited. They chose men of worth and ability [for public office]. They practiced good faith and cultivated good will. Therefore people did not single out only their parents to love, nor did they single out only their children for care. They saw to it that the aged were provided for until the end, that the able-bodied had employment, and that the young were brought up well. Compassion was shown to widows, orphans, the childless and those disabled by disease, so that all had sufficient support.[4]

In this beautiful passage, we see the divergence between a Confucian ideal of how history should proceed and what the reality of a Confucian China has been. In the ideal as Confucius is said to have described it, men of ability were chosen for public office, and not just men of high birth or correct lineage, as was and would be the case in every Chinese dynasty; in the ideal, a kind of universal love was practiced, and not just the particularistic ethics of the household, as became the norm; and in the ideal, all had sufficient support, instead of the persistent reality when one aspires to distribute resources in a manner that at best results in the least hardship rather than the broadest good.

Confucianism has generally had more to say about well-being than about its inverse, and this results in a view of poverty as the lack of one or more of life's necessities, a list that would include the obvious staples of food, clothing, shelter, and security of one's person, as well as the distinctively Confucian additions of harmonious family relations and good government. The list of what is needed for a good life is thus far not remarkable.

What is remarkable in Confucianism, however, is the priority of these necessities of a good life, and it is here that we observe a certain Confucian ambivalence toward poverty. Confucianism maintains that, of life's most basic needs, good government, construed as a state that enjoys the confidence of the people, is more important than either food or military defense, as the following exchange between Confucius and one of his disciples makes clear (*Analects* 12:7):

> Zigong asked about governing. The Master said, "Simply make sure there is sufficient food, sufficient armaments, and that you have the confidence of the common people."
>
> Zigong said, "If sacrificing one of the three things became unavoidable, which would you sacrifice first?" The Master replied, "I would sacrifice the armaments."

---

[4] Translation by Michael Nylan in Xinzhong Yao, *Routledge Curzon Enclyclopedia of Confucianism*, vol. I (London: RoutledgeCurzon, 2003), 369.

Zigong said, "If sacrificing one of the remaining two things became unavoidable, which would you sacrifice next?" The Master replied, "I would sacrifice the food. Death has always been with us, but a state cannot stand once it has lost the confidence of the people."[5]

Put slightly differently, being well fed, warmly clothed, and appropriately lodged are fundamental, but ultimately it is instruction in human relations that is Confucianism's highest goal, for this is what distinguishes humans from animals. Providing for the human capacity to grow in the direction of goodness is the state's highest responsibility, as this is what will enable one to recapture one's original and innate goodness (*Mencius* 3A:4).

This counterintuitive set of priorities is also reflected in a remarkable conversation Confucius had with two of his best students, Zilu and Ran Qiu, regarding what they believed they would accomplish if they were suddenly entrusted with the administration of a state. Zilu articulates the more noble ideal:

If I were given charge of a state of a thousand chariots – even one hemmed in by powerful states, suffering from armed invasions and afflicted by famine – before three years were up I could infuse its people with courage and a sense of what is right.

But Ran Qiu expresses the more practical goal:

If I were given charge of a state sixty or seventy – or even fifty or sixty – square *li* in area, before three years were up I could see to it that the people would have all they needed. As for instructing the people in ritual practice and music, this is a task that would have to await the arrival of a gentleman.[6]

In other words, alleviating the people's hardship – seeing to it that the people have "all they need" – is an important goal, and is fundamental to good governing, but the highest goals are to inspire the people with the ritual traditions of a great past and to instruct them in human relations.

Just as poverty can have numerous dimensions, it can have various causes. Confucians recognize that government can be a cause of poverty as well as its potential solution when, for example, rulers tax their subjects abusively and thereby drive hard-working agriculturalists to the brink of subsistence. Other government-provoked causes of poverty can include poor instruction regarding agronomy, incorrect calendrical calculations, inadequate provision of the seeds and iron tools needed for effective cultivation, and poor planning of various sorts.

---

[5] *Confucius Analects*, trans. Edward Slingerland (Indianapolis: Hackett, 2003), 128. Slingerland includes Wang Yangming's comment on this passage: "Once you have lost the hearts of the people, how can the rest be relied upon? Even if you have grain, would you even get to eat it?"

[6] Ibid., 123.

Confucianism insists that rulers practice humane taxation policies, so as not to burden peasant-cultivators unnecessarily. To do otherwise will invite ruin, because abused peasants will abscond, leaving their fields untilled and the government's tax coffers unfilled. The epitome of enlightened land reform and taxation traditionally extolled by Confucianism is that of the well-field. Under this system, land was to be divided into nine equal-sized fields, eight of which are farmed privately, with the ninth central field (containing the well) farmed collectively, its yield set aside as the eight families' tax (*Mencius* 3A:3).

One of the Chinese government's traditional tools for combating famine brought on by increases in the cost of food during times of scarcity has been the ever-normal granary – a strategic reserve of foodstuffs built up during ordinary harvests in order to create stocks that the government can then release when times take a turn for the worse. The ever-normal granary has long been identified as a Confucian institution, though the attribution has as much to do with Confucianism's penchant for planning as it does with any specific textual reference. Provisioning the granary was the king's responsibility, and so any lapse in its effectiveness could be construed as grounds to question whether a true king is on the throne.

This in turn begs the question of how one is to know when this true king reigns? Mencius's definition of these conditions is the most extreme: he writes that when men of seventy have silk to wear and meat to eat, and the common people suffer from neither hunger nor cold (*Mencius* 1A:7), a true king sits on the throne. Conversely, Mencius regards the king who harms humanity as a bandit (1B:8) and, in this sense, proposes a state that exists for the people, even if it is not governed by these same people. Mencius insists that rulers not embrace their subjects' welfare out of some instrumental concern but rather because such care is the only acceptable moral alternative. In his text's opening words, Mencius goes so far as to chastise King Hui of Liang for thinking about what might profit him or his kingdom rather than about what is humane and what is righteous.

Traditional Confucianism imagines society to be like an organism, with each person a component with a specific role to fill. This society is highly stratified, and because everyone has an ordered place, the society may be deemed to be functioning well when all of its constituent parts – all its individuals within all its homes – are correctly performing their assigned roles. This is what Confucians mean when they say that the Way is prevailing, something Confucians believe occurred at a number of times in the past, and something that rulers are to aspire to resurrect in the present. Confucians style this Way variously, but most commonly call it the Way of Heaven (*tian*), the Way of the Kings (or Former Kings), and the Way of the Sages (or Sage Kings).

Like the limbs and organs in a human body, the individual components in this organism, that is, you and I, are interconnected through our relationships horizontally with all of humankind and vertically to Heaven itself as

the source of life. As Zhang Zai (1020–77) expressed this interconnected-
ness in an inscription he wrote on the west-facing window of his lecture hall,
"Heaven is my father and Earth is my mother, and even such a small creature
as I finds an intimate place in their midst.... All people are my brothers and
sisters, and all things my companions."[7]

Within this organism of society, Confucianism regards poverty as an aberration, though it would not regard inequality in the same way, or as Mencius
said, "It is the nature of things to be unequal."[8] In later centuries the civil
service examination system served as something of a social leveler or equal-
izer of opportunity, but there is only a limited sense of equality of opportunity
in traditional Confucianism. This is because the very concept of opportunity
is inconsistent with the traditional Confucian understanding of the destiny
(*ming*) that represents the endowment of individuals and kingdoms alike.
The only self-determination that you and I would have enjoyed in traditional
times is the freedom to do the task to which we have been born, which is one's
lot. As Mencius (3A:4) states on the hierarchy that is Confucianism's logical
consequence, "There is the work of great men and there is the work of little
men.... Those who labor with their minds govern others and are supported by
them; those who labor with their strength are governed by others and support
those others."[9]

There is thus nothing inherently wrong with a king enjoying luxuries not
available to his subjects. After all, performances of the correct musical pieces
at designated times of the year and the execution of a host of elaborate rituals
to mark the change of seasons and other important occasions were part and
parcel of a monarch's completion of his part in what Confucianism imagined
to be an integrated cosmic order: Heaven above will deliver the rain and sun-
shine needed for agriculture and will change the seasons in a timely manner;
the Earth below will then bring forth its bounty of food, salt, and iron; but all
of this will happen if and only if humankind fulfills its responsibility of good
government and administration. Of all humans, the king is understandably
the most important in this regard, yet even the king does not enjoy unlimited license, and Confucius speaks of the importance of royal frugality, especially in straitened circumstances, emphasizing that the emotional sincerity
of ritual actions is ultimately more important than their degree of ornateness
and ostentation. As the Confucian Fan Zhongyan (989–1052) expressed this,
the cultured have a responsibility to be the first to worry about the world's
troubles and the last to enjoy its pleasures.

The king has the cosmic authority conferred by Heaven to call on the labor
of his subjects for the good of the kingdom, but, cautions Confucius, this must

7 Wing-tsit Chan, trans. and comp., *A Source Book in Chinese Philosophy* (Princeton, NJ:
   Princeton University Press, 1963), 497.
8 Ibid., 70.
9 Ibid., 69.

be done only at seasonable times so as to minimize disruption to agriculture (*Analects* 1:5). As Confucius put this in reference to a government minister celebrated for his virtue (5:16), "in the way he cared for his people, he displayed benevolence; and in the way he employed the people, he displayed rightness."[10]

There is also ambivalence in Confucianism regarding its principles' universality and particularity. Confucianism has tended for most of its history to see the principles of enlightened rulership as part of the universal endowment of a benign Heaven and thus not as something contingent upon specific time or place. It is in this respect difficult to imagine circumstances under which the Confucian conception of poverty would depend upon specific historical circumstances, as if to say that poverty could be acceptable under certain circumstances but not others. At the same time, Confucianism has traditionally been inward-looking if not actually xenophobic, and so Chinese Confucianism has typically been indifferent to the socioeconomic conditions under which others might live.

High-Risk Groups

Confucianism is concerned about class but does not create fine distinctions and tends to divide individuals broadly and sharply into officials and nonofficials. Nonofficials, in turn, can be subdivided into peasant cultivators or agriculturalists, artisans, and merchants, all of whom are important in different ways.

Of all these, only peasant-cultivators are taxed, because the fruit of their labor is the easiest to predict and quantify. Mencius's rationale for not taxing the activities of merchants was to encourage them to store their goods within the walls of one's kingdom, which should then increase the supply of goods for all (2A:5), and one can imagine a similar rationale for not taxing the output of artisans, and thereby attracting their services. Peasant-cultivators are thus at once the most vulnerable to poverty and the most protected of classes. They are the most vulnerable because, then as now, their livelihood can be disrupted by the vagaries of nature as easily as by the vagaries of man. The ever-normal granary is one way in which the state can assist in buffering cultivators against the inevitable year-by-year variation in crop yields. But peasants were always vulnerable to changes in taxation or agricultural policies, either of which could easily wreak havoc on a peasant-cultivator's household, driving many of them into poverty.

Conversely, Confucian political economy emphasizes the importance of protecting peasant-cultivators, because the fruit of their labor allows for population growth and a corresponding increase in tax revenue. The well-being of the peasant-cultivator is thus a key concern for the Confucian

---

[10] *Confucius Analects*, 46.

monarch. If a king abuses his agriculturalists, they can seek relief by escaping to a neighboring realm, taking their productive labor and the promise of its fruits elsewhere. One corollary to this is the fact that the Confucian tradition, despite drawing clear distinctions between responsibilities of men and women in both private and public spheres, does not explicitly feminize poverty, seeing poverty as an issue that is gender blind. The Chinese tradition, by contrast, has disadvantaged women in a host of material ways, limiting their rights to own or inherit property and discouraging widows from remarrying.[11]

Volition

Confucianism proposes a cosmos governed by Heaven, a morally impartial force of nature with the power to bless or to withhold blessing from a specific regime, household, or individual. As noted, when Heaven withholds its blessing, the seasons will be disrupted, there will be too much or too little rainfall or heat, the next harvest will be affected, households will be unable to meet their tax obligations, a regime will weaken under this lack of resources, and eventually a successor will arise to topple it and take its place. This is what the Chinese tradition regards as a dynastic cycle, and it thus becomes impossible for Confucianism to imagine a realm in which a tyrant or despot can succeed for long in inflicting hardship upon the people. Without Heaven's mandate (*ming*), this regime will surely sooner or later fall, and a more benevolent regime will take its place. The key to this change, however, is that Heaven does not act arbitrarily but only in response to human activity in its principal area of responsibility of government. In order to address problems of financing the government, a Confucian king has the option of lowering his expenses but not that of increasing taxes on the peasantry. Equally plausible to the Confucian imagination as a cause of poverty is a realm in which a king's or a government's inability to restrain spending is compounded by some easily imaginable monarchic missteps: expensive formalism in rituals and sacrifices, disregard of the state granary, indifference toward land reform, reckless aggression toward neighboring states, using corvée (forced) labor at seasonally inopportune times, and so on. These are cases where the impoverishment of peasant-cultivators is again directly traceable to human volition, and where the consequential poverty is an undeserved hardship for those most profoundly and directly affected.

---

[11] While it may seem questionable to distinguish between a Confucian tradition and a Chinese one, another example may help to clarify the distinction. Confucianism has heavily emphasized learning as an activity that improves the individual, but it has spoken of virtue as the primary criterion for governing. As a result, using an exam system to determine who qualifies for government office is profoundly Chinese but scarcely Confucian, and Confucius himself would have rejected utterly the notion that one can measure an individual's goodness by measuring his knowledge of texts that speak about goodness.

Furthermore, owing to the absence of anything resembling a democratic public sphere in classical Confucianism, that is, a sphere of contestation in which individuals and their communities might participate in the selection of a state's leaders, it is difficult to imagine circumstances in which anyone other than a state's rulers might be held responsible for the contributions of that state's policies to the impoverishment of its people. This in turns means that, according to Confucianism, poverty will ultimately always have a human origin, and the poor in this respect are always to some extent victims.

Goals

Thus, for Confucianism the very existence of poverty is problematic, and it becomes both a cosmic and a moral imperative for those in authority to address it. Rulers have a number of responsibilities in this regard. They are expected to employ ritual specialists to see to it that ceremonial is correct in both form and substance. They are obliged to employ authorities on the historical record to inform them of instances of poverty or hardship in the past, and what the earliest kings did to address these problems successfully. And they are to follow the guidance of the past, the assumption being that so long as the correct principles are followed, what worked once will work again.

When we look with modern eyes at the question of whether it is a moral obligation to alleviate poverty, we distinguish between poverty as something one aspires ultimately to eliminate and poverty as something whose effects one wishes to mitigate. Classical Confucianism makes much the same distinction. As we have seen, to the extent that it is defined at all within the tradition, poverty is defined as the inverse of well-being. Thus, to provide relief for the conditions of poverty is sufficient as a place to begin, because when men of seventy have silk to wear and meat to eat, and when the common people suffer from neither hunger nor cold, one will know that a true king is on the throne. But poverty will be eliminated not when its conditions are relieved but when its root causes are addressed.

Further, there is generally little in classical Confucianism to suggest that the alleviation of poverty requires the sacrifice of other human goods, the exceptions being such items as unnecessarily lavish ceremonial performances at the court, and a tendency for Confucian-inspired rulers to adopt sumptuary legislation restricting certain extravagances. Examples of the latter would address who can wear silk or ride in a palanquin, one assumption being that by reducing such extravagance at higher levels there could be more available to all at the lower levels.

We also recall, however, that in the Confucian hierarchy of human needs, good government is ultimately more important than alleviating the people's physical needs or even in providing for their defense, and so one can conclude that willful disregard of the principles of humane government is even more contemptible than willful disregard of the conditions of the people's well-being.

To this point I have discussed classical Confucianism generally, essential-izing what was in fact a polyphonic tradition. Though some specialists would likely find room for disagreement, I have posited that Confucians of virtually all stripes would agree on such matters as how poverty is to be defined, who is affected by it, and who bears responsibility for it.

In the remainder of this chapter, we discuss a different set of ques-tions: what can be done to combat poverty, who is responsible for these efforts, and how broad-reaching this moral imperative is. To answer these, it will be important to acknowledge a broader range of possible responses within the classical Confucian tradition. Confucius, Mencius, and Xunzi (313–238 BCE) had different perspectives on the question of human nature, and these differences are reflected in their respective understandings of the appropriate remedies or strategies for dealing with poverty and other social ills. The Chinese tradition has hallowed a lineage that goes from Confucius through Mencius eventually to Zhuxi, branding Xunzi a heterodox inter-preter of the master. Of the three, however, Xunzi was possibly the most widely admired and followed in his own age, when no one questioned his credentials as a Confucian.

Each of the three sought to apply a combination of ritual, educational, and self-cultivational strategies to alleviate social ills, and the contrast between them is the most apparent in Confucius's two students. Believing in human nature's innate goodness, Mencius regarded morality as natural and instinc-tive. To the extent that poverty is the consequence of unrighteous rule, what is needed is a time of healing for the wounds that this inhumanity inflicted. Stop the damage, and natural regenerative forces will operate, restoring social har-mony and the people's attendant well-being. Mencius's moral optimism led him to conclude that the proper end of education was to help us to recover our lost goodness through self-cultivation.

Xunzi, by contrast, regarded morality as artificial and learned behavior. Under the tempering weight of training in tradition and civilization, and using teachers as models, we learn to overcome our instinctive competition and strife and to behave in socially constructive ways. For Xunzi, self-cultivation means not nurturing what is within but rather subduing it. Of all the ancient Confucians, Xunzi perhaps most appreciated how crucial the support of the people was to the ship of the state. He was also the most pragmatic in seeking practical solutions to societal ills, that is, solutions of a sort that someone less than a true king might be able to implement.

Not surprisingly, Confucius's positions were ultimately somewhere between the positions of these two, being so balanced that interpreters as dif-ferent as Mencius and Xunzi could each claim authenticity for their opposing views. Confucius valued ritual and music, no less than self-cultivation and reflection, seeing both the potential for goodness inherent in human nature and the problems in one's nature that need to be overcome. As a result, we find in Confucius's writings an attractive balance between the idealistic and the pragmatic, as when he wrote, "By nature people are similar; they diverge as the result of practice."[12]

In the following sections, we consider how these three classical Confucians would have answered the questions of how to combat poverty and whose responsibility it is to do so, and by examining all three I hope to convey the range of possible perspectives with legitimate claim to being *Confucian*. By way of conclusion, I use the example of contemporary urban homelessness, speculating on how these three might counsel their local authorities. My purpose in doing so is not to suggest that Confucius, Mencius, and Xunzi ever imagined anything like the social blight that afflicts portions of so many downtowns around the world. Instead, I hope to show both the potential utility of their insights and those insights' limitations.

Remedies

There was no disagreement among Confucians regarding the fact that a ruler cannot be indifferent to the hardships of the people, but there was a range of Confucian opinion regarding how best to address this. Confucius himself was mindful of the problem of poverty, as were his students, who saw famine as one of the most formidable challenges for a true prince to overcome. At the same time, they regarded alleviating the people's needs as ultimately less challenging than instructing them in ritual or music (*Analects* 11:26). Overcoming poverty requires a nobility of spirit in the administration of the land.

Confucius's model ruler takes his responsibility for ruling seriously and practices frugality as a way of showing affection to his subjects. The model ruler does not rule by the coercive instruments of laws or ordinances, punishments or sanctions, but rather by moral suasion and personal example. By dint of this moral force, relationships within the household (private) and within the realm (public) are rectified, households have their primordial harmony restored, and in a self-regulating manner society as a whole (re)attains an Edenic equilibrium.

According to Confucius, the model ruler's tools include ritual and music, which is another way of saying a civilization's cultural traditions. It is culture, in the form of education, that both brings pleasure and enhances character. Culture is like water for the plant that is a person's inner nature: use it appropriately, and moral and material growth will be the result.

When we look at Confucius's dictum (*Analects* 2:15), "Learning without thinking is a waste of time, but thinking without learning is reckless," we see Confucius's balanced emphasis on both interiority and exteriority. On the one hand, we are to cultivate our interior realm – or human nature – where indeed much goodness resides. On the other hand, we are also to allow ourselves to be transformed by the external weight of a great civilizational tradition.

[12] *Confucius Analects*, 200.

Mencius viewed this somewhat differently. Like Confucius, he regards society as a composite, with an ordered place for each and every individual in each and every household. He differs from Confucius, however, in believing that these varied individuals with their varied destinies and missions all share the same identical good nature, a nature that is good in the same way that water flows downhill. Mencius wrote of a nature that is so good as to make morality instinctive and natural, a nature that cannot bear to see the suffering of others.

The ruler's task in all this is not to concern himself narrowly with just the material dimension of society's ills, though Mencius was mindful of his own idealism and, as we have seen, counseled rulers regarding such matters as having farmers plow deeply and weed carefully (1A:5). More important is for the king to see to it that humanity and righteousness prevail, and that the people's most basic domestic relationships are honored. Within the administration of his government, the king is responsible for employing the worthy and competent, so that his government will have the people's respect, and for seeing to it that both taxes and punishments are reduced so that the burdens on the people are kept to a minimum. This, Mencius tells us, is what humane kingly government is all about.

That poverty exists at all would for Mencius be evidence of damage, though the damage might as easily be within the impoverished individual as with the society as a whole. Either way, if the damage is ever to heal, whatever has caused the damage, that is, the harm, must first cease. Mencius used the metaphor of a mountain, which, if protected from the erosion caused by human interference and allowed to regenerate, will recover from all the damage brought upon by thoughtless harmful behaviors. So too with humans: remove the source of the damage, and watch the healing, that is, the elimination of poverty, begin.

Xunzi was in many ways the most pragmatic and historically grounded of the three, and the contrast with Mencius's idealism could scarcely be more pronounced. Where Mencius saw the proper object of learning to be recovery of a lost goodness, and where Confucius advocated a balance between learning and thinking, Xunzi saw value only in learning, and this for its capacity to refashion our instincts in socially constructive ways. Under the influence of teachers and rulers, human rapaciousness can be harnessed and reined in, so that potentially damaging social energies will be channeled into more constructive purposes.

For Xunzi, good government was humankind's most fundamental responsibility, and if we attend to this correctly, all the rest will fall into place. Rulers need their people's support just as boats need water to stay afloat, but the way to order one's kingdom is by embracing the same principles that informed the past. Because human nature does not change, neither will these principles. Xunzi thus invoked an image of former kings using ritual to contend with the chaos that arises when humans are allowed to pursue their desires in an unrestrained manner. Along with learning, ritual becomes critical to humans fulfilling their very humanity.

Poverty for Xunzi thus is a natural and, to this extent, inescapable consequence of human nature, though it can be overcome. Using the policies of the early kings will help kings today to make model subjects out of their populace and, along the way, to alleviate if not altogether eliminate poverty.

Scope and Priorities

Any assessment of the scope and priorities of Confucian social thought will generate conflicting perspectives between Confucianism's universalistic and particularistic tendencies. Clearly, poverty is a problem for the Confucian ruler, for whom the alleviation if not actual elimination of want is a crucial piece of evidence in any claim to possessing the mantle of Heaven's mandate and to being a true king.

This can be thought of as a universal moral principle, and in support of this perspective, we recall the inspirational words of Zhang Zai, who maintained, "Heaven is my father and Earth is my mother, and even such a small creature as I finds an intimate place in their midst." This suggests that a good Confucian will sympathize with the hardship of others wherever they might be, but to suggest this is also to overlook Confucianism's particularistic ethics and the historical experience of Confucianism in China.

Though he stoked the memory of an Edenic moment in the past when universal love prevailed, Confucius did not advise his contemporaries to treat the parents of others as if they were one's own parents, or the children of others as if they were one's own children, as did his rivals in the Mo-ist camp. As we have noted, Confucianism stresses the relationships within the household as the primary foundation for future growth, the advantage being that this provides a realizable goal, a place to begin as it were, and a means to measure progress. One begins at home and then proceeds outward; as Mencius phrased this, "Treat with respect the elders in my family, and then extend that respect to include the elders in other families. Treat with tenderness the young in my own family, and then extend that tenderness to include the young in other families."[13]

The Confucian focus is thus fundamentally situational. As individuals, our primary obligation is to attend to the needs of those within our household before we concern ourselves with poverty or hardship in families elsewhere. As rulers, our primary concern is with poverty in our own kingdoms, and not at all on poverty in kingdoms elsewhere. The inward-looking tendencies of both Confucianism and Chinese civilization generally make it difficult to imagine circumstances under which Confucians would be exercised by poverty in alien lands, which would more likely be seen as evidence of the moral

---

[13] Chan, *Source Book in Chinese Philosophy*, 61.

inferiority of the alien regime. The absence in this respect of a broader altruism in traditional Confucianism is striking. In this particular subset of questions regarding the scope and priorities of the effort to combat poverty, the differences between Confucius and his principal interpreters are too narrow to warrant separate discussion.

Responsibility and Conditionality

Differences exist, however, when we come to discuss who is responsible for doing what to combat poverty. All Confucians would agree that it is ultimately the ruler's responsibility to lead the way in this fight, but the traditional king would not have had the same range of options as the leader of a contemporary social-democratic state, and this necessarily tempers our speculations.

For example, aside from certain state monopolies on salt and iron, the taxation of agriculture was the traditional Chinese state's principal source of revenue, and both commerce and manufacturing (artisanal activity) were generally untaxed. Because the peasant-cultivator would have been the first to feel the pains of a poor harvest rippling through the agrarian economy, the Confucian ruler could not propose an increase in taxes on the propertied wealthy, because they paid tax only on their land's agricultural product, and such a tax increase would necessarily trickle down to burden precisely those already in distress. Making matters worse, the largest landowners often enjoyed exemptions of various sorts from proportionate taxation of their lands. Raising taxes on those whose circumstances one is seeking to alleviate would be an obvious folly.

In modern times, one can imagine private philanthropic organizations – and even certain individuals – stepping forward to address the needs of society's neediest, but classical Confucianism allowed no space for the kind of civil society represented by private organizations. This is because Confucianism imagined the realm as a vast family, with the ruler as the parent of the people, and just as Confucianism imagined no sphere of privacy for relationships within the household, it made no room for private organizations or voluntary associations within the state or society at large.[14] This vacuum in turn deprived the poor in China of virtually any form of philanthropic aid other than clan based, at least before the rapid spread of Buddhism from the sixth century CE.

The means available to the traditional Confucian ruler to address poverty were thus limited. As already noted, he was expected to maintain the ever-normal granary and to employ it as a humanitarian mechanism during times

[14] The private academy being one notable exception. I develop this argument in my "Confucian Perspectives on Civil Society and Government," in *Civil Society and Government*, ed. Nancy L. Rosenblum and Robert C. Post (Princeton, NJ: Princeton University Press, 2002), 334–59.

of poor harvests. He could attempt land and tax reform of the well-field sort, but history did not recommend this approach, because none of the traditional Confucian societies of East Asia ever succeeded in implementing this or any other comparably egalitarian system, or such low rates of taxation on crops. Royal injunctions regarding deep plowing or careful weeding have their limits, as does royal frugality. The Confucian ruler was of course expected to economize in a manner proportionate to the needs of the day, but even here there were obvious limits as to what was practicable during the most difficult of times.

These may be thought of as the practical or instrumental means available to the Confucian ruler to address the problem of poverty, but recall also that the Confucian ruler was expected to give priority to reforming the people by means of ritual, music, education, and the rectification of relationships. Though Confucianism is typically reticent regarding the specifics of how such social transformation is to come about, one imagines something akin to a pre-modern cultural-social renaissance with broadly salutary impact on domestic relationships. Through the perfection of the family households throughout the realm, the ruler is able to address poverty successfully wherever it is to be found.

Here, one senses meaningful variation in the respective approaches of Confucius, Mencius, and Xunzi. Confucius would surely be the most balanced of the three, seeking a combination of the reform of the individual subject and the reform of the gentleman-ruler. Confucius does not tell us how this change will come about and simply assumes that the success of these efforts in the past will assure their efficacy in the present.

Mencius is the most idealistic, though it would have been in character for him to make an effort to offer specifics on a variety of practical matters. Mencius would regard poverty as akin to an illness, would focus principally on diagnosing the ailment, and would then work to eliminate its cause or source. His assumption is that healing will occur naturally and that, by removing the toxin, the wise ruler will have restored an environment in which unimpeded growth in the direction of goodness becomes possible for one and all. Mencius would thus expect to overcome poverty through a process of societal and individual healing.

Xunzi we imagine to be the most pragmatic, and to our eyes he is the also most familiar, using what were already time-tested policies. Xunzi seeks ways to incentivize socially constructive behavior and to discourage the selfishness, rapacity, and strife that generate all social ills, including poverty. Xunzi sees education – learning – as the answer to both society's and the individual's ills, though, in a world of radically limited opportunity, it is difficult to see how education would alleviate poverty as it is to imagine how royal ceremonial could do so. Xunzi would see laws and their attendant rewards and punishments as the natural allies of education in the effort to change the world.

Conclusion and Case Studies

Whether or not we can say how *Confucianism* would respond to poverty in the present, I hope that we are now sufficiently prepared to speculate on how some leading ancient Confucians might approach it today. By way of conclusion, then, I offer some exceedingly brief and altogether speculative thoughts on how our trio of ancient Confucians might address one specific example of homelessness, and what are often styled "street sweeps."

For one year in the mid-1970s when I was in graduate school, I walked at least twice a day past a supermarket on a busy corner of New York's Upper West Side. A man lived day and night in the alley next to the market, surviving on the canned food and produce that the store discarded, and also the coins that passersby sometimes pressed into his hands, this despite the fact that I never saw him even once solicit assistance. From the perspectives of traditional Confucianism, what are the state's or local government's responsibilities toward this man and his neighbors? Confucius, I suspect, would hope that a *junzi* – a trained and qualified gentleman – in authority will eventually reunite this fellow with his family. But the sage Confucius would also likely have found something admirable in the man's self-sufficiency, something made possible through the essentially painless altruism of the market.

Mencius probably would have welcomed seeing representatives of the state enjoining the official philanthropy of the modern welfare state. However, regarding our example as a kind of patient, such state welfare would likely be for Mencius a temporary strategy until a more comprehensive healing of the man's character might be brought about. Mencius's model ruler would likely be unsurpassed in his interventionism, actively interceding on behalf of the physical and psychological well-being of our man beside the supermarket.

Xunzi would certainly be the most authoritarian in his approach, though the consequences he intends are every bit as humane as those of Confucius and Mencius. Xunzi would approve of the modern paternalistic regime, which would regard our example more as a problem than a patient. Xunzi would assert reeducation, which in this context would likely mean a kind of enforced vocational rehabilitation and attendant loss of individual liberty, as the solution. His approach is in its basics just as paternalistic as that of Mencius, though it appears to come from a less charitable impulse.

My second question for case study concerns two varieties of "street sweeps." In one, vagrants, homeless, and other unfortunate street people are rounded up and taken elsewhere as a cosmetic means of addressing downtown urban poverty. This often occurs before major civic events like an Olympics, or in preparation for the state visit of a high-ranking dignitary. In the other, street people are rounded up and taken either voluntarily or involuntarily to shelters whenever the state deems outdoor conditions to be potentially hazardous or even lethal. One might typically see this in the winter when temperatures drop below a predetermined level or when snow or the weather makes outdoor life exceptionally forbidding.

Confucius, I suspect, would see a kind of ironic justice in having the presence of homeless street people embarrass a ruler on the occasion of a state visit or ceremonial occasion. Let this be visible to all, and let it be to the ruler's shame, Confucius might well have opined. I suspect that Mencius might view the state visit as an opportune occasion to move a ruler belatedly into the kind of humanitarian intervention that in his view should have already been attempted. A true king would have attended to this without the need for a prod from the state occasion, but under a true king the problem would presumably have been fixed (cured) long ago. Xunzi, one supposes, would see a street sweep related to a state visit as an entirely appropriate gesture, having the doubly salutary qualities of honoring the visiting dignitary in this internationally recognized ritual manner, while "cleansing" the capital of a kind of blight. One senses that Xunzi would feel right at home in the official residences of any number of contemporary metropolitan mayors and governors.

The humanitarian street sweep in which the homeless are forcibly evacuated *for their own good* is where one senses a distinction between the consequentialist and deontological analyses of our sagely Confucian trio. Confucius, Mencius, and Xunzi would in fact all surely agree that, when necessary to do so for their own good, forcibly removing the most vulnerable from exposure to the elements is what should be expected of a humane and benevolent state headed by a ruler who understands a ruler's most fundamental parental responsibilities.

It is their intentions or perspectives, however, that would surely differ. Confucius would likely feel as a parent does, regretting that such a drastic step is necessary at all, but recognizing that it is to the best for all concerned. Mencius, I imagine, would at some profound level take satisfaction in this demonstration of our most fundamental humanity as it finds expression in humanitarian concern. Xunzi, one suspects, would simply see this as doing exactly what is to be expected of today's ruler qua ruler, neither more nor less.

7

Poverty and Morality

A Feminist Perspective

Nancy J. Hirschmann

Feminism is not a moral discourse per se, in many people's views, but a political one. It is centered on power: the power that men have over women, and the
resulting lack of power that women have over property, in the determination
of laws, in the practice of political authority, over their own lives, over their
children, and over their own bodies. Moreover, to a large extent, feminism
is dedicated to practical issues rather than "ethics" per se as a formal discourse: domestic violence, sexual assault, sexual harassment, pornography,
pay equity, and job discrimination are more central issues to feminism than,
say, questions of "the good."[1] Feminism also, of course, has far more eso-
teric leanings into literary theory, philosophies of the body, and the meta-
question of "the meaning of woman" itself. Issues of "the body," defining
sexual identity and sexual desire, and the relationship between gender and
sex are not generally considered "moral" issues, even though they are highly
philosophical.[2]

But these various forms of feminism do have an obvious moral component,
and morality underlies most of these other kinds of arguments: it is essentially

[1] This is not to deny that many feminist philosophers are interested in ethics; nor, indeed,
that some Feminist philosophers interested in ethics tie this interest to practical political
issues. For instance, see Eva Kittay and Diana Meyers, eds., *Women and Moral Theory*
(Savage, MD: Rowman and Littlefield, 1982); Fiona Robinson, *Globalizing Care: Ethics,
Feminist Theory, and International Relations* (Boulder, CO: Westview Press, 1999);
Claudia Card, ed., *Feminist Ethics* (Lawrence: University Press of Kansas, 1991); Mary
Daly, *Gynecology: The Meta-ethics of Radical Feminism* (Boston: Beacon Press, 1978);
Sarah Hoagland, *Lesbian Ethics* (Palo Alto: Institute of Lesbian Studies, 1988). It is true
that work on ethics per se constitutes a small percentage of work in feminist theory and
philosophy, but a point I will be making in this paper is that many, if not most, of the "practical" issues feminists confront are also ethical issues because they have to do with unjust
inequalities of power.
[2] See, for instance, Judith Butler, *Bodies That Matter: On the Discursive Limits of "Sex"*
(New York: Routledge, 1995); Diana Fuss, *Essentially Speaking: Feminism, Nature, and
Difference* (New York: Routledge 1989).

a demand for the recognition that women (no matter how you define them) be treated as full human beings. That is, at its base, the essence of feminism, the recognition of women's full humanity and their treatment as moral equals, not just of men of their own demographic (because racism and classism ensure that many men are also discriminated against), but of men of the privileged group. Throughout the history of philosophy and political thought, women have been considered lesser human beings, from Aristotle's theory that women had no souls and contributed nothing to reproduction except to serve as incubators, to Rousseau's argument that women must be subordinate to their husbands, to Rawls's argument that male heads of families were the appropriate subjects of justice.[3] The moral foundation of feminism, I maintain, is the requirement that we recognize and honor the full humanity of women. I do not here enter into a detailed philosophical argument defending the claim that women's humanity is downgraded even today, but many of the facts that I report here about women and poverty will substantiate my claim. Amartya Sen's argument for the millions of "missing women" – girls who were presumably aborted or killed at birth, or died in childhood because of abuse and neglect, simply because they were girls – is only the most overt evidence that this claim is justified and that women are throughout the world and throughout history considered less valuable as human beings, less capable of controlling their own lives, not to mention the lives of others, less worthy of the rights and entitlements that states and societies routinely grant men.[4] However, poverty is a topic that reveals and supports this assertion, and as I talk about poverty from a feminist perspective, I accept this as the moral foundation of feminism: feminism seeks to establish the full humanity of women in a world that seeks to deny it.

Poverty is not a topic that a large number of feminists write on from a theoretical perspective, much less a moral one. Although the holy trinity of "gender, race, and class" is recited as a mantra by feminists who proclaim the importance of "intersectionality" and who seek at least to acknowledge that the category "woman" contains a great diversity along various vectors of identity and experience, feminist theorists have not done a very good job of analyzing class in general and poverty in particular. Poverty is, of course, a key

3 This is not to deny that there is feminist potential in the arguments laid out by the latter two; Aristotle is a more difficult case. See Susan Moller Okin, *Justice, Gender and the Family* (New York: Basic Books, 1989); Nancy J. Hirschmann, *Gender, Class, and Freedom in Modern Political Theory* (Princeton, NJ: Princeton University Press 2008); Elizabeth V. Spelman, *Inessential Woman: Problems of Exclusion in Feminist Thought* (Boston: Beacon Press, 1988); Elizabeth Wingrove, *Rousseau's Republican Romance* (Princeton, NJ: Princeton University Press, 2000).
4 Amartya Sen, "More Than 100 Million Women Are Missing," *New York Review of Books* 37, no. 20 (December 20, 1990); Martha Nussbaum, *Sex and Social Justice* (New York: Oxford University Press 1999). I do not even mention here the vast feminist literature on pornography because it is often dismissed as ideologically suspect (in circular fashion).

political issue for women and for feminist scholars, in that women's economic inferiority has arguably stemmed from, and in turn perpetuated, the ongoing and sustained political inequality of women: their exclusion from participation in public life, their exclusion from the rights and status of citizenship, their lack of voice and influence in the determination of public policy. But, as I argue, it is also clearly an ethical issue.

As is the case for other perspectives represented in this volume, poverty from a feminist perspective starts with lack of financial resources. A lack of money certainly ties to issues of inequality, entitlement, resources, health, dependency, exclusion, and hardship;[5] but these frequently stem from the initial lack of financial wealth. And in this, women do suffer comparatively to men throughout the world. Women earn less money than men to begin with; in the relatively progressive Western democracies, women earn approximately three-quarters of what men earn, even when they perform the same jobs.[6] Similar disparities can be demonstrated throughout the world.[7] More women than men live in poverty in the United States and around the world. In the United States in 2001, 12.9 percent of the female population lived below the poverty level; 28.3 percent (4.1 million) of female householders live in poverty; and more than two-thirds of food stamp recipients are female-headed households.[8] In 1968 women's poverty rates were 55 percent higher than men's; ten years later, in 1978, women's poverty rates were 72 percent higher than men's. This dropped to 47 percent higher in the 1980s, and in 2000 the female poverty rate was only 26 percent higher than the male rate. But these figures mask the fact that women still make up about 57 percent of the U.S. poverty population, which is about the same as it was in the 1970s.[9]

Internationally, of course, the conditions of poverty are frequently more dire, particularly in Africa and Asia, and the numbers are worse. According to the United Nations' WomenWatch, "more than 1 billion in the world today, the great majority of whom are women, live in unacceptable conditions of

5 Paul Spicker, "The Rights of the Poor: Conceptual Issues," in *Poverty and the Law*, ed. Peter Robson and Asbjorn Kjonstad, Oñati International Institute for the Sociology of Law (Oxford: Hart Publishing, 1988), 4–5.
6 John Iceland, *Poverty in America: A Handbook* (Berkeley: University of California Press, 2003), 89.
7 Karina Batthyány and Sonia Corrêa, "Health, Gender and Poverty in Latin America," 11–12, Women and Gender Equity Knowledge Network of the WHO Commission on Social Determinants of Health, https://www.who.int/social_determinants/resources/health_gender_poverty_latin_america_wgkn_2007.pdf.
8 Reneé E. Spraggins, "Women and Men in the United States: March 2002" (Washington, DC: U.S. Census Bureau, U.S. Department of Commerce), http://www.census.gov/prod/2003pubs/p20–544.pdf; Carmen DeNavas-Walt, Bernadette D. Proctor, and Robert J. Mills, "Income, Poverty, and Health Insurance Coverage in the United States: 2003" (Washington, DC: U.S. Census Bureau), http://www.census.gov/prod/2004pubs/p60–226.pdf.
9 Iceland, *Poverty in America*, 88.

poverty."[10] Johnston, Taylor, and Watts put the number slightly lower, claiming that 1.3 billion people live in poverty, 70 percent of whom are women.[11] The World Bank, by contrast, puts the figure higher: "Of the world's 6 billion people, 2.8 billion – almost half – live on less than $2 a day, and 1.2 billion – a fifth – live on less than $1 a day."[12] Obviously, part of the problem involves how one measures poverty; Glewwe and van der Gaag note that "different definitions of poverty select different population groups as poor."[13] Though "less than a dollar a day" seems a standard benchmark for dealing with the "Third World," it is obvious that different countries must define poverty differently in keeping with the level of economic development, currency value, and so forth. As John Iceland points out, "Poverty is by its nature at least somewhat relative. People are poor when others think of them as poor."[14] Defining poverty for women is further complicated by access to information; Moghadam points out that "the claim that the majority of the world's poor are women cannot be substantiated" because of difficulties in gathering gender-related data in the poorest communities and the ways in which access to women by outsiders is frequently limited through patriarchal control. But she nevertheless points out that "the disadvantaged position of women is incontestable."[15] John Dernbach argues, "In industrial countries, unemployment is higher among women than among men, and women constitute three-fourths of unpaid family workers. Thus, in addition to poverty, women are less able than men to break free from deprivation."[16] As Tazul Islam simply puts it – expressing a theme that runs throughout not just "feminist" analyses of poverty but that of the World Bank and other international organizations as well – "Women are poorer and more deprived than men."[17]

Such poverty is closely linked to lack of education, with studies showing a direct link between the education of girls and their better life prospects as adults, including reproductive outcomes.[18] Yet girls are much less likely than

[10] http://www.un.org/womenwatch/directory/women_and_poverty-3001.htm.

[11] R. J. Johnston, Peter Taylor, and Michael Watts, *Geographies of Global Change: Remapping the World* (Malden, MA: Blackwell Publishers, 2002), 10.

[12] World Bank, *World Development Report, 2000/01*, chap. 1, "The Nature and Evolution of Poverty," 3, http://siteresources.worldbank.org/INTPOVERTY/Resources/WDR/English-Full-Text-Report/ch1.pdf.

[13] Paul Glewwe and Jacques van der Gaag, "Identifying the Poor in Developing Countries: Do Different Definitions Matter?" *World Development* 18, no. 6 (1990): 803.

[14] Iceland, *Poverty in America*, 23.

[15] Valentine M. Moghadam, "The Feminization of Poverty and Women's Human Rights," SHS Papers in Women's Studies/Gender Research, UNESCO, Gender Equality and Development Section, Division of Human Rights, Social and Human Sciences Sector, Paris, July 2005, 1.

[16] John Dernbach, *Stumbling toward Sustainability* (Washington, DC: Environmental Law Institute, 2002), 165.

[17] Tazul Islam, *Microcredit and Poverty Alleviation* (Burlington, VT: Ashgate, 2007), 47.

[18] WomenWatch, United Nations, http://www.un.org/womenwatch/asp/user/list.asp-ParentID=3001.htm; see also Connect World, http://www.connect-world.net/

boys to receive education, and women experience higher rates of illiteracy than men. According to UNICEF, of the world's illiterate population (875 million), two-thirds – 583 million – are women. Many girls who live in sub-Saharan Africa, South Asia, East Asia, and the Pacific are prevented from going to school; and "the reason for a lot of girls not going to school is prejudice – which means they are seen to not be good enough – because they are girls."[19] In Malawi, "poverty ... is compounded by poor education. Illiteracy rates are alarmingly high, and girls often drop out of school early. The prevailing belief in this area is that the role of a female in society is to marry, have many children, raise the children, and look to her husband for guidance in all matters.... Women are definitely second-class."[20] Moghadam notes that families spend more on health care and education for boys than for girls.[21] Similarly, Islam notes that "disparity in literacy rates between poor men and women is also pronounced especially in the rural areas of Bangladesh. Parents in Bangladesh are less likely to send their daughters to school than their sons. The direct and indirect costs of education are higher for girls and the benefits for parents are remote and uncertain."[22] According to Dernbach, "In developing countries, women make up 60 percent of the illiterate adults; female enrollment at the primary education level is 14 percent less than male enrollment and female wages are only three-fourths of male wages."[23] In some countries, such as Cameroon, girls are less likely than boys to be issued birth certificates, which are needed to enter school; the cost of obtaining birth certificates later is prohibitively high. In Botswana, girls who become pregnant are forced to leave school; reentry policies require that the girl produce a birth certificate for her baby; but this process "can take so long as to make the effort of going back to school worthless."[24]

All this brings us to an additional factor to consider in defining what poverty means from a feminist perspective: it goes beyond financial to social conditions, status, and power within a given society. This is something that poverty studies not focused on gender recognize: access to markets, opportunities, education, health services, and infrastructure is a contributing cause and measure of poverty, and poverty is both an objective experience of lack of resources and a subjective experience of relative deprivation.[25]

Global_Themes/Poverty/Facts_on_poverty.html. See also Amartya Sen, *Development as Freedom* (New York: Knopf, 1999), 101.

[19] UNICEF, "Getting Girls into School," http://www.unicef.org.nz/school-room/education/girlseducation.html.

[20] Sue Makin, "Saving Mothers, One at a Time," *New York Times*, July 15, 2008, http://kristof.blogs.nytimes.com/2008/07/15/maternal-health-in-malawi/index.html.

[21] Moghadam, "Feminization of Poverty," 16–17.

[22] Islam, *Microcredit*, 48.

[23] Dernbach, *Stumbling toward Sustainability*, 165.

[24] *FAWE News* 8, no. 3 (July 2000): 20.

[25] Sen, *Development as Freedom*; World Bank, "World Development Report (WDR), 2000/2001: Attacking Poverty," http://web.worldbank.org/WBSITE/EXTERNAL/

Indeed, Arya and Roy point out that "poverty [is] a process of social exclusion, rather than ... a condition that can be captured through a set of statistical indicators."[26]

But from a feminist perspective, gender inequality is a factor that overlaps and complicates these other factors. Indeed, poverty is to some extent *caused by* gender and inequalities in gender relations. "Women," for instance, "own less than 15 per cent of land worldwide" because, at least in part, "in some countries, women cannot legally own property separately from their husbands, particularly in parts of Asia and sub-Saharan Africa. Lacking legal title to land and property, women have virtually no collateral for obtaining loans and credit, thus limiting their economic options." In other cases, even though women can legally own and inherit property, "custom dictates that men control it and that it passes only to male heirs on a man's death. It is difficult or impossible in these circumstances for women to exercise their property rights in practice."[27] Poverty and sexism interact in social conditions such as prostitution and sex trafficking, into which poverty can force women, whether by "choice" as a means of survival or because poverty enhances, if not creates, vulnerability to fraudulent coercion into sexual slavery.[28]And of course sexism always compounds and deepens poverty, preventing women's escape from it; as Dernbach puts it,

Poor women suffer from the same deprivations as men. They too must cope with joblessness, lack of income, and decreased life expectancies. However, women

---

TOPICS/EXTPOVERTY/0,,contentMDK:20194762~pagePK:148956~piPK:216618~the SitePK:336992,00.html.

[26] Sadhna Arya and Anupama Roy, "When Poor Women Migrate: Unravelling Issues and Concerns," in *Poverty, Gender and Migration: Unraveling Issues and Concerns*, ed. Sadhna Arya and Anupama Roy (Thousand Oaks, CA: Sage Publications, 2006), 20.

[27] International Center for Research on Women, "Reducing Women's and Girls' Vulnerability to HIV/AIDS by Strengthening Their Property and Inheritance Rights," *ICRW Information Bulletin* (Washington, DC: International Center for Research on Women, May 2006), 18, n. 35. See also Bina Argawal, "Gender and Command over Property: A Critical Gap in Economic Analysis and Policy in South Asia," *World Development* 22, no. 19 (1994): 1455–78. Argawal notes "among the Jaffna Tamils in Sri Lanka, under the *Thesawalami* legal code a married woman needs her husband's consent to dispose of land which she legally owns" (p. 1466). Similarly, in Uganda, "women's existing rights of access to and use of land are deeply embedded in the country's cultural and social systems regulated through marriage and kinship ties, deeply entrenched in patriarchal traditions and values.... If a woman separates from her husband and returns to her parents' home she loses all rights to land irrespective of her contributions to its development." Mary Mayende, "Women's Land Tenure and Access to Financial Services in Uganda," United Nations Department of Economic and Social Affairs, posted January 19, 2005, http://esa-conf.un.org/WB/default.asp?action=9&boardid=31&read=1915&fid=314.

[28] Jagannath Adhikari, "Poverty, Globalisation and Gendered Labour: Migration in Nepal," in Arya and Roy, *Poverty, Gender, and Migration*, 93; Arya and Roy, "When Poor Women Migrate," 32; Rekha Shrestha, "How Unskilled Tag Helps Artful Traffickers Beat Law," *Himalayan Times* 25 (August 2003): 1.

typically have additional obstacles such as unequal opportunities to education and health services as well as to the productive assets by which they can hope to break free from the shackles of poverty.[29]

Religion is often a factor that pushes the sexism that ensures women's poverty. Although Sohail H. Hashmi maintains in his chapter that Islam dictates charity for the poor and redistribution of wealth, he also notes that the Qur'an indicates that inequalities in wealth are God's will. In some fundamentalist states and cultures, these inequalities are powered by sexism; women are subjected to such harsh restrictions by virtue of their gender that they are often condemned to poverty in the event of the death of fathers, husbands, or brothers. This situation is clearest in cases such as Afghanistan under the Taliban, where women were not permitted to leave the house not only without the *burqa* but without male relatives accompanying them, a rule rarely excepted even for women who had lost their male relatives to military fighting. Such extreme patriarchal norms – invoked in the name of Islam – clearly prevented all women from engaging in self-sustaining economic activity and, in the case of widows, from leaving the house to buy food, even if they had money with which to buy it.[30] In less extreme cases, women's economic activity is often still severely limited.[31] In India, families may become impoverished through excessive dowry demands for the marriage of their daughters, despite dowry practices being prohibited by law.[32]

It hardly needs stating that women have relatively little formal political power to change these conditions compared to men throughout the world. Though some European countries such as France have legally mandated gender equity in candidacy and representation, women constitute an average of 20 percent of national legislatures (reduced to 19 percent if Nordic countries are excluded). Other Western democracies have even fewer women legislators: the United Kingdom has only about 12 percent female legislators; in the United States, women constitute 16 percent of both the House and Senate, and unlike the United Kingdom or Germany, the United States has never had a female executive. Similarly, "women make up only 16 per cent of members of national parliaments in Africa and Asia and 9 per cent in the Arab States.

[29] Dernbach, *Stumbling toward Sustainability*, 165.
[30] See Nancy J. Hirschmann, *The Subject of Liberty: Toward a Feminist Theory of Freedom* (Princeton, NJ: Princeton University Press, 2003).
[31] See for instance Arlene Elowe MacLeod, *Accommodating Protest: Working Women, the New Veiling, and Change in Cairo* (New York: Columbia University Press, 1991), in which she shows that even in contemporary Cairo, where fundamentalism cannot be said to prevail, and some, particularly single, women often wear Western clothes, married women are pressured not to work, even when women's incomes raise the family from the lower to middle class.
[32] Uma Narayan, *Dislocating Culture: Identities, Traditions and Third World Feminism* (New York: Routledge, 1997).

These percentages are well below what is believed to be a 'critical mass' for women to influence policy and spending priorities."[33]

Feminists are particularly interested in the ways in which gender influences these issues of social status and power, and particularly the ways in which women, because they are women, suffer from greater levels of poverty, or suffer more greatly from the same levels of poverty as men. The most obvious point of vulnerability for women is their reproductive capacity, as pregnant women need more resources such as food and health care.[34] But an equally important factor is women's inferior status in the family, in which they do the majority of the work and yet do not maintain the majority of the power and control over family decision making. Many nations lack laws prohibiting domestic violence, and some cultures claim as a "cultural value" that husbands have a right to "discipline" their wives. Though domestic violence is not necessarily a direct "cause" of poverty, women who seek to escape violence are often thrown into poverty, particularly when they also lack property rights, education, and skills to enable them to support themselves economically.[35]

Women's inferior status in the family is coupled ironically with their primary responsibility for it; as Tazul Islam notes about women and poverty in Bangladesh, "If one of the family members has to starve" because there is inadequate food, "it is almost an unwritten law that it has to be the mother.... Women have to manage home and family with virtually nothing to manage with."[36] Sylvia Chant describes a common scenario: "Maricris, an 18-year-old single woman living at home with her mother and two younger sisters (father is in jail on charge of murder), gets no rest at all. For the last four years she and her next youngest sister of 15, have sold snack foods from a pushcart in Carbon Market (the centre of vegetable trading in Cebu), between 6 p.m. and 6 a.m., seven days a week, earning just US$1.75 a day, and committing half the

---

[33] Inter-Parliamentary Union, "Women in National Parliaments: Situation as of 31 January 2007" (Geneva, 2007), 20, Inter-Parliamentary Union Website, http://www.ipu.org/wmn-e/world.htm (accessed February 12, 2007). On France's "parité" movement, see Joan Wallach Scott, *Parité!: Sexual Equality and the Crisis of French Universalism* (Chicago: University of Chicago Press, 2005); on the importance of female legislators to the creation of legislation that is "woman friendly," see Kathleen Casey and Susan J. Carroll, "Welfare Reform in the 104th Congress: Institutional Position and the Role of Women," in *Women and Welfare: Theory and Practice in the United States and Europe*, ed. Nancy J. Hirschmann and Ulrike Liebert (New Brunswick, NJ: Rutgers University Press, 2001), 111–32.

[34] This claim hardly needs documentation, but on the state of Palestinian women who are pregnant or nursing, for instance, see U.N. News Center, February 15, 2005, http://www.un.org/apps/news/story.asp?NewsID=13358&Cr=&Crl.

[35] See Hirschmann, *The Subject of Liberty*, chaps. 4 and 5; Rosemary Ofeibea Ofei-Aboaguy, "Altering the Strands of the Fabric: A Preliminary Look at Domestic Violence in Ghana," *Signs: Journal of Women in Culture and Society* 19, no. 2 (1994): 924–38; United Nations Population Fund, *The State of the World Population* (New York: United Nations, 2000), chap. 3, "Ending Violence against Women and Girls."

[36] Islam, *Microcredit*, 47.

proceeds to their mother. Despite catching up on some sleep during the day, Maricris maintains: 'we still have time to do the household chores, including the laundry.' More disturbing still, perhaps, than these actual examples of gender difference, is that many people do not see fit to comment, simply accepting this as the 'natural' order of things."[37]

This inequality within the family, most particularly in the context of poverty, is decidedly a moral issue: "If poverty is to be seen as a denial of human rights, it should be recognized that the women among the poor suffer doubly from the denial of their human rights – first on account of gender inequality, second on account of poverty."[38] Equality is a cornerstone of feminist thinking and feminist theory: equality with men, to be sure, but also equality among women, equality with one another. Feminists recognize, if they do not always successfully address, the ways in which race, class, sexuality, ethnicity, and geography intersect with gender to produce radical differences among women: differences to which more privileged women may – even if indirectly or unintentionally – contribute. Certainly, the circumstances of women's poverty clearly demonstrate my starting assumption, that women are considered as discounted humans, not of equal moral worth, simply by virtue of their gender. That this sexism may be compounded by racism, classism, ethnocentrism, religious prejudice, and colonialism does not negate the impact that gender itself has on women's experiences of inferiority. There is thus a moral responsibility for feminist theorists to attend more to poverty and class inequality from a theoretical and ethical perspective. It should, of course, be noted that feminists who are not interested in political and moral theory do write about women and poverty, particularly scholars in area studies, comparative politics, and other social science fields. Some of these scholars, such as anthropologist Valentine Moghadam, specifically point out various aspects of poverty that are relevant to moral inquiry, such as her claim quoted earlier that women's poverty is a denial of women's human rights.[39] But as Christine Sylvester dryly notes, the highly theoretical field of "postcolonial studies," including a number of feminists, may claim that it is highly concerned with the "voice" of "the subaltern," but not so much with "whether the subaltern is eating."[40]

Philosopher Martha Nussbaum may be the proverbial exception that proves the rule. Nussbaum adopted Amartya Sen's capabilities approach to consider

---

[37] Sylvia Chant, *Gender, Generation and Poverty: Exploring the "Feminisation of Poverty" in Africa, Asia and Latin America* (Northampton, MA: Edward Elgar, 2007), 255–56.
[38] Moghadam, "Feminization of Poverty," 1.
[39] Ibid.
[40] Christine Sylvester, "Development Studies and Postcolonial Studies: Disparate Tales of the 'Third World,'" *Third World Quarterly* 20, no. 4 (1999): 703. The notion of "the voice of the subaltern" is most closely associated with feminist postcolonial theorist Gyatri Spivak, "Can the Subaltern Speak?" in *Marxism and the Interpretation of Culture*, ed. Cary Nelson and Larry Grossberg (Urbana: University of Illinois Press, 1988), 271–313.

women's experiences of poverty in one small area of India.[41] The capabilities approach operates from the basic notion that humans have a fundamental, perhaps even "natural," right to a number of basic conditions of life, such as clean water, conditions for health, work, leisure, and so forth. In examining extremely poor cultures – in Nussbaum's case, a particular region in the state of Kerala, India – she is able to develop a moral argument against poverty, and for the moral obligation of states and international agencies to help end it. Nussbaum considers how the conditions of dire poverty, such as widespread illiteracy, high infant mortality rates, shortened life expectancies, poor or nonexistent public utilities (including water), and inadequate medical care, translate into particularly harsh oppression for women and children, through child marriage, dowry murders, and forced prostitution – all of which are legally prohibited but culturally practiced. Taking a "universalist" feminist perspective, she is highly critical of Western feminists who are so afraid of the pitfalls of moral absolutism that they shy away from arguments about international poverty; in the name of respect for "cultural difference," Western feminists stop themselves from critiquing other societies, even when it entails abandoning women to their suffering.

Respecting "culture," Nussbaum points out, often ends up meaning respecting men's power to subordinate women, who "lack essential support for leading lives that are fully human" because they are kept poor, illiterate, powerless, and subordinate.[42] This, she claims, is an abandonment of not only the political project that underlies feminism but the moral imperative to help other women as well. By emphasizing "capabilities" rather than "functionings," Nussbaum asserts, feminists can avoid the dangers they fear of moral absolutism and the imperialist history of telling other cultures what to do, while supporting the needs of women in those cultures. The capabilities argument is not that people have to do specific things to be free or to constitute themselves as "fully human," but rather that they have to have the ability and the resources to do these things if they want to. It involves recognizing the fact that women too frequently do not participate in defining the "cultural values" and rules that subordinate them to men. By pointing out that women do not participate to the same extent as men and the poor do not participate to the same extent as the wealthy in defining the norms that set the parameters for choice, Nussbaum argues that the capabilities approach can provide for a basic threshold of fundamental capabilities that empowers women to lay claim to voice.

The issue of women's participation in defining the terms of their membership under conditions of poverty and the treatment of poverty as a moral issue are similarly, if more fully, developed in the literature on public assistance

---

[41] Martha Nussbaum, *Women and Human Development: The Capabilities Approach* (Cambridge: Cambridge University Press, 2000).
[42] Ibid., 4.

in Western democratic countries, generally called "welfare." In the 1990s a number of feminist moral theorists very actively engaged the debates over welfare reform, particularly in the United States, but also in Europe. Feminist philosophers such as Eva Kittay, feminist legal theorists such as Martha Fineman, and feminist political theorists such as Nancy Fraser, Joan Tronto, and myself wrote about a variety of ethical issues pertaining to welfare, and thereby to poverty, such as the nature of "care" in the work women do in families; the moral importance of women's care work for social networks and indeed to humanity as a whole, and what obligations society owes women for such work; the ways in which terms like "dependency" become defined so as to bias against women's experience and work in the family; and the meaning of freedom and equality in a world where women are structured to engage in such labor within a context wherein it is universally devalued and uncompensated.[43]

Welfare is, of course, central to any feminist consideration of poverty in the West, from both a political and a moral standpoint. In 2002, 69 percent of all adult Food Stamp participants in the United States were women; 46 percent of women participants were in the key childbearing and career-launching years of ages eighteen to thirty-five. Women living in poverty are almost always mothers, because motherhood frequently hampers women's ability to work for wages and makes them economically vulnerable to husbands or other intimate partners.[44] Ninety percent of adult recipients of Temporary Assistance to Needy Families (TANF) are women, and three-quarters of them are between twenty and thirty-nine years of age – again, prime working years but also prime years for the rearing of small children. Additionally, 61.4 percent of adults receiving Supplemental Security Income payments were women.[45]

The vast majority of welfare recipients are single mothers. That fact means that public assistance policies reflect collective social attitudes and moral ideals surrounding children, as well as women. Feminists are not the only theorists concerned about children, of course, but the work of feminist theorists and philosophers points to a variety of ethical issues that are raised by poverty from a feminist perspective. What sorts of rights and expectations are children entitled to in their life prospects? And what responsibilities do their parents

---

[43] See Martha A. Fineman, "Dependencies," 23–37; Nancy J. Hirschmann, "A Question of Freedom, A Question of Rights? Women and Welfare," 84–107; Eva Feder Kittay, "From Welfare to a Public Ethic of Care," 38–64; and Joan Tronto, "Who Cares? Public and Private Caring and the Rethinking of Citizenship," 65–83, in Hirschmann and Liebert, *Women and Welfare*; Nancy Fraser and Linda Gordon, "A Genealogy of Dependency: Tracing a Keyword of the U.S. Welfare State," *Signs: A Journal of Women and Culture in Society* 19, no. 2 (1994): 309–36.

[44] Okin, *Justice, Gender and the Family*, esp. chap. 5, "Vulnerability by Marriage."

[45] Health Resources and Services Administration, "Women's Health USA 2004" (Washington, DC: U.S. Department of Health and Human Services, 2004), http://mchb. hrsa.gov/whusa04/pages/ch1.htm.

have as individuals for providing for those rights? Are parents entitled to support from the state to help them provide resources for their children, or is it up to parents to provide for them on their own? If the latter, then how do we balance the rights of children with the bad luck they may have experienced in being born into poor circumstances that they did nothing to cause?

Such questions obviously dovetail with broader ethical questions concerning women's rights: what responsibilities do men have to create conditions that are equitable for the rearing of children such that women do not pay a disproportionate price? We know that after divorce, women's average standard of living declines significantly while men's increases; women are often plunged into economic hardship by divorce, a fact that the state does little to prevent in its inadequate attempts to ensure men's payment of child support. "No fault" divorce laws, under the guise of gender equality, fail to recognize that a couple's decision that the woman should stop paid work to devote full-time care to the home translates into lesser earning power following a divorce, lower lifetime earnings, less money for retirement, and jeopardized health coverage.[46]

It might appear that the poverty experienced by women and girls in the Third World makes the issue of poverty experienced by women on public assistance in the United States and Europe seem trivial by comparison. But because, as I previously indicated, the majority of feminist work on poverty in the developing world tends to focus not on moral considerations but rather on factual and pragmatic issues, operating out of sociology, comparative politics, and political economy,[47] attention to the Western welfare debates is helpful in understanding poverty from a feminist moral perspective. Insofar as that indicates a limited view of poverty from a feminist perspective, that itself may be an important lesson to attend to. But looking at these policies provides insights into what feminists do, should, and must say about poverty in all contexts.

A key moral issue to confront is the ways in which welfare discourse is a discourse of "character" rather than economics, under the rubric of "personal responsibility." It blames the poor for being poor, it blames women for being unmarried, and it blames feminism for the ability of women to be unmarried. Family "caps" penalize any mother who gets pregnant while she is on public assistance by refusing to increase her benefits to accommodate the extra child, the implication being that women would otherwise reproduce limitlessly in order to gain wealth. Accordingly, cash and benefit incentives are offered

---

[46] Martha Albertson Fineman, *The Illusion of Equality: The Rhetoric and Reality of Divorce Reform* (Chicago: University of Chicago Press, 1991).

[47] For instance, see Sally Engle Merry, *Human Rights and Gender Violence: Translating International Law into Local Justice* (Chicago: University of Chicago 2006); Chant, *Gender, Generation and Poverty*; Amalia L. Cabezas, Ellen Reese, and Marguerite Waller, eds., *The Wages of Empire: Neoliberal Policies, Repression, and Women's Poverty* (Boulder, CO: Paradigm Publishers, 2007).

for women to use Norplant, a long-term contraceptive implanted under the skin of a woman's forearm. Forced labor is another prominent feature; the Personal Responsibility Work Opportunity Reconciliation Act (PRWORA) mandated that states institute work requirements for recipients, in some cases forcing them to take minimum wage jobs at the cost of forgoing advanced education and training for better-paying jobs that could lift participants out of poverty.[48]

These policies are often claimed to have been a "success" in that welfare rolls declined dramatically before the turn of the twenty-first century, a decline that continued through the first decade of the twenty-first century until the most recent economic downturn in 2007 and 2008.[49] But reasons for such reduction vary widely: some claim that the strong economy of the 1990s helped welfare recipients move into jobs that hold the promise of continued economic independence, while others claim that many have been pushed off welfare prematurely because the complicated rules have been misinterpreted by administrators, so that recipients do not apply for the benefits to which they are entitled.[50] But insofar as this "success" has come not by helping women but by punishing them, then all of these policies, from a feminist perspective, are morally wrong. They treat women as not just second-class citizens but as second-class human beings.

This problem is illustrated in welfare's emphasis on marriage, with studies showing that female single-headed households are more likely to be poor than families headed by men in heterosexual marriages. Certainly, marriage is a fine institution, offering much of value to men, women, and children that helps us be better persons: affective life, living in relationship, sharing, cooperation, love. (Disclosure: I have been in a monogamous marriage to the same man for more than twenty years, never divorced.) Thus, providing resources to help married couples succeed in their relationship is a good thing. But the emphasis on marriage under PRWORA and the punitive requirements placed on single mothers – requirements that in some states are lifted if the woman marries[51] – help create the problem that they are supposed to solve. By putting extremely difficult burdens on single mothers, forcing them into minimum

---

[48] I explore welfare in greater detail in *The Subject of Liberty*, chap. 5. Also see Gwendolyn Mink, *The Wages of Motherhood: Inequality in the Welfare State, 1917–1942* (Ithaca, NY: Cornell University Press 1995) and *Welfare's End* (Ithaca, NY: Cornell University Press 1998); Kathryn Edin and Laura Lein, *Making Ends Meet: How Single Mothers Survive Welfare and Low-Wage Work* (New York: Russell Sage Foundation, 1997).

[49] It also varies by state. Stephen Ohlemacher, "Welfare Rolls Keep Growing, Despite Years of Overhauls," Associated Press, February 26, 2007.

[50] Douglas J. Besharov and Peter Germanis, "Welfare Reform – Four Years Later," *Public Interest*, no. 140 (Summer 2000): 17–35; Marcia K. Meyers, "How Welfare Offices Undermine Welfare Reform," *American Prospect* 11, no. 15 (2000): 40–45.

[51] Linda McClain, *The Place of Families: Fostering Capacity, Equality, and Responsibility* (Cambridge, MA: Harvard University Press, 2007).

wage jobs rather than providing skilled training, and failing to provide adequate support for health care, child care, and transportation – the three largest obstacles to women's working – welfare reform ensures that most women will remain poor. The moral message is not subtle, for the policies penalize single mothers for failing to cohere to the Western, white patriarchal system of power encoded in the "traditional" patriarchal family and for claiming "I count, too, as an equal human being." If women stand up for themselves and refuse to remain married to their husbands because of abuse, infidelity, or other mistreatment, welfare policy says they must be disciplined by taking the worst possible jobs, doing so while performing the truly difficult job of single parenting, under the extremely daunting conditions of poverty. Is this not a clear message that these women are not worthwhile human beings? When marriage is not something that helps humans, but hurts them (as in domestic violence or infidelity), then the continued demand that parties remain in the marriage means that the institution is more important than the people in it. That poses a serious moral challenge to the policies that promote it under such conditions.

Thus, for example, the George W. Bush administration spent hundreds of millions of dollars on "marriage education," which encouraged women to be obedient and subservient to husbands, disempowering them to challenge abuse.[52] But hardly any money was allocated for programs to prevent domestic violence, much less for drug rehabilitation or employment programs for men to make them appropriate and capable "providers." States have made greater efforts to secure child-support payments from errant fathers, though such efforts are usually the result of pressure on the woman and any payment from the father is offset by a similar reduction in her monthly payment; thus, saving money is the object of such policy, not making women's burden of raising their children any lighter. Moreover, for women who have had to run away from their partners to escape abuse, forcing them to identify their children's fathers enables the men to in turn locate the women, thus making them vulnerable to abuse.[53] Worst of all, programs that would help to genuinely end poverty, particularly the Earned Income Tax Credit, are grossly underfunded. Clearly,

---

[52] The president's original proposal was for $1.5 billion, but in actuality, $500 million has been spent. Robert Pear and David Kirkpatrick, "Bush Plans $1.5 Billion Drive for Promotion of Marriage," *New York Times*, January 14, 2004; Barbara Ehrenreich, "Let Them Eat Wedding Cake," *New York Times*, July 11, 2004; McClain, *The Place of Families*; Wendy Pollack, "Marrying Uncle Sam? The Problem with the Bush Administration's 'Marriage Promotion' Agenda," October 7, 2003, National Organization for Women Web site, http://www.now.org/issues/economic/welfare/100703marriage.html.

[53] Some states created a domestic violence exception after incidents of violence resulted from such cases. But not all states did so. See Laura Lein, Susan E. Jacquet, Carol M. Lewis, Patricia R. Cole, and Bernice B. Williams, "With the Best Intentions: Family Violence Option in the Lives of Women Receiving Welfare," *Violence against Women* 7, no. 2 (2001): 194.

Nancy J. Hirschmann

such programs would help married working men living with their wives and children; but they would help single working mothers even more.[54]

Similarly, the discourse that work is the solution for poverty is not in itself problematic as long as we do not oversimplify it to a reductive equation. But that is often what happens under welfare policies. Thus, despite the decline in welfare rolls, the 2006 TANF reauthorization made work requirements even stricter, as if the poor needed to be squeezed even harder. But work requirements fly in the face of the fact that, even before PRWORA, most women on public assistance already worked for wages and have cycled on and off welfare. What keeps women out of the labor market is not an unwillingness to work but rather the inability to earn adequate income to pay for childcare, the unavailability of health insurance through their employers, or the burdensome difficulties of transportation when a woman lives in the city, where her children also go to school, while the jobs are in the suburbs.[55] By taking a stereotype based on distortion – the "welfare queen" who is too lazy to work but cunning enough to manipulate the system – as the "reality" of the "normal" welfare recipient, the lived reality of poor women is ignored, and the humanity of those women is thereby discounted and denied. Most poor women are not poor because of laziness or character defect but because of a sexist system that foreshortens market opportunities and makes the market unattractive to them by virtue of harassment and discrimination when compared to the idealized vision of the stay-at-home mom, a vision that turns into nightmare when women are denied the resources to protect themselves. Women end up all too frequently "kidding ourselves," to borrow a phrase from Rhona Mahoney, about the outcomes of the choices they make because of inadequate information.[56] I would put it more strongly, however, that women are socialized to make such poor choices in an effort to sustain patriarchal power.

Finally, the failure to recognize childrearing as "work" that is socially vital similarly relegates women's experiences and labor to the realm of the inessential, which political theorists have done since ancient times. This leads to inconsistent and even hypocritical policies. Consider the way that conservative discourse in the 1990s excoriated white middle-class mothers who worked for being "selfish" for not giving up their careers to raise their children, while at the same time condemning as "lazy" poor black mothers who were on public assistance to take care of their children full time. The fact that the white women being condemned held managerial and professional positions, while the kind of jobs that welfare mothers were forced to take as part of PRWORA's work requirements were generally minimum wage,

Heidi Hartmann and Hsiao-ye Yi, "The Rhetoric and Reality of Welfare Reform," in Hirschmann and Liebert, *Women and Welfare*, 160–76.

Ford Fessenden, "The Big Commute, in Reverse," *New York Times*, February 23, 2008.

Rhona Mahoney, *Kidding Ourselves: Breadwinning, Babies, and Bargaining Power* (New York: Basic Books, 1995).

Poverty and Morality: A Feminist Perspective   149

inadequate to support a family, only deepens the inconsistency. Such contradictory discourses play off of double standards so commonly accepted that
most people do not even see them as such. The fact that many middle-class
working women – even married women – would not even *be* middle-class and
able to stay off public assistance if they did not work is completely elided as
class becomes the acceptable focus for racist sexism. What it reveals, however,
is a dynamic of gendered power that feminists, at the least, morally condemn,
for both positions seek to keep women subordinated and dependent on men
within a traditional patriarchal nuclear family. In the new poverty discourse,
women are the problem, men are the solution; or more accurately, feminism
and the demand for gender equality, for the recognition of women's full and
equal humanity, are the problem, patriarchy is the solution.

All of these points raise important moral as well as political issues for
feminists. Perhaps the most important from a feminist view is the way in
which others decree how women in poverty must behave in order to receive
inadequate government support. This disallows women's ability to understand their own situation and think for themselves. In this, the situation of
welfare reform is not that different from poor women in other countries who
are controlled by husbands, fathers, and villages; only in this case it is the
state, the agency that is supposed to help, that ends up being the perpetra-
tor of women's disempowerment and continued poverty. Its failure to help
is a moral failure, a failure to recognize and respect women's fundamental
human right to shape their own lives, as John Stuart Mill put it, "pursuing
our own good, in our own way."[57]

Liberal Theory on Gender and Poverty

My invocation of Mill is not coincidental, for this failure can be traced to many
of the founding figures of liberalism itself. The twin foci of work requirements
and population control in particular have long been a staple of liberal political philosophy, dating back to John Locke in the seventeenth century, Adam
Smith in the eighteenth, and John Stuart Mill in the nineteenth. The history
of political theory provides some sources that are useful to contemporary
thinking about poverty from a feminist perspective, particularly relating to
the difficulties that feminist theorists and philosophers face in taking on the
issue of poverty. Given the emphasis of such theory on freedom and equality, the centrality of the individual, and the importance of the family, these
theories provide useful insights into where contemporary attitudes and values
about women and poverty come from, how they have developed, and what
sorts of assumptions they encode. As Andrew Levine argues in his chapter
on Marxism in this volume, canonical political theorists like Locke and Mill

[57] John Stuart Mill, "On Liberty," in *On Liberty and Other Essays*, ed. John Gray (New
York: Oxford University Press, 1991), 17.

are clearly "moral theorists" as well, and considering their theories can reveal some important insights into the place of gender in poverty.

John Locke's well-known *Two Treatises of Civil Government* (1690) attends very little to poverty; indeed, he maintained that class inequality was something to which men consented, because it was the only way for everyone to be better off.[58] But his lesser known "Essay on the Poor Law" (1699) addresses poverty issues more directly. Locke argued that the poor's dependency on parish relief was creating severe tax burdens on the middle class, and he sought a more efficient and regulated system of poor relief.[59] Even more alarming than the cost, however, was the corruption that spurred such dependency. "Poor Law" was written at the end of the 1690s, in the last of Britain's "seven barren years," a period in which pauperism was extremely common and 2 percent of the British population owned 65 percent of the land.[60] But even so, Locke claimed that poverty resulted not from a lack of economic opportunities, but rather from laziness and corruption, "the relaxation of discipline and corruption of manners; virtue and industry being as constant companions on the one side as vice and idleness are on the other."[61] In other words, Locke blamed poverty on the moral corruption of the poor, not on systematic economic inequality: or rather, the inequality was systematic only insofar as it revealed differences in moral health, or "character."

God has given us property in the person and rationality, as Locke argued in the *Second Treatise*, and so "the true and proper relief of the poor ... consists in finding work for them, and taking care they do not live like drones upon the labour of others."[62] Locke conceded that there are some on parish relief (which taxed members of the parish and provided cash assistance to the poor, who could spend the money as they saw fit), such as the ill and infirm, who are genuinely unable to support themselves. Most poor people could support themselves, however, either entirely (particularly in the case of able bodied male drunkards) or at least partially (such as destitute widowed mothers of small children). Forcing such people to labor was essential, for they were clearly able to work.

Women suffered equally from laziness and corruption, and Locke insisted that women work as well, including mothers. Though childrearing is burdensome enough to prevent women from working out of the home full time, Locke

58 John Locke, *Two Treatises of Civil Government*, ed. Peter Laslett (Cambridge: Cambridge University Press, 1994), 2.50.
59 John Locke, "An Essay on the Poor Law," in John Locke, *Political Essays*, ed. Mark Goldie (London: Cambridge University Press, 1997), 183. See also Hirschmann, *Gender, Class, and Freedom*, chap. 2.
60 Henry Richard Fox Bourne, *The Life of John Locke*, vol. 2 (London: Scientia Verlag Allen, 1969), 376; John Marshall, *John Locke: Resistance, Religion, and Responsibility* (Cambridge: Cambridge University Press, 1994), 158.
61 Locke, "An Essay on the Poor Law," 184.
62 Ibid., 189.

maintained, it does not completely fill their days: women have many "broken intervals in their time" during which they "earn nothing" and "their labour is wholly lost."[63] Feminist readers of the *Two Treatises* will see a convenient shift in argument in the "Poor Law." For in the former, Locke argues that the rigors of childbirth disable women from participation in the same activities as men; a human female is "capable of conceiving" almost immediately after giving birth, "and de facto is commonly with Child again, and Brings forth too a new Birth long before the former is out of a dependency." By contrast, in the "Poor Law" Locke argues that because "More than two children at one time, under the age of 3 years, will seldom happen in one family," then women are not normally overly burdened by pregnancy and childcare.[64] At the same time, and rather contradictorily, Locke believed that poverty was caused by too many children; "a man and his wife, in health, may be able by their ordinary labour to maintain themselves and two children."[65] Most poor families have more than two, however. Locke seeks a solution that will enable poor women asking for parish relief to be productive; and the solution that Locke hit on was to take children out of the home altogether.

In particular, Locke recommended that children aged three to fourteen be placed in "working schools," which were basically wool spinning factories.[66] Doing this would accomplish several things at once. First, it would enable both parents to work for wages, particularly mothers, by freeing them of care-taking responsibilities. Second, it would further reduce the cost to the parish of supporting these "excess" children because they would be contributing to their own upkeep by producing wool. Third, it would provide direct support for these children, which they otherwise would not obtain from their impov-erished parents, for the children would not be paid in wages, which would only be lost to drunken fathers, but in food, specifically, bread, water, and, "in cold weather, if it be thought needful, a little warm water-gruel." For, the efficient Locke noted, "the same fire that warms the room may be made use of to boil a pot of it."[67]

But more is at stake for Locke than protecting the property rights of the wealthy and middle class, or even maximizing capitalist efficiency. Rather, it is character that is at issue; specifically, the development of industry and ratio-nality. Not only did the existing form of parish relief rob the industrious who paid the poor rates. It also robbed those on relief, for by not working, such individuals' reason would deteriorate (or never develop); by living "upon the labour of others" they would become "drones," less than human.[68] Through

[63] Ibid.
[64] Ibid., 182.
[65] Ibid., 191.
[66] Ibid., 182, 192.
[67] Ibid., 191.
[68] Ibid., 189.

their labor, by contrast, laborers would develop reason sufficiently to know that working hard is the right thing to do, that work is key to achieving as much contentment out of life as their lot will allow. So they would be "reasonable" beings, sufficiently rational to know to follow their leaders and obey the law, even if they were not rational enough to be express consenters and active parties to the social contract.

Locke did not see himself as hostile to poverty and the poor, then. Rather, he was hostile to laziness and corruption, whether they manifested themselves in the poor or rich. Indeed, he was quite scornful of those who used their inherited wealth as an excuse for idleness.[69] By contrast, he seemed to express respect for hardworking laborers. If those dependent on parish relief were poor because they were lazy and corrupt, then the cure for poverty was to change their character. In adults, this was a hard business, because their character was already largely formed – hence the requirements of forced labor. But in children, the secret was establishing the correct "habitudes." Hence the point of the working "schools" in Locke's view is to build health, mental discipline, reason, and strength of character. Working schools would habituate poor children to work and teach them its value – specifically, "the children will be kept in much better order, be better provided for, and from infancy be inured to work, which is of no small consequence to the making of them sober and industrious all their lives after."[70] The true evil that needs to be rooted out, according to Locke, is not poverty per se, but irrationality, which leads to poverty. Locke linked industry and rationality very closely such that industry – the use of property in your person (labor) to acquire property in the form of land or goods – was taken as evidence of rationality, and propertylessness was evidence of a lack of rationality. Hence, those on parish relief, who were by definition not industrious (because otherwise they would be self-supporting), were also not rational.

Writing two centuries later, John Stuart Mill similarly linked poverty with irrationality and poor character, blamed excessive reproduction and overpopulation, and included women in the scope of his reforms. But whereas Locke blamed men and women equally, Mill, a staunch feminist, tended to believe that poor women were the victims of their husbands' bad character and bad choices; and to the extent that women's character was bad, it was the result of sexist oppression. Provide women with equal rights, and they would lay claim to moral virtue, reduce the number of children they had, get jobs if necessary, and save the world. Nevertheless, women were affected by poverty even more than men.

In the first place, poverty made women more vulnerable to men's violence. Mill believed that poor women were more likely to be physically abused

---

[69] John Locke, "Some Considerations of the Consequences of the Lowering of Interest and the Raising the Value of Money," in *Locke on Money*, ed. Patrick Hyde Kelly (New York: Oxford University Press, 1991), 206–342.

[70] Locke, "An Essay on the Poor Law," 190.

than wealthier women. In a series of articles for the *Morning Chronicle* that Mill coauthored with Harriet Taylor between 1846 and 1851, they note that most men, in all classes, are "impressed with the belief of their having a *right* to inflict almost any amount of corporal violence upon *their* wife or *their* children."[71] But it is particularly "the universal belief of the labouring class, that the law permits them to beat their wives – and the wives themselves share the general error."[72] Similarly, in the *Subjection of Women* (1869) Mill singles out the "thousands" of men "among the lowest classes in every country, who, without being in a legal sense malefactors in any other respect, because in every other quarter their aggressions meet with resistance, indulge the utmost habitual excesses of bodily violence towards the unhappy wife, who alone, at least of grown persons, can neither repel nor escape from their brutality"[73]

Poor women are also more vulnerable to excessive reproduction, which Mill at least tacitly suggested was another form of male abuse. In *Subjection*, Mill repeatedly made reference to the fact that, under current matrimonial law, where women had no property rights, no right to divorce, and no way out, women were their husbands' sexual victims: as a result, "however brutal a tyrant she may unfortunately be chained to ... he can claim from her and enforce the lowest degradation of a human being, that of being made the instrument of an animal function contrary to her inclinations."[74] In addition to the immoral assault on women's individual integrity and rights, however, this situation of inequality has even larger social consequences. For Mill saw overpopulation as the primary cause of poverty: too many workers competing for too few jobs drive down wages. And this problem is a result of men's selfishness and immorality: "Poverty, like most social evils, exists because men follow their brute instincts without due consideration," reproducing at will without regard to whether they can support their children, much less considering for the long term effects of too many workers on the economy.[75] Unregulated sexual reproduction among the poor and laboring classes is both a moral problem and a political economy one. Mill compares someone who

---

[71] John Stuart Mill and Harriet Taylor, "The Law of Assault," in John Stuart Mill, *Collected Works*, vol. 25: *Newspaper Writings, December 1847–July 1873*, ed. Ann P. Robson and John M. Robson (Toronto: University of Toronto Press, 1986), 1173. Although Taylor is not named as coauthor in the *Chronicle* or Mill's bibliography, Robson indicates that the series of essays was coauthored by Taylor. See prologue to "The Acquittal of Captain Johnstone," in John Stuart Mill, *Collected Works*, vol. 24: *Newspaper Writings, January 1835–June 1847*, ed. Ann P. Robson and John M. Robson (Toronto: University of Toronto Press, 1986), 865. See also Hirschmann, *Gender, Class, and Freedom*, chap. 5.

[72] "The Law of Assault," 25:1174.

[73] Mill, *The Subjection of Women*, in *Collected Works*, vol. 21: *Essays on Equality, Law, and Education*, ed. John M. Robson (Toronto: University of Toronto Press, 1984), 287.

[74] Ibid., 285.

[75] John Stuart Mill, *Principles of Political Economy: With Some of Their Applications to Social Philosophy*, in *Collected Works*, vol. 3: *Principles of Political Economy, Part II*, ed. John M. Robson (Toronto: University of Toronto Press, 1965), 367.

"has a large family and is unable to maintain them" to "a man who is intemperate in drink"; the latter "is discountenanced and despised by all who profess to be moral people," yet many feel that the former is justified in asking for charity.[76] This sort of illogical reasoning is morally wrong, Mill claims, and destructive to society.

Mill was a strong supporter of the Poor Law of 1834, which sent the able-bodied poor to the workhouse, where they were "stigmatized by loss of civil rights and strongly discouraged from procreation," in contrast to the disabled, who received "outdoor relief" – that is, cash assistance or food – and were not stigmatized.[77] The trope of the "deserving" and "undeserving" poor thus took a particular form for Mill: deserving was not a function solely of how one became poor (whether through laziness, disability, or fraud) but also of one's ability to labor to raise oneself out of poverty. Labor was key to improving character. Accordingly, Mill's reform efforts provided for more "indoor" relief, because it would ensure that the able-bodied would work, whereas "parish allowances [end up] subsidizing him [the laborer] in a mode which tends to make him careless and idle."[78] "So long as the poor-rate is available to him, he will accept of nothing which is only to be obtained by real work."[79]

For most contemporary liberals and feminists, such views, particularly of reproduction, smack of the worst kind of paternalism, completely inhibitive of personal liberty and women's autonomy. But Mill in fact excoriates those who advocate reproduction as a fundamental right, who "see hardship in preventing paupers from breeding hereditary paupers in the workhouse itself. Posterity will one day ask with astonishment, what sort of people it could be among whom such preachers could find proselytes."[80] For such attitudes implicitly accepted "the base doctrine, that God has decreed there shall always be poor."[81] Mill instead believed that poverty could be ended if the poor could be reconstructed and made to make the right choices. For even if poverty is a result of humans' "brute instincts," humans are not determined by those instincts; "society is possible, precisely because man is not necessarily a brute. Civilization in every one of its aspects is a struggle against the animal instincts."[82] Hence, Mill claimed that support of reproductive freedom for the poor involved "misplaced notions of liberty," for true liberty required not just doing what one wants but recognizing what one should want, what is in one's long-term interest, which is something that poverty often prevents one from seeing. Even though the circumstances of poverty create bad characters that result in bad choices that perpetuate their poverty, it is possible

76 Ibid., 368.
77 Editor's note to Mill, *Political Economy*, 3:444.
78 Ibid., 358.
79 Mill, "The Proposed Irish Poor Law," in *Collected Works*, 24:1072.
80 Ibid.
81 Mill, *Political Economy*, 3:369.
82 Ibid., 367.

to change their character and their choices. Accomplishing this, however, clearly required public policy, governmental oversight and administration of poor relief. Private charity might enable people to survive poverty but would not end it, in part because the charitable wealthy took a fatalistic attitude about the poor, needed to feel superior to them, and had an interest, though a generally unrecognized one, in perpetuating poverty precisely to sustain those feelings of superiority. Moreover, the toughness that was required of a poverty policy was not in keeping with the presumed sentiments of charity.

For women, such "liberty" is absent. This longtime advocate of birth control is also thinking about the women who are forced to give birth. In fact, shortly after criticizing "those [i.e., not just "men"] who have children when unable to support them," Mill notes, "It is seldom by the choice of the wife that families are too numerous; on her devolves (along with all the physical suffering and at least a full share of the privations) the whole of the intolerable domestic drudgery resulting from the excess. To be relieved from it would be hailed as a blessing by multitudes of women who now never venture to urge such a claim, but who would urge it, if supported by the moral feelings of the community."[83] Indeed, Mill goes so far as to say, "There would be no need ... of legal sanctions" against reproduction if women were granted equality; "Let them cease to be confined by custom to one physical function as their means of living and their source of influence, and they would have for the first time an equal voice with men in what concerns that function."[84]

Feminism, Poverty, and Liberalism

The similarities between Locke's and Mill's accounts of poverty are fairly evident, particularly the linking of poverty to character failings and inferior rationality, the attribution of individual fault as the cause of poverty, the role of the state as the reformer of character by requiring labor, and the control of reproduction – in Locke, by putting children in working schools, in Mill, by state regulation of marriage, thereby reducing childbearing. And both theorists display many themes, tropes, and "solutions" that cohere eerily with late twentieth-century welfare and poverty policies as they pertain to women, such as limiting reproduction. What is perhaps more interesting are the echoes between these liberal discourses and poverty in countries that do not share the liberal tradition. For instance, Mill's argument that giving women equal rights, and most particularly by granting them education, will empower them to choose to have fewer babies is the most basic standard of many international aid organizations. Literacy, as Sen first noted, is the single most important correlate of women's ability to control their own reproduction.[85]

[83] Ibid., 372.
[84] Ibid., 372–73.
[85] Sen, *Development as Freedom*.

6

156 Nancy J. Hirschmann

Mill particularly offers us the ethical insight that poverty and gender go hand in glove, and that powerlessness in one sphere facilitates, indeed magnifies, powerlessness in the other. Moreover, he is able to help us identify the circularity of gender and poverty. If all that women earn while married becomes, through laws of coverture or "traditional" practices of patriarchy, their husband's property; if women are prevented by law from leaving abusive husbands; if they are denied education and access to professions so as to be able to earn decent incomes that can support them and their children, then women are destined to be poor unless they are lucky enough to maintain the favor of an economically self-sufficient man. But this, Mill reasoned, put even such "lucky" women in positions of terrible vulnerability and inequality: women are more subject to domestic violence, sexual assault, and other forms of abuse. That, he says, is simply wrong. The moral dimensions of Mill's argument are, indeed, the most powerful, even if they are not the only ones.[86] The trapped situation in which poverty places poor women is therefore doubly damning, for they are poor through no fault of their own, and yet are completely denied the tools to get themselves out.

This is similarly true of many poor women today; they are poor through no fault of their own, but the state either actively restricts their ability to get themselves out of poverty, as is often the case under Western welfare policies, or does too little to enforce women's legal rights in the face of contrary customary practices, as is the case in many areas of the Third World.[87] The state thus has a moral obligation to provide them with appropriate resources to help them escape. In contemporary terms, I would say that Mill's argument suggests that the state is obligated to provide employment supports that can help women accomplish the goals of self-sufficiency that the state claims it seeks. If women are to escape poverty, they need affordable on-site childcare; improved transportation; pay equity (do we still have to ask for that?); and opportunities for higher paying jobs, including training and education.

Locke perhaps offers insight into the failings of contemporary poverty discourse more than he gives us a way to address them, though he indirectly offers one solution: education. Locke's "working schools" are hardly something to be emulated, but they point to the link between education and work; hence feminists seek greater funding of higher education for women and better technical training for better-paying jobs. Such support in the Third World is often for much lower levels of education, given the high rates of illiteracy among poor women, but the connection between education and wealth is no

[86] In Nancy J. Hirschmann, "Mill, Productive Labor, and Women's Work," *American Political Science Review* 2, no. 2 (May 2008): 199–213, I argue that most feminist attention to Mill's writings have focused on the moral aspects of his argument for women's equality, but that attending to the political economy aspects are just as important. Here, I am pushing that argument a bit further, by suggesting the moral implications and foundations of Mill's economic arguments.
[87] See particularly Mink, *Welfare's End*.

less important. In the United States, poor teenage girls need to be provided with the kind of education that gives them hope for a better life, and an incentive (as well as the know-how, currently denied them under "abstinence only" programs) not to get pregnant at an early age. Similarly, in the Third World, literacy and reduced reproduction tend to go hand in hand.

Reproduction is a key moral issue for feminists, and it is clear that most twenty-first-century feminists would reject Locke's and Mill's attempts to limit and control women's reproduction. (Indeed, Locke's "working schools" would seem to be the ancestor of former U. S. representative Newt Gingrich's suggestion that poor children be taken from their parents and put into orphanages.)[88] Control of women's bodies by men historically has been key to women's subordination, and control by themselves key to their autonomy.[89] We must remember, of course, that Mill was a strong advocate of birth control, and of women's controlling their own bodies, and birth control in his lifetime was fairly primitive. Today, women theoretically have many more options as long as the technology is made available to them, including safe abortion. A feminist approach to poverty must include a moral mandate that birth control and abortion be made available to poor women. Greater access of young girls to condoms would reduce the frequency of teenage pregnancy and sexually transmitted diseases, which are spreading to younger and younger people, particularly in Africa, thereby diminishing their life chances for escaping poverty themselves.[90]

But perhaps the most important feminist moral requirement is to include poor women in the construction of social policies that affect their lives. This is something that is implicit in Mill's argument, in that he believes he is speaking not only *for* poor women but *on* their behalf as well. Their lack of representation meant that they had nobody to stand up for them, and he believed that that was what he was doing. However, given the oppressive conditions of poverty, he suggested, poor women might not be trusted to know what is in their own best interests. This was clearly Locke's thinking as well: if poverty is a sign of poor rationality and poor character, then it is logically impossible to expect the poor to help themselves. Similarly, upper-class white male politicians who crafted welfare "reform" of the 1990s made many pronouncements about poor women, about who they were, what they wanted, and why they were poor, that had no relation to the reality of poor women's lives and existence.

Most contemporary feminists reject such views, but perhaps they should not. Is it really so surprising that a life of poverty will have effects on the

---

[88] Robert Scheer, "Returning to the Bad Old Days of Orphanages," *Los Angeles Times*, December 11, 1994.

[89] Linda Gordon, *Pitied but Not Entitled: Single Motherhood and the History of Welfare, 1890–1935* (New York: Free Press, 1994).

[90] T. R. Eng and W. T. Butler, eds., *The Hidden Epidemic: Confronting Sexually Transmitted Diseases* (Washington, DC: National Academy Press, 1997).

psychology and self-conceptions of poor women? Martha Nussbaum has argued that the "adaptive preference" phenomenon, where individuals adapt their desires and preferences to the limited options that are available to them, means that poor women will be unable to imagine a life different from the deprived one they lead. Other feminist scholars have documented a lack of self-esteem and confidence, depression, and erasure of identity among women on welfare.[91]

Where Locke and Mill – as well as U.S. welfare reform – get it wrong, however, is the lines of causation: it is not such character failings that cause poverty. Rather, the conditions of poverty cause the psychology. And even there, "the psychology" is really a very small part of it: as Nussbaum shows, providing very little improvement to the lives of the very poor produces exponential increases in happiness, self-value, and imagination. Microcredit is a particularly clear example of this: the assumption that the poor will not pay back loans, and therefore are not creditworthy, is a claim about psychology rather than fact. The Grameen bank has proved that the poor can and will pay back loans, and there is even evidence now that loans and banking services can be offered to the poor on a for-profit basis. Similarly, if the money spent on marriage education had instead been allocated to provide low-cost loans to help poor women buy used cars to ease their transportation difficulties from cities where they lived to suburbs where the jobs were, work requirements of welfare reform would have been considerably less onerous, and more women would have succeeded at obtaining and keeping better-paying jobs that had a real chance of helping them escape poverty. Such commonsense ideas – on-site (or near-site) affordable childcare, health insurance, transportation, education, training, and equal rights in the workplace – do not seem to be so difficult to grasp, at least intellectually. Why they seem to be difficult to implement may attest to our own moral failings.

That failing returns us to the last moral dimension that I wish to highlight concerning poverty from a feminist perspective, and that is the importance of recognition and voice. Western feminists working on welfare stress the need to ask poor women to participate in making policy that affects them. The rationale for this is twofold, the first being practical: feminist scholarship on welfare in particular demonstrates the "kitchen table wisdom" of poor women on public assistance – their insights into the problems with the program, into what is needed to alleviate the difficulties caused by poverty, and into what is needed to lift them out of poverty.[92] All you have to do, these feminists maintain, is ask the women, and you will get some smart, commonsense public

---

[91] Marta Elliott, "Impact of Work, Family, and Welfare Receipt on Women's Self-Esteem in Young Adulthood," *Social Psychology Quarterly* 59, no. 1 (1996): 80–95; Robin Rogers-Dillon, "The Dynamics of Welfare Stigma," *Qualitative Sociology* 18, no. 4 (1995): 439–56.

[92] Lisa Dodson, "At the Kitchen Table: Poor Women Making Public Policy," in Hirschmann and Liebert, *Women and Welfare*.

policy prescriptions. But the second rationale is the dignity that comes from being consulted and asked.

This, too, holds relevance for poverty in the Third World. Indeed, microcredit illustrates the overlapping vectors of financial and social dimensions of poverty that I have traced throughout this essay. It has done enormous good in helping the poor, and particularly poor women, obtain small loans that enable them to establish small businesses that allow them to earn a subsistence living. This financial improvement in turn brings about improvement in their social situation: particularly important is that women's bargaining power in the family in making decisions and in demanding respectful treatment is greatly enhanced because of their economic power. Their self-value is thereby increased, and their self-understandings of what they can do, and who they are, are shifted. Their capabilities, to borrow from Sen and Nussbaum, are enhanced.

Certainly microcredit, often touted as a cure-all for poverty, has its limits. It helps raise women out of poverty but only to a certain level, in a sense to a less bad level of poverty. It alone, absent other sorts of financial services such as programs to enhance voluntary savings, cannot truly lift people out of poverty. Nor has it been very successful in assisting the poorest of the poor, but only those at higher levels.[93] What microcredit does, however, is support the fundamental feminist argument that poor women need to be empowered to make their own decisions. By making direct loans to women to enable them to start small businesses, microcredit offers more than simply money: it offers women a way to take control of their lives, at least to some degree, and to be active participants in shaping their futures. More than money is required to end poverty, and more than money is required to end sexism; both require changing social norms, attitudes, and practices. But money, microcredit has shown, is an important building block. Yet at the same time, microcredit also demonstrates the power of sexism and classism: it shows that very little is needed to reduce poverty, that the poor do not simply need money thrown at them, but assistance to their own efforts to make their lives better. So why are we not giving it to them? That may be the most important moral issue of poverty, and not just from a feminist perspective.

[93] Islam, *Microcredit.*

8

Hinduism and Poverty

Arvind Sharma

The religion and poverty of India are her two primary materials, of which the whole structure of her society has been – and is still being – built. In relation to them, other considerations seem flippant.

Ronald Segal, *The Anguish of India*

Hinduism is the name given to the most widely prevalent religious tradition of India, whose followers constituted about 80 percent of India's population in 2001.[1] Hinduism has been a prominent feature of the Indian landscape over the centuries, although its origins are shrouded in antiquity. Some trace it as far back as 3000 BCE on the basis of archaeological finds in the region of Harappa in the Punjab that already display features we now associate with Hinduism; others date it from around 1200 BCE, the date usually assigned to its earliest available literary text, the RgVeda. Still others date it from around the fourth century BCE, applying the term Vedism rather than Hinduism to the prior period. According to this view, Hinduism represents a transformation of Vedism under the impact of the new religions of Buddhism and Jainism, whose emergence is usually placed in the sixth century BCE.

Hinduism, as a continuous religious tradition of such antiquity, invites the appellation of eternity in its own eyes; this would be one way of explaining its own term for itself: *sanātana dharma*, often translated as eternal religion. But whether eternal or not, it has certainly been a continuous tradition. This point is important for our present discussion because the country we now call India has, in the course of its long history, undergone many vicissitudes of economic fortune, and Hinduism has been a party to all of them, on account of its own long history. This historical fact, as we shall see, complicates the discussion of poverty in Hinduism because one could as well choose to discuss the topic of Hinduism and *prosperity*, since in its long run Hinduism has been associated with both. The issue is further complicated by the fact that India was a British

---

[1] Data from the Government of India, http://censusindia.gov.in/Census_Data_2001.

colony for about two hundred years from circa 1757 to 1947. It is a widely cited statement that "India enjoyed 17.6 percent of the world's industrial production in 1830, while Britain's share was 9.5 percent. By 1900 India's share had declined to 1.7 percent while Britain's had grown to 18.6 percent."[2] How is this reversal to be accounted for? Indian scholars tend to blame it on imperialism, and British scholars on Hinduism.

The fact is that when India became independent in 1947 it was massively characterized by both Hinduism and poverty.[3] Some pushed this correlation to the point of causation, so much so that the low rate of economic growth in the post-Independence period was characterized by many as the Hindu rate of growth.[4] Thus,

India's low rate of economic growth until the 1980's, at 3.5 per cent per annum, was characterized by Raj Krishna as "Hindu rate of growth." Several scholars seriously believed that the Hindu "other-worldliness" was a major factor in India's low economic performance, at least before the reforms of the nineties. Fortunately for Hinduism, nobody advocated eradication of Hinduism as the basis for the reforms! Instead, unnecessary controls and over-bureaucratization of the economy were perceived as the major issue for the low performance of the past. The reforms were based on this perception, and it worked.[5]

The issue whether the apparent lack of India's growth in the post-Independence and even the pre-Independence period has something to do with the Hindu scriptural value system had been raised earlier. Two such scholars who did so are Max Weber and K. W. Kapp, and this view may therefore be described as the Weber-Kapp thesis. I have previously examined that question and concluded that the Hindu scriptural law system was too versatile and diverse to yield such a conclusion.[6] More recently, Deepak Lal[7] has confirmed this conclusion in his two-volume work *Hindu Equilibrium*.[8] The crux of the matter, as pointed out earlier, is that historically Hinduism can also be associated with prosperity rather than poverty. India was a Hindu country in the fourth century BCE and one of the remarkable features of Megasthenes' account of India, as he found it in fourth century BCE, is its allusion to the agricultural productivity of India in particular and to economic prosperity in general. This is obvious from the fragments of his work preserved by Strabo[9]

---

[2] Gurcharan Das, *India Unbound* (New York: Random House, 2002), 61.
[3] Ramachandra Guha, *India after Gandhi* (New York: Harper Collins, 2007), 467.
[4] M. V. Nadkarni, *Hinduism: A Gandhian Perspective* (New Delhi: Ane Books India, 2006), 380.
[5] Ibid.
[6] Arvind Sharma, *Hindu Scriptural Value System and the Economic Development of India* (New Delhi: Heritage Publishers, 1980).
[7] Deepak Lal, *The Hindu Equilibrium*, 2 vols. (Oxford: Clarendon Press, 1989).
[8] Nadkarni, *Hinduism*, 379–80.
[9] J. W. McCrindle, *Ancient India as Described by Megasthenes and Arrian*, 2nd ed. (Calcutta: Chuckervertty, Chatterjee, 1960), 52–53.

and Diodorus Siculus[10] in the first century BCE.[11] The Greek accounts thus ascribe a fairly high level of material prosperity to India, including absence of famines. What is more, they offer an explanation of such an exemption in terms of the cultural mores of the people.

But, further, there are usages observed by the Indians which contribute to prevent the occurrence of famine among them; for whereas among other nations it is usual, in the contests of war, to ravage the soil, and thus to reduce it to an uncultivated waste, among the Indians, on the contrary, by whom husbandmen are regarded as a class that is sacred and inviolable, the tillers of the soil, even when battle is raging in their neighborhood, are undisturbed by any sense of danger, for the combatants on either side in waging the conflict make carnage of each other, but allow those engaged in husbandry to remain quite unmolested. Besides, they neither ravage an enemy's land with fire, nor put down its trees.[12]

These statements however need to be taken with a grain of salt. For although the Greek observers were struck by the richness of India's natural resources and the skill of its population in exploiting them, and the Arthaśāstra confirms their impression,[13] it is also clear that when Megasthenes declared that famines in India were unknown, "he certainly wrote in this particular from inadequate knowledge."[14] The Arthaśāstra (IV.3), even if not a contemporary document although ascribed by tradition to this period,[15] contains suggestions for averting famines – a fact confirmed by the two plaque inscriptions found in Mauryan Brāhmī: at Sohgaura in Groakhpur district, U.P., and at Mahasthagarh in the Bogra district of Bengal, which refer to the establishment of granaries as safeguards against famine. Moreover, according to the Jaina tradition, Candragupta Maurya, at whose court Megasthenes was the Seleucid ambassador, is supposed to have abdicated and migrated to

---

[10] Ibid., 29–30, 30–31.

[11] Ibid., 30.

[12] Ibid., 31–32. Apparently even the mantic arts were pressed into service in this respect. Diodorus, writing of the caste of "philosophers," remarks: "To the people of India at large they also render great benefits, [when, gathered together at the beginning of the year, they] forewarn the assembled multitudes about droughts and wet weather, and also about propitious winds, and diseases, and other topics capable of profiting the hearers. Thus the people and the sovereign, learning beforehand what is to happen, always make adequate provision against a coming deficiency, and never fail to prepare beforehand what will help in a time of need. The philosopher who errs in his predictions incurs no other penalty than obloquy, and he then observes silence for the rest of his life" (ibid., 38–39).

[13] K. A. N. Sastri and P. C. Bagchi, "Government, Society and Art of the Mauryan Empire," in *A Comprehensive History of India*, vol. 2, ed. K. A. Nilakanta Sastri (Bombay: Orient Longmans, 1957), 73.

[14] A. L. Basham, *The Wonder That Was India* (New Delhi: Rupa, 1999 [1967]), 192.

[15] See T. Trautman, *Kauṭilya and the Arthaśāstra* (Leiden: Brill, 1981); H. C. Raychaudhuri, "A Note on the Date of the Arthaśāstra," in *The Age of Imperial Unity*, ed. R.C. Majumdar (Bombay: Bharatiya Vidya Bhavan, 1968 [1951]), 285–87; Surrendra Nath Mital, *Kauṭilīya Arthaśāstra Revisited* (New Delhi: Centre for Studies in Civilizations, 2000).

the south with his Jaina guru Bhadrabāhu, "who had predicted that a famine would rage in North India for a period of twelve years. As tradition sometimes makes mention [of] an event after it has occurred ... it is not unlikely that this continuous famine began somewhere about the close of Candragupta's reign and lasted for some years thereafter."[16]

Similarly, inspiring as the spectacle of tillers plowing the fields even as the soldiers are at one another's throats nearby may be, no such specific detail is mentioned in the Indic sources. It is instructive that this passage from Megasthenes is itself cited as evidence that in "ancient times non-combatants went generally unmolested in India."[17] It is nevertheless true that the tenor of the texts is in keeping with the general picture. The Manusmṛti (VII.90–93) lays down rules for fair play in battle, and the Arthaśāstra (XII.1) distinguishes between righteous conquest (*dharmavijaya*), larcenous conquest (*lobhavijaya*), and demonic conquest (*asuravijaya*).

The Greek assessment of the Indian economic scene, although not wholly accurate, seems, however, to have been substantially correct. While not literally true, it was "on cogent ground that Megasthenes based his well-known and oft-quoted" but not literally true "statement that famine has never visited India,"[18] for "towards the close of the fourth and the beginning of the third century B.C. contemporary Greek observers were struck by the abundance of India's agricultural and mineral resources, the skill and industry of its inhabitants and the number of its flourishing cities."[19]

If Megasthenes was stuck by abundance in India, the Europeans in India at the beginning of the nineteenth century were struck by features that can only be called its polar opposites. The *Oxford History of India*, after describing the destitute condition of the cultivator and the merchant, records the desperate scene:

The social and cultural state of the country declined along with its political fortunes. The state of the county was in nothing more clearly revealed than in the spread of social diseases whose germs always lurk within civilized societies ready to multiply and break forth should favourable conditions arise. The most obvious of these was dacoity, of which the Pindaris were the supreme example. The dislocation of society drove adventurous, hopeless, or embittered spirits to lawless life. They formed the material for princely armies or robber bands, each of whom recruited from the other as fortunes rose and fell. The landless or uprooted man looking for a leader and reckless from despair was a typical figure of the time.[20]

---

[16] Sastri and Bagchi, "Government, Society and Art of the Mauryan Empire," 48.
[17] P. V. Kane, *History of Dharmaśāstra*, vol. 3, 2nd ed. (Poona: Bhandarkar Oriental Research Institute, 1973), 210.
[18] U. N. Ghosal, "Economic Conditions (Post-Mauryan)," in Sastri, *A Comprehensive History of India*, 2:455–56.
[19] Ibid., 455.
[20] Percival Spear, *The Oxford History of India*, 4th ed. (New Delhi: Oxford University Press, 2004), 575.

No wonder then, as K. M. Panikkar notes succinctly,

James Mill, who wrote the first great History of British India, was convinced that the Hindus had no history before the Muslims and they were always in the same abject condition as that in which the British found them in Bengal in the eighteenth century.[21]

The contrast between the pictures drawn by Megasthenes and James Mill is difficult to overlook. What is all the more remarkable is the fact that, just as Megasthenes took prosperity to be India's permanent condition (if his insistence on the absence of famine may be so construed), James Mill also took poverty to be Indian's permanent condition – a belief that gave rise to the association of Hinduism with poverty.

According to Angus Maddison,[22] the economic historian, India was the world's largest economy from first century CE until 1500 CE, when China began to compete for this position. It was India's fabulous wealth that made Western nations seek it out as a trading partner, although it is by no means certain that this wealth was evenly distributed and the economy productive in the modern sense.[23] This commercial interest took on imperial overtones when the British East India Company won the battle of Plassey in 1757, which paved the way for British rule over India.

We now proceed from a historical to a conceptual engagement with the issue. Before such a step is taken, however, it might be useful to indicate the sources of these concepts. They are drawn from Hindu literature, which is conventionally divided into two categories, called *śruti* or Revelation and *smṛti* or Tradition. The main subcategory within *śruti*, which consists of the revealed texts known as the Vedas, is that of the Upaniṣads, also known as Vedānta. The Bṛhadāraṇyaka Upaniṣad belongs to this class. Tradition or *smṛti* is the other main category, and material from four subcategories or classes from within this category has been drawn upon. To the first class belong texts on Hindu statecraft, the most famous of which is the Arthaśāstra, already alluded to. The next class consists of texts known as Dharmaśāstra, or law books, which serve as guides to the Hindu way of living. The most famous of these, the Manusmṛti, has also been already alluded to. The third class consists of the so-called national epics of India – the Rāmāyaṇa and the Mahābhārata. A fourth class consists of texts called the Purāṇas, which are a storehouse of stories about the gods, legendary sages, and kings. These texts broadly fall in a period extending from a few centuries before the Christian

---

[21] K. M. Panikkar, *The Foundations of New India* (London: George Allen & Unwin, 1963), 67.

[22] For details, see Angus Maddison, *Contours of the World Economy, 1–2030 A.D.: Essays in Macroeconomic History* (Oxford: Oxford University Press, 2007).

[23] For conditions from the seventeenth to the nineteenth century, see Angus Maddison, *Class Structure and Economic Growth: India and Pakistan since the Moghuls* (London: Allen & Unwin, 1971), chap. 2.

era until around the tenth century. The texts classified as *śruti* or Revelation belong to an earlier period, stretching from circa 1200 BCE to a few centuries before the common era.

Definitions

Certain distinctions are important for understanding how poverty is understood within Hinduism. One such distinction is between involuntary and voluntary poverty and the other is between involuntary poverty and destitution.

Involuntary poverty reflects the situation in which one is poor because one cannot help it. One would prefer not to be poor, but one cannot avoid being so. Such involuntary poverty represents a scarcity of resources. This is what we usually mean by poverty, and such poverty is condemned in Hindu ethical discourse. There is a very strong tradition within Hinduism, however, of renouncing the things of the world for the sake of the spiritual pursuit. Such an attitude is institutionalized within Hinduism in the context of *sannyāsa*, which consists of a formal act of renouncing association with the things of the world by donning the ochre robe, whereby one signals to society at large that one has opted out of the trappings of wealth and embraced poverty as a lifestyle, as more suitable for the spiritual pursuit. People who take *sannyāsa* in Hinduism come from all walks of life and have included princes and rich merchants. Such renunciants are supposed to subsist by begging, as they pursue their religious life. Such voluntary or ascetic poverty may be either of the eremitic or cenobitic kind. In the former case, one wanders alone; in the latter case, one is the member of a monastic order. The West is familiar with the cenobitic form of poverty through the Christian monastic tradition. The Buddhist monastic tradition is also largely cenobitic in its orientation. The Hindu tradition, however, sets much more store by the eremitic tradition compared to these, although cenobitic monasticism is also well established within it and may well have been inspired by the Buddhist example.

This distinction is vital in thinking clearly about the role of poverty within Hinduism. The inability to distinguish between the two has misled observers in the past into claiming that poverty is a cherished value in Hinduism, in such a way as might make Hinduism hostile to its removal through economic development. Nothing could be further from the truth. The Hindu pantheon contains a goddess of prosperity called Lakṣmī. Economic well-being is prized within Hinduism, and the pursuit of wealth is considered a legitimate goal of human endeavor. It comes under the category of *artha*, which, along with *kāma, dharma,* and *mokṣa* constitute the four legitimate goals of human life, which are collectively referred to by the word *puruṣārtha*. In contrast to *artha*, but not necessarily in opposition to it, *kāma* refers to the pursuit of sensual pleasures and *dharma* to the pursuit of virtue. *Dharma, artha,* and *kāma* are sometimes referred to as the "ordinary norms," the pursuit of which would seem self-evident to a rational human being. Hinduism allows, however, for the pursuit of another goal called *mokṣa* or liberation, which is sometimes referred to as the extraordinary norm. It consists of seeking spiritual fulfillment. Those who seek *mokṣa* often take *sannyāsa* and thus embrace voluntary poverty. One way of looking at this distinction between involuntary and voluntary poverty would be to distinguish between poverty as an economic fact and poverty as a spiritual value. It is possible to confuse the two. Some historians have argued that when, in medieval times, India fell victim to foreign rule, resulting in the collapse of the established order, many people started taking *sannyāsa* as a way of escaping from the harsh realities of the world. Some have further argued that it is for this reason that Sikhism, a form of Indic religiosity that arose at this time, does not countenance the practice of renunciation.

The location of poverty in terms of the four *puruṣārthas* is thus crucial in defining the Hindu perspective on poverty. While one is pursuing *dharma*, *artha*, and *kāma*, one seeks prosperity to be successful in this pursuit, but if one seeks *mokṣa* by renouncing the world, then one embraces a life of poverty. *Mokṣa*, however, can also be sought while living in the world and this point has been much emphasized in modern Hinduism. It is nevertheless true that the pursuit of liberation or salvation is often carried out by renouncing the world and its comforts by adopting *sannyāsa*.

This distinction between voluntary and involuntary poverty is also of relevance in the context of *dharma* or righteous living. While the pursuit of wealth as *artha* is certainly accepted, it was also thought that the more virtuous might nevertheless wish to lead an austere life as reflecting a higher level of personal morality. This comes out clearly in the lifestyle of Mahatma Gandhi, which upheld the dignity of poverty.[24]

Another important distinction in the context of Hinduism is that between poverty and destitution. It may not always be possible to remove poverty because it is a relative concept. But in destitution, in the form of lack of food, clothing, and shelter, poverty acquires an absolute character. The ruler was expected to provide *indirect* help to the unemployed or the poor but render *direct* help to those destitute, such as the widow, the handicapped, the helpless, or the invalid.[25] These two distinctions also help us make sense of contemporary economic trends. The noted Indian thinker Ashis Nandy writes:

All poverty has been dehumanized during the last fifty years. There were people previously who lived a reasonably healthy and creative life, despite being poor. People in the monasteries were always poor. Many writers and artists were poor. Teachers were expected to be poor, or, at least, austere. The Brahmins in India, the much maligned Brahmins, were expected to live austerely and were sometimes poor. There was some vague awareness, amidst all the hypocritical glorification of poverty, that social status didn't have much to do with money. There was some space

---

[24] M. K. Gandhi, *Hindu Dharma* (Ahmedabad: Navajivan Publishing House, 1958), 47–48.
[25] Basham, *The Wonder That Was India*, 89.

for some degree of austerity, voluntary poverty. This gave some dignity to those who were left behind in the rat race of life. They could identify with those who were voluntarily poor and live with a modicum of self-respect.[26]

One can clearly see the distinction between voluntary and involuntary poverty at work here. Similarly, the distinction between poverty and destitution comes into play in the next set of remarks:

Now, we have rubbished this concept of poverty and collapsed it with destitution. The earlier poverty allowed you to live an austere life in a minimally healthy fashion because the lifestyle of the poor and that of the rich were different. The rich were supposed to have many clothes; the poor only a few. As a result, in the tropics at least, you could remain poor but reasonably clean. Similarly, the rich ate one kind of food, the poor another. The rich lived in one kind of house, the poor in another. But the poor at least had coarse grains to grow, roots and berries to collect and eat, and mud huts to live in. It was a hard life, but it was not undignified. Unlike the destitute, the poor did not have to starve to death on the pavements of prosperous cities.[27]

The contemporary significance of this distinction lies in the fact that globalization might reduce poverty but increase destitution.[28]

High-Risk Groups

The relationship of poverty to the caste system in India may enable one to address the issue of high-risk groups, although the issue not only is complex but also may turn out to be contentious.

For our purposes, the caste system, as it is known, may be described as representing the confluence of two Indic terms: *varṇa* and *jāti*. Varṇa refers to the four classes into which Hindu society has been traditionally divided: the Brāhmaṇas, the priests and intellectuals; the Kṣatriyas, the rulers, including warriors and bureaucrats; the Vaiśyas, who consist of traders, artisans, and agriculturists; and the Śūdras, the labor class. The former "untouchables" formed a subdivision of this last category of Śūdras according to most accounts. This idealized structure of the four *varṇas* also subsumed various *jātis*. The *jātis* were endogamous, commensal, and often craft-exclusive groups, which numbered anywhere from four thousand to eight thousand, to which the individuals belonged usually by virtue of their birth. These *jātis* constituted the lived social reality, and each was notionally connected to a *varṇa*, although this point, as well as the order of priority among them, could be a matter of dispute. Hindu texts in general talk much about the *varṇa*, but much less about the *jātis*. Textual scholars therefore tend to focus on *varṇa* and anthropologists on *jāti*, but it seems fair to say that the combined reality

[26] *Talking India: Ashis Nandy in Conversation with Ramin Jahanbeglo* (New Delhi: Oxford University Press, 2006), 134.
[27] Ibid., 134–35.
[28] Ibid., 136.

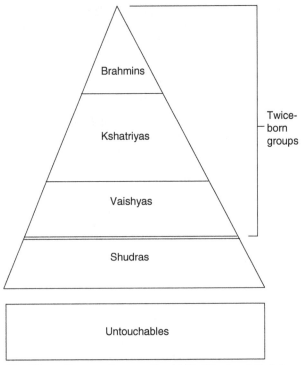

FIGURE 8.1. The Varṇa System. *Source*: David R. Kinsley, *Hinduism: A Cultural Perspective* (Englewood Cliffs, NJ: Prentice-Hall, 1982), 124.

represented by the two terms is foundational to what has come to be known as the caste system (see Figures 8.1 and 8.2).

On the basis of certain Hindu normative texts such as the Manusmṛti, one could initially argue that the lowest class, referred to generally as *Śūdras*, would fall into the high-risk group, and so also would include *women*, who are equated with them in sociological discourse, because both these classes of people were formally denied access to the revealed texts of Hinduism known as the Vedas. This privilege belonged to the male members of the three higher castes knows as *dvijas* or twice-born. Incidentally, the category of *wasp* is said to have been framed on the analogy of the *dvija*, a point that might help render the category less exotic.

The Manusmṛti, for instance, contains the following verse (10.129):

Even a capable *Śūdra* must not accumulate wealth; for when a *Śūdra* becomes wealthy, he harasses Brahmins.[29]

---

[29] Patrick Olivelle, *The Law Code of Manu* (New York: Oxford University Press, 2004), 189.

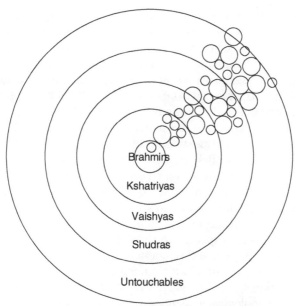

FIGURE 8.2. *The Varṇa and Jāti System*: The *jati* system. The five concentric circles represent the four *varnas* and the untouchables. Each small circle represents a *jati*. The closer to the center a *jati* is located, the higher it is in the system. Some *jatis* are shown within two *varnas* to indicate the gradual shift of an entire caste in the overall system. The *jatis* that are shown overlapping the outer circle represent tribal groups that are in the process of becoming associated with the Hindu social system by adopting Hindu practices and beliefs. *Source*: David R. Kinsley, *Hinduism: A Cultural Perspective* (Englewood Cliffs, NJ: Prentice-Hall, 1982), 126.

This clearly puts the *Śūdras* in the high-risk category. This text also contains the following verse (9.3):

Her father guards her in her childhood, her husband guards her in her youth, and her sons guard her in her old age; a woman is not qualified to act independently.[30]

This would mark women as well in the high-risk category so far as poverty is concerned. The same text, however, speaks of *Śūdra* kings (4.61) and *Śūdras* with wealth (11.34). It also allows women to possess their own wealth in the form of *Śtrīdhana* or women's wealth (3.52; 9.194). It is worth noting that the temple in which Ramakṛṣṇa (1836–86), the well-known mystic of modern India, had his famous mystical experiences had been built by a *Śūdra* widow.

From this point of view, the order of the enumeration of the four *varṇas*, generally deemed hierarchical, is also of some relevance. It is quite obvious that the order is *not* based on *wealth*. Were it based on wealth, the *Vaiśyas*

---

[30] Ibid., 155.

would qualify for the first position. Nor is it based on *power*. Were it based on power, the *Kṣatriyas* would qualify for the first position. It is also not based on *humility*. Were it based on humility, the *Śūdras* would qualify for the first position. But it is *Brāhmaṇa* who tops the list, which seems to suggest that the order is based on ritual purity. Or perhaps, on both ritual and moral purity, given the fact the former is said to be impossible without the latter.[31] Thus, the highest caste need not be the dominant caste in a village.

This *disjunction* between status and wealth (and power), which is widely recognized as a feature of this system, complicates our discussion of the risk factor of poverty being facilely equated with caste *ideologically*, and the fact that the life of voluntary poverty was recommended for the Brahmin confirms this. However, *anthropologically* and *historically* the relationship is still tenable because many Brahmins took to secular pursuits. What made the lower castes high risk in this respect was their *theoretical* dependence on the higher castes whom they were expected to serve, but once again, *historically and anthropologically*, they come through better off.[32] Similarly, it was the legal dependence of a woman on the male members of the family – father, husband, and son – that made her financially vulnerable. On the other hand, both textual and anthropological evidence attest to her right to what is called *strī-dhana* or women's property.[33]

Volition

The role of volition in Hinduism needs to be carefully understood before this concept can be understood in relation to poverty. Volition in Hinduism can be exercised in two contexts. The first is provided by the domain of mundane ordinary existence represented by quotidian life. Most of us feel that we exercise our volition when we act in daily life, as when we decide to take one route rather than another to the place we are going, or decide to read a Russian rather than an American novel, or choose to marry June rather than Jane, or prefer job offer X to job offer Y. So does the Hindu, but for the Hindu the context is thicker than for, say, a Westerner, because most Hindus implicitly believe in the doctrine of *karma* and rebirth. Volition has to do with actions, and the consequences of our action, but when the scale on which it is to be viewed is the context of not one life but several lives, then it becomes fraught with greater consequence than if its effects were for all practical purposes confined to one life. We exercise our volition on the basis of our character, and our character is molded by our actions. This is obvious, but what is not

---

[31] See M. Hiriyanna, *The Essentials of Indian Philosophy* (London: George Allen & Unwin, 1947), 204, n. 10.
[32] Ram Sharan Sharma, *Śūdras in Ancient India: A Social History of the Lower Order Down to circa A.D. 600* (Delhi: Motilal Banarsidass, 1980).
[33] Anant Sadashiv Altekar, *The Position of Women in Hindu Civilization from Prehistoric Times to the Present Day* (Delhi: Motilal Banarsidass, 1956), 219.

obvious to a non-Hindu is also obvious to a Hindu – that his character, in this life, has not been molded only on the basis of his experiences in this life but also those in a previous life, or even previous lives. And, further, that the consequences of his or her actions will ramify through future lives. Because our existence in the various lives is determined by karma or the moral quality of our lives, the nature of our karma has an important bearing on our prosperity in future lives. What it boils down to is that financial integrity becomes a very important factor in the situation. The following rebirth story illustrates this point well:

When he went off to battle, a certain army officer kept his money – two thousand rupees – in trust with a Rawalpindi merchant who was under contract to supply rations to the troops. One day during the Kabul uprising, the officer was killed under bizarre circumstances: he was unable to stop the mare he was riding from heading directly into the enemy lines. No matter how hard he reined in the usually trustworthy animal, she would not alter her deadly course, and a hail of fire killed both horse and rider.

The government sent the officer's belongings to his relatives, who knew nothing about the sum of money he had left with the merchant. The merchant, for his part, mentioned the money to no one, and kept it as if it were his own.

Twenty years later he was living in Saharanpur, running a small shop. One night, as he was entertaining some old friends, his guests heard sobs and piteous cries coming from the next room. The merchant explained that this was his daughter-in-law, mourning her husband who had died only a few days before. The guests offered their condolences, but expressed surprise that the merchant was entertaining them when he, too, should be mourning his son's death. In reply, the merchant told them the following story:

"Twenty years ago, after my return from Rawalpindi, I married, and my wife gave birth to a son. When he had grown up, we arranged a marriage for him, but immediately after the wedding he became gravely ill, and nothing we did would cure him. Finally, I brought a Muslim clergyman to try to heal him. The clergyman recited some words and I immediately gave him two and one half rupees, which was all I had in my pocket at that moment. I then asked my son how he felt. He said that he was about to die and he explained.

"Twenty years ago," he told me, "I left two thousand rupees in your safekeeping just before I was killed in the Kabul uprising. You kept the money, and so I was reborn as your son to recover it. The two and one half rupees you had in your pocket were all that was left of that money, and when you passed them on to the priest in payment for the services he had rendered to me, our account was squared.

"The mare that rode so willfully directly into enemies lines, was reborn as my wife, and because of the way in which she made me die, she will have to grieve at my passing. That will square my account with her."

"So," the merchant said, "the officer is dead and the mare is crying. For whom should I mourn, the mare or the officer? Therefore, gentlemen, be good enough to enjoy your meal."[34]

---

[34] "Whom Should I Mourn," *Darshan* 14 (May 1988): 59.

So much for the ordinary or material context in which volition is exercised. Volition can *also* be exercised in Hinduism, and this presents the second context of its exercise, when volition is directed not toward achieving *dharma*, *artha*, and *kāma* but rather *mokṣa*. The principles, however, governing the exercise of such volition in the two contexts vary. In the first case, volition is directed toward seeking prosperity in the world; in the second case, it is directed toward moving away from the snares of the world. As is famously asserted within the tradition, chains are still chains even if they be made of gold. While exercising volition in the first context, one is likely to choose prosperity and even achieve it, but it is a golden chain. In order to become really unfettered one must pursue the second course, which often involves living a life of voluntary poverty.

So while poverty is connected to volition in both the cases, its exercise differs radically in the two cases.

To revert now to the first case: it is clear that poverty in this life could be a consequence of the acts performed by us in another life. This should not, however, lead us to conclude that such poverty is a case of "undeserved hardship that befalls people through no fault of their own." Our impoverished state in this life may be a result of our actions performed in a former life, but it is not undeserved because it is we ourselves who performed those actions which are responsible for our present condition. It could be argued that this doctrine (at least potentially) is fatalistic because if poverty in this life was thus preordained, it leaves no room for the exercise of freedom. M. Hiriyanna responds cogently to this argument by pointing out that there is no external agent such as Fate constraining the individual, and that one's *own* deeds produce one's "fate," which thus turns out to be something one has control over.[35]

The doctrine of karma sounds uncomfortably close to fatalism to the Western ear, but, for the informed Hindu, it has the opposite implication. The westerner thinks that someone is poor because of the deeds performed in the *past*, from which there is no escape. The Hindu thinks however that there is no escape from trying to eradicate it, because how one acts in the *present* will determine the future.[36] Thus, poverty may be preordained, but it is not undeserved. It is very important to recognize here, similarly, that inevitability of result does not imply immutability of outcome. It is inevitable that good deeds will contribute to prosperity. But it is up to us to perform good *or* bad deeds. Which is to say that if one started performing that karma now which leads to prosperity, then, in due course, prosperity in the future will be as inevitable as poverty is in the present.

Nor does one have to put up with poverty in the present because the doctrine of karma has two sides to it: what has happened is the result of our past actions *and* what will happen is also the result of our present actions.

---

[35] Hiriyanna, *The Essentials of Indian Philosophy*, 47.
[36] See Arvind Sharma, "Karma, Rebirth and the Problem of Evil," *Philosophy East & West* 58, no. 4 (October 2008): 573–76.

The Hindu perspective is more inclined to side with the statement that "poverty is more often a deserved, if unintended, consequence of an individual's (or community's) own avoidable shortcomings." The question may be raised as to how does one apportion the blame (or divide the credit) between the individual and the community. The soteriology of Hinduism tends to be individualistic, and we have seen how the doctrine of karma emphasizes individual responsibility. It does allow room for the communal dimension, however, especially in such a context as the present one. For instance, the ruler and the ruled have a karmic connection.

This point is elaborated by M. V. Nadkarni. We noticed earlier how one could ascribe to the doctrine of karma

"radically individualistic implications ... that no one could be held responsible for what happened to one and that in turn, no one could be held responsible for what happened to anyone else; determined as each was by his and her own *karma*." If, for example, poverty, illiteracy and disease are attributed to only the past *Karma* of the suffering of individuals, there would be no case for social action and responsibility. Daya Krishna who referred to this criticism also, however, observes that parallel to it there was also the theory of "kings' sharing in the merits and demerits earned by his subjects through the performance of good and bad deeds.... They thus developed a theory of the collective community of moral agents, in which there was joint sharing in the fruits of action." Since every one has freedom of will, it results in *karma* not only of the acting individual but also has an impact on others. This is inevitable in a society of interacting individuals. Action of one can create poverty for another, and also can relieve it in others. As such there is moral responsibility for each other, as well as community responsibility for each other, as well as community responsibility to relieve poverty, hunger, disease and unhappiness. The *Gītā* teaches that each should perform his/her own duty/work selflessly with *loka-saṅgraha* in mind, which has a liberating impact. Failure to do so binds us to the Law of *Karma*, earning negative *karma* or demerit.[37]

Or even from an individualistic perspective:

'If we see some one suffering and do nothing to help the person by adopting the view "that is his karma," expressing in Hindu jargon the Western attitude that "that is his problem," then one has to remember that when it is our turn to suffer, we too will receive no succour on the same argument that it is our *Karma*. But if we help others when they suffer we too will be helped when we suffer.[38]

Goals

The alleviation of poverty is not morally optional in Hinduism (although a misinterpretation of the doctrine of karma and rebirth could make it appear

[37] Nadkarni, *Hinduism*, 53.
[38] Arvind Sharma, *Hinduism for Our Times* (New Delhi: Oxford University Press, 1996), 30–31.

that way, as explained earlier). It is a moral imperative in keeping with the concept of *dharma*. In Hinduism it is a requirement of justice, but of metaphysical rather than moral justice. It is a moral duty that involves metaphysical justice according to a major school of Hindu philosophy. According to this system, the reality underlying the world is the same so that we are all ultimately one, and the sense of separateness is misleading. This point has been articulated clearly in the Swadhyaya movement, started by Dada Pandurang Shastri Athavale (1920–2003), who was awarded the Templeton Prize for progress in religion in 1997. He takes the two well-known articulations of the Hindu school of philosophy known as Vedanta – *aham brahāsmi* (I am the ultimate reality) and *tat tvam asi* (You are that ultimate reality) – as his starting point and focuses on the second.

The second law is [that] every man is my brother. Swadhyaya is Vedanta philosophy in practice. It offers a way to look upon all faiths with love. It could play a key part in enlightening humanity. It is one thing to understand and accept the idea of God within, but it is another thing to live it. As the individual swadhyayees begin to translate the idea of an indwelling God into words and deeds, they and their communities begin to transform themselves. This transformation may be called the Swadhyaya way of life. It challenges the conventional wisdom of the developmentalists and the secularists as well as the liturgical and formulistic wisdom of the clerics and theologians.[39]

The elimination of poverty and the alleviation of poverty are not dichotomized in traditional Hinduism. It is a matter of resources and agency. Those who have only enough resources to alleviate poverty should alleviate it even if they cannot eliminate it; those who have the resources to eliminate it should do so. There is the suggestion, however, that *mokṣa* may be a goal for achieving the alleviation or elimination of poverty, which might well be suspended. This Hindu position is cogently articulated by the Tibetan saint Milarepa (twelfth century) in the present context as follows:

In the Scriptures the ability really to benefit others is regarded as a very high and rare virtue, the last and most sublime flowering of a mature development of perfect wisdom. Eight hundred years ago Milarepa, the great Tibetan saint, was asked by his disciples "if they could engage in worldly duties, in a small way, for the benefit of others." Milarepa replied: "If there be not the least self-interest attached to such duties, it is permissible. But such detachment is indeed rare; and works performed for the good of others seldom succeed, if not wholly freed from self-interest. Even without seeking to benefit others, it is with difficulty that works done even in one's own interest are successful. It is as if a man helplessly drowning were to try to save another man in the same predicament. One should not be over-anxious and hasty in

---

[39] Raj Krishna Srivastava, ed., *Vital Connections: Self, Society, God: Perspectives on Swadhyaya* (New York: Weatherhill, 1998), 11–12. For an even more forthright exposition of this view, see Arthur Osborne, ed., *The Teachings of Bhagavan Raman Maharshi in His Own Words* (Tiruvannamalai: Sri Ramanasramam, 1971), 108–9.

setting out to serve others before one has oneself realized the Truth in its fullness; to do so, would be like the blind leading the blind. As long as the sky endures, so long will there be no end of sentient beings for one to serve; and to every one comes the opportunity for such service. Till the opportunity comes, I exhort each of you to have but the one resolve, namely to attain Buddha-hood for the good of all living beings."[40]

Those who take this position and regard spiritual development as a higher value do so not only because their own single-minded pursuit of *mokṣa* is promoted in this way but also because the ultimate good one can render to another is ultimately spiritual rather than material (no matter how much material good may be desirable immediately) and that one can hardly hope to lead another to *mokṣa* if one has not attained it oneself. There is also the suggestion that until one achieves *mokṣa*, one remains an imperfect agent and cannot really produce the best outcome for imperfect actors. Perhaps a modern illustration will be helpful here. A would-be doctor can always act as a nurse, but in order to be a doctor, he or she will have to concentrate on studying, at the expense of nursing the patients in the present, so that ultimately he or she can be of even greater use to the patients as a doctor in the future.

Remedies

The obligation to alleviate poverty in Hinduism is quite universal and is epitomized in the way one is supposed to treat a guest, who is significantly called *atithi* or a visitor who turns up without appointment, although the term is now used to refer to all guests. It is the supreme duty of the householder to take care of any guest according to the Manusmṛti (3.105–14).[41]

Hospitality can, however, only mollify poverty; it cannot really alleviate or eradicate it. One should not be led to assume that the householder's duty stops with offering hospitality. The role of the person in the stage of life known as the householder for alleviating poverty is also widely celebrated in Hinduism. The same Manusmṛti (6.87–90) declares the superiority of the householder over the other stages of life in the following terms:

Student, householder, forest hermit, and ascetic: these four distinct orders have their origin in the householder.... Among all of them, however, according to the dictates of vedic scripture, the householder is said to be the best, for he supports the other three. As all rivers and rivulets ultimately end up in the ocean, so people of all the orders ultimately end up in the householder.[42]

Such a householder is enjoined to perform the five great sacrifices (*pañca mahāyajñas*) daily. The first three pertain to the worship of Brahman,

[40] Cited by Edward Conze, "Buddhism: The Mahāyāna," in *The Concise Encyclopedia of Living Faiths*, ed. R. C. Zaehner (Boston: Beacon Press, 1967), 300–1.
[41] Olivelle, *The Law Code of Manu*, 51.
[42] Ibid., 105.

ancestors, and gods. The fourth one, called *bhūta-yajña*, involves "the worship of all things living, by scattering grain and other food on the threshold for animals, birds, and spirits," while the fifth, called *puruṣa-yajña*, involves the "worship of men, by showing them hospitality."[43]

The real initiative for the alleviation and elimination of poverty, however, comes from the king or the state.

Scope and Priorities

The scope for the removal of poverty is universal, although the effort is sometimes directed to the condition of the practicing Brahmin, for whom hunger was a health hazard. It applies to all the castes and classes and to all nationalities and societies.

Some Hindu texts could be adduced "in support of a global campaign to end hunger and prevent preventable disease over efforts by societies to overcome less extreme levels of property and vulnerability." The *Bhāgavata-Purāṇa* contains the following account of Rantideva, which is widely celebrated:

During a period of devastating famine in his kingdom King Ranti Deva spent the whole of his wealth in feeding the hungry and the distressed. Deeply pained by the sufferings of his people and by way of atonement, the King undertook a fast for forty-eight days and did not take any food or even water during that period. On the forty-ninth day, when he was satisfied that almost all the hungry and the distressed in his kingdom had been well looked after, he decided to break his fast. Just as he was about to do so by taking a morsel of food and a cup of water he heard the piteous cry of a person of low caste Pulkasa as he is called in the Purana, asking for water to quench his thirst. The king was then in the midst of his ministers and councilors. He stopped tasting the water placed before him and ordered that the cup be given to the Pulkasa. The people around him remonstrated strongly at this suicidal act on the part of the king. It was pointed out by them that it was too much on his part to take the risk of sacrificing his life for the sake of a Pulkasa after this long fast for nearly forty-eight days. Immediately afterwards, the king began to take the morsel of food. Even for that food there came a guest at his doors. At this stage, Ranti Deva made the famous pronouncement: I do not seek from the Supreme Lord the Highest Bliss attended with the eight powers of *siddhis*. Nor do I care for *apunarbhavam* or cessation of the cycle of births and deaths. But my only desire is to be present in all beings, undergo suffering with them and serve them so that they may become free from misery.

In the next verse he continues to say: "Hunger, thirst, fatigue, loss of strength in limbs, distress, languor, grief, disappointment, delusion – all these undesirable features of my distressed soul have all disappeared upon my giving water to one who was suffering from acute thirst."[44]

43 Basham, *The Wonder That Was India*, 170.
44 Balsubramania Iyer, *Hindu Ideals* (Bombay: Bharatiya Vidya Bhava, 1969), 60–61. See Bhāgavata-Purāṇa 9.21.

Responsibility and Conditionality

The responsibility for removing poverty seems to rest on oneself, on others, and on the state, according to Hinduism. The activist interpretation of karma emphasizes one's economic well-being. As Balasubramania Iyer explains,

Artha is the foundation upon which the whole structure of life has been built and all the other purusharthas can be achieved only by the fulfillment of this primary purpose in life. The word Artha has a very wide significance as in the Artha Sastra, the Science of Polity for the political and economic structure of a State. But the meaning of the word, when used in the context of the purushartha of the individual is that which I have already indicated, acquisition of wealth for livelihood and material comforts. Indian thinkers have always regarded the economic factor as an essential element of human life. There is no sin in the acquisition of wealth nor is there any virtue in poverty. Indian thought does not advocate asceticism or renunciation of wealth for all but the chosen few. It does not contemplate asceticism as part of the normal good life. *"Anāyasena maraṇam vinā dainyena jivanam"* (to live and die with ease) is our daily prayer. Our seers do not look down upon the efforts to increase a man's wealth. The great talented lady-moralist of the Tamil land, Avvai said, "Go even across the billowy ocean and acquire wealth." *Arthakarī ca vidyā* (learning should bring wealth) says the Vidura Neeti. In the Bhagavad Gita the Lord characterizes the *artharthi* who worships God for the sake of wealth as a noble person.[45]

Perhaps it should be pointed out here that the voluntary poverty is advocated in Hinduism for those who lead priestly and spiritual lives, such as practicing Brāhmaṇas, and those who have renounced the world and adopted the fourth stage of life called *sannyāsa*. The third stage of life, the *vānaprastha*, also requires a simple lifestyle. But people of *varṇas* other than the Brāhmaṇa, and in other *āśramas* (or stages of life) than the last two, may freely engage in the pursuit of wealth. And that covers the masses.

How *artha* or wealth should be disposed, once earned, is also discussed.

One should collect wealth following what is right and such wealth obtained righteously should be divided into three parts: one should secure both *dharma* and *artha* with one-third of the wealth acquired, one-third should be spent on *kāma* (i.e. chaste sexual life and enjoyment of other pleasures not in conflict with *dharma*) and one-third he should increase. Manu (VII.99 and 101) prescribed similar rules for the king.[46]

The responsibility of dealing with poverty also in some measure rests with others, to the extent that charity alleviates it. Two pieces of evidence are particularly interesting in this regard. The first is found in the Bṛhadāraṇyaka Upaniṣad (v.2.1–3). It contains the literary conceit that the heavenly roll of

---

[45] Iyer, *Hindu Ideals*, 238–39.
[46] P. V. Kane, *History of Dharmaśāstra*, vol. 5, part 2, 2nd ed. (Poona: Bhandarkar Oriental Research Institute, 1977), 239 (emphasis added).

thunder repeats the sound Da, Da, Da but that its didactic significance varies with the group that hears it. For the gods, the sound Da stands for *dāmyata*, or self-control. For the demons, it stands for *dayadhvam*, or compassion. For the humans, however, it stands for *datta*, that is to say, be charitable.[47] The second piece of evidence is found in the Manusmṛti. Charity, which naturally implies the alleviation of poverty for the recipient, is reinforced by the view found in the *smṛti* texts of Hinduism that the chief virtue suitable for a particular age varies with time (Manusmṛti I.85) [48] and that in our present age this virtue is charity (Manusmṛti I. 86).[49]

One can, however, do only so much for oneself, and others can do only so much for others. The state is where the buck stops, so to speak. It is interesting to note in this context that, while in modern times the state performs the triad of executive, judicial, and legislative activities, "one great difference between ancient and modern societies is that legislative action of the king was extremely limited in ancient times."[50] This fact, however, did not prevent the state in ancient India from taking care of the poor and the destitute. "The king is also called upon to support helpless and aged people, the blind, the cripple, lunatics, widows, orphans, those suffering from diseases and calamities, pregnant women by giving them medicines, lodging, food and clothing according to their requirements. Vide Vas. 19.35–36, Viṣṇudharmasūtra III.65, Matsya 215.62, Agni 225.25, Ādiparva 49.11, Sahbā 18.24, Virāṭaparva 18.24, Sānti 77.18."[51] According to P. V. Kane, the noted scholar of Hindu jurisprudence, such provisions anticipate the concept of the welfare state.[52]

An examination of these provisions sheds interesting light on the issue of conditionality. It seems that those who were able-bodied were expected to earn their keep. The Rajanīti-Prakāśa quotes

Śaṅkha-Likhita to the effect that even kṣatriyas and vaiśyas who cannot maintain themselves by the methods prescribed by the śāstras for them should approach the king who should help them with the means of livelihood and they should work for the king in the manner laid down for them and that śūdras also should apply their skill and crafts for the benefit of the king when so maintained.[53]

In the case of able-bodied women, the position is less clear. The Rajanītiprakāśa quotes the Viṣṇudharmottara to the effect that the king is required to "honour and protect chaste women [*pativratā*]," implying financial help but with no quid pro quo. In the Arthaśāstra,

[47] See S. Radhakrishnan, ed., *The Principal Upaniṣads* (Atlantic Highlands, NJ: Humanities Press, 1992), 289–90.
[48] See Olivelle, *The Law Code of Manu*, 18.
[49] Ibid., 19.
[50] Kane, *History of Dharmaśāstra*, 3:98.
[51] Ibid., 59.
[52] Ibid., 59–60.
[53] Ibid., 59.

In the instructions to the king's superintendent of Weaving we are told that the staff of the royal weaving and spinning establishments should be made up of indigent women – a motley collection, including widows, cripples, orphans, beggar-women, women who failed to pay fines and were compelled to work them off, and broken-down prostitutes. These were all of low class and worked under male overseers.[54]

Conclusion

The relationship between poverty and morality, and Hinduism, can be analyzed diachronically as well as synchronically. When it is analyzed diachronically, the economic history of India comes into play. When it is analyzed synchronically, the overarching templates of Hinduism, such as the doctrines of karma and dharma, of *varṇa* and *jāti* (caste), of the stages of life (*āśramas*), of the goals of life (*puruṣārthas*), and of the Ages (*yugas*) and its understanding of the role of the state help frame the issue.

---

[54] Basham, *The Wonder That Was India*, 179–80.

9

The Problem of Poverty in Islamic Ethics

Sohail H. Hashmi

The problem of poverty occupies a central place in Islamic ethics. Indeed, it is arguably the first social issue that the Qur'an addresses, beginning with some of the earliest revelations received by the prophet Muhammad. The claims of the poor and the obligations of the wealthy are moral issues taken up by hundreds of Qur'anic verses. Likewise, the *hadith* literature is rich in moral admonitions and practical instructions that reflect, according to Islamic tradition, the Prophet's teachings and reforms on this subject.[1] Two of Islam's five pillars of faith bear directly or indirectly on the issue of poverty: *zakat*, which is the duty of the rich to pay alms to the poor; and *sawm*, or fasting during the month of Ramadan, which is intended in part to cultivate empathy for the destitute. Islamic law devotes considerable attention to the institution of *waqf*, or charitable trusts, which has provided the foundation for Muslim philanthropy over the past thirteen centuries.

The centrality of poverty and its alleviation in the earliest Islamic sources no doubt reflects the importance of this issue in the seventh-century Arabian society in which Islam emerged. Yet the problem of poverty in Islam has never been more acute than at present, with Muslims constituting large numbers of the world's poorest. Stagnant economies, chronic unemployment or underemployment of young people, and corrupt or inept governments that pilfer or mismanage development funds have all factored into Islamic revivalism. One of the most prominent intellectual aspects of this revivalism is the development during the past fifty years of "Islamic economics." Social justice concerns – the argument that Islamic ethics have become divorced from economic practices because of Muslim infatuation with Western ideologies

---

[1] The *hadith* literature consists of collections of oral traditions relating Muhammad's words and actions. In Islamic orthodoxy, the *hadith* is considered second only to the Qur'an as a source of Islamic theology, law, and ethics. Yet, because the *hadith* collections were compiled beginning in the second century after Muhammad's death, some Muslims question their authenticity and thus the normative value of many specific traditions.

and institutions – underlie the burgeoning literature of Islamic economics. If there is a central thesis in this literature it is that the Islamic economic system is neither entirely laissez faire capitalism nor classless, propertyless communism. The ideal Islamic system lies somewhere in between, ranging in the arguments of theorists from a liberal welfare state to a more interventionist socialist state.[2]

This chapter offers a survey of how Muslim thinkers over the centuries have grappled with the problem of poverty. The "problem" may be divided into three ethical concerns: Why poverty? Who are the poor? What are the best means to alleviate poverty? The first question – embracing such existential issues as why poverty exists, whether it is willed by God or the result of human action (or inaction) – has historically received little direct attention from Muslim thinkers. An Islamic "theology of poverty" can be plumbed, I believe, from the Qur'an and *hadith*, and I outline one at the outset.

The other two questions – on who are the poor and how to alleviate poverty – receive extensive treatment in the classical sources. Building upon moral-legal injunctions and admonitions in the Qur'an and *sunna* (recorded practices) of the Prophet and the first four "rightly guided" caliphs, legists dealt at length with these issues in the jurisprudential (*fiqh*) literature. This literature preserves the internal debates of the jurists and their different rulings on specific points of law. But it also demonstrates that the four principal schools of Sunni jurisprudence and the dominant school of Shi'i jurisprudence agreed broadly on the general ethical approach to identifying the poor and to dealing with poverty, including the assignment of responsibilities to society and state. This classical legacy, enshrined as *shari'a*, or divinely sanctioned Islamic law in the minds of many Muslims today, still remains relevant and even determinative for Islamic economics and for contemporary legislation in a number of Muslim states.

Why Poverty?

According to Islamic tradition, Muhammad received the first Qur'anic revelation around the year 610 CE at the age of forty during a spiritual retreat in the hills surrounding Mecca. He was at the time a successful businessman, a member of the dominant Quraysh tribe, a respected member of the community, with a contented family life. Muslim biographies of the Prophet are vague on why he felt the need to withdraw from his townspeople, but the earliest Qur'anic revelations provide possible answers. The Qur'an begins to

[2] See the surveys by Muhammad Nejatullah Siddiqi, "Muslim Economic Thinking: A Survey of Contemporary Literature," in *Studies in Islamic Economics*, ed. Khurshid Ahmad (Leicester, UK: Islamic Foundation, 1981), 191–315; and Mohamed Aslam Haneef, *Contemporary Islamic Economic Thought: A Selected Comparative Analysis* (Petaling Jaya, Malaysia: Ikraq, 1995).

develop from its initial verses a theme that would run through the course of
the entire revelation over the next twenty-three years: faith in God means
service to humanity, and one of the greatest forms of service is compassion
toward the poor and the needy. Qur'an 74:43–44 declare that on the Day of
Judgment sinners will be those who did not pray or "feed the indigent." Qur'an
111:2 initiates the criticism of the wealthy who reject Muhammad's call. Their
wealth will avail them nothing in the hereafter. They spend their days boast-
ing of the wealth they squander, rejecting the "steep path" of righteousness
that calls for freeing the slave or feeding the orphan and the downtrodden
(Q. 90:6, 12–16).

So often does the linkage between faith in the true God and acts of
charity appear in what are widely believed to be the earliest verses that
several Western Islamicists surmise significant economic motivations for
Muhammad's vocation.[3] According to this narrative, Muhammad's Mecca
was a flourishing religious and commercial center in Arabia; the Ka'ba drew
pilgrims from throughout the peninsula for worship, and it was an important
stop for caravans plying the coastal route from Yemen to Syria. Mecca's leading families were exploiting gods and mammon to amass significant wealth.
In W. Montgomery Watt's memorable line, "The Qur'an appeared not in the
atmosphere of the desert, but in that of high finance."[4] Watt and others suggest that the growth of an affluent mercantile class in the half century before
Muhammad began the call to Islam opened a widening gap between rich
and poor. Tribal solidarity and an ethos of shared wealth was giving way to
increasing individualism and less concern of the rich for the poor.[5] Two *suras*
(chapters) warn Muhammad himself to resist this trend in his own conduct: Q.
80, which opens with the words, "He frowned and turned away… " referring
to the Prophet's response to a blind man who approached him seeking spiritual guidance while he was busy in conversation with a rich man; and Q. 93,
which contains pointed references to Muhammad's humble origins:

Did He not find you an orphan and give you sustenance? And He found you astray
and gave you guidance. And He found you in need and gave you wealth. So deal not
harshly with orphans. And do not turn away the needy. And proclaim the bounties
of your Lord!

Watt concludes that Islam arose in response to a "malaise" in Meccan society
produced by fundamental changes in economic relationships without a con-
comitant change in religious or ethical values.[6]

---

3 See Charles C. Torrey, *The Commercial-Theological Terms in the Koran* (Leiden: Brill,
   1892); Hubert Grimme, *Mohammed* (Munster: Aschendorff, 1892); Henri Lammens, *La
   Mecque à la veille de l'Hégire* (Beirut: Imprimerie Catholique, 1924); W. Montgomery
   Watt, *Muhammad at Mecca* (Oxford: Clarendon Press, 1953).
4 Watt, *Muhammad at Mecca*, 3.
5 Ibid., 72–73.
6 Ibid., 20.

Watt's thesis was strongly challenged by Patricia Crone in *Meccan Trade and the Rise of Islam*. She argues that there is no historical basis for the claim that seventh-century Mecca was a bustling mercantile center experiencing an upheaval in social relations, specifically in growing class distinctions. Instead, the historical evidence suggests that Meccan society was rather stable and content. The Qur'an's concern with poverty is, therefore, the result of Muhammad's subjective assessment of his society and his self-image as a reformer. "It was ... *Muhammad*," Crone writes, "who disrupted traditional kinship ties with his preaching."[7]

The contending viewpoints on what may be called the economic motivation thesis for Muhammad's vocation ultimately rest on differing views regarding the historicity of the Qur'anic text. Crone rejects the Qur'an as a credible historical source for Muhammad's Mecca; Watt generally accepts it. Neither view, however, undermines the claim that the needs of the poor and disadvantaged are central to Islamic ethics, and this is the result of the attention the Qur'an lavishes on this issue. Regardless of the reason, as far as the Qur'an is concerned, poverty is a problem. As Watt writes: "The Qur'an provides an analysis of the situation – not complete, but sufficient for practical purposes – and a guide to action."[8] In other words, the Qur'an never develops a systematic response to the question, Why poverty? but focuses instead on ways to address poverty. It is not a book of philosophy but primarily a book of practical morality. Still, there are hints of an answer within the Qur'an that provide a point of departure for discussion of this issue.

The Qur'an repeatedly declares: "To God belongs dominion over the heavens and the earth" (e.g., Q. 2:107, 3:189, 5:17, 67:1). "Dominion" is a rough translation of the Arabic word *mulk*, which connotes the sense of ownership, possession, sovereignty – qualities both physical and metaphysical. In terms of property rights, Qur'anic commentators have historically understood these verses as meaning that God is the ultimate owner of all things on earth and only He has complete and unassailable rights of disposal. Man can claim only a contingent right of ownership, as the servant of God (*'abd Allah*) and as His steward or vicegerent on earth (*khalifa*; see Q. 2:30, 6:165). "The earth is God's. To such of His servants as He pleases does He give it as a heritage" (Q. 7:128).

The task of Muslim scholars over the centuries has been to define the parameters of human property rights, to balance the claims of the individual and the community as a whole (*umma*). Before we turn to a detailed account of how this balance has been struck, it is important to note that ulema of the classical period carved out a broad moral and legal sphere for individual property rights. Nothing in the Qur'an suggests that human beings ought not

[7] Patricia Crone, *Meccan Trade and the Rise of Islam* (Princeton, NJ: Princeton University Press, 1987), 233.
[8] Watt, *Muhammad at Mecca*, 79–80.

amass property; indeed, its underlying premise is that people have a right to do so. The *hadith* literature contains abundant, explicit sanctions for individual property rights, including the Prophet's statement in his Farewell Sermon, delivered shortly before his death: "Verily your lives and your possessions are as inviolable as the sacredness of this day of yours, in this month of yours, in this town of yours."[9]

With property rights come inevitable social inequalities. The Qur'an states that such disparities are God's will and part of the great moral test that is life: "He has raised you in ranks, some above others, so that He may try you in the gifts that He has given you" (Q. 6:165). "God enlarges or restricts the sustenance to whomever He pleases. [Those granted abundance] rejoice in this worldly life, but this worldly life is of little comfort in the Hereafter" (Q. 13:26). As in other domains of human existence where God "wills" something, these and other verses raise difficult questions about predeterminism versus free will in Islamic theology. This issue featured prominently in fierce debates among rival theological schools during the early Islamic centuries.[10] It is a subject too vast to probe in any depth here. What we can say, though, is that in terms of Qur'anic ethics, the verses suggesting that one's lot in life is divinely predestined are counterbalanced by numerous others calling for humans to struggle, to work, to make and spend wealth – subject, of course, to the constraints God imposes on what is lawful and unlawful.[11] Q. 4:29 exhorts: "O you who believe! Do not consume your property in false pursuits, but let there be among you trade in good faith." God in His omniscience knows what choices we will make and in what material and spiritual conditions our lives will end. But His omnipotence is not so absolute and exclusive as to rule out all human agency during the course of our lives. We are not fated to live and die in the same circumstances in which we were born. Through our choices, we shape our own destinies; without this choice, the notion of individual responsibility that is central to the Qur'an's notion of this life as a trial or test for the life to come would be meaningless (see, e.g., Q. 6:164, 17:15, 39:7). Yet, our choices are not limitless; we are constrained by the "hand that we are dealt." Given different natural endowments, talents, aptitudes, or just the good fortune of having been born in a particular time, place, and family, some people will fare better than others always. Wealth is acquired, transmitted to heirs, or lost according to God's plan for each individual. "Do not envy the way that God has made some of you excel over others," counsels

9 Muhammad ibn 'Abdallah Khatib al-Tabrizi, *Mishkat al-Masabih*, 4 vols., trans. Mawlana Fazlul Karim (New Delhi: Islamic Book Service, 1998), 3:587.

10 See W. Montgomery Watt, *Free Will and Predestination in Early Islam* (London: Luzac, 1948); Harry A. Wolfson, *The Philosophy of the Kalam* (Cambridge, MA: Harvard University Press, 1976), chap. 8.

11 See Maxime Rodinson, *Islam and Capitalism*, trans. Brian Pearce (Austin: University of Texas Press, 1981), esp. chap. 4, "The Influence of Muslim Ideology Generally in the Economic Field."

Q. 4:32. "Men should have a portion of whatever they have earned, while women should have a portion of whatever they have earned. Ask God for some of His bounty. God is aware of all things."

Because poverty and wealth are not entirely the result of human actions – that is, they are not always earned – the Qur'an and *hadith* attach no moral value to either. It is not whether one is rich or poor that is morally significant; it is what one does with one's wealth or poverty. Both are means or instruments – like many others in the Qur'an – that God uses to try human beings. The pauper and the rich man will both face divine judgment on an equal footing for what their souls earned in this earthly life.

But the clear message given by the Qur'an and *hadith* is that extremes of poverty or wealth distract from the moral, God-conscious life. The ideal is the median, the life of self-sufficiency, closer to the poor than to the rich. The servants of God, according to Q. 25:67, are "those who, when they spend, are not extravagant or miserly, but stand firmly in between." According to one famous *hadith*, particularly popular among Sufi exponents of the ascetic life, the Prophet is supposed to have said, "Faqri fakhri" (My poverty is my pride).[12] And according to another *hadith*, the Prophet prayed: "O God! make the provision of the family of Muhammad just sufficient."[13] Numerous *hadiths* state that the poor will enter paradise ahead of the rich and that the majority of those in paradise will be those who were poor on earth.[14] The riches of the wealthy, though they are acquired entirely by lawful means, are nevertheless obstacles to their salvation. Their wealth is "cleansed" by acts of charity and the payment of the alms tax, *zakat*, a word derived from the root *z-k-y*, meaning in part "to purify" or "to justify" (see Q. 9:103). The Qur'an presents *zakat* along with *salat* (prayer) as two links in the chain that binds all the prophets to each other (Q. 2:83; 19:31, 55; 21:73).

The root *z-k-y* has another meaning as well: to thrive, to increase, to grow. *Zakat* could, therefore, be seen as a means to enlarge one's own soul (see Q. 91:9–10) as well as to increase the spiritual well-being and material prosperity of the community. For the present discussion on the reasons for poverty, this meaning of *zakat* can be explicated by a Qur'anic verse key to all discussions of distributive justice in Islam: "What God has bestowed on His messenger from [the property] of the people of the townships belongs to God, to His messenger and to kindred and orphans, the needy and the wayfarer, in order that it [wealth] not make [merely] a circuit among the wealthy of you" (Q. 59:7).[15] The final line suggests the metaphor of a continuous cycle of giving

---

[12] See Annemarie Schimmel, *And Muhammad Is His Messenger* (Chapel Hill: University of North Carolina Press, 1985), 48.

[13] Khatib al-Tabrizi, *Mishkat al-Masabih*, 1:273.

[14] Ibid., 1:264–65.

[15] Qur'anic commentators generally understand the "people of the townships" as the Banu Nadir, a Jewish tribe living near Medina that surrendered in 625 to Muslim forces without fighting and was subsequently expelled by Muhammad. Because their landed property was

and receiving, the goal of which is to distribute – to expand – the communal wealth. *Zakat* is merely one way to ensure that wealth circulates. As an obligatory aspect of the faith, *zakat* is the principal means among others to counteract the human urge toward greed, miserliness, or hoarding (all strongly condemned in Q. 3:180, 9:34, 64:16), which threatens to disrupt the cycle and thereby restrict the growth in communal wealth.

Ibn Khaldun (d. 1406) presents in the *Muqaddima* an account of what happens when extravagance and greed rule society. His grand sociological theory of the rise and fall of civilization is not based on specific Qur'anic texts, but it is informed by and illustrates religious lessons. The *Muqaddima* also contains by far the most detailed and incisive premodern Muslim analysis of the causes of poverty. Ibn Khaldun begins his cyclical theory of civilization with Bedouin culture, spare in its needs, with few social inequalities, and as a result morally strong and resilient. The harshness of desert life, however, pushes the nomadic Bedouin toward sedentary culture. Sedentary society makes possible economic prosperity and the pursuit of luxury. Over time, urban civilization reaches its limits, and then begins to decline. The state (or, more precisely, the ruling dynasty) increases its taxes on the people to finance its mounting expenses. The ruler must raise enough revenue to finance himself, his large entourage, and the militia that secures his power.[16] Higher taxes translate into higher prices.

The expenditures of sedentary people, therefore, grow and are no longer reasonable but extravagant. The people cannot escape this (development) because they are dominated by and subservient to their customs. All their profits go into (their) expenditures. One person after another becomes reduced in circumstances and indigent. Poverty takes hold of them.[17]

In contrast to the virtuous poor of the Qur'an and *hadith*, Ibn Khaldun's poor are a bitter and immoral lot. Addicted to luxury, they turn to "lying, gambling, cheating, fraud, theft, perjury, and usury" in misguided efforts to maintain their former lifestyles. Rulers and ruled both descend into an equality of debasement and vice. "If this (situation) spreads in a town or nation, God permits it to be ruined and destroyed. This is the meaning of the word of God: 'When we want to destroy a village, we order those of its inhabitants who live in luxury to act wickedly therein. Thus, the word becomes true for it, and we do destroy it' [Q. 17:16]."[18] So the cycle of civilization, of poverty

gained without fighting, it was treated as *fay'*, belonging in its entirety to the Prophet (i.e., the Islamic state) to disperse in accordance with the terms of the verse. *Fay'* is contrasted with *ghanima*, the normal spoils of war, of which the Islamic state's share is only one-fifth and the rest is dispersed to the fighters.

[16] Ibn Khaldun, *The Muqaddimah: An Introduction to History*, trans. Franz Rosenthal (New York: Pantheon, 1958), 2:92.

[17] Ibid., 2:293.

[18] Ibid., 2:294.

and wealth, begins anew. Clearly, Ibn Khaldun the historian was pessimistic about the potential for human beings to escape from what he saw as inexorable social forces, even as Ibn Khaldun the Muslim jurist and statesman sought to mitigate those forces through application of Islamic law and ethics.

Who Are the Poor?

The Qur'an employs a number of terms to designate those who are economically disadvantaged or financially insecure. Some, such as *'a'il* (Q. 93:8) and *mahrum* (Q. 51:19, 70:25), appear only a few times. Others appear repeatedly on lists of those entitled for individual, communal, or state support. Q. 2:177 presents one of the most detailed of such lists when it includes in its description of righteous Muslim behavior: "To spend of your substance out of love for Him, for your kin [*dhu al-qurba*], for orphans [*yatama*], for the needy [*masakin*], for the wayfarer [*ibn al-sabil*], for beggars [*sa'ilin*], and for the ransom of slaves [*riqab*]." The *yatama* (orphans) are frequently included in lists of the needy (e.g., Q. 2:177, 4:2–6, 76:18), although sometimes it is to admonish their guardians to be scrupulous in handling their property (e.g., Q. 4:2, 17:34, 59:7).

Generally, however, the Qur'an uses the terms *fuqara'* and *masakin* when referring to the poor and needy who have a claim on the wealthy Muslim and on Muslim society as a whole. Most importantly, both terms appear in the key verse Q. 9:60 that lists those entitled to receive *zakat*: "Charities [*sadaqat*] shall go to the poor [*fuqara'*], the needy [*masakin*], the workers who administer [*zakat*], those whose hearts have been reconciled [i.e., new or potential converts], those in bondage [i.e., to free slaves] and in debt, those [engaged] in the cause of God, and the wayfarer. Such is God's commandment. God is Omniscient, Most Wise." The first point to note is that this verse employs the plural of the general term for charity, *sadaqa*, but interpreters understand the verse as dealing specifically with *zakat*, the obligatory alms tax, because of the declaration at the end that this is "God's commandment."[19] Second, the list of *zakat* recipients includes groups of people who are not obviously poor, so the original intent of *zakat* may have been broader than simply poverty relief. Nevertheless, the poor and needy appear first and second on the list of eight deserving categories, and historically *zakat* has been most closely associated with the distributive justice goals of Islam. A number of *hadiths* purport to confirm this link, as in the well-known instruction that the Prophet gave to his newly appointed governor of Yemen, Mu'adh ibn Jabal: "*Zakat* will be taken from their rich [*aghniya'*] and will be given to their poor [*fuqara'*]."[20]

---

[19] Muhammad Ali, *The Holy Qur'an* (Columbus, OH: Ahmadiyyah Anjuman Isha'at Islam, 1995), 399, n. 1069.
[20] Khatib al-Tabrizi, *Mishkat al-Masabih*, 2:40.

But the Qur'an does not provide specific criteria for identifying or differ-entiating between the *fuqara'* and the *masakin*. That task was left to the early Qur'anic exegetes, who explicated Qur'anic terms, and the classical legists, who elaborated the laws governing the collection and distribution of *zakat*. Most scholars agreed that the distinction lay in the severity of poverty or in the relative capacity to ameliorate their condition, but there was little agree-ment on whether the *fuqara'* or the *masakin* were the more impoverished or incapacitated.[21] Some suggested that *fuqara'* were the "hidden poor," those who stoically and silently bore their poverty (see Q. 2:273), whereas *masakin* were the "open poor" because they resorted to begging.[22] Ultimately, the exact distinction between the two was considered largely irrelevant because Q. 9:60 clearly indicates that both categories are entitled to *zakat*. The more important concern then was to define the criteria separating the poor and needy from the rich (*aghniya'*), those who qualify for *zakat* versus those who pay *zakat*. This issue in turn yielded a large, complex, and inconsistent body of rulings.

Classical jurists divided into two camps, broadly speaking, on how to define the rich versus the poor. The first group, identified principally with the Hanafi school of law, favored an approach based on identifying and act-ing on some absolute measure of poverty. The poverty threshold was defined by ownership of property up to a certain limit, termed the *nisab*. According to juristic tradition, the *nisab* was, in most cases, fixed for different types of property by the Prophet himself.[23] Thus, the jurists generally agreed that the *nisab* for livestock was five camels, forty sheep, thirty cows, and so on. *Nisab* levels were similarly fixed for other types of "apparent wealth," such as land and agricultural produce. For "hidden wealth," in which were grouped such assets as money, jewelry, and commercial goods, the *nisab* was set at 20 dinars (equivalent roughly to 85 grams) of gold and 200 dirhams (approximately 595 grams) of silver. According to the Hanafi school, if a person owned any of these assets in amounts equal to or greater than the *nisab* for a full lunar year – after providing for his and his dependents' basic needs of food, shelter, and clothing – he was considered wealthy (*ghani*, sing. of *aghniya'*) and was liable to pay *zakat* upon the surplus wealth. Such an individual could not be

[21] Ibn Rushd, *Bidayat al-Mujtahid (The Distinguished Jurists' Primer)*, 2 vols., trans. Imran Ahsan Khan Nyazee (Reading, UK: Garnet Publishing, 1994), 1:322; Yusuf al-Qardawi, *Fiqh az-Zakat: A Comparative Study*, trans. Monzer Kahf (London: Dar al-Taqwa, 1999), 344; Ingrid Mattson, "Status-Based Definitions of Need in Early Islamic *Zakat* and Maintenance Laws," in *Poverty and Charity in Middle Eastern Contexts*, ed. Michael Bonner, Mine Ener, and Amy Singer (Albany: State University of New York Press, 2003), 31–52.
[22] Abu 'Ubayd ibn Sallam, *Kitab al-Amwal (The Book of Revenue)*, trans. Imran Ahsan Khan Nyazee (Reading, UK: Garnet Publishing, 2002), 548; Al-Qardawi, *Fiqh az-Zakat*, 343–44; Michael Bonner, "Poverty and Economics in the Qur'an," *Journal of Interdisciplinary History* 35, no. 3 (Winter 2005): 399.
[23] See Khatib al-Tabrizi, *Mishkat al-Masabih*, 2:47–56.

considered poor or needy and, therefore, could not receive *zakat*. Otherwise, the Hanafis reasoned, an individual might find himself both paying *zakat* and receiving it, violating the Prophet's instruction that *zakat* be taken from the rich and given to the poor.[24]

The second group, consisting of the other three schools of Sunni jurisprudence – namely, the Malikis, Shafi'is, and Hanbalis – as well as the Ja'fari school of Twelver Shi'ism, applied a needs test rather than a property test to determine whether a person was poor or rich. In the early juristic sources, "needs" (*hajat*) were never systematically or consistently defined. The jurists agreed that no person should be allowed to go hungry or naked, but beyond this, necessities seem to have been defined on a sliding scale, with some scholars defining them narrowly as what is needed to sustain life and others understanding them more expansively to include the requirements of an individual's social class or accustomed way of living. Whereas the Hanafi approach disqualified people from receiving *zakat* if they owned the *nisab* beyond meeting their needs, the other schools did not apply any strict limit to the wealth a needy person could own. As al-Shafi'i (d. 820) is reported to have said: "Judging by money alone is not fair, because a person may be considered rich, when, in fact, his wealth and earnings are below what is needed for his personal and family expenses."[25] In effect, the majority favored an approach based on relative rather than absolute notions of poverty.

The Shafi'is and Hanbalis held that anyone possessing at least half the wealth sufficient for him and his dependents when the *zakat* was collected could not be considered poor and was thus ineligible to receive *zakat*. The author of *'Umdat al-Salik* (The reliance of the traveler), a compendium of Shafi'i jurisprudence, elaborates that

what [the poor person] has is insufficient to sustain him to the end of his probable life expectancy if it were distributed over the probable amount of remaining time; *insufficient* meaning it is less than half of what he needs. If he requires ten dirhams a day, for example, but the amount he has when divided by the time left in his probable life expectancy is four dirhams a day or less, not paying for his food, clothing, housing, and whatever he cannot do without, to a degree suitable to someone of his standing without extravagance or penury, then he is *poor* – all of which applies as well to the needs of those he must support.[26]

The Malikis and Ja'faris suggested that the relevant criterion was whether or not an individual possessed enough wealth to satisfy his and his dependents' needs for an entire year. In both cases, however, the definition of need was

---

[24] Ibn Rushd, *Bidayat al-Mujtahid*, 1:321; *The Hedaya: A Commentary on the Mussulman Laws*, 2 vols., trans. Charles Hamilton (New Delhi: Kitab Bhavan, 1985), 1:60–61; Mattson, "Status-Based Definitions of Need," 35–36.

[25] Al-Qardawi, *Fiqh az-Zakat*, 349.

[26] Ahmad ibn Naqib al-Misri, *'Umdat al-Salik (The Reliance of the Traveller)*, ed. and trans. Noah Ha Mim Keller (Evanston, IL: Sunna Books, 1991), 267 (emphasis in original).

on a case-by-case basis and could embrace those who possessed assets well beyond the *nisab* but still fell short of meeting their particular requirements during any given year. Conversely, it could exclude from the list of *zakat* recipients those who did not possess the *nisab* for any asset yet earned enough to satisfy their specific needs. As a result of this approach, the same individual could be both a recipient and a payer of *zakat*, or neither a payer nor a recipient, because the criteria for determining the payment and the receipt of *zakat* were separate.

The early jurists also dealt at some length with the issue of the deserving versus undeserving poor. On the basis of numerous *hadiths*, the majority held that *zakat* should not be distributed to any person who is physically fit but chooses not to work when suitable employment is available. As clarified in *'Umdat al-Salik*, "suitable" employment means work befitting a person's physical capabilities, temperament, and social standing: "If ... an individual were an important personage unaccustomed to earning a living by physical labor, he would be considered 'poor.'"[27] The Hanafis again are an exception in arguing that it is permissible to give *zakat* to an individual who chooses not to work though suitable employment is available, but, they add, in accepting charity, the able-bodied person commits sin.[28] The legists agreed that penury resulting from monasticism or complete devotion to religious pursuits did not warrant payment of *zakat*. Yet, students devoted to the study of Islam did deserve support from the *zakat* funds. Some scholars added the caveat that only outstanding students who could be expected to benefit society through their learning should be eligible.[29]

The jurists disagreed as well regarding the distribution of *zakat* to poor non-Muslims. The majority held that because *zakat* was collected from Muslims only, only Muslims should be its recipients.[30] Dissenters pointed to the general language of Q. 9:60, which states simply that *zakat* is for the poor and needy without reference to faith, and to records of the Prophet and the rightly guided caliphs distributing state funds to a few non-Muslim poor. Muslim writers today seem generally to have embraced the minority position. The influential Egyptian jurist Yusuf al-Qaradawi writes that poor Muslims receive priority for *zakat*, but nothing bars non-Muslims from receiving it if the needs of Muslims have been met. Moreover, Qaradawi notes, the restrictions on aid to non-Muslim poor placed by classical jurists applied only to *zakat*; no bars were placed on other forms of individual charity or state assistance.[31]

[27] Ibid.
[28] Al-Qaradawi, *Fiqh az-Zakat*, 350–51.
[29] Al-Misri, *'Umdat al-Salik*, 268; al-Qaradawi, *Fiqh az-Zakat*, 353.
[30] Ibn Rushd, *Bidayat al-Mujtahid*, 1:329, claims that Muslim jurists unanimously agree that *zakat* cannot be paid to non-Muslims.
[31] Al-Qaradawi, *Fiqh az-Zakat*, 448–52; see also Afzal ur-Rahman, *Economic Doctrines of Islam*, 4 vols. (Lahore: Islamic Publications, 1995), 3:235–36.

In theory, the collection and distribution of *zakat* was in the hands of administrators appointed by the state. Accordingly, on an individual or family level, the determination of poverty or wealth lay in the hands of these officials. The rule, based on Prophetic *hadiths*, was that the declaration of wealth or poverty was largely a matter of individual conscience, and that the *zakat* official should err on the side of generosity in judging someone poor or not. In *Ahkam al-Sultaniyya* (Ordinances of government), al-Mawardi (d. 1058) writes that the collector could "chastise" someone caught paying less than his due, but he does not elaborate further. In determining the *zakat* owed, the collector could assess only "apparent" wealth; he was required to accept the word of the payee regarding "hidden" wealth. "If the official errs in dividing the alms, giving it to those who are not entitled to it, he is not held responsible for distributing it to those who disguise their wealth."[32]

Al-Mawardi later assigns the task of dealing with the undeserving poor to another functionary, the *muhtasib*, or market supervisor. "If he sees signs of wealth on [someone] even though he asks people for charity, he should inform him that it is forbidden to the person who does not need it, without objecting to his conduct in case he is poor in reality. If the beggar is strong and able to work, he should rebuke him and order him to practice a trade; if he persists in begging, he should punish him until he gives that up." But this is the limit of the *muhtasib's* authority in such cases, al-Mawardi concludes. Any further action against the indolent and undeserving beggar requires the intervention of higher authorities.[33]

In practice, the role of Muslim states in collecting and disbursing *zakat* seems to have diminished after the ninth century. Compliance with the *zakat* requirement of Islamic faith, as with the broader moral obligation of charity, became largely an act of individual piety. Community leaders such as the local imam or village headman and institutions such as the mosque or Sufi orders assumed the function of intermediaries between rich and poor. As a result, what had always been a rather informal system for determining who was poor and needy became even more so. Local communities decided who in their midst did or did not deserve aid.[34] This situation remains largely unchanged today, even among those Muslim states where *zakat* has been officially revived as a government function. Although a centralized bureaucracy exists in many of these countries to collect and disburse *zakat*, local *zakat* committees effectively decide who gets relief. Faced with large numbers of obvious poor who depend on such aid for bare subsistence, local officials can have little use for

---

[32] 'Ali ibn Muhammad al-Mawardi, *al-Ahkam al-Sultaniyya wa'l-Wilayat al-Diniyya (The Ordinances of Government)*, trans. Wafaa H. Wahba (Reading, UK: Garnet Publishing, 1996), 139.

[33] Ibid., 269.

[34] See, for example, the studies of local institutions and practices in Bonner et al., *Poverty and Charity in Middle Eastern Contexts*.

the recondite debates of the classical jurists. Yet, even in the large body of writings by modern Muslim jurists and economists, clear – let alone new or distinct – definitions of poverty in an Islamic framework are scarce.[35]

Modern Muslim jurists and economists have also demonstrated a reluctance to tackle the prominence of women among the poorest in Muslim societies.[36] This is the result, no doubt, of the generally conservative approach of Muslim scholars, whether they are jurists or economists, to gender-related issues. The literature in Islamic economics largely rehearses the provisions made in Islamic law and morality to establish the financial independence and security of women. These measures were indeed far-reaching in their social implications and represented significant advances for women's status, not just in comparison with pre-Islamic Arabian society, but with most premodern societies as well. The Qur'an secures property rights for women (Q. 4:7), and all schools of Islamic law agreed that a woman's property is exclusively her own. Before a woman marries, she is entitled through her guardian to demand of her future husband a dower (*mahr* or *sadaq*) that when paid becomes her own property. On the basis of Qur'anic verses (Q. 2:236–37; 4:4, 19–21, 25) and a number of *hadiths*, Islamic law prohibits the husband from claiming any portion of this dower during marriage or in the event of divorce following the consummation of marriage.[37] While married, a woman is entitled to full maintenance (*nafaqa*) for herself and her children from her husband. Most jurists defined maintenance not just as the provision of basic necessities but a standard of living commensurate with the one she had enjoyed before marriage.[38] The husband can make no claims upon his wife's wealth, even if it is

[35] In general, Muslim jurists today tend to repeat uncritically definitions of poverty provided by classical jurists more than a millennium ago. See, for example, al-Qardawi, *Fiqh az-Zakat*, 343–65. Muslim economists tend to rely on measurements of poverty current in the international development literature. For example, a lengthy recent study titled *Islamic Economic Institutions and the Elimination of Poverty*, ed. Munawar Iqbal (Leicester, UK: Islamic Foundation, 2002), contains a number of chapters drawing on World Bank and UN indices, but with little discussion of how these relate to early Islamic definitions of poverty.

[36] Poverty statistics for countries rarely disaggregate numbers according to gender, and this makes accurate conclusions about the percentage of female versus male poor difficult. There are, however, a number of indicators that do confirm the greater incidence of female poverty in Muslim countries, such as the number of female-led households below the poverty line and female life expectancy, illiteracy, education, and average income. The Gender-related Development Index (GDI) produced by the UN Development Program provides a useful measure of gender inequalities by factoring in gender differences in life expectancy, education, and income. In the GDI figures for 2005, released as part of the *Human Development Report, 2007/2008*, only five Muslim-majority countries – all small, oil-rich principalities – ranked in the top fifty most developed, that is, having low levels of gender inequality. See http://hdrstats.undp.org/indicators/268.html (December 11, 2008).

[37] Ibn Rushd, *Bidayat al-Mujtahid*, 2:20–36; al-Misri, *'Umdat al-Salik*, 533–35; *Hedaya*, 1:122–57.

[38] John Esposito and Natana J. Delong-Bas, *Women in Muslim Family Law*, 2nd ed. (Syracuse: Syracuse University Press, 2001), 23–26; Mattson, "Status-Based Definitions of Need," 44–47.

considerable, to pay for family expenses. Indeed, according to the majority of scholars, a man cannot pay any portion of his *zakat* to his wife, children, elderly parents or any other person for whom he is obliged to provide maintenance. A wealthy woman, however, may disburse *zakat* to her needy husband, children, or other family members because she is under no obligation to support them financially.[39]

These legal provisions did make it possible for women in many Islamic societies to avoid material hardship and in some cases to amass considerable fortunes. Records of philanthropic endowments (*waqf*) – including mosques, schools, hospitals, hospices, and public fountains – as well as registers of landed property attest to the presence of wealthy women throughout Islamic history. But these same records indicate that women became philanthropists or proprietors of estates largely through gift or inheritance from males. Societal conventions did not permit them to be actively engaged publicly as entrepreneurs or investors except on the lowest of levels or through male agents. Moreover, the documentary evidence suggests that women, especially widows, divorcées, and orphans, were always disproportionately represented among the recipients of charity and public support.[40] Today, abandoned women, divorcées, and widows with dependent children remain consistently the most common recipients of *zakat* funds.[41]

Women's poverty is, in many cases, the result of societal customs that are ascribed to Islam but in fact have little grounding in religion or are direct contraventions of *shari'a* stipulations. Women are the poorest Muslims because in many countries they receive less education than men, and adult illiteracy rates for women far outpace those for men, in spite of Islamic injunctions that both men and women should be educated. As a result, women are consigned to low-paying jobs, if they receive any income at all.[42] In many cultures, the dower that is a woman's right is paid instead to her father or other male guardian, or it is not paid at all during the marriage, forcing the woman to claim it in court upon divorce or the death of her husband. Women's share of inheritance and other property rights are often not respected by societal conventions or by local courts.

But women's poverty in Muslim societies is also the result of conservative and misogynistic interpretations of ambiguous Qur'anic verses or various Prophetic *hadiths*. A particularly controversial Qur'anic passage states: "Men are guardians [*qawwamun*] of women because God has

[39] Ibn Sallam, *Kitab al-Amwal*, 532–36; al-Qardawi, *Fiqh az-Zakat*, 457–58.
[40] Leila Ahmed, *Women and Gender in Islam* (New Haven: Yale University Press, 1992), 102–12.
[41] See, for example, Grace Clark, "Pakistan's Zakat and Ushr System from 1979 to 1999," in *Pakistan 2000*, ed. Charles H. Kennedy and Craig Baxter (Lanham, MD: Lexington Books, 2000), 153.
[42] For data on women's education, illiteracy, and percentage in the workforce, see UN Department of Economic and Social Affairs, *The World's Women, 2005: Progress in Statistics* (New York: UN Publishing Section, 2006).

favored some more than others and because they spend out of their wealth. Therefore, the righteous women are obedient [*qanitat*], guarding in the unseen that which God has guarded" (Q. 4:34). This verse raises a number of difficult interpretive issues centering on the terms *qawwamun* and *qanitat*. Because of its context, the verse has commonly been viewed as pertaining to the mutual rights and obligations of husbands and wives. Classical commentators understood the verse as prescribing the role of "guardian" or "provider" to the husband because God made men superior to women and because men are enjoined to provide materially for their wives and children. So long as the husband fulfills his function as breadwinner, the wife must obey him in all Islamically lawful requests and should focus on her role as mother and homemaker. This reading of the verse is still widely embraced by conservative commentators and jurists. Q. 4:34 thus provides today, as it has throughout Islamic history, a key religious justification for the exclusion of women from the workplace and from public life in general. More broadly, it has been used to cultivate a culture that views women as mentally and physically inferior to men and as wards of men throughout the course of their lives.

Such an ethos may prevent large numbers of Muslim women from suffering the privations of poverty because they are adequately provided for by husbands or male kin, but it has proved inadequate for too many women in the past and in the present. Q. 4:34 has, accordingly, been at the center of a new, feminist Qur'anic exegesis that seeks, among other things, to improve the material situation of Muslim women.[43] The gist of this commentary is that this verse and the Qur'an as a whole does not countenance any innate male superiority to women. Men are *qawwamun* over women only insofar as they financially provide for them. There is no Islamic bar to women providing financially for their husbands or families (as indeed the Prophet's first wife, Khadija, did when they were married). If they do so, logically they would be *qawwamun* over their husbands. Or if the couple agrees to share financial responsibilities for their families, then both husband and wife jointly and equally assume the role of guardian or maintainer. In short, the Muslim feminists' reading of Q. 4:34 challenges traditional, patriarchical notions of gender relations that perpetuate the structural poverty that traps many Muslim women. Rereading this verse is an important first step in altering deeply ingrained and religiously justified societal mores. But other *shari'a* stipulations must also be addressed if women's poverty is to be truly alleviated.

---

[43] See in particular Amina Wadud, *Qur'an and Woman: Rereading the Sacred Text from a Woman's Perspective* (New York: Oxford University Press, 1999), 69–74; Asma Barlas, *"Believing Women" in Islam* (Austin: University of Texas Press, 2002), 186–87; Kecia Ali, *Sexual Ethics and Islam: Feminist Reflections on Qur'an, Hadith, and Jurisprudence* (Oxford: Oneworld, 2006), 117–20.

How to Alleviate Poverty?

If in Islamic ethics, as asserted earlier, no individual is predestined by God or by fate to be trapped in unending poverty, then neither is any society of human beings. Just as poverty and wealth are results in part of individual choices, so also are they results of societal choices. As the favorite Qur'anic verse of Muslim reformers states: "God does not change the condition of a people until they change themselves" (Q. 13:11). Islamic morality and law accordingly call for a range of measures to combat poverty. They include voluntary as well as obligatory measures. Individual Muslims as well as societies and states bear the responsibility.

Sadaqa is the general term used by contemporary Muslims for the wide range of voluntary (or, more accurately, supererogatory) charity, in distinction to *zakat*, the obligatory alms tax. In early Islamic usage, however, the distinction was blurred. As observed earlier, the Qur'an itself uses the term *sadaqat* in the key verse generally understood as dealing with *zakat*, Q. 9:60. Other instances of *sadaqat* in the Qur'an are ambiguous (e.g., Q. 2:271), as indeed are certain verses containing *zakat* (e.g., Q. 5:55, 33:39), at least according to some commentators.[44] The same interchangeability in terms is observed in the *hadith* literature. Al-Mawardi states flatly that "the two terms *sadaqa* and *zakat* are synonyms for one and the same thing."[45] Yet the Qur'an does use *sadaqa* and *zakat* together in Q. 58:13 in a way that distinguishes voluntary charity from *zakat* (see also Q. 2:177). This ambiguity of usage in the Qur'an and *hadith* may be satisfactorily resolved, as some classical writers suggested, by accepting *sadaqa* as the broader term for all charity, one encompassing a particular type, *zakat*.

What is unambiguous in the Qur'an and *hadith* is that voluntary acts of charity bring the giver closer to God and expiate sins; they are thus intrinsic to Muslim piety. "Every Muslim has to give in charity," the Prophet declares in a well-known *hadith*.

The people asked, "O Messenger of God! If someone has nothing to give, what should he do?" He said, "He should work with his hands and benefit himself and also give in charity (from what he earns)." The people further asked, "If he cannot find even that?" He replied, "He should help the needy who appeal for help." Then the people asked, "If he cannot do that?" He replied, "Then he should perform good deeds and keep way from the evil deeds and this will be regarded as charitable deeds."[46]

Furthermore, the Qur'an and *hadith* provide general guidelines on such questions as who is most entitled to an individual's charity, how charity ought

---

44 T. H. Weir and Aron Zysow, "Sadaka," in *Encyclopaedia of Islam*, 2nd ed. (Leiden: Brill, 1995), 8:709.
45 Al-Mawardi, *al-Ahkam al-Sultaniyya*, 127.
46 Al-Bukhari, *Sahih al-Bukhari*, 9 vols., trans. Muhammad Mushin Khan (Beirut: Dar al-Arabia, 1985), 2:301.

to be disbursed, and how much of one's wealth should be expended in charitable pursuits. Giving to the "near poor" is more meritorious than giving to the "far poor," that is, one's needy kinfolk (apart from dependents who have a prior claim to maintenance) should be the first beneficiaries, followed by close neighbors, then the Muslims of one's town, and so on. Charity is to be given in humility, with no expectation of benefit or gain to the giver except for God's favor (Q. 2:262–64). According to Q. 2:271, giving charity in secret – so that "the right hand does not know what the left hand has given," as related in one *hadith* – is preferable to giving it openly.[47] With regard to how much should be given, the Qur'an lauds the unbridled generosity of some Medinans who welcomed and supported the Meccan immigrants "even though they themselves were in dire need" (Q. 59:9), while also enjoining moderation: "Do not tie your hand to your neck [in miserliness], nor stretch it out to its utmost reach, so that you become blameworthy and destitute" (Q. 17:29; see also 6:141, 25:67, 17:26). These verses led to disagreement among classical jurists on whether any maximum limits should be applied to *sadaqa*. Because the hagiographical literature on the Prophet, his wives, and his closest companions emphasized their unsparing generosity, so much so in the case of Muhammad that he is said to have left no property to his heirs, the jurists generally held that *sadaqa* could be unlimited. The important reservation was that the giver first fulfill all obligations to himself and his dependents, so that in giving charity he and his family should not themselves join the ranks of those deserving it.

Over the course of Islamic history, one of the most common and effective means of dispensing charity to the poor has been through the institution of charitable trusts (*waqf*, pl. *awqaf*) by the wealthy. The *waqf* finds no direct roots in the Qur'an or *hadith*, but it appears to have emerged within the first Islamic century as a way of fulfilling the charitable requirements of Islamic faith and perhaps other, less pious motives as well, such as prestige, providing a steady means of income to one's descendants, and circumventing inheritance laws.[48] Any Muslim could endow a *waqf* by designating a source of revenue to be used for some public good in perpetuity. Thus, landed property was frequently set aside as a *waqf* for the building and upkeep of some charitable institution and to provide the income of people hired (which could include the donor's relatives) to supervise it. Through *awqaf*, the poor might be fed in public kitchens, the thirsty provided clean drinking water in public fountains, needy children educated in mosque schools, and the sick treated in hospitals. A particularly successful *waqf* could draw further endowments from subsequent donors so that not only was its life extended but its services were also diversified. A few institutions did survive for centuries, but most *awqaf* rarely

---

[47] Ibid., 2:287.
[48] See Amy Singer, "Charity's Legacies: Reconsideration of Ottoman Imperial Endowment-Making," in Bonner et al., *Poverty and Charity in Middle Eastern Contexts*, 295–313.

survived one or two generations beyond their founders, often falling prey to confiscation by rulers or the venality of those designated to maintain them.

In 1826 the Ottoman state brought most *awqaf* under the jurisdiction of a central ministry in an effort to curb the abuse and excesses that had come to be associated with this institution. This process of nationalization and limitation of *awqaf* was replicated during the late nineteenth century by European colonial powers and in the early twentieth century as postcolonial Muslim states gained independence. In contemporary Muslim societies, *waqf* plays a much more limited role in poverty relief than in centuries past. Since the late 1960s, however, it has seen a revival of sorts as one aspect of the resurgence of religious identity and activism in most Muslim countries. Islamic movements spearheaded the establishment of *awqaf* such as mosques, schools, canteens, and medical clinics as part of their grass-roots mobilization efforts. Muslim states have responded with a range of policies. Debt-ridden states, such as Egypt or Pakistan, have tacitly, though warily, welcomed the assumption by nonstate actors of welfare obligations that they are unable or unwilling to assume. Most countries have navigated a middle course between complete privatization and total nationalization of these *awqaf* by legislating administrative regulations to prevent abuse in private foundations, as in the case of Turkey, or by creating GONGOs (government-organized nongovernmental organizations) to provide ongoing services or emergency relief, as in the case of Saudi Arabia.[49]

Apart from voluntary efforts to relieve poverty, the Islamic tradition contains an array of obligatory measures as well. Distributive justice in Islam is not simply a recommendation; it is a requirement of faith. The Qur'an describes the righteous as those who acknowledge that "in their wealth, the beggar and destitute have a right [*haqq*]" (Q. 51:19; see also 70:24). In order to ensure that wealth circulate not just among the rich (Q. 59:7), the Qur'an lays the basis for a number of institutions that were developed in the practice of the Prophet and his earliest successors, and later elaborated by the classical expositors of the *shari'a*. These include the laws of inheritance, the prohibition of usury, and, of course, *zakat*.

The Qur'anic injunctions regarding inheritance (*wiratha*) provide for a wide distribution of the deceased's estate. The beneficiaries for whom specific shares are stipulated in the Qur'an may be called the first-degree heirs; they include spouses, children, surviving parents, and siblings (see Q. 4:11–12, 176). Beyond these, jurists detailed the portions that more removed family members could claim: second-degree heirs include agnatic relatives, and third-degree heirs include extended female relatives.[50] Two aspects of the inheritance laws

[49] Jonathan Benthall and Jerome Bellion-Jourdan, *The Charitable Crescent: Politics of Aid in the Muslim World* (London: I. B. Tauris, 2003), 29–37; see also the detailed survey of contemporary practice in "Wakf," in *Encyclopaedia of Islam*, 2nd ed. (Leiden: Brill, 2002), 11:63–99.

[50] Afzal ur-Rahman, *Economic Doctrines of Islam*, 2:61–67.

reinforced the principle of maximum dispersal of an estate, particularly so that it might benefit the poor and needy in a community: First, every person has a right to will up to one-third of his estate to individuals not specified in the Qur'an, allowing for generosity to needy distant relatives, orphans, servants, or neighbors. Second, Q. 4:8 asks heirs to give some of their inheritance as charity to the poor and needy when they receive this unearned wealth.

Male and female beneficiaries are allocated specific shares, and the fact that the verses appear in the fourth chapter, al-Nisa' (The Women), indicates the importance laid on women's inheritance rights – a departure from pre-Islamic Arabian custom that bequeathed everything to male relatives. Certain Arab tribes, such as the Quraysh of Mecca, departed from the norm in allowing women to inherit; as Islamic sources tell us, the Prophet's first wife, Khadija, had acquired a considerable fortune through the skilled parlaying of her inheritance from two previous husbands into trade.[51] But it is unclear how formalized or widespread the practice of female inheritance was in Mecca. What the Qur'an does is precisely to formalize women's inheritance claims for all Muslims.

The general Qur'anic principle, based on Q. 4:11, is that females receive one-half the share of their male counterparts in the same level of kinship to the deceased (i.e., wife and husband, daughter and son, mother and father). This inequality has been explained by commentators with reference to the greater financial obligations upon men, who bear the sole responsibility for maintaining their wives, children, and elderly parents, especially their mothers. There is no commensurate financial obligation for women, so the inheritance they receive is entirely their own.[52] This explanation, and the Qur'anic principle of distribution, rely again on the idea that men will fulfill their obligations as providers (*qawwamun*) for their wives, daughters, and mothers. If they fail in this obligation, society will provide for them through the various social welfare provisions of Islamic law and morality. Yet, for Muslim feminists today, such guarantees are inadequate in both principle and practice. They criticize the inherent patriarchy underlying these provisions; they point out that in practice the discriminatory inheritance scheme is unfair to single women, divorcées, or widows, and especially so for those supporting children. Amina Wadud writes that the Qur'an lays down only two fundamental principles regarding inheritance: women should inherit, and shares should be distributed equitably. In her argument, the specific shares allotted are not fixed but are only possible combinations that can be reshuffled according to the overriding principle of fairness. "'Equity' in distribution ... must take the actual *naf'a* (benefit) of the bereft into consideration.... If in a family of a son

---

[51] See W. Montgomery Watt, *Muhammad at Medina* (Oxford: Oxford University Press, 1956), 290.

[52] See, for example, Sayyid Qutb, *In the Shade of the Qur'an*, trans. and ed. Adil Salahi and Ashur Shamis (Leicester, UK: Islamic Foundation, 2001), 3:51–52.

and two daughters, a widowed mother is cared for and supported by one of her daughters, why should the son receive a larger share?"[53]

The Qur'anic ban on usury (*riba*) is a second important means of preventing large concentrations of wealth. Q. 2:275 contrasts legitimate trade with usury and the following verse contrasts usury with charity, declaring that God will deprive the former of any growth while multiplying the benefits of the latter. Q. 3:130 expands upon the condemnation of usury found in these possibly earlier verses by outlawing it altogether: "O you who believe! Devour not usury, doubled and multiplied, but fear God that you may [truly] prosper." The ethical principle enunciated in the verses dealing with *riba* seems clear enough: lending money on interest to those in need violates the Qur'an's injunctions regarding charity for the destitute and the unimpeded circulation of wealth in society. Q. 2:280, without specifically mentioning *riba*, emphasizes to creditors an ethic of unbridled generosity: "If the debtor is in difficulty, grant him time until it is easy for him to repay. But if you remit it by way of charity, that is best for you, if you only knew."

Yet these verses also raise the complicated issue of what exactly the Qur'an is prohibiting as *riba*. This issue invariably looms large in the contemporary literature on Islamic economics, where no distinction is drawn between usury and interest, and thus the prohibition on *riba* translates into a ban on all forms of interest. Proponents of Islamic banking have therefore expended a great deal of time and energy in finding ways to make modern Islamic finance "*shari'a* compliant" while still being able to function in a global financial system that rests on interest-based transactions of all sorts. Their Muslim opponents argue that the Qur'anic *riba* is not interest in the modern commercial sense, but usury of an excessive sort that increased a debt exponentially when the debtor failed to repay the principal on time. Thus, the reform that the Qur'an was trying to implement was to liberate people from potentially a lifetime of debt and servitude to rapacious moneylenders.[54]

The debate is protracted, heated, and well beyond the confines of this chapter; what is germane to the present discussion are the claims made by both sides regarding the impact of usury or interest on Islam's distributive justice goals. Abu al-A'la Mawdudi (d. 1979), a seminal exponent of Islamic economics, writes that "usury [by which he means all interest] develops miserliness, selfishness, callousness, inhumanity and financial greed in the character of man.... It blocks the free circulation of wealth in the society, and diverts the flow of money from the poor to the rich."[55] Another prominent theorist, Afzal ur-Rahman, argues that "the abolition of interest is absolutely necessary to maintain the level of investment at a speed conducive to social welfare."[56]

[53] Wadud, *Qur'an and Woman*, 87–88.
[54] Fazlur Rahman, "*Riba* and Interest," *Islamic Studies* 3, no. 1 (March 1964): 6–7.
[55] Abu al-A'la Mawdudi, *Economic System of Islam* (Lahore: Islamic Publications, 1984), 165–66.
[56] Afzal ur-Rahman, *Economic Doctrines of Islam*, 3:118.

In an early critique of such views, Fazlur Rahman (d. 1988) writes that the "Welfare Cooperative Commonwealth" envisioned by the Qur'an would make interest and the present banking system "quite superfluous." But, he continues, when contemporary Muslim societies are so far removed from the ideals of the Islamic economic system, "it would be suicidal for the economic welfare of the society and the financial system of the country and would also be contrary to the spirit and intentions of the Qur'an and *Sunnah* to abolish bank interest."[57]

Islamic commercial banking began to develop in the mid-1970s, and today financial institutions offering alternatives to conventional interest may be found in some sixty countries. Initially, the Islamic alternatives offered were generally two types of profit-and-loss sharing known as *mudabara* and *musharaka*. Because these forms of finance involved uncertainty for the lender, a third alternative, *murabaha*, quickly supplanted the other two. Under such transactions, the bank takes possession of the goods that are being bought by the borrower and then "sells" them to the borrower on a deferred payment schedule – with a suitable markup for costs incurred in time and effort. The bank's possession could be for only a few seconds, and so to its critics *murabaha* is an interest-bearing transaction in all but name. Only Iran, Pakistan, and Sudan have outlawed conventional interest. In all other countries, Islamic finance competes with interest-based banking, and the results are clearly not in favor of Islamic banking. Not only are conventional banks flourishing in Muslim countries, but large American- and European-based institutions are thriving in both the Islamic and non-Islamic sectors by diversifying their offerings to include *shari'a*-compliant services for devout Muslim clients.[58]

Much of the debate on interest-free banking is irrelevant to the concerns and needs of the poorest Muslims. Their lives are rarely touched in a direct way by the availability of a bank providing *shari'a*-compliant services. For the poor, it is the lack of collateral as much as the prospect of paying interest that bars them from taking out loans. This is the problem addressed by micro-financial institutions (MFIs). Following a model developed in the 1970s by the Bangladeshi economist Muhammad Yunus and his Grameen Bank, MFIs lend money to the poor by replacing traditional collateral with compulsory savings during the term of the loan and group responsibility for loan repayment. Some limit or target their lending to women and impose restrictions on how the loaned money may be spent. Most MFIs in Muslim countries operate as secular institutions, and they do charge interest at rates generally higher than those of conventional banks but lower than what the poor would obtain from local moneylenders. Consequently, many countries have seen the emergence of Islamic MFIs, which operate in much the same way as other MFIs,

---

[57] Fazlur Rahman, *"Riba* and Interest," 41.
[58] Timur Kuran, *Islam and Mammon: The Economic Predicaments of Islamism* (Princeton, NJ: Princeton University Press, 2004), 7–19.

but instead of charging interest, they offer loans through *murabaha*. Thus, Islamic microfinance faces the same criticisms that are leveled against Islamic banks generally on the one hand and MFIs generally on the other, including claims that the impact of MFIs in poverty reduction is only slight and that they do little to remove their borrowers from a "debt trap."[59] Nevertheless, even though today they lag far behind their secular counterparts in numbers and capital, the Islamic MFIs show signs of gaining strength through greater investment and more professional management.

Finally, we come to *zakat*, arguably the primary instrument in Islamic ethics for poverty alleviation and distributive justice. As with the juridical criteria governing who owed *zakat* and who was entitled to receive it, the rates by which *zakat* was calculated and the rules for its disbursement were grounded in the *sunna* of the Prophet. According to *hadiths*, the Prophet had stipulated *zakat* rates for a wide range of goods, and these were meticulously tabulated by the classical jurists. All legal schools held that gold and silver are taxed at the rate of 2.5 percent. The rates for livestock are enumerated according to the type and number of animal; for example, the *zakat* on up to twenty-five camels is one sheep for every five camels, and then a female camel between one and two years old for twenty-five to thirty-five camels, a female camel between two and three years old for thirty-six to forty-five camels, and so on. Agriculture is taxed at the rate of 10 percent for land that is naturally watered and 5 percent for land that requires irrigation.[60]

As discussed earlier, the classical jurists differed on the criteria defining rich and poor, and these disagreements reverberate in their contending views on the goals of *zakat* disbursement. The Hanafis generally held that *zakat* payments be made to the poor so that they reach the *nisab*; thus, the Hanafis fixed the maximum payment to any individual at two hundred dirhams of silver or its equivalent. The other schools of law applied a more flexible approach based on their needs-based measure of poverty. The Shafi'is and some Hanbalis held that the goal of *zakat* is to remove permanently, whenever possible, the recipient from poverty. As the second caliph, 'Umar ibn al-Khattab, is said to have ordered: "When you give to them, make them wealthy."[61] The Malikis and most Hanbalis argued that *zakat* be paid so that the needs of the poor are met for one full year. These last two opinions need not be mutually exclusive, as Yusuf al-Qaradawi writes. Giving craftsmen, farmers, and others the means to earn their own living for a year will, it may reasonably be hoped, make them self-sufficient thereafter. Those who are physically incapable of

---

[59] For a debate on the efficacy of MFIs in Bangladesh, see M. Kabir Hassan and Dewan A. H. Alamgir, "Microfinancial Services and Poverty Alleviation in Bangladesh: A Comparative Analysis of Secular and Islamic NGOs," and comments by Abulhasan M. Sadeq in Iqbal, *Islamic Economic Institutions and the Elimination of Poverty*, 113–86.

[60] Ibn Rushd, *Bidayat al-Mujtahid*, 1:295–313; al-Qardawi, *Fiqh az-Zakat*, 64–338.

[61] Ibn Sallam, *Kitab al-Amwal*, 515.

supporting themselves or their families will require indefinite support, which could be disbursed through annual or other regular payments.[62]

As in many other areas of Islamic law, the legal provisions regarding *zakat* were never fully implemented in practice. The third caliph, 'Uthman ibn Affan (r. 644–56), made a significant change in *zakat* collection when he decreed that state collectors should tax only "apparent" wealth; the wealthy were left free to calculate and pay *zakat* on "hidden" wealth either to the state or directly to needy recipients. As a result, *zakat* in the following centuries became largely a tax on agricultural lands and produce.[63]

'Uthman's revision of earlier practice may have resulted from growing popular discontent with rapacious and corrupt tax collectors. Indeed, under Umayyad and Abbasid rule, the number of Sunni jurists who accepted that some or all *zakat* be paid directly by the rich to the poor progressively grew. In the Ja'fari school of Shi'ism, the collection of *zakat* was considered the prerogative of the imam, but with the disappearance of the Twelfth Imam in 874, this along with all other functions of the imam was considered to have lapsed, and the individual Shi'a was left free to pay *zakat* privately or to an agent of his own choosing. Over the following centuries, as Twelver Shi'a ulema began to assert their role as agents of the Hidden Imam, they claimed the responsibility to receive and dispense *zakat* in Shi'a communities while also accepting the legitimacy of private payments.[64] The result of these developments was historically to limit the impact of *zakat* on poverty alleviation; *awqaf* and other forms of voluntary charity (*sadaqa*) became the principal and most effective means for aiding the poor.[65]

Beginning in the late nineteenth century, a reexamination of *zakat* was undertaken by Muslim reformers in a number of countries as part of their efforts to reconceptualize Islamic institutions and thereby revitalize Muslim societies. These efforts were invigorated by the advent of Islamic economics, in which *zakat* invariably figures prominently in conceptualizations of the Islamic economic system. Pressure from Islamic movements played a major role in the institutionalization of *zakat* as a state function in a number of Muslim countries, including Saudi Arabia, Libya, Yemen, Malaysia, Pakistan, and Sudan. Even in Muslim countries where *zakat* is not officially assessed, the collection and distribution of *zakat* funds is a quasi-state function because it is performed by *zakat* committees attached to local mosques, which are under the supervision of a central government ministry. Large amounts of money are also collected annually by Muslim charities based in Europe and

[62] Al-Qardawi, *Fiqh az-Zakat*, 360–61.
[63] Aron Zysow, "Zakat," in *Encyclopaedia of Islam*, 2nd ed. (Leiden: Brill, 2002), 11:409; Timur Kuran, "Islamic Redistribution through *Zakat*: Historical Record and Modern Realities," in Bonner et al., *Poverty and Charity in Middle Eastern Contexts*, 277.
[64] Moojan Momen, *An Introduction to Shi'i Islam* (New Haven: Yale University Press, 1985), 77, 189, 207, 298.
[65] Kuran, "Islamic Redistribution through *Zakat*," 281–82.

North America. At least a half-dozen organizations in the United States accept *zakat* payments, including the Islamic Society of North America, the largest Muslim organization in the country. Many organizations now provide convenient on-line calculators for assessing the *zakat* due on one's assets and electronic payments through the Internet.

Yet, despite the renewed interest in *zakat* and the fulfillment of this obligation by millions of Muslims, the evidence indicates that it has had no appreciable impact on reducing poverty in the contemporary Muslim world. The reasons are familiar: confusion and inconsistency in assessing *zakat*, evasion in paying it, and corruption and inefficiency in distributing the proceeds. The search for solutions by Muslim intellectuals and activists has yielded, characteristically, widely divergent and contested proposals.[66] All recognize that reform is needed. The conservative approach argues that the rules governing *zakat* are fixed and cannot be changed; it is reform of the individual, society, and state that is necessary for the Islamic system to work. The modernist approach emphasizes the need for reform of *zakat* itself; an institution developed fourteen centuries ago for a mercantile and agricultural economy requires rethinking for an industrial and postindustrial age. If *zakat* is indeed to function as the primary Islamic institution for redressing poverty, the way forward, it seems to me, requires a combination of both approaches.

---

[66] See Kuran, "Islamic Redistribution through *Zakat*," 284–89; Mawdudi, *Economic System of Islam*, 216–77, 295–310; al-Qardawi, *Fiqh az-Zakat*, 331–38; Sayyid Qutb, *Social Justice in Islam*, trans. John Hardie and Hamid Algar (Oneonta, NY: Islamic Publications International, 2000), 303–5; Zysow, "Zakat," 419–20.

IO

Jewish Perspectives on Poverty

Noam Zohar

Judaism is a religious tradition focused on a particular people; hence, I report on some practices and institutions of Jewish communities. But the communities were inspired and guided by the covenantal tradition – by allegiance to the Torah (Instruction), seen as God's revealed words. Thus, my exposition consists by and large in describing and analyzing teachings of the Torah. When at certain points I trace the application of these teachings in Jewish life, this is only to illuminate a norm or an ideal; I am not attempting to produce a history of such applications.

Jewish religion is grounded in Scripture, that is, in the twenty-four books of the Hebrew Bible. But the foundational work of Rabbinic Judaism is the Mishnah (compiled in the Galilee, evidently as an orally recited text, c. 200 CE). While some of its clauses closely follow biblical law (at times, with bold modifications), others contain numerous independent teachings. The Rabbis recognized this duality of core texts and emphasized that the "Written Torah" must be joined with the "Oral Torah." The latter contains not only the Mishnah but also accompanying works, including collections of *midrash* – detailed and often free-flowing biblical interpretations and commentaries. The classical Rabbinic tradition culminates in the twenty-volume Babylonian Talmud. Here each clause of the Mishnah is explored in detail, and reasons are provided for the different opinions in myriad arguments (mostly left unresolved). Following the Mishnah, the bulk of the Talmud is dedicated to normative discourse, called *halakhah*; but about a third of it is devoted to *aggadah*: stories, lore, homilies and more.

Thus, in order to discuss a topic from the perspective of the Jewish tradition, it is often helpful to trace a kind of narrative, beginning with the foundational "five books of Moses" (the Pentateuch), which contain biblical law (but also much else) and with the other parts of Scripture: The Prophets and the Writings (the latter include, inter alia, the Psalms and Proverbs). Thence one may proceed to Rabbinic literature (described in the previous paragraph) and beyond that to post-talmudic Judaism. In the Middle Ages and down to early modern times, Judaism had become markedly decentralized; its adherents lived in dispersed, mostly urban Jewish communities, each enjoying some degree of autonomy in relation to the surrounding polity. Across these communities, a shared allegiance to the Talmud[1] was accompanied by a pluralism of interpretations and local practices. The communities were connected in a loose but comprehensive cultural network, sustained by constant literary intercourse. Thus, for example, the halakhic code of Maimonides (twelfth century), the Mishneh Torah, quickly gained broad influence, even if its authority was rarely accepted without reservations.

The Jewish community normally exercised coercive authority over its members, but it is important to recognize that not all halakhic norms were seen as warranting coercion. Many sections of *halakhah* pertain to personal morality and ritual observance; in most such matters, individual Jews were deemed accountable only before God's "heavenly court." In the realms of both private and public law – notably including taxation – halakhic norms were enforced by rabbinic and communal courts.

The political changes of the eighteenth and nineteenth centuries brought an end to the political authority of halakhic law, as Jews came to be formally emancipated as citizens in modern states. Adherence to traditional teachings among contemporary Jews is thus a matter of personal commitment, and varies greatly among Jewish individuals and denominations. The state of Israel is a basically secular democracy, and Jewish religious strictures formally have no claim to power; still, they affect Israel's laws and social practices by informing the majority culture and public discourse.

Definitions and Volition: Poverty, Suffering, and Virtue

The word *'oni*, which in modern Hebrew denotes "poverty" as a social phenomenon (and the condition of the people trapped within it), carries a different meaning in the Hebrew Bible. There it means "suffering" or "misery," specifically that produced by causes other than indigence, such as childlessness or oppression.[2] A word formed from the same root, as a verb in the strong transitive construction (*'innah*), means "to torture" or "to oppress," used, for example, in the story of Pharaoh and the Israelites in Egypt (Exod. 1:11–12).

Strikingly, however, the cognate adjective-noun *'ani* – also formed from the same root (and written with the same letters, distinguished from *'oni* only by the vocalization) – specifically denotes the indigent in all of its appearances in

[1] This allegiance was not shared by the Karaites, a group with sometimes broad membership who came to be defined as a deviant sect by the eventually dominant Rabbanites. See Michael Walzer et al., eds., *The Jewish Political Tradition*, vol. 1: *Authority* (New Haven: Yale University Press 2000), 344–55; vol. 2: *Membership* (New Haven: Yale University Press 2003), 344–59.
[2] The King James Version and its cognates consistently translate the word as "affliction" in its eight appearances in the Pentateuch; other translations vary.

the Pentateuch. Such a denotation for a word whose literal meaning is something like "miserable" clearly reflects a recognition that indigence is a primary cause of misery.

In later biblical books, however – especially Psalms and Isaiah – *'ani* commonly means one who is in a markedly hapless condition, such as a victim of illness or of injustice, often juxtaposed with his evil oppressors. The psalmist sometimes calls himself *'ani* and invokes God's help against his enemies. In the last chapter of Isaiah, God says: "Yet to such a one I look: to the poor and brokenhearted, who is concerned about My word" (66:2); the same term is employed in comforting the Israelite collective: "Unhappy,[3] storm-tossed one, uncomforted!" (54:11).

Although such usage is found especially in this later stratum of the biblical literature, it echoes classical promises of divine help for the vulnerable, for example: "You shall not abuse a poor and destitute laborer, whether a fellow countryman or a stranger in one of the communities of your land. You must pay him his wages on the same day, before the sun sets, for he is poor and urgently depends on it; else he will cry to the Lord against you and you will incur guilt" (Deut. 24:14–15). This orientation has its roots in prebiblical Near Eastern cultures, where a supplicant will standardly present himself before the gods as a vulnerable victim of his unjust foes. A presumption of divine empathy toward, and affinity with, the poor is expressed in God's commandment in one of the earliest biblical sections, the so-called Book of the Covenant: "If you lend money *to My people, to the poor among you*, do not act toward them as a creditor: exact no interest from them" (Exod. 22:24; emphasis added). (Note the expectation for *imitatio dei*: paralleling God's attitude, empathy must be shown by those with the means to make interest-free loans.)

This leads to a particular stance with regard to the moral assessment of poverty or, more precisely, of the poor. The question has sometimes been raised whether poor people are in some way themselves responsible for their condition. Such "responsibility" might be understood in naturalistic terms: one has become poor, say, because of laziness, failure to plan for the future, and the like. But within a worldview proclaiming divine Providence, such responsibility might be perceived rather in terms of divine retribution: one is afflicted with poverty as punishment for his or her sins.

The aforementioned biblical perspective, however, points in the opposite direction. The poor can expect divine support not only on account of compassion toward their plight but also – more importantly – because poverty is associated with virtue. To some degree, this is implicit in the contrast of the oppressed poor with their evil oppressors.

It would be an exaggeration to posit that, for these biblical authors, affluence necessarily indicates ill-gotten gains. But certainly for some of them,

---

3 The people are depicted in female imagery, thus this word is in the female form: *'aniya*.

possession of riches is associated with hubris – a moral and religious vice. Thus, the prophet Zephaniah describes the redeemed Israelite community in the future Jerusalem:

> For then I will remove the proud and exultant within you,
> And you will be haughty no more on My sacred mount.
> But I will leave within you a poor, humble folk,
> And they shall find refuge in the name of the Lord.
> The Remnant of Israel shall do no wrong and speak no falsehood;
> A deceitful tongue shall not be in their mouths.

> (Zeph. 3:11–13)

The two adjectives employed here to describe the community of the righteous are *'ani* and one of its chief cognates, *dal*. If these denote poverty here, then the message is clear: hubris is a vice of the rich, whereas poverty is identified with the virtue of humility. And the last two lines seem to go beyond that, associating poverty with truthfulness as well, and suggesting by contrast that the rich are not only haughty but also deceitful.

In this realm of discourse, poverty is indeed seen as resulting – at least in part – from voluntary choices, but these are by no means seen as faulty. On the contrary, poverty signifies virtue, whereas riches may indicate acts of injustice, and in any event are likely to produce hubris.

In numerous biblical verses, there is fluidity in the terms themselves; the received text in several instances is uncertain between the similar forms *'ani-'anav* (in the singular) and *'aniyim-'anavim* (in the plural), denoting respectively the poor and the meek. Thus, the psalmist's promise that "the humble [*'anavim*] shall inherit the land" (Ps. 37:11) was interpreted in ancient times as referring to "the poor" (*'aniyim*), and this, together with cognate verses in Isaiah (61:1–2 and 66:2), provided the background for the beatitudes that open the Sermon on the Mount: "Blessed are the poor in spirit; for theirs is the kingdom of heaven. ... Blessed are the meek, for they shall inherit the earth"[4] (Matt. 5:3, 5).

It is striking that, despite a general tendency to explain suffering and misfortune in terms of divine retribution, the biblical authors – in all their differences – consistently shy away from asserting that the poor's suffering and deprivation constitute punishment for their sins. Consider the book of Proverbs, the greatest repository of optimistic faith in divine providence, which it tends to describe in terms of natural causation. The book often condemns laziness and, in a characteristic statement, asserts: "A Lazy man craves, but has nothing; the diligent shall feast on rich fare" (Prov. 13:4).

---

[4] Almost certainly, the original Hebrew for "meek" is the very same word, *'anavim*; and the word rendered as "earth" is the same as that rendered "land" in this citation from Psalms. On all this, see D. Flusser, "Blessed Are the Poor in Spirit," in his *Judaism and the Origins of Christianity: Collected Papers* (Jerusalem: Magnes Press, 1988), 102–14.

Yet the poor are never condemned as implicitly sinful. On the contrary, Proverbs – just like Psalms and the prophets – repeatedly expresses a moral preference for the humble and poor over the haughty and rich, for example: "Better to be humble and among the lowly ['aniyim-'anavim] than to share spoils with the proud" (Prov. 16:19).

Likewise, Deuteronomy proclaims that "there shall be no needy among you – since the Lord your God will bless you ... if only you heed the Lord your God and take care to keep all the instruction" (Deut. 15:4–5). Yet in the next passage, emphasizing the duty to help the poor, it goes on to say: "For there will never cease to be needy ones in your land, which is why I command you: open your hand to the poor and needy kinsman in your land" (Deut. 15:11).

A similar approach prevails in Rabbinic Judaism. In a polemical exchange attributed to Rabbi Akiva, the foreign interlocutor suggests that God surely has destined the poor to suffer their fate, as otherwise He would have done something to alleviate it:

This is the question that the evil Tornosrufus asked Rabbi Akiva: If your God loves the poor, why does He not provide for them? [Akiva] replied: In order that we may be saved, through them, from judgment in Gehinom [hell]. He retorted: On the contrary, that will condemn you to Gehinom! Let me offer you a parable. To what is this comparable? To a king who was displeased with his servant and put him in jail, commanding that he be given no food or drink. A person took action and provided [the servant] with food and drink; when the king hears of this, will he not be displeased with [that person]? Now you are called "servants," as written, "For it is to Me that the Israelites are servants" [Lev 25:55]. Rabbi Akiva replied: Let me offer you a parable. To what is this comparable? To a king who was displeased with his son and put him in jail, commanding that he be given no food or drink. A person took action and provided [the son] with food and drink; when the king hears of this, will he not send [that person] a gift? Now we are called "sons," as written, "You are the children of the Lord your God." (Deut. 14:1) (Babylonian Talmud, Bava Batra 10a)[5]

The suggestion that God refrains from directly helping the poor, so as to leave room for meritorious human action, is stated expressly in a later Rabbinic text. Midrash Tanchuma on Exodus 20:1 offers a creative interpretation of Psalms 61:8, reading the verse not simply as part of David's prayer to God, but rather as an exchange:

David proclaimed before the Holy One: ... Master of the universe, render Your world level, making rich and poor equal! He responded: ... If they will all be rich, or all poor, who will be capable of giving in kindness?[6]

Here again, any suggestion that the poor have brought about their own condition, or that they somehow deserve it, lies entirely outside the realm of discourse.

---

5 The translation of this and of all other rabbinic texts is my own.
6 The Hebrew term here is *hesed*.

In concluding this section, let me return briefly to the issue of definition. This is tied closely to the question of terminology; in addition to the cognate *dal* mentioned above, biblical Hebrew has many words that serve as close synonyms. The classical homiletic collection on the subject of helping the poor, section 34 of Leviticus Rabbah, catalogs seven terms, exploring their different nuances, and these provide elements of a broad definition. I will not attempt distinct translations of the seven terms, but rather of their expositions:

'ani – that is the plain meaning. *evyon* – as he yearns for everything.

misken – as he is held by all in contempt. *rash* – as he has lost [all] property. *dal* – as he is cut away from [all] property. *dakh* – as he is depressed; he sees an item [of food] and does not eat, sees an item [of drink] and does not drink. *makh* – as he is under everyone, situated like a doorstep. (Leviticus Rabbah 34:6)

Note the several aspects of existence in poverty. According to this midrashic exposition, two of the terms express an objective situation – lack of property (the word denotes both movables and nonmovables). Two others express subjective deprivation and yearning, one focusing on hunger and thirst, the other encompassing everything desirable. And two emphasize deprivation of social status, comprising both the emotional-relational aspect of constant contempt and the behavioral reality of being always "stepped upon."

These three distinct aspects of poverty are spelled out here in a hortatory effort to evoke empathy and move the audience to action. But they also suggest a multifaceted definition of poverty, as each of them provides independent grounds for empathy and for a call to ameliorative action. Thus, a person might be poor, requiring help, on account of either (1) unsatisfied needs/ yearnings, (2) marginalization and humiliation, or (3) lack of property.[7]

High-Risk Groups: Land, Patriarchy, and the Life of Study

For most of the biblical period, the social-economic setting is that of an agricultural society, and the poor are chiefly those without land – hence, the conjunction of the poor and the sojourner in commandments such as:

And when you reap the harvest of your land, you shall not reap all the way to the edges of your field, or gather the gleanings of your harvest; you shall leave them for the poor and the stranger: I am the Lord your God. (Lev. 23:22)

7 It might be argued that lack of property should not count as a problem in itself, unless it entails deprivation in terms of needs or social status. The text seems to suggest, on the contrary, that even if a person suffers no such deprivation – because, say, his needs are taken care of, and he is treated decently – he is still deemed poor on account of lacking property. Perhaps this is because, although suffering no immediate deprivation, he lacks security and a measure of self-sufficiency. Indeed, in her detailed analysis regarding the proper definition of the poverty line, Jill Jacobs suggests that "the property threshold be high enough that a family living exactly on this line will always have some amount of savings in the bank." See J. Jacobs, "Toward a Halakhic Definition of Poverty," *Conservative Judaism* 57, no. 1 (2004): 3–20, at 16.

Those without land commonly made their living as laborers. Note, for example, the following injunction with regard to a day laborer, automatically conceived as "poor":

> You shall not abuse a laborer – poor and needy – whether a fellow countryman or a stranger in one of the communities of your land. You must pay him his wages on the same day, before the sun sets, for he is poor and urgently depends on it; else he will cry to the Lord against you and you will incur guilt. (Deut. 24:14–15)

According to the biblical narrative, the Land of Israel was originally apportioned to all adult males. The size of tribal holdings was determined in proportion to the number of individuals in each tribe, to ensure the equality of the freeholders' initial holdings. Yet the vicissitudes of agricultural and economic life were sure to produce inequalities in the long run, as economic failure forced some to sell their land. The law of the Jubilee is designed to correct such maldistribution, restoring everyone to his ancestral land – yet this was clearly no more than utopian legislation, as is evident from prophetic outcries such as that of Isaiah:

> Ah, those who add house to house and join field to field,
> Till there is room for none but you to dwell in the land!

> (Isa. 5:8)

Thus, the agricultural economy of biblical Israel was bound to relegate some people who were originally freeholders to the class of poor, landless laborers, there to join immigrants (*gerim* – "sojourners," often translated as "strangers") who by definition had no share in the ancestral, tribal lands. On a declarative level, such sojourners are entitled to full equality before the law (cf. Lev. 19:33–34). In practice, they are commonly listed among the poor and needy; this situation, in combination with their lacking the support of an extended family, made them vulnerable to abuse.[8]

Because the land was distributed only to males, women – especially those not attached to a man – constituted another vulnerable group. Although the daughters of Zelophehad were able to secure a right to female inheritance of a man who dies without sons, that remains an exception; the land is normally transferred from father to son(s). A woman depends for financial security upon her husband; hence, the widow is commonly mentioned as being liable to mistreatment and in need of aid and sustenance.

Postbiblical Jewish practice and rabbinic law introduced comprehensive changes in the economic arrangements pertaining to marriage. Employment of a marriage contract (*ketubah*) was defined as obligatory. A central clause of this contract was designed to establish a measure of economic security for

---

[8] For a knowledgeable but historically uncritical description of the Jubilee and its context, see Frank Loewenberg, *From Charity to Social Justice* (New Brunswick, NJ: Transaction, 2001), 107–10.

the wife upon divorce or upon the husband's death – fundamentally, through a high-priority lien on a parcel of land. In combination with other changes, women's economic disadvantage was alleviated but by no means eradicated.

Moreover, Judaic divorce law continues to this day to serve as a significant factor contributing to the feminization of poverty. This is due to a traditional conception of marriage as "acquisition": divorce essentially consists of the husband releasing his wife, and his consent is required to set her free. Such power often gives rise to extortion, whereby a woman will surrender property or entitlements in order to obtain her freedom. This tends to exacerbate the general phenomenon of deterioration in the economic standing of women (and their children) in the wake of divorce.

Another group liable to be poor consists, somewhat surprisingly, of those who devote their lives to the study of Torah (the divine Teaching). Study of Torah is traditionally perceived as the supreme vocation, and in rabbinic Judaism scholars constitute the social and even political elite.[9] Nevertheless, a classical third-century statement reads:

This is the path of Torah: Bread with salt shall be your food, and water by measure shall you drink; you shall sleep upon the earth and live a life of deprivation, toiling in the Torah. If you do so – you will be blessed and happy: blessed in this world, and happy in the world to come…. And yearn not for the royal table, for your table is greater than theirs and your crown greater than theirs; your employer can be trusted to pay you your reward. (Mishnah Avot 6:4)

Thus, an individual who devotes his life to the supreme calling of Torah study ought not cultivate any expectations of worldly reward. Yet, in reality, in many medieval and early modern Jewish communities, scholars enjoyed the status of a religious elite, and this was often accompanied by relative economic prosperity. From that perspective, the preceding passage possibly describes "the *path* of Torah," that is, the student's situation during the long years of study en route to becoming an accomplished scholar.

In contemporary Israel, however, perpetual study has been promulgated as a way of life not only for a scholarly elite but for whole segments of the (male) ultra-orthodox population. In these circles, wives – commonly allowed only a restricted education – are expected to support their husbands and their (often numerous) children, supplementing modest stipends allotted to the men engaged in a life of study. Arguments abound about how a welfare state should deal with such elective poverty (though it is not elected by the children, and arguably neither by the wives, who have little choice but to follow their prescribed gender role – nor even by the husbands, who are following the dictates of an authoritarian society, internalized from infancy).[10]

9 Cf. Walzer et al., *Authority*, 244–306; *Membership*, 131–49.
10 See M. Friedman, "The Ultra-Orthodox and Israeli Society," in *Whither Israel? The Domestic Challenges*, ed. Keith Kyle and Joel Peters. (London: Royal Institute of International Affairs; I. B. Tauris, 1993), 177–201.

Thus, in a society shaped by Judaic traditions, groups more liable to be poor include immigrants and aliens, women, and – paradoxically – those committed to the supreme religious ideal of a life of study.

Goals: Extensive Alleviation, Not Eradication

In the Jewish tradition, alleviating poverty is by no means merely a matter for supererogation. It is certainly a moral imperative, or rather – in this tradition's terms – a *mitzvah*, God's commandment. Is it, as such, a requirement of justice? The answer depends on how one defines "justice" as distinct from that which is a requirement of morality and of the Torah. The duty to help the poor is called *tzedakah*, derived from the same root as the Hebrew word for justice, *tzedek*. Furnishing *tzedakah* is obligatory on both the individual and the communal levels.

But could fulfilling this obligation be enforced? Here we find an intriguing debate among medieval authorities. Some held that members of the community could be taxed for *tzedakah*, just as for other communal necessities (such as paying the king's taxes or constructing and maintaining a synagogue). Others insisted on retaining a realm of (partial) political freedom, within which individuals can exercise their free will, answering God's commands (or at least some of them) without human compulsion. Actual practices diverged: in some locations, the communal *tzedakah* fund – the primary source for meeting the basic needs of the poor – was financed by a regular tax; in others, by votive donations (though undertaking such donations was not, of course, free from social pressure).

Eradicating poverty seems never to have been a goal or even an ideal. Even the pietistic community of the Essenes, who rejected private property, subscribed to an ideal of equality in virtuous poverty rather than aspiring to a shared affluence. And the Rabbis expressly rejected this ideal, derogating those who maintain "mine is yours and yours is mine" (Mishnah Avot 5:10) and defending instead the legitimacy of private property – even while fully expecting generous giving to others.

With regard to alleviating poverty, the goals of *tzedakah* are diverse, relating to the different aspects of the problem. The human needs that must be met include not only basic sustenance and clothing but also the range of items necessary for a minimally decent life. This is nicely expressed in the talmudic instructions to the managers of the *tzedakah* fund:

Our rabbis taught: If an orphan boy and an orphan girl ask for provision, provision is made [first] for the orphan girl and [only] then for the orphan boy, because it is a man's practice to go seeking, but it is not a woman's practice to go seeking. If an orphan boy and an orphan girl ask [for support in order] to get married, [arrangements are] made [first] for the orphan girl's marriage and [only] then for the orphan boy's, because a woman's shame is greater than a man's.

Our rabbis taught: If an orphan boy asks [for support in order] to get married, [the officers] rent him a home and set up a bed and all [necessary] utensils, and then [arrange] for him to marry a woman. As written, "lend him sufficient for whatever is needed for him" (Deut. 15:8): "sufficient" – that is a home; "whatever is needed" – that is a bed and table; "for him" – that is a wife, as written, "I will make a fitting helper for him" (Gen. 2:18).

Our rabbis taught: "sufficient" – you are obligated to provide for him, but you are not obligated to make him rich. (Babylonian Talmud, Ketubot 67 a–b)[11]

This last comment is an explicit reflection of the previously mentioned stance: traditional Judaism has not adopted a goal of eliminating poverty. The biblical promise (cited earlier) that "there shall be no needy among you" was not expected to be fulfilled before the messianic era, which lies beyond the horizon of accessible history. In the meantime, the opposite statement (in the next passage, also cited earlier), that "there will never cease to be needy ones in your land," was seen as describing the prevailing reality. It was only within the context of the modern Zionist movement that a sustained effort emerged to eradicate poverty – along with private property. The socialist Zionists figured prominently among those segments of the Zionist movement who perceived it in redemptive (if not messianic) terms: a human initiative to bring about what had been heretofore believed to lie outside the scope of human agency in history. Their ideal of an egalitarian, close-knit community famously took form in the *kibbutz* movement, whose communities (mostly secular, some religious) persevere with partial success to this day.

A strong egalitarian, social-justice tendency (though not quite as radical as in the original *kibbutz* movement) has also been espoused by many Jews in the modern era, both as individual citizens and as members of ideological groups and movements, whether secular or religious. This too has sometimes been placed in the context of redemptive visions, often stated in terms of *tikkun olam* – "repairing the world"[12] – inspired by the prophetic critiques of Isaiah and his contemporaries and by trends in Hassidic spirituality.[13]

Remedies: Modes and Limits

Modes of Helping the Poor
Providing *tzedakah* – help for the needy – is seen as a definite obligation, falling upon each individual who has the capacity to help. However, providing for

---

[11] Translation from Michael Walzer et al., eds., *The Jewish Political Tradition*, vol. 3: *Community*, forthcoming.
[12] This modern sense of *tikkun olam* is vastly expanded as compared to the term's original meaning in rabbinic and medieval usage, as reflected in the next section.
[13] For a brief summary of these prophetic critiques, see Loewenberg, *From Charity to Social Justice*, 57–58.

the basic needs of the poor was seen also as a communal responsibility, and Jewish communities did so through two complementary mechanisms: a daily operation of food collection and distribution, and a *tzedakah* fund that made weekly disbursements to all poor residents. In most communities, collections for both these resources effectively amounted to taxation for welfare spending. The duty to help is, however, not exhausted or defined in solely financial terms. Traditional teachings regarding the mode and purpose of providing *tzedakah* are instructively summarized by Maimonides in his *Mishneh Torah*:

7. There are eight levels of providing *tzedakah*, each one superior to the next. The highest, supreme level is one who supports an Israelite who has come by hard times, by handing him a gift or a loan, or entering into a partnership with him, or finding work for him, in order to strengthen his hand, so that he would have no need to beg from other people. Concerning such a one Scripture says, "you are to sustain him, like a stranger or a sojourner, that he may live with you" (Lev. 25:35) – meaning: sustain him, so that he will not lapse into poverty.

8. Below this is he who provides *tzedakah* to the poor in such a way that he does not know to whom he has given, nor does the poor person know from whom he or she has received – for this constitutes the fulfilling of a *mitzvah* for no ulterior motive.... Roughly on this level is he who contributes to the *tzedakah* fund. One should not, however, contribute to the *tzedakah* fund unless he knows that the person in charge of it is trustworthy, wise, and capable of managing it properly....

9. Below this is he who knows to whom he is giving, while the poor does not know from whom he or she is receiving. For example, the great among the Sages would set out secretly and cast money into the doorways of the poor. This is the proper way to act; it is the desirable manner of providing *tzedakah*, if those in charge of the *tzedakah* fund are conducting themselves improperly.

10. Below this is the case where the poor person knows from whom he or she is receiving, yet remains unknown to the giver. For example, the great among the Sages used to place money in a fold of cloth which they would throw over their shoulder, whereupon the poor would come behind them and take without being exposed to humiliation.

11. Below this is he who provides *tzedakah* directly to the poor before being asked.

12. Below this is he who provides *tzedakah* to the poor after being asked.

13. Below this is he who gives the poor less than what is proper, but with a friendly countenance.

14. Below this is he who gives with a frowning countenance.

(Mishneh Torah, Gifts to the Poor 10:7–14)

The highest level of helping is achieved when a person is given support to prevent him or her from becoming destitute. As is evident from other items on the list, Maimonides accords the highest priority to preventing loss of self-respect; enabling the needy to preserve or to regain self-sufficiency is thus far preferable to providing aid in a persistent state of dependency.

Recognizing that many will nevertheless be in such a state, the overriding concern here is to minimize the humiliation of dependence – and also the self-congratulation or even arrogance of the person providing help. The communal fund (if ideally managed) is regarded as approaching the highest level of *tzedakah* not on account of its efficacy in enforcing collection, in securing funding for meeting basic needs, or in providing broad and just distribution – but rather on account of its bureaucratic anonymity. In this regard, Maimonides's position may be somewhat idiosyncratic. The ubiquity of the *tzedakah* fund in Jewish communities more likely reflects a recognition that it is imprudent and irresponsible for the community to rely entirely on individual goodwill for meeting the basic needs of the poor. Still, the provisions of the fund were commonly supplemented by individual giving, which alone could not make any significant headway toward providing "whatever is needed."

In any event, the value perspective enunciated in Maimonides's eight-level scale has undoubtedly been central in Jewish approaches to dealing with poverty. In contemporary terms this would translate, I think, into a strong endorsement of programs enabling the unemployed to acquire skills and gain employment, thus escaping economic dependency and reestablishing their sense of dignity. Overall, mutual insurance schemes ("social security"), with their (well-founded) sense of entitlement, should be preferred to straightforward welfare distributions. And looking at the two lowest levels, it seems clear that it might be better to offer a bit less in terms of financial help if that means a better kind of human interaction. Or, to put the same point negatively, if an increase in the amount distributed can be achieved only in a way that will markedly increase emotional abuse, it may not be worth pursuing.

Limits

Is there a limit on what may be required or imposed? The classical halakhic discussion of this question focuses on the "redemption of captives" – that is, paying for the liberty of fellow Jews taken captive (for ransom or for sale as slaves) in the course of military conquests or in raids by brigands. Broadly speaking, this is an instance of *tzedakah*, distinguished both by the urgency of the situation (captives are deemed to be in grave danger of abuse and even death) and by the great expenditure needed. The point of departure for the Rabbinic discussion of limits is the Mishnah's statement:

Captives should not be redeemed in excess of their price, on account of *tikkun `olam* [the proper ordering of social affairs]. (Mishnah Gittin 4:6)

This implies that excessive payments for redeeming captives are liable to produce disarray in society's affairs. The Talmud explores what might be at stake:

The question was raised: This [issue of] *tikkun `olam* – is it because of the [financial] strain on the community, or is it perhaps so that they [potential captors] should not come and take more and more captives? (Babylonian Talmud Gittin 45a)

According to *Rashi*'s classical commentary (Rabbi Shelomo Yitzhaki, France, eleventh century), which reflects the adjoining talmudic discussion, an important normative issue hangs on this question. For, on the first interpretation ("because of the strain on the community"), there should be no limit imposed on redemption from private funds, "if he has a rich father, or other relative, who wishes to redeem him for a great sum, without having the strain fall upon the community."

Subsequent codification seems to have endorsed the second understanding, which emphasizes the future dangers implicit in acceding to outrageous demands, rather than an immediate concern for exhausting communal resources.[14] This would appear to render the entire discussion irrelevant to our dilemmas of welfare finance. After all, here the demand for greater spending stems from unintended and undesired personal or social failings, rather than from the ruthless will of extortionists.[15]

In fact, however, the halakhic endorsement of the concern for future hostage taking and escalating demands does not imply a rejection of consideration for "the strain on the community." It is only that the refusal to bow to excessive demands goes *beyond* such consideration, prohibiting even the use of private funds. Still, if it is proposed to use community funds, the prohibition is overdetermined, reflecting also a valid concern for avoiding an excessive "community strain," even when faced with the life-threatening consequence of leaving a captive individual unredeemed.

How is this powerful concern for avoiding a great "community strain" to be characterized? *Rashi* explains: "We ought not strain the community *and drive it into poverty* for the sake of these individual [captive]s" (emphasis added). We have already seen that the welfare requirements of *tzedakah* do not envision eradicating the gap between the poor and the affluent, so it comes as no surprise that a limit on social spending is set well before communal resources are depleted. However, in a tradition that attaches enormous value to life-saving, there was evidently a need to explain why avoiding communal impoverishment should be deemed more important than preserving individual lives. An explanation offered by Rabbi M. Sofer (Hungary, nineteenth century) suggests a definition that might be useful for our exploration of the issue of limits on welfare spending: "Especially in our times, when Israel are subject to their foes, [avoiding an excessive] strain upon the community comes under the category of `life-saving.'"[16] Because community funds are needed

---

[14] Compare A. L. Mackler, "Judaism, Justice, and Access to Health Care," *Kennedy Institute of Ethics Journal* 1 (June 1991): 146–47.

[15] Having said that, I wonder how to respond to a conceivable counterclaim that ironclad commitments to welfare spending encourage poverty: that "they will come and take more and more." This would be plausible, at most, only for instances of poverty that are deemed voluntary.

[16] Responsa Hatam Sofer, vol. 5 (H.M.), section 177.

to maintain collective security,[17] depleting these funds cannot be permitted even for the sake of rescuing the life of one individual.

A similar argument can plausibly be made, it seems, regarding the use of public funds in contemporary societies. Modern welfare spending, just like the redemption of captives, can demand vast expenditures; and any significant strain upon public funds is likely to cause cuts in spending in other critical areas. A definition of the limit on taxation for welfare spending made in terms of avoiding "impoverishing the community" should not be interpreted literally, in the sense of reducing all members of the community to a common poverty. Rather, it requires preserving communal resources sufficient to meet other crucial needs besides welfare.

The Obligation to Help: Scope and Priorities

For the larger part of its history, the Jewish people existed in discreet communities, more or less loosely affiliated at a local level, with a deep sense of general solidarity across lands and continents. A prevailing norm states, "The poor of your town take precedence over the poor of another town." This has two distinct applications: we must care for the local poor before sending off help to the poor of other communities; and local distributions should not be made available to poor people who are not residents (i.e., wanderers), or should be available to them only selectively. For the most part, it was the second application that had the greater impact, as the loose nature of intercommunal links – in combination with various hazards – made the issue of sending substantial aid over any considerable distance relatively rare. The common form of competition for welfare resources was therefore between the local poor, asserting an entitlement to the care and resources of their own community, and itinerant claimants. The accepted rule was that the weekly disbursement from the *tzedakah* fund is provided only to residents, whereas the daily food distribution will be made to anyone. Responsibility toward local residents might encompass Jews and non-Jews together ("on account of the ways of peace"), insofar as they were prepared to cooperate in the collections and distribution of welfare funds.[18]

In the realm of personal giving, the precedence of community members or neighbors yields to a stronger set of particular duties – those toward one's immediate and extended family: "A poor person who is one's relative takes precedence over any other [claimant]" (Mishneh Torah, Gifts to the Poor 7:13).

Over against all this, the beneficiaries of "redemption of captives" were normally fellow Jews from far away, transported from the location of hostilities

---

[17] Sofer cites a medieval precedent involving payment "to the ruler," codified in Rabbi Joseph Caro's *Shulhan 'Arukh*, Y.D. 251:14; such payments by the Jewish community were basically in exchange for protection.

[18] Cf. Walzer et al., *Membership*, 483.

to the land of their captors or to markets in prosperous and relatively secure areas.

The question of responsibility of a larger scope – toward wholly alien political (or religious, or ethnic) communities or toward their individual members – lies beyond the horizon of virtually all Jewish authors. True, the messianic vision – as described by the prophet Isaiah (2:1–4) – includes a system of global adjudication, with a kind of world court in Jerusalem, producing universal peace. But even the nations that "shall study war no more" will, according to this vision as well as others, retain their distinct national identities.[19]

Thus, even the messianic world is imagined as containing boundaries, with national communities each retaining its identity and its existence as a distinct polity. In other words, the Jewish tradition overall does not envision a unified global community. The idea of international distributive justice, or even of *tzedakah* duties toward faraway persons is, I believe, not encountered in traditional sources. Persistent boundaries entail a persistent division of moral responsibility: each community is responsible for the poor within it. The problem of great disparities between wealthy and poor nations does not arise; perhaps this is due (at least in part) to the fact that the messianic age is imagined as exceedingly prosperous, with the fields and fruit trees producing abundantly – perhaps more than enough for all.

Responsibility and Conditionality

Can the poor be expected to alleviate their own condition, for example, by seeking work? Even the book of Proverbs, which makes a repeated point of condemning laziness, consistently insists on the importance and value of helping the poor. The option of making demands upon the poor (namely, "go work") is explicitly rejected in Rabbinic discourse. The classical homiletic collection mentioned earlier repeats the following retort in two separate contexts:

[If, when asked by a poor man for money], a rich man replies: "Won't you go work [so as] to eat? Look at [your] shins, look at [your] thighs, look at [your] flesh!" – The Holy One says to him: "Not only did you not give him [anything] of yours, you [even] cast an evil eye upon that which I gave him?!"[20]

The question "Who is morally responsible for doing what to combat poverty?" has been addressed to a significant degree in my discussion. To reiterate, communal mechanisms and resources (collected as taxes) were used primarily for community-wide provision for basic needs, whereas private giving would be

---

[19] See my "Contested Boundaries: Judaic Visions of a Shared World," in *Boundaries and Justice: Diverse Ethical Perspectives*, ed. S. Hashmi and D. Miller (Princeton, NJ: Princeton University Press, 2001), 237–48.

[20] Leviticus Rabbah 34, clauses 4 and 7; the text goes on to warn the rich man that he will therefore lose his fortune.

the main source for more extensive provisions ("whatever he needs"). The latter was, however, expected to go first of all to the donor's relatives.

Above and beyond this dichotomous, partly complementary arrangement, it is essential to realize the crucial role played by voluntary societies. Many welfare functions – requiring both extra funds and service in person – became the responsibility of purpose-specific societies (e.g., the sick-care society, the burial society, the society for the education of orphans). These societies arose in the medieval communities; which of them, if any, existed in a given community depended on local initiative, and their specific aims and mandates – as determined in their charters – varied greatly. Their income came in part from fees paid by their members, but often also from levies or taxes on particular activities or transactions, confirmed and enforced by the community and its authorities.

II

Liberal Egalitarianism and Poverty

Darrel Moellendorf

Liberal egalitarianism is an account – or, more accurately, a family of accounts – of the justice of political, social, and economic institutions.[1] There are several fundamental moral commitments that most liberal egalitarian theorists share. One is to moral individualism – in other words, that moral duties are primarily owed to individuals and only derivatively (if at all) to the groups or corporate bodies made up of individuals. Another is that the rights and liberties of individuals are highly important. This is the liberal strain in the accounts. Although there is disagreement about whether some claimed rights are actually rights, and about the exact content, extent, and importance of others, there is little disagreement about the moral importance of certain core individual rights and liberties, such as freedoms of conscience and religion; freedom from invidious discrimination on the basis of race, ethnicity, gender, or sexual orientation; the rights to free speech and assembly; and the right to participate as an equal in the political process. The importance of such rights is usually understood as proscribing the achievement of social goals, however desirable, by means that would violate individual rights. Although they take rights seriously, most liberal egalitarians, unlike natural rights theorists, would not affirm the existence of natural rights. Liberal egalitarians can be distinguished from classical liberals or libertarians in particular in part by a rejection of natural rights to property, whether in oneself or the world. A third commitment, the egalitarian strain in the accounts, is that socioeconomic inequalities must be limited in order to be just.

Insofar as liberal egalitarian accounts of justice typically address the morality of political, social, and economic institutions, they provide the basis for judgments concerning the justified use of coercive power by public institutions. For example, one very general way to think about the liberal egalitarian

[1] While completing this chapter I enjoyed the support of the Deutscher Akadmischer Austausch Dienst and the hospitality of the Institut für Interkulturelle und Internationale Studien at Universtität Bremen. I am deeply grateful to both organizations.

approach to poverty is that it is usually, although not necessarily solely, in virtue of its egalitarian commitment that eradication of poverty is endorsed, but that its liberal commitment constrains what public agencies may permissibly do to prevent or eradicate poverty and limits the kind of justifications that public agencies may use to express their concern. For example, a liberal egalitarian appalled at severe poverty would nonetheless typically believe it to be unjust for a public agency to compel citizens into prolonged servitude to eradicate the poverty, and for such an agency to justify policies directed toward bringing persons out of poverty on grounds that it would be pleasing to God, even if it is the case that many citizens, including the liberal egalitarian, reasonably believe this.

There might seem to be an incoherence in the fundamental commitments of the liberal egalitarian account if these require preventing or alleviating poverty but constrain how that can be done. Perhaps other moral accounts – for example, Confucianism – also require that institutions promote socioeconomic equality. Why must that promotion be limited out of respect for individual liberty? Alternatively, other moral accounts, such as libertarianism, also maintain that individual liberty and conscience should be respected. On what grounds then could those who take liberty seriously argue that institutions should equalize, to some extent, the socioeconomic conditions of persons? These twin commitments that distinguish liberal egalitarianism from other accounts seem to require some kind of reconciliation.

The most influential attempt at such reconciliation in recent political philosophy is that of John Rawls.[2] Rawls's account is complicated, and the justificatory method evolves over the course of his career. This makes it very difficult to summarize his account briefly and adequately, but some of the basic approach can be highlighted, and doing so will serve to illustrate one important way in which the apparent tension between liberty and equality is handled and to introduce readers to the most influential recent theorist in the tradition.

In his later account, Rawls assumes the freedom and moral equality of persons and attempts to defend an account of justice – the moral principles that apply to the fundamental institutions of society – that will delimit the fair terms of social cooperation among such persons. Insofar as among persons there is a reasonable pluralism about basic matters of religious and ethical conviction, fair terms of social cooperation can be justified best by a method that relies fundamentally on obtaining agreement among persons, rather than being deduced from moral premises that some might reasonably reject. But because the content of the agreement will be influenced by whether some

---

[2] The most important works of John Rawls in this regard are the following: *A Theory of Justice* (Cambridge, MA: Harvard University Press, 1971, rev. 1999), page numbers in these notes will refer to the revised edition; *Political Liberalism* (New York: Columbia University Press, 1993); and *Justice as Fairness: A Restatement*, ed. Erin Kelly (Cambridge, MA: Harvard University Press, 2001).

have bargaining advantages over others, the moral validity of the agreed-upon principles depends upon there being a fair process that generates them.

This concern about the fairness of the process leads Rawls to advocate an agreement entered into by persons who lack any knowledge about themselves that would make them able to submit proposals for principles that would justify institutions privileging themselves or their group. This can be appreciated by noting that if persons are able to use their bargaining position to establish privileges, the content of any agreement could turn out to support existing institutions, even if they are fundamentally unjust. So the agreement that Rawls takes as justifying principles of justice is a hypothetical one, not an actual one. He calls the justificatory argument "the original position"; and the constraints on self-knowledge are due to what he terms "the veil of ignorance." The hypothetical agreement of the persons – parties – in the original position behind the veil of ignorance expresses what we would actually agree to if we deliberated fairly without trying to privilege ourselves. The original position is then a thought experiment to help those of us concerned about the fair terms of social cooperation understand what fair deliberation requires and which principles for social cooperation such deliberation would yield.

Now, plainly much depends upon what the parties in the original position do and do not know about themselves. One way to think about what sort of knowledge should be excluded is to reflect upon our convictions concerning what sorts of bargaining threats would constitute an unfair advantage in such a deliberative process. If a party were able credibly to threaten that, unless institutions advantaged people like her, members of her group would veto any agreement, the resulting agreement would be biased in favor of such a group. However, if the parties know nothing about themselves, then they have no basis on which to agree to any principles at all because they do not even know what to consider worth regulating by fair terms of cooperation. Rawls, of course, recognizes this problem and responds by making the parties ignorant of any of the circumstances of their social or natural fortune; they know nothing about their race, ethnicity, sex, social class, religious affiliation, or natural abilities. But he assumes that they affirm the goodness of certain things – he calls them "primary goods" – normally needed by everyone to live as free and equal persons in society. He takes these to include basic rights and liberties (including freedoms of thought and conscience), the freedoms of movement and occupational choice, the powers and prerogatives of offices and positions of authority, income and wealth, and social bases of self-respect (the institutions that support attitudes of self-worth and self-respect). These are the goods that constitute the content of principles of justice and that institutions should regulate.

Rawls argues that in the original position the parties would agree on the following principles of justice:[3]

---

[3] The statement of these principles evolves over time. This is a final version appearing in *Justice as Fairness*, 42–43.

1. Each person has the same indefeasible claim to a fully adequate scheme of equal basic liberties, which scheme is compatible with the same scheme of liberties for all.
2. Social and economic inequalities are to satisfy two conditions.
   a. They are to be attached to offices and positions open to all under conditions of fair equality of opportunity.
   b. They are to be to the greatest benefit of the least advantaged members of society.

These principles provide a reconciliation of the commitments to liberty and equality. Lest one think that practical conflicts between liberty and equality would still prove to be intractable, Rawls argues that under normal conditions the first principle takes priority over the second.

Rawls makes several different arguments in defense of these principles, but the one that is rooted in the original position procedure involves the claim that, because of the uncertainty of their social position and the indeterminate possibility that it could be poor, parties in the original position would endorse only principles that ensured that those in the worst position were as well-off as they could be. This sort of reasoning is called *maximin reasoning*; and whether it is rational to employ seems to depend on one's circumstances. Rawls argues that the original position constitutes the appropriate circumstances and that the reasoning would lead the parties to endorse the principles stated earlier rather than other possible principles, such as a utilitarian one.

To appreciate the reconciliation of liberty and equality that Rawls makes, it is necessary to observe that he does not argue that there is a deeper moral principle that is the basis of both commitments. Instead, he argues that the appropriate justificatory procedure would produce both commitments and would order them by prioritizing liberty. So, the threat of incoherence is not answered purely theoretically, by proving that principles of liberty and equality are both logically entailed by some more basic principle, and therefore not in contradiction. Rather, the answer has a basis in practical reason. If we seek principles for fair terms of cooperation in a society characterized by a reasonable pluralism of religious and ethical views, it is appropriate to employ a procedure involving hypothetical agreement. The outcome of such a procedure, according to Rawls, is an affirmation of principles of both liberty and equality.

There is a Kantian lineage to the Rawlsian reconciliation. The eighteenth-century philosopher Immanuel Kant argued that morality has its basis in practical reason. According to Kant, one of the expressions of the categorical imperative, the fundamental principle of morality, enjoins one to "so act as if he were through his maxim always a legislating member in the universal kingdom of ends."[4] Rawls's development of the original position as a model of

---

[4] Immanuel Kant, *Grounding for the Metaphysics of Morals*, (438) trans. James W. Ellington in Immanuel Kant, *Ethical Philosophy* (Indianapolis: Hackett, 1983), 11.

procedural fairness that generates principles of justice is a descendant of the
Kantian idea that respect for persons requires acting on maxims that would
be legislated by members of a kingdom of ends. Basic respect for individual
persons is characteristic of the moral individualism of contemporary forms of
liberal egalitarianism.

The Kantian lineage of much of contemporary liberal egalitarian thinking is often consciously worked up as an alternative to utilitarianism, which
advocates actions and policies that produce maximal aggregate utility or happiness. Utilitarians have good reasons to condemn some forms of poverty
insofar as the happiness accruing to the poor from wealth transfers from the
rich would more than offset the unhappiness experienced by the rich. The
best-known contemporary proponent of a utilitarian approach to poverty is
Peter Singer. In a seminal article on morality and world poverty, Singer maintains that individuals are obliged to give to the poor of the world up to the point
at which they would sacrifice something "of comparable moral importance."[5]
This view seems to follow from the utilitarian injunction to seek maximal
aggregate happiness or minimal unhappiness. Despite the eloquent attempts
of the great nineteenth-century utilitarian John Stuart Mill to defend the
importance of individual liberty in his *On Liberty*, most contemporary liberal
egalitarians have judged that utilitarianism's goal to maximize utility leaves
individual's rights vulnerable to the whims of the majority. Rawls, for example, rejects the utilitarian approach of aggregating utility on grounds that it
"does not take seriously the distinction between persons."[6] The criticism is
directed precisely at the aggregating method of utilitarianism, which would
have us pursue social goals on grounds that they would maximize happiness
rather than that they would express respect for individuals.

Definitions of Poverty

The egalitarian liberal commitment to poverty reduction rests on commitments to either equality or liberty (or both). Because of this rather indirect
relationship between the primary commitments of liberal egalitarianism and
poverty, and because liberal egalitarian theories are primarily normative
(moral) and not empirical (descriptive), definitions of poverty are not at the
forefront of these accounts. In many cases, one can only surmise the definitions based upon other features of the account. One very important exception
to this, however, is in the writings of Amartya Sen, who, as a developmental
and welfare economist, has discussed poverty extensively and with very influential results.

For reasons that will be clearer in the next section, Sen argues that the
proper aim of distributive justice is to equalize capabilities or freedoms

---

[5] Peter Singer, "Famine Affluence and Morality," *Philosophy and Public Affairs* 1 (1972): 231.
[6] Rawls, *Theory*, 24.

among persons. This view has come to be called *the capabilities approach*. Sen contends further that the considerations that favor capabilities also apply in the measurement of poverty.

The basic failure that poverty implies is one of having minimally adequate capabilities, even though poverty is also *inter alia* a matter of inadequacy of the person's economic means (the means to prevent the capability failure). Consider the example ... of the person with a high metabolic rate, or large body size, or a parasitic disease that wastes nutrients. He is less able to meet minimal nutritional norms with the same level of income, compared with another person *without* those disadvantages. If he is to be seen as poorer than the second person, despite the same income, the reason lies in his greater capability failure.[7]

Sen concludes that poverty should not be conceived of as a low income but as income inadequacy – that is, income that is inadequate for conversion into basic capabilities. In other words, a person is impoverished not merely when her income falls below some established level but when her income is inadequate to support a basic set of human capabilities.

For other liberal egalitarians, the primary object of distributive justice is resources. Ronald Dworkin is the chief proponent of this view.[8] Its significance for definitions of poverty is that in contrast to the capabilities approach, Dworkin's view would seem to be compatible with a traditional identification of poverty as income that falls below some stipulated level. Rawls offers an account that distributes several different primary goods. In contrast to Dworkin's resource account, Rawls's might be considered pluralistic. His account of distributive justice concerns the distribution of wealth and income and of opportunities to obtain positions of privilege. Insofar as the Rawlsian account is concerned with the distribution of wealth and income, it seems consistent with taking poverty as income below some established threshold.

High-Risk Groups

Sen argues that the equality achieved by equalizing primary goods or resources obscures an important source of remaining inequality, namely, in the capabilities of persons to convert resources into functionings.[9] Two persons with the same bundle of goods or resources might have very different capability

---

[7] Amartya Sen, *Inequality Reexamined* (Cambridge, MA: Harvard University Press, 1992), 111. Sen's discussion of poverty measurement is not by any means limited to the virtues of the capabilities account. He is also concerned with how well indices can capture changes in poverty. See Amartya Sen, *Poverty and Famines* (Oxford: Oxford University Press, 1981), chaps. 2 and 3, and James E. Foster and Amartya Sen, *On Economic Inequality*, expanded ed. (Oxford: Oxford University Press, 1997), "Annex A.6."

[8] The resource equality account is set out in several of the chapters of Ronald Dworkin, *Sovereign Virtue* (Cambridge, MA: Harvard University Press, 2000), which includes several previously published articles devoted to the account.

[9] See, for example, Sen, *Inequality*.

sets because of the existence of different physical needs or capacities. Sen levels two criticisms against accounts such as Dworkin's and Rawls's. First, approaches that seek to equalize goods or resources systematically confuse the means for the ends of justice. Second, the capability approach is sensitive to a kind of pluralism to which these other approaches are not, namely in the conversion of resources to capabilities. Hence, according to Sen, accounts of justice that require that institutions provide a certain distribution of income can prove to be insensitive to the needs of some persons who are particularly vulnerable, or at high risk, because of differences in their conversion of incomes to capabilities.

Differences in the conversion of incomes to capabilities might have either a biological or social basis. Sen contends that causes of both kinds come into play when analyzing women's poverty – understood as income inadequate to convert to basic capabilities. Such poverty might result from the demands of pregnancy and neonatal care, sexist stereotyping, the demands of work and childcare, and inferior incomes. The point Sen presses is that to the extent that institutions are sensitive only to income levels, they might be insensitive to important inequalities between men and women.[10] Martha Nussbaum has also raised this criticism in several published works.[11]

Both Rawls and Dworkin have responded, not, however, to Sen's charge about the insensitivity of their accounts to women's poverty in particular, but to the claimed inadequacy of their accounts more generally. Rawls's account might seem particularly vulnerable to Sen's first criticism because he admits the instrumental value of primary goods: they simply are "all purpose means that are generally necessary to enable citizens adequately to develop and fully exercise their two moral powers, and to pursue their determinate conceptions of the good."[12] This claim, however, forms the basis of Rawls's response that indeed he recognizes that certain capabilities are morally important – namely, "the capabilities of citizens as free and equal persons in virtue of their moral powers."[13] In response to the second claimed advantage of the capability approach, Rawls asserts that differences between persons can be accommodated in the application of moral principles in the legislative process where a great deal of empirical information is relevant, rather than at the highest level of the justification of moral principles. In responding to both of Sen's claimed advantages of the capabilities approach, Rawls seems to be attempting to narrow the difference between him and Sen rather than to reject the capabilities approach fundamentally.

[10] This and related points are also discussed in Amartya Sen, *Development as Freedom* (New York: Alfred A. Knopf, 1999), chap. 8.

[11] See, for example, Martha Nussbaum, *Sex and Social Justice* (Oxford: Oxford University Press, 1993) and *Women and Human Development* (Cambridge: Cambridge University Press, 2000).

[12] Rawls, *Justice as Fairness*, 57.

[13] Ibid., 167.

Dworkin's response raises what he takes to be two fundamental criticisms of Sen's capability approach.[14] First, it would be impossible to equalize multiple capabilities for functioning without equalizing with respect to matters that people value very differently. This challenges the claim that by so equalizing capabilities one has achieved equality at all. Second, Sen is uncomfortably pushed toward either equality of welfare or equality of equal resources, even though he would like his account to be distinguished from both, which he takes to be inadequate. Sen distinguishes these two accounts as accounts of the equalization of achievements (welfare or utility) and the equalization of the means to achievements (goods or resources).[15] Sen claims that the latter are superior insofar as they are closer to an assessment of the freedom of agents, not merely their conditions. Dworkin claims that one feature of equal welfare accounts is that they take all the responsibility for a person's welfare to be social responsibility; there is no personal responsibility for one's choices. Now, Dworkin contends that if Sen's account posits social responsibility for equalizing all capacities for personal states such as self-respect and happiness, regardless of a person's ambitions, tastes, and choices, it extinguishes personal responsibility for choices, just as equalizing welfare does. But if Sen's account involves social responsibility to equalize only those capacities that are not the result of personal choice, then "it is not an alternative to equality of resources but only that same ideal set out in a different vocabulary."[16]

Volition

Liberal egalitarian theories are normative theories. As such, with a few exceptions, they do not usually offer extensive accounts of the causes of poverty. They are not therefore usually involved with considering explanations that clarify the extent to which poverty is the result of individual choice. But Dworkin's response to Sen suggests that a central point of debate between liberal egalitarians concerns the extent to which individual choice makes one responsible for one's inferior social position. Indeed, Dworkin takes it to be a central virtue of his resource account that it allegedly captures our commonsense moral intuitions that persons are individually responsible for their choices but not their circumstances.[17] This view has come to be called *luck egalitarianism* in the literature.[18] According to luck egalitarians, the point of egalitarian institutions is to compensate persons for their bad luck with respect to their natural and social circumstances. But luck egalitarians argue that person ought not to be compensated for their bad choices. The idea is

[14] Dworkin, *Sovereign*, 299–303.
[15] Sen, *Inequality*, 32.
[16] Dworkin, *Sovereign*, 303.
[17] Whether or not there is such an intuition has not gone unchallenged. See, for example, Samuel Scheffler, "Egalitarianism," *Philosophy and Public Affairs* 31 (2003): 5–39.
[18] Cf. Elizabeth Anderson, "What Is the Point of Equality?" *Ethics* 109 (1999): 287–337.

that persons are not responsible for their circumstances but are responsible for their choices.

Dworkin's version of luck egalitarianism rests fundamentally on a distinction between circumstances (including resources) and personal characteristics (such as choices, ambitions, and character). There are two fundamental features of Dworkin's egalitarian account: a hypothetical initial auction of resources and hypothetical insurance schemes against certain kinds of misfortune. Both features are thought experiments, the results of which are to be used to give an account of a distribution of resources that would be equal. Such an account would then guide the construction of real egalitarian institutions.

The initial auction assumes that there are no preexisting moral entitlements to resources and employs a standard of equality that Dworkin calls "the envy test." The latter holds that a necessary condition of an equal division of resources is that no one prefers someone else's bundle of resources to her own. The test builds social appraisal into the standard of equality rather than making the appraisal entirely impersonal. The worth of a person's bundle of resources then is a function of how others value it. Employing this standard, Dworkin argues that an equal initial distribution of resources would be the distribution produced by an auction of all resources in which the purchasers have been provided with equal allotments of currency. What anyone comes to possess is a function of what she is willing to pay for it, where the cost of it is established by the extent to which others value it. One must either pay the socially established price of an item or readjust one's preferences. In effect, then, one chooses how much of one's currency one will spend for an item in the auction; and one is responsible for that choice.

An initially equal distribution will not, however, remain equal because of several factors. Some persons will be more talented than others in making what others are willing to purchase; some will be more willing to take gambles in the use of resources; and, of those who gamble, some will be more successful than others. Insofar as gambling is a matter of choice, Dworkin is not concerned with the inequalities that it would produce. Inequalities due to natural talents are, however, a different matter. Talents of mind and body are matters of circumstance, not choice. Moreover, their use can impose costs on others by making the productive labor of the others comparatively less attractive. Talents are not, however, to be treated in exactly the same manner as external resources that are subject to an initial auction. Dworkin claims that this would penalize the talented by forcing them to pay a great deal for the use of their body and minds and would result in distributions that would fail the envy test. Moreover, the development of one's natural talents is a matter of choice and ambition. So, although the unchosen and cost-imposing nature of talents must be equalized, this must not impose costs on the talented that would fail the envy test and ignore the role of ambition (choice) in the development of talents.

How should the initial hypothetical auction be augmented in order to appropriately produce equality of resources given differential talents? Dworkin advocates a hypothetical insurance market in which the purchasers seek to insure against the possibility – but unknown likelihood – that their talents will not produce economic rents. Dworkin argues that, in such a market, normally prudent persons would buy insurance only against the possibility of having very low earning power from one's talents. If this is the case, then it could be modeled by a real distributive mechanism, which putatively is both choice sensitive and resource insensitive, in the form of an income tax and transfer scheme that covers people for low income due to less demanded talents at the rate of the hypothetical insurance market. Such a scheme would be more appropriate than private insurance because in actuality people do have some knowledge about how much their talents are likely to fetch on the market and what sort of access they will have to institutions, such as schools, to help them develop their talents. Such knowledge would distort a private insurance market in ways that would defeat treating talents as matters of unchosen circumstance requiring equalization to some extent.

This summary of Dworkin's view illustrates a strain of egalitarian thinking that tries to take inequality-producing individual choices as sources of just inequality. This is a controversial view. Not all egalitarian thinking rests so heavily on the distinction between luck (circumstances) and choice. It is already clear that the issues surrounding volition in egalitarian thinking overlap with those involved with responsibility. I survey a few alternative accounts in the section on responsibility and conditionality.

Poverty is most acute in the developing world. Nearly half of the world's population lives in abject poverty on less than $2 purchasing power parity (PPP) per day.[19] Worse still, 1.15 billion people live on less than $1 PPP per day.[20] An estimated 1.3 billion people lack access to clean water; and 840 million children are malnourished.[21] The United Nations International Children's Emergency Fund reports that 30,500 children under five die every day of mainly preventable causes.[22] Increasingly, liberal egalitarians are discussing these matters. Some are concerned with the causes of global poverty.

Rawls, for example, claims that the causes of wealth and poverty lie in the political culture and the religious, philosophical, and moral traditions that

---

[19] World Bank, *Global Economic Prospects and the Developing Countries* (2002), 30, http://www.worldbank.org/prospects/gep2002/chap1.pdff. A value of $2 PPP means the local currency equivalent of what one could purchase with $2 in the United States. Recently the World Bank has recalculated the PPP formulas, and there is controversy about how to calculate it or whether it is even a useful indicator of poverty.

[20] Ibid.

[21] United Nations Development Programme, *Human Development Report, 1999*, 28, http://hdr.undp.org/reports/global/1999/en/.

[22] United Nation's International Children's Emergency Fund, *The State of the World's Children* (2000), http://www.unicef.org/sowc00/.

230   *Darrel Moellendorf*

support public institutions and political virtues.[23] Thomas Pogge challenges
this view, not by rejecting the claim altogether but by seeking to undermine
its explanatory adequacy.[24] According to Pogge, Rawls's account ignores both
historical factors, such as the role of slavery and colonialism, and current
institutional features of the global order. His analysis of the current global
order involves an account of two features that produce strong incentives for
actions that degrade and corrupt domestic political cultures. These are the
international borrowing and resource privileges that accrue to any group possessing control over the instruments of state power no matter how the group
comes to office or exercises its power. These privileges allow the group to
borrow freely in the country's name and to exercise control over the natural
resource base of the country. Because the privileges exist regardless of how a
group achieves, or wields, power, the borrowing privilege establishes incentives to attempt coups, to engage in civil wars, and to rule corruptly in all societies, and the resource privilege provides additional incentives of these sorts
in resource-rich countries. Hence, the existence of severe poverty in underdeveloped countries is evidence of an injustice in the global order and directs
responsibility to those who maintain that order.

Goals

In contrast to some other moral traditions, liberal egalitarian support for
the goal of eradicating poverty derives from other fundamental moral commitments. Often, although not always, it is based on the commitment of distributive justice to limit socioeconomic inequalities. To be sure, this latter
commitment is not identical to a commitment to eradicate poverty.[25] The ideal
of equality is comparative. Assessing whether it has been realized requires
comparing persons' conditions. Egalitarian thinking typically concerns
whether, or to what extent, it is permissible for one person to have more than
another. I have canvassed various versions of this in the works of Dworkin,
Rawls, and Sen. Alternatively, the antipoverty ideal is not comparative.
Assessing whether antipoverty policies realize their goal involves measuring
persons' conditions against some impersonal index – a poverty line – below
which persons are judged to be impoverished and above which not. The antipoverty ideal alone could tolerate unlimited inequality just so long as persons
do not fall below the poverty line. Alternatively, a version of egalitarianism
could conceivably prohibit improvements as measured against the impersonal
poverty line if they require increasing inequalities between persons. Such a
version would reject poverty eradication in the name of egalitarianism. No
such version of liberal egalitarianism is, however, advocated by any major

---

[23] John Rawls, *The Law of Peoples* (Cambridge, MA: Harvard University Press, 1999), 108.
[24] Thomas Pogge, *World Poverty and Human Rights* (London: Polity Press, 2002).
[25] See also Sen, *Poverty and Famines*, chap. 2.

liberal egalitarian theorist. As a case in point, consider the second part of the second of Rawls's two principles of justice. It is referred to as *the difference principle*. The difference principle is both egalitarian in limiting inequality and maximally antipoverty, insofar as it requires that institutions ensure that the least advantaged members of society are better off than the least advantaged members in any other feasible institutional arrangement. Hence, if poverty can be eliminated, it must be.

Some egalitarian liberal accounts emphasize a different antipoverty-related goal, based upon the liberal strain in the account. This is the goal of fulfilling basic human rights. Henry Shue provides one of the more prominent versions of this argument.[26] Shue takes a moral right to provide (1) the rational basis for a justified demand (2) that the actual enjoyment of a substance be (3) socially guaranteed against standard threats. A basic right is a person's minimal moral demands on others. Shue argues that persons have a basic moral right to subsistence involving the enjoyment of unpolluted air and water; adequate food, clothing, and shelter; and minimal preventative care. This right requires social provision of subsistence at least to those who cannot provide for themselves.

Shue's argument that there is a right to subsistence is also an argument for its basic character. The argument assumes that persons have other rights, which guarantee, for example, liberty of conscience or freedom of speech. No one can fully enjoy such rights if she lacks the essentials for a fully healthy and active life. The means of subsistence are then necessary to the enjoyment of other rights. A right to subsistence is a basic right because the enjoyment of the matters protected by the other rights depends on the enjoyment of subsistence. The antipoverty commitment expressed by this argument is directed against only the most severe forms of depredation, namely those that prevent the enjoyment of other rights. An argument such as this is in principle also open to classical liberals, or libertarians, who reject the egalitarian commitments of liberal egalitarians, although typically libertarians reject this argument on grounds that rights can impose only negative duties of noninterference, not positive duties of provision of some good. Shue rejects this criticism by claiming that even fulfilling negative duties – say, not to harm – requires the provision of resources to support the police and a criminal justice system.

Pogge also develops a rights-based antipoverty account, which invokes Article 25 of the Universal Declaration of Human Rights:[27]

Everyone has the right to a standard of living adequate for the health and well-being of himself and of his family, including food, clothing, housing, medical care, and necessary social services, and the right to security in the event of unemployment,

---

[26] See Henry Shue, *Basic Rights: Subsistence, Affluence, and U.S. Foreign Policy*, 2nd ed. (Princeton, NJ: Princeton University Press, 1996).
[27] Pogge, *World Poverty*.

sickness, disability, widowhood, old age or other lack of livelihood in circumstances beyond his control.[28]

Pogge argues for what he calls an "institutional understanding" of rights, which takes individuals and governments to have responsibilities to organize an institutional order in which persons have secure access to the objects of their human rights. Hence, a right to a standard of living adequate for health and well-being generates duties on persons to reorganize society so as to secure access to such a standard of living for other persons. He argues that the international borrowing and resource privileges, discussed in the previous section, result in extensive human rights violations, for which persons living in powerful countries are responsible.

Remedies

Most liberal egalitarians judge all existing capitalist societies (some more than others) as unjust because of their deep and pervasive inequalities. However, because liberal egalitarian theorists are primarily concerned with the normative task of justifying principles of justice, the vast majority tend to spend comparatively little time on empirical matters such as which institutional arrangements will best satisfy those principles and therefore remedy the injustices. Once again, an important exception to this is Sen's work in developmental economics. Typically liberal egalitarians endorse institutions that either adjust market distributions, limit intergenerational wealth transfers, limit the extent of private ownership of capital, or some combination of these.

Dworkin tends to favor the first of these three arrangements. Arguing on behalf of a progressive income tax scheme, he contends that "the consequences of protracted unemployment or extremely low income are sufficiently serious that most prudent people of average means would insure against those consequences to some degree: they would attempt to buy coverage that would at least enable them to sustain life with some dignity – provide food, decent shelter, and a minimum level of medical care for themselves and their family."[29] An income tax and transfer scheme that models the payments of a hypothetical insurance scheme against little-demanded talents serves to equalize resources and protects against falling into abject poverty. Other liberal egalitarians seek to adjust market distributions by distributing the fruits of an income tax scheme by means of an unconditional universal basic income grant.[30] The arguments for a basic income grant tend be both normative and efficiency based. A basic income to the poor would both alleviate poverty and

---

[28] Universal Declaration of Human Rights, Article 25, http://www.un.org/Overview/rights.html (accessed February 12, 2008).
[29] Dworkin, *Sovereign*, 335.
[30] The chief proponent of this view is Philippe van Parijs. See his *Real Freedom for All: What If Anything Can Justify Capitalism* (Oxford: Oxford University Press, 1998).

reduce inequality. Removing means testing, and all other conditions, would reduce various bureaucratic inefficiencies and remove perverse incentives to not seek work in order to maintain public assistance. Brian Barry endorses both progressive income taxation and an unconditional basic income as parts of a comprehensive social democratic arrangement, which also comprises strong trade unions to curb the power of capital, universal healthcare, and public education of a high quality.[31]

In contrast to the social democratic remedy, Rawls prefers either what he refers to as "property owning democracy" or "liberal socialism." The main social and economic institutions of property-owning democracy include mechanisms that ensure a wide disbursement of capital, in particular progressive estate taxes and an expenditure (sales) tax,[32] but that also ensure fair equality of opportunity in education and insulate the political system from economic inequalities through public financing of campaigns. Rawls distinguishes between property-owning democracy and social democracy (or the welfare state) by characterizing the former as instituting a widespread initial distribution of wealth and capital ownership and the latter as redistributing wealth after it has been amassed in the hands of a small class of wealthy persons.[33] The version of socialism that Rawls takes to be the strongest rival to property-owning democracy includes social ownership of the means of production, multiparty democracy, market competition between firms, and worker self-managed firms.[34]

Several liberal egalitarians offer other institutional suggestions. Michael Walzer argues that egalitarianism should seek not to equalize holdings in some good, what he calls "simple equality," but rather to prevent the tyranny of one kind of good over others. This alternative he refers to as "complex equality," which – roughly – involves seeking to prevent persons who are privileged in their holdings of goods of one kind from converting that into a privilege in the holding of a good of another kind.[35] For example, in circumstances of complex equality a person would not be able to convert her privileged economic position into a position of superior political power, or vice versa. In criticizing the pursuit of simple economic equality, Walzer argues that it would create monopoly elsewhere: "But then state power itself will become the central object of competitive struggle. Groups of men and women will seek to monopolize and then use the state in order to consolidate their control of other social goods."[36]

---

[31] Brian Barry, *Why Social Justice Matters* (London: Polity, 2005).
[32] Rawls, *Justice as Fairness*, 161.
[33] Rawls, *Theory*, xiv–xv.
[34] Rawls, *Justice as Fairness*, 138. A defense of a model of socialism along these lines can be found in David Schweikart, *Against Capitalism* (Cambridge: Cambridge University Press, 1993).
[35] See Michael Walzer, *Spheres of Justice* (New York: Basic Books, 1983), chap. 1.
[36] Ibid., 15.

Walzer takes there to be spheres of human interaction, each with its own goods and each governed by distinct distributive principles. So, whereas freedom of exchange might be the appropriate guiding norm of rational agents in the marketplace, it is not among members of the political community who rightly are concerned with one another's security and welfare. In that sphere, a norm of need fulfillment is appropriate. Complex equality rejects attempts to constrain inequalities in one sphere, say the economy, through regulation issuing from another, say the political system, but requires preventing domination by means of capitalizing on inequalities within one sphere to seek advantage in another. Hence, Walzer argues that political communities must not let economic inequalities result in political domination, in which the needs of the co-members of political society are not met.[37] The concern to prevent domination, then, involves an antipoverty commitment. Poverty is less an injustice in the economic sphere than an injustice between the economic and political. For if need-fulfillment institutions and programs do not supplement market distributions, then economic activity will confound the political moral requirement to attend to the needs of members of the political community.

Pogge argues that the international borrowing and resource privileges could be undermined by constitutional precommitments at the state level and that absolute poverty could be eliminated by a global tax on resource extraction. The constitutional precommitments involve states making constitutional amendments that would reduce incentives to undemocratic assumption of power. One amendment would maintain that the debts incurred by state leaders who come to office undemocratically not be paid back at public expense. This would discourage lenders from offering loans to putchist regimes for fear of a refusal to pay back the loans by a later democratic government. Another amendment would stipulate that only democratically elected regimes could enter into legally binding contracts to transfer ownership of public property. This puts multinational corporations seeking contracts to extract resources on notice that the legality of the contract will be challenged at a later date if the government signing it came to office undemocratically. Additionally, Pogge defends a global institution that he calls a "global resource dividend." A GRD would be generated by a tax on the resource extraction. The tax would be set at a small percentage of the value of the extracted resources. The moral idea is that no state, or group of citizens of a state, can claim exclusive ownership of the resources that exist within their territory. Moreover, directing a small percentage of the value of the resources exploited can go a long way toward reducing the worst aspects of global poverty. For example, Pogge estimates that a $2 per barrel tax on crude oil extraction could generate more than 18 percent of the revenue needed to raise the income of the world's poorest population to $2 per day.

Over the years, Sen has extensively discussed a variety of policies that would facilitate social and economic development in underdeveloped societies

---

[37] Ibid., chap. 3.

and thereby contribute to alleviating global poverty.[38] In general, he contrasts two different approaches to development – one that he calls "growth mediated," the other "support led."[39] The former seeks development and poverty reduction through rapid economic growth and requires that the growth yield investment in employment and social services. The latter seeks development through investments in social services and the maintenance of democratic institutions. Sen discusses the virtues of the support-led approach extensively in his writings. He argues that the historical evidence indicates that investments in education and primary healthcare are especially useful in producing economic growth and raising people out of poverty. Political freedoms are also very important in part because there has never been widespread famine in a well-established democracy. He also argues that social and educational programs that empower women reduce birthrates and therefore help to reduce poverty.

Scope and Priorities

Until recently the vast majority of the work of liberal egalitarians has been concerned with inequalities within states or domestic society. Over the past three decades, this concentration has been changing, a result, in part, of confronting the fact that not only is there severe poverty in the developing and underdeveloped world but inequality globally is profound. The United Nations Development Programme notes that the total income of the world's richest 1 percent of people is equal to that of the poorest 57 percent.[40] The assets of the richest three people in the world are more than the combined GNP of all of the least developed countries.[41] These huge inequalities have dramatic effects on the life prospects of persons. One important example of this is longevity. According to the World Health Organization, "Over 60% of deaths in developed countries occur beyond age 70, compared to about 30% in developing countries."[42]

As a response to global inequality, several liberal egalitarians have argued that Rawls's robustly egalitarian principles of distributive justice can be applied globally.[43] Rawls disavows such an application. Moreover, he does not even believe that global poverty per se is unjust. He does, however, defend

---

[38] Many such proposals can be found in Sen, *Development as Freedom*.

[39] Jean Drèze and Amartya Sen, *Hunger and Public Action* (Oxford: Oxford University Press, 1989), chap. 10. See also Sen, *Development as Freedom*, chap. 2.

[40] United Nations Development Programme, *Human Development Report, 2002*, 19 http://hdr.undp.org/reports/global/1999/en/pdf/chapterone.pdf.

[41] Ibid., 38.

[42] Colin Mathers et al., *Global Burden of Disease in 2002: Data Sources, Methods and Results*, World Health Organization, Discussion Paper 54, 44, http://www3.who.int/whosis/menu.cfm?path=whosis,burden,burden_estimates&language=english.

[43] See, for example, Brian Barry, *The Liberal Theory of Justice* (Oxford: Oxford University Press, 1972), 128–33; Charles Beitz, *Political Theory and International Relations* (Princeton, NJ: Princeton University Press, 1979); Darrel Moellendorf, *Cosmopolitan*

a principle of assistance to what he terms "burdened societies."⁴⁴ These are
societies lacking in sufficient "political and cultural traditions, the human
capital and know-how, and, often, the material and technological resources
needed to be well-ordered."⁴⁵ Poverty eradication is not the primary goal of
assistance, although it might sometimes be instrumental in achieving the goal
of fostering a liberal or decent society.

Part of the reason that Rawls has for this view rests on an account of the
causes of poverty globally. He takes these to be primarily domestic and therefore rejects the assignment of responsibility to noncompatriots. Rawls seems
to reason that, in the domestic case, principles of justice guide institutions in
order to ensure fair terms of cooperation among individual persons; but in the
international case, this is not necessary because persons do not cooperate with
one another sufficiently; hence, principles of justice ensure the fair terms of
cooperation between societies, each of which is responsible for the well-being
of its individual citizens. Such reasoning would explain why the justificatory
procedures that Rawls employs for the domestic case and the international
case are so different. In the domestic case, the original position contains
parties that represent the interests of persons. But in the international case
the original position contains parties that represent the interests of liberal
or decent societies. From this original position, Rawls contends that eight
principles of international justice – the Law of Peoples – would be affirmed.
These include, among others, respect for sovereignty, nonintervention, self-
defense, respect for a minimal set of human rights, and a duty of assistance to
burdened societies.

The set of eight principles that Rawls defends, and the argument that he uses
to do so, have received significant attention and criticism. Pogge argues that
even if the parties in the original position are representatives of societies, not
individual persons, it is unclear why, if deliberating behind a veil of ignorance
about their wealth and resources, they would not choose an egalitarian distributive principle.⁴⁶ A concern for the possibility of being a weak and vulnerable society – maximin reasoning – would seem to support such a choice, and
an interest in self-determination would not bar it because greater resources
among the poor would seem to increase the capacity for self-determination.

Justice (Boulder, CO: Westview Press, 2002); Thomas Pogge, *Realizing Rawls* (Ithaca,
NY: Cornell University Press, 1989); R. G. Peffer, *Marxism, Morality and Social Justice*
(Princeton, NJ: Princeton University Press, 1990); David A. J. Richards, "International
Distributive Justice," in *Ethics, Economics and the Law*, ed. J. R. Pennock and John W.
Chapman (New York: New York University Press, 1982), 219–52; and T. M. Scanlon,
"Rawls' Theory of Justice," in *Reading Rawls: Critical Studies on Rawls' "A Theory of
Justice,"* ed. Norman Daniels (Stanford: Stanford University Press, 1989). 169–205.
⁴⁴ Rawls's account of assistance to burdened societies is developed in *Law of Peoples*
(Cambridge, MA: Harvard University Press, 1999), 105–20.
⁴⁵ Ibid., 106.
⁴⁶ Thomas Pogge, "An Egalitarian Law of Peoples," *Philosophy and Public Affairs* 23
(1994): 195–224.

Another problem concerns the relationship between the principle of respect for human rights and principles of egalitarian distributive justice. If representatives of liberal societies would endorse a human rights principle, then why would they not endorse global egalitarian principles as well? Alternatively, if they would not endorse the latter, then why the former?[47]

Several aspects of globalization call into question Rawls's background assumption that fair terms of cooperation are needed only between societies and not between persons. One is increased economic integration. There are now global markets in labor, resources, consumer goods, and investment opportunities. The institutions of the World Trade Organization govern the vast majority of international trade. Successful development strategies are typically led by the development of manufacturing sectors producing for foreign markets.[48] Foreign direct investment (FDI) is very often a requirement of domestic financing as well as financing from third-party countries.[49] This makes FDI increasingly important in the economic development of countries. But generally the globalization of investment has been associated with an increase in job insecurity and increased inequalities within states.[50] Increased economic integration has been associated with a trend toward increased global inequality, but measurement controversies abound here.[51] To borrow and adapt a term from Walzer, the economic sphere seems both larger than and relatively independent of the multiple spheres of national politics.

Rawls is by no means the only liberal egalitarian theorist who believes that distributive principles are limited by state borders. Several theorists defend coercion accounts, which take either the content or strength of distributive duties to depend upon whether the other person is a fellow member of a coercive (state) legal system.[52] Usually these accounts emphasize two coercion-producing aspects of legal systems – namely, that they sanction violators and that the sanction is the product of the rules of the legal system. Coercion

---

[47] See Moellendorf, *Cosmopolitan Justice*, 7–29, for a discussion of this and related criticisms.

[48] See the thorough discussion of such strategies in Ha-Joon Chang, *Kicking Away the Ladder: Development Strategy in Historical Perspective* (London: Anthem Press, 2002).

[49] Victor S. F. Sit, "Globalization, Foreign Direct Investment, and Urbanization in Developing Countries," in *Facets of Globalization: International and Local Dimensions of Development*, ed. Shahid Yusuf, Simon Evenett, and Weiping Wu, World Bank Discussion Paper No. 415 (Washington, DC: World Bank, 2001), 12–13.

[50] Cf. Guy Standing, *Global Labour Flexibility: Seeking Distributive Justice* (New York: St. Martin's Press, 1999), pt. III.

[51] Cf. Branko Milanovic, *Worlds Apart* (Princeton, NJ: Princeton University Press, 2005), chap. 8.

[52] Important accounts include Michael Blake, "Distributive Justice, State Coercion, and Autonomy," *Philosophy and Public Affairs* 30 (202): 257–96; Richard W. Miller, "Cosmopolitan Respect and Patriotic Concern," *Philosophy and Public Affairs* 27 (1998): 202–24; and Thomas Nagel, "The Problem of Global Justice," *Philosophy and Public Affairs* 33 (2005): 113–47. For a response to Blake, Miller, and Nagel, see Darrel Moellendorf, *Global Inequality Matters* (Basingstoke: Palgrave Macmillan, 2009), chap. 2.

accounts often maintain that coercion is justified if and only if the institutions also uphold the principles of egalitarian distributive justice. The upshot is that because compatriots participate in a common legal system that deliberately coerces persons into obedience to the norms, and noncompatriots do not, duties of egalitarian justice exist between compatriots but not (or not as strongly) between noncompatriots.

This account might be challenged on two grounds. It might be responded that international institutions and treaty law, for example, the laws of the World Trade Organization, also coerce individuals.[53] But I believe that the more fundamental challenge is to the claim that legal sanction is not necessary for duties of egalitarian distributive justice. This challenge asserts that the claim that legal sanction is necessary for duties of egalitarian distributive justice confuses instances of necessary conditions for the more general conditions. The more general conditions are that individual persons have no reasonable alternative but compliance with the norms of association and that those norms are changeable by deliberate social action. It makes no significant moral difference whether the lack of reasonable alternative is due to punishment or, say, starvation or whether the situation is the product of legislation or, say, years of conventional commercial practice. If this is the case, the global economy governed by norms of market competition (as well as WTO rules) is plausibly sufficient for the generation of duties of egalitarian distributive justice. It should be noted that, although coercion accounts generally reject the global application of principles of egalitarian distributive justice (or their equal strength with domestic applications), not all of the accounts deny the existence of duties to prevent severe poverty. Michael Blake's account, for example, maintains that equal respect for the autonomy of persons requires egalitarianism domestically but insurance against debilitating poverty globally.[54]

There are other accounts of the basis of global egalitarian principles that are not contingent on features of the global economy. Charles Beitz and Brian Barry both argue that there is no nonarbitrary way to assign ownership of natural resources to any set of persons smaller than the set that contains everyone in the world.[55] Hence, the income associated with sale of the rights to exploit resources should be equally distributed to all. The practical implication of these egalitarian liberal accounts overlap significantly with left-libertarian accounts that assert that all persons possess an equal natural property right in the earth's land or natural resources.[56] Presumably, such an equal distribution

---

[53] See, for example, Barry, *Why Social Justice Matters*, 29.

[54] Blake, "Distributive Justice, State Coercion, and Autonomy."

[55] Charles R. Beitz, *Political Theory and International Relations* (Princeton, NJ: Princeton University Press, 1979), 136–43, and Brian Barry, "Humanity and Justice in Global Perspective," in *Ethics, Economics, and the Law*, ed. J. Roland Penncock and John W. Chapman (New York: New York University Press, 1982), 219–52.

[56] Cf. Henry George, *Progress and Poverty* (New York: Robert Schalkenbach Foundation, 1962). For a recent application to matters of global justice, see Hillel Steiner, "Just Taxation

of ownership income would go a long way toward mitigating the most severe instances of poverty globally. Others, such as Simon Caney and Kok-Chor Tan, argue that principles of distributive justice are not necessarily contingent on institutional arrangements at all. Hence, if it is the case that there are sound arguments for egalitarian principles of distributive justice domestically, then the arguments are equally sound in application to the global setting.[57]

Responsibility and Conditionality

Liberal egalitarian theories of social justice offer accounts of the fair distribution of goods (understood broadly). Accounts of social and individual responsibility are not always explicit in these theories. Accounts of social responsibility can be plausibly inferred by employing the reasonable assumption that social responsibility is directed toward the provision of institutions that ensure a fair distribution. It might be further inferred (by lack of an alternative source of responsibility) that when a person's share of the goods is within the latitude allowed by just institutions, responsibility for her condition is an individual matter.

Interpreting Dworkin requires no such inferences. He is explicit about the assignment of social and individual responsibility under just institutions. He rejects an egalitarianism that seeks to equalize the utility or welfare of persons on grounds that it would render society responsible for individual choices, tastes, and preferences. If a person develops expensive tastes and is not happy unless these are satisfied, then rendering her welfare equal to that of a person with much more modest tastes would require significant differences in expenditure. Dworkin maintains there is no social responsibility to incur this cost of equalizing welfare because the individual is responsible for her tastes. Because he takes natural talents as resembling external resources in some respects, he advocates an income tax as a means of transferring from the talented to the less talented. It is, however, controversial whether such an institution could sufficiently distinguish talents, for which individuals are not responsible, from efforts, for which they are.

Dworkin's account of responsibility can be contrasted with other egalitarian accounts. Some versions of egalitarianism seek to equalize opportunities but leave persons responsible for the realization of their opportunities. One version of this is the first part of Rawls's second principle of justice, a principle he calls "fair equality of opportunity." This principle is more egalitarian than a formal equal opportunity principle that merely requires that persons

---

and International Redistribution," in *Global Justice*, ed. Ian Shapiro and Lea Brilmayer (New York: New York University Press, 1999), 171–91.

[57] See Simon Caney, *Justice beyond Borders* (Oxford: Oxford University Press, 2005), 121–22; and Kok-Chor Tan, "The Boundary of Justice and the Justice of Boundaries," *Canadian Journal of Law & Jurisprudence* 19, no. 2 (July 2006): 319–44, and his *Justice without Borders* (Cambridge: Cambridge University Press, 2004), 175.

not be discriminated against in education and employment. Fair equality of opportunity requires that persons of approximately equal natural talents and abilities have approximately equal opportunity sets throughout their youth so that their access to positions of privilege as adults is not significantly determined by social factors such as race, gender, religion, or even their parents' social class and wealth.

Notice that fair equality of opportunity leaves the responsibility to individuals to choose to make something of the opportunities by the employment of their natural talents. As such, neither the choice nor the talent set are a matter of social responsibility. It is not necessarily unjust if two equally talented persons have unequal social positions as long as the difference is due to the choice to act on some opportunities that both have and not due to unequal opportunities. It also is not necessarily unjust if people of different talent sets have different social opportunities. Barry defends a version of equality of opportunity that expands social responsibility by holding that differences in effort alone (not in natural talents) can justify unequal outcomes.[58] His account of the assignment of social and individual responsibility, then, although opportunity- and not resource-based, is similar to Dworkin's.

Fair equality of opportunity is not, however, a stand-alone principle according to Rawls. It is one part of what he calls the "democratic conception equality," which includes the difference principle (the second part of the second principle of justice), which requires that inequalities be to the maximum benefit of the least advantaged. The effect of adding this principle to fair equality of opportunity is to reduce the range of justified inequalities on the basis of choice and talent. Even if the least advantaged are disadvantaged in part because of their talents or their choices about whether to develop them, economic institutions that permit such disadvantages are just only if there is no alternative institutional arrangement in which the least advantaged persons of that alternative society would have greater wealth and income. Therefore, the scope of social responsibility is enlarged.

Democratic equality does not, however, extinguish either talents or choice as the basis of justified inequalities. In effect, the least well-off persons are fully responsible for their inferior position only if there is not an alternative possible arrangement in which the least well-off would be better off. Hence, although personal choice might render a person at least partially responsible for being less well-off than other members of her society, it does not necessarily render her fully responsible for her deprivation. If there is an alternative social arrangement in which the least well-off persons would be better off, then the least well-off person in the actual society is not responsible for the extent of her deprivation that falls below the persons in the possible society.

This has important consequences for responsibility for poverty. Imagine the following scenario. The society contains (among others) groups of persons

---

58 Barry, *Why Social Justice Matters*, 37–45.

A and B. A is affluent, while B lives in poverty. Are persons in B responsible for their poverty or is the society responsible? Imagine an alternative institutional arrangement, which could be arrived at by reforming or radically reconstructing the society in which A and B live. In this alternative society, other persons might constitute the group of the less affluent. Persons in group C are the least affluent but are not impoverished. Assume that they are less affluent than A but more affluent than B. Then, according to the difference principle, the condition of B is unjust. We can infer that even if persons in B are responsible for being less affluent than persons in A, they are not responsible for the extent of the deprivation that they suffer that is greater than C's. Hence, even if they are individually responsible for being in a subordinate position, they are not responsible for being impoverished. If social institutions can prevent the poor from being impoverished, then society is responsible for doing this.

Conclusion

Liberal egalitarians generally agree that poverty is a mark of injustice in social institutions. But the liberal egalitarian accounts of why that is the case are many and varied. For some it follows from their egalitarian distributive commitments, for others from their commitments to human rights. The disagreements, however, do not stop there. They also concern the scope of the egalitarian and antipoverty commitments, whether duties of these sorts are owed only to compatriots or to noncompatriots as well. I have surveyed several of the most influential accounts and debates. Many others also merit consideration but cannot be discussed here. The depth and range of disagreements might strike some as a reason to despair about the capacity of liberal egalitarianism to be adequate in the details. On the contrary, it seems to me to be evidence of a rich and vibrant tradition, generating the kind of debate that offers hope for genuine moral understanding.

12

Marxism and Poverty

Andrew Levine

Religions, Emile Durkheim tells us, are systems of practices and beliefs that maintain social cohesion by inculcating norms and rules of conduct.[1] Their function is to join individuals together into societies. So conceived, they need not be theistic; thus the "primitive" religions he studied were, at most, pretheistic, and the religions of the scientific age that Durkheim, along with other positivists, envisioned will not be theistic either. But all religions that persist for significant periods of time would have ethical traditions associated with them; after all, establishing rules that guide individual conduct is what religions do. Thus, all the so-called world religions have ethical traditions. But this is less true of traditions of thought that are not exactly religions in their own right. Natural law theories, which intersect with some of the world religions – Catholic Christianity, especially – occupy a different conceptual space. Natural law theory is a kind of moral philosophy – like utilitarianism or Kantianism, to cite pertinent modern examples. A moral philosophy is a philosophical theory, not an ethic. It can help shape ethics, but the connections are seldom direct. The situation is different yet again with political movements – feminism, liberalism (in its egalitarian and libertarian versions), and Marxism, insofar as they do not rise (or fall) to the level of religions in Durkheim's sense. In its (big-C) Communist version, Marxism was more susceptible than the others to taking a religious turn. Thus, it was not uncommon for opponents, and sometimes also neutral observers, to call Communism or some version of it – Stalinism or Trotskyism or even Leninism – religions. Needless to say, this was not a description self-identified Marxists welcomed. It is questionable, too, how apt it was. Insofar as there is anything to the description, it pertains to an aberrant phenomenon within the larger Marxist political and theoretical tradition, one that is plainly at odds with the letter and spirit of Marx's thought. Thus, it makes more sense to group Marxism

[1] Emile Durkheim, *The Elementary Forms of Religious Life*, trans. Karen E. Fields (New York: Free Press, 1995). Durkheim claimed to have identified an essential structural property all religions share: a categorical distinction between sacred and profane realms.

with liberalism than, say, with Catholicism or Islam or, as Stalin's critics would have it, Eastern Orthodoxy.

Within each of the (mainly) political movements just identified, there are convergences of viewpoints, though they are sometimes evident only at high levels of generality. There are also considerable theoretical disagreements. Thus, it is not unusual to find self-identified feminists, liberals, and Marxists (along with proponents of other political "isms") appealing to a variety of moral philosophical traditions for support. In these instances, the idea that they have an ethical tradition or traditions associated with them is extremely problematic. This is especially true of Marxism.

The terminology I have been assuming is fairly standard. It can be confusing, however, because it is not universally employed and because one of its key components, "moral philosophy," is misleading. I should therefore define my terms directly. By a "moral philosophy," I mean a philosophical theory of the right and the good (as these notions bear on what we ought to do). Aristotle, Hobbes, Kant, Mill, and many others advanced moral philosophies in this sense. Moral philosophies can and generally do underwrite "ethical theories" – guides to conduct pitched at an abstract level. Some, but not all, of these ethical theories are "moral theories." Moral theories, as distinct from moral philosophies, are ethical theories that depend fundamentally on "the moral point of view," the point of view of impartiality or generality or universality or agent neutrality (where these are alternative descriptions of the same idea). That idea is that conduct should be assessed from no particular agent's vantage point, but from the vantage point of agency as such. Hobbes, Kant, and Mill were moral theorists in this sense; Aristotle was not.

Moral theory is peculiar to the "Western" philosophical tradition, though I would not be surprised if other philosophical traditions developed similar notions. The moral point of view emerged in a world shaped, in part, by the Judaism – or proto-Judaism – of the Prophetic period. It finds its first clear, though still primitive, articulation in the so-called golden rule; in other words, in the sacred writings of Christianity. Ancient Greek ethics had no notion of impartial deliberation, though the Socratic and post-Socratic aspiration to provide rationally compelling theories can be enlisted in support of the idea. Moral theory has been the predominant mode of ethical thought in the West at least since the early modern period. Even holdouts from earlier strains of Christian (or Jewish and perhaps also Islamic) "traditions" have more or less been brought on board. There have also been prominent critics of morality, though obviously not of ethics itself. Nietzsche was perhaps the best known. In a very different way, Marx, too, was a critic of morality.

Marx and Moral Philosophy

Marx's relation to moral philosophy was quite attenuated. After breaking with his "erstwhile philosophical conscience" (Young Hegelianism) in his early twenties, he had virtually nothing to say about the subject. Years later, in developing a theory of history, historical materialism, moral theories were treated – at least implicitly, along with other "forms of consciousness" – in the way that legal and political "superstructures" were. The general idea is that they are as they are because they are functional for reproducing an under-lying (infrastructural) "economic base." "Base" and "superstructure" (or superstructure plus forms of consciousness) are metaphorical descriptions. What historical materialism does is identify real structures it calls "modes of production." It then periodizes history as a succession of modes of pro-duction. Thus, it purports to give an account of history's real structure. It also purports to identify an endogenous process leading from one mode of production to another – in the absence of exogenous interferences or other factors that preempt the unfolding of this dynamic. Ethical thinking, being part of consciousness, plays a role in this story; it helps to maintain modes of production. This role is causal, not epiphenomenal, as some have imagined. It could hardly be otherwise if forms of consciousness stabilize and reproduce the economic base.

In his Young Hegelian period, Marx faulted moral theories – or, more pre-cisely, Hegelian theories of Right (*Recht*) – precisely for their universality. His point was that principles of Right ignore real societal (class) divisions, submerging them in a *false* universality. In doing so, they reinforce class dom-ination by obfuscating its reality – indeed, by advancing a "moral view of the world" that implicitly denies that these divisions exist. Thus, long before the base/superstructure component of his theory of history emerged, Marx anticipated one of its key tenets – and, in so doing, he made himself a critic of morality. Decades later, Nietzsche would fault the moral view of the world by impugning the very notion of universality, not just its real world applications. His aim was to overcome (supersede) morality by incorporating its "negation" of pre-Christian ethical standards into a yet undeveloped "higher" unity. This is, of course, a Hegelian formulation. It has lately been fashionable to read vestiges of Hegelianism in Nietzsche's formulations as ironic rhetorical ges-tures. Whether or not this is so, Marx's point was less radical, and not at all *anti*-Kantian. His claim was just that this side of communism, where class divisions are finally overcome, morality can be and often is a snare and an illusion.

Marx may have abandoned moral philosophy, and disparaged morality, but it is plain, even from his later work on other subjects, that his moral phil-osophical, and moral, convictions never disappeared. Orthodox Marxism, the Marxism of the Second International and then of official Communism (and also Trotskyism and Maoism) took Marx's (ambivalent) disparagement of morality to heart. But, from roughly the 1950s through the 1980s, when Marxism fell into an eclipse from which it has yet to emerge, considerable attention has been expended on uncovering the moral philosophical under-pinnings of Marx's thinking. What has become clear is that, apart from Marx's claim about the real world of morality, there is nothing particularly innovative about his moral philosophical commitments. The reasons to dwell on them have more to do with the insight they provide on Marx's views on other topics than on moral philosophy per se.

I have argued elsewhere that "alienation," a key metaphysical *and* moral philosophical concept in Marx's early (Young Hegelian) writings, is roughly "heteronomy" in Kant's sense and, therefore, that Marx advanced a Kantian conception of *unfreedom*.[2] It was to end alienation that Marx first proposed (small-c) communism as a political objective. If I am right about what alienation is, it follows that Marx too defended a generally Kantian conception of freedom (as autonomy). Not long ago, the connection between Marx's early and later writings was a lively topic of debate.[3] However, it soon became clear that this question had more to do with politically motivated accounts of Marx's intellectual trajectory than with analyses of Marx's writings. So-called Marxist humanists endeavored to join Marx's Young Hegelianism to his mature reflections on political economy and related matters. Those who wanted to assume the mantle of Marxist (or Marxist-Leninist) orthodoxy advocated, instead, for an "epistemological break," as Althusser called it. But the facts on the ground were never in doubt. As a Young Hegelian, Marx did advocate views that were connected historically and conceptually with Kantian moral philosophy. When Marx turned from philosophy to other subjects, he never repudiated these earlier views. It is therefore fair to say that, under the skin, Marx remained a Kantian (or rather a Young Hegelian descendant of Kant) to the end, even if he was reluctant to admit it.

The Young Hegelians made much of Kant's claim, seconded by Hegel,[4] that Kantian moral philosophy defended the idea of freedom – specifically, the conception of freedom found in Rousseau. It would be only slightly facetious to say that, for the Young Hegelians, Rousseau "discovered" that idea, Kant worked it out, and Marx and the others believed it or at least wanted to put it into practice. I would add that Marx never stopped wanting to put it into practice, at least insofar as he remained a (small-c) communist. Marx was famously loath to say much about communism, to prescribe "recipes for the cook shops of the future." But it is clear that, for him, communism did what the *Rechtstaat* of Hegelian political philosophy falsely purported to do – it realized the idea of freedom. Communism, according to *The Communist Manifesto*, is a "realm of freedom" – where "the condition for the free development of each is the free development of all." Because the freedom Marx

2 Andrew Levine, *Engaging Political Philosophy: From Hobbes to Rawls* (Malden, MA: Blackwell, 2002), chap. 6.
3 An influential proponent of the idea that Marx's early writings were non-Marxist was Louis Althusser. See, for example, Louis Althusser, *For Marx*, trans. Ben Brewster (New York: Pantheon, 1969).
4 See, for example, G. W. F. Hegel, *The Phenomenology of Mind*, trans. J. B. Baillie (New York: Humanities Press, 1966), III, C, a ("The moral view of the world").

had in mind was the conception of freedom that Kant defended, his moral philosophy was Kantian. To be sure, he was no longer interested in contributing to the development of Kantian moral philosophy after he broke with Young Hegelianism, not even in the attenuated way that he had previously. He turned his attention instead to understanding and changing real world conditions in ways that bring humanity closer to Kant's vision of an ideal moral order. He remained dedicated, in other words, to exploring how "the moral vision of the world," constituted by a "harmony of rational wills," could have *actual*, not merely *possible*, applicability.

The other towering moral philosophical figure affecting Marx's thinking was Aristotle. In this instance, there is no question of an "epistemological break"; Marx's Aristotelianism was consistent, and there has never been any reason, political or otherwise, to deny it. Aristotelianism is implicit in Marx's philosophical anthropology – particularly, his view of the good. For Aristotle, the world consists of discrete kinds, each with potentialities awaiting realization. Aristotle's core normative contention was that it is good, good in itself, for these potentialities to be realized; in other words, for each natural kind to become "excellent" in its own way. In Marx's view, it is similarly good when human beings become, as it were, all that they can be – as they will, Marx thought, provided History's trajectory is not deflected away from the course his theory of history, historical materialism, predicts. That theory identifies an endogenous process that would lead to a (small-c) communist future, provided it is not overwhelmed by exogenous causal factors.[5] In his more Kantian moments, freedom mattered to Marx for its own sake; in his more Aristotelian moments, it mattered because it is necessary for self-realization. Had Marx been more interested in moral philosophy, he might have found ways to integrate these thoughts. For his own purposes, however, there was no need, inasmuch as these distinct ways of thinking converge in humanity's communist future. Communism, the realm of freedom, supposes abundance and therefore freedom from burdensome toil. It also supposes persons disposed more to act for the sake of human solidarity than their own interests (egoistically conceived). It is, in short, a realm of uncoerced – freely (autonomously) chosen – cooperation. These conditions are indispensable, Marx reasoned, if human beings are to become all that they potentially are.

Most natural kinds self-realize without regard to their historical situation. A flower becomes all that it can be provided it is supplied with the right soil in which to grow, the right amount of sunlight, the right amount of moisture, and so on. Its place in human history is obviously irrelevant; so is its place in natural history. Human beings, on the other hand, are inserted into a historical process. Therefore, the nature of their special excellence changes as human history advances. Being history's final epochal stage, communism provides the richest imaginable conditions for human self-realization. Communist

---

[5] I elaborate on this contention in *Engaging Political Philosophy*.

men and women have more opportunities to set ends before themselves than even the most privileged precommunist men and women, and they have the most means available for realizing their ends. Marx's rare speculations about daily life in communist societies – for example, his claim that people will hunt in the morning, fish in the afternoon, and philosophize (be "critical critics") at night – is hopelessly utopian, if only because the polymorphous development of all capacities is impossible given the constraints of time and human limitations. But perhaps some more modest approximation is realizable under conditions of real freedom for all.[6] This is what Marx hoped. This is why it is fair to see him standing on the shoulders not only of Kant but of Aristotle as well. However, in this instance, too, he was not an Aristotelian philosopher, carrying on that tradition in the way that, for example, Thomas Aquinas did. He was instead just a devotee, intent on making the world safe for the kind of excellence Aristotelian moral philosophy envisioned.

From Marx to Marxism

In the last years of Marx's life, "Marxism" began to coalesce into a distinct tendency within the workers' movement. It was for this reason that Marx felt obliged to proclaim that he was not a Marxist.[7] His hesitations notwithstanding, Marxism quickly became the major socialist tendency in Europe and, in short order, throughout the rest of the world. The period between 1889, when the Second International was founded, and the outbreak of the First World War was, as Leszek Kolakowsi put it, Marxism's "golden age."[8] It was in this period that a kind of orthodoxy, the Marxism of the Second International, crystallized.

The Bolshevik Revolution transformed that golden age forever, giving rise to new orthodoxies. But Second International Marxism would probably not have survived much longer in any case; if nothing else, changes in world capitalism, as it entered a revivified imperialist stage, made aspects of the old orthodoxy anachronistic. Thus, from the beginning of the twentieth century, there were dissident or at least nonorthodox Marxist thinkers who challenged aspects of Second International and then Communist orthodoxy. Dissidence increased as the decades wore on, especially as the Marxist orthodoxy of the golden age became transformed into Stalinist orthodoxy. Many erstwhile Marxists abandoned the fold altogether; others developed a slew of diverse and sometimes incompatible reconstructions of Marxist theory.

---

[6] The expression comes from Philippe Van Parijs. See *Real Freedom for All: What (If Anything) Can Justify Capitalism?* (Oxford: Oxford University Press, 1995).

[7] Marx is reputed to have several times declared that he was not a "Marxist." The best evidence for him having actually uttered the words "je ne suis pas marxiste," as is often claimed, is a letter from Friedrich Engels to C. Schmidt, dated August 5, 1890.

[8] See Leszek Kolakowski, *Main Currents of Marxism: The Golden Age*, trans. P. S. Falla (Oxford: Oxford University Press, 1978).

Twentieth-century Marxism drew more on contemporaneous philosophical currents than on Marx's own philosophical (or moral philosophical) commitments. Some of the "Austro-Marxists" – Victor Adler, Otto Bauer, Karl Renner, and especially Max Adler – were exceptions inasmuch as their overriding philosophical commitments also derived from Kant. But their Kantianism, or rather neo-Kantianism, had more to do with the intellectual milieu in which they lived than with any intention on their part to develop Marx's own positions. Most other Western Marxists adhered to philosophical currents that did not even emerge until decades after Marx's death: phenomenology, existentialism, and structuralism, or on strains of neo-Hegelian thinking that diverged considerably from Marx's own Young Hegelianism. Twentieth-century Marxism was, in any case, not particularly focused on moral philosophical issues, though some Western Marxists – not just the Austro-Marxists but Georg Lukács and Jean-Paul Sartre, among others – did promote views about "What is to be done?" In this sense, one could ascribe distinctive views about ethics to them. But their ethics do not so much derive from Marx or from classical Marxism as from ways of thinking that are independent of Marxism, as in Sartre's case, or, as in Lukács's, from reflections on Bolshevism – in other words, on a political departure from Marx's thinking and from the orthodoxy of Marxism's golden age. It is telling that even those who would insist most adamantly that Leninism is a continuation of classical Marxist theory and practice emphasize its innovative aspects – hence, the designation "Marxism Leninism."

Western Marxism was largely a creature of what analytical philosophers disparagingly call "continental philosophy." These philosophical currents, applied to Marxist themes, tended to encourage programmatic posturing over painstaking elaborations and assessments of particular theses. Not so "analytical Marxism," an intellectual tendency that emerged in the English-speaking world in the 1970s and that briefly flourished for roughly the next decade and a half.[9] Analytical Marxism bore little connection to self-identified Marxist political tendencies. Unlike most Western Marxists, its practitioners were therefore unaccountable to any political constituency. On the other hand, they were very accountable to academic constituencies and therefore adhered closely to the disciplinary norms of analytical philosophy, empirical social science, and mainstream economic theory. Philosophers led the way. They did so at a time when moral, social, and political philosophy came increasingly under the sway of the form of egalitarian liberalism developed by John Rawls. It is hardly surprising therefore that, as Marx's positions, along with those of orthodox Marxists, were subjected to scrutiny in accord with prevailing academic norms, Marxism, or rather Marxist moral philosophy, collapsed into Rawlsian liberalism. By the time analytical Marxism had

[9] For further elaboration, see my *A Future for Marxism? Althusser, the Analytical Turn and the Revival of Socialist Theory* (London: Pluto Press, 2003).

more or less run its course, it seemed that, from a moral philosophical point of view, there was nothing distinctively Marxist left. Without quite saying as much, most analytical Marxists came to believe that, insofar as a focus on Marxian themes provides any special insight into notions of justice or exploitation or equality or any other topic of concern to moral philosophers, it is only because of the empirical findings Marxist social science brings to bear on these matters.[10] Thus, analytical Marxism failed to establish a Marxist moral philosophy. However, unlike other strains of Western Marxism, which also failed to develop a distinctive Marxist moral philosophy, analytical Marxists made moral philosophical issues central concerns. In so doing, they made clear what other Western Marxists implicitly understood: that there is no Marxist moral philosophy to develop. Although the issues are not quite the same, they also made clear that there is no distinctive Marxist ethic either.

Bolshevik Ethics

But what is true of the whole is not quite true of all of the parts. Thus, Bolshevism did, in a way, promote a distinctive (though hardly unique) ethic. That would be the straw man ethic of popular moral theorizing – where "the end justifies the means." This is an unfortunate characterization. What else would justify the means, as Sidney Morgenbesser used to quip? The real issues have to do not with what determines what (inasmuch as it is a truism that, as Kant put it, "to will the end is to will the means thereto"), but with what, if anything, should constrain means in political contexts. An extreme position – examined cogently in Jean-Paul Sartre's play *Dirty Hands* (*Les mains sales*) – holds that the only constraints worth taking into account are strategic, not moral, ones; that anything goes, provided it is efficacious for some defensible – and sufficiently momentous – end. What makes Sartre's treatment of the problem interesting is that the position he investigates applies not only to actions that morality proscribes (like lying or killing) but also to self-identifications and other ingrained features of persons' characters. In other words, integrity and authenticity are as much at issue as right and wrong actions. *Dirty Hands* investigates those who would turn themselves entirely into instruments of revolution, along with those who would hold something back, not because they question the revolution's importance (that is assumed) but for reasons that count as ethical (and perhaps also moral). The situation is complicated, even for those who would hold nothing back. As Sartre's dramatization makes clear, there are both ethical and epistemological dimensions

---

[10] Because analytical Marxists also maintained that there is no distinctively Marxist social scientific methodology, the idea that these distinctive positions are in some theoretically pertinent sense distinctively *Marxist* is also tenuous. Marxist social science yields findings that elude other social scientific tendencies because of the questions its investigators address, not because of the methods they deploy.

to being a "professional revolutionary" in the Bolshevik sense. It is one thing to place oneself entirely at the disposal of a historical calling, and something else to place oneself at the disposal of some ostensibly infallible arbiter of historical callings. When Sartre wrote *Dirty Hands*, this was a timely issue. The parties of international Communism in the age of Stalin represented themselves as indispensable for humanity's leap into "the realm of freedom." Their thinking was of a piece with Saint Cyprian's who declared that "outside the Church, there is no salvation," but with the crucial difference that Communist politics is *not* about saving oneself or anything else of concern to the morally scrupulous; it is about moving History along to its final end (*telos*). The party's role was to direct its militants to do what History requires; a task that, by its own lights, only it can fulfill. Outside the party, there is no revolution. This description may seem a caricature. But it is not far from the popular understandings of the time.

The "dirty hands" ethic Sartre examined is a species of what Max Weber called "an ethic of responsibility."[11] Weber contrasted that ethic with an "ethic of ultimate ends." Weber's ethical convictions were neo-Kantian. He did maintain that the Sermon on the Mount puts forward a paradigmatic example of an ethic of ultimate ends. But he might as well have said that the Sermon on the Mount, or at least its golden rule, anticipates Kantian ethics. In any case, it is clear that, for Weber, an ethic of ultimate ends is a Kantian ethic – where, as in one of Kant's formulations of the categorical imperative, persons are treated as ends in themselves and never as "means only." Were reason fully in control, individuals' wills would be in harmony – and there would be no need for coercive (i.e., political) coordination. But, because reason is not in control, politics is indispensable: it is the only "solution" to the problem of moral or, what comes to the same thing for Kant, rational recalcitrance. For as long as human beings remain recalcitrant – in other words, for all time – there will be a need for politics, and therefore for people for whom politics is a "vocation." Weber maintained that, for those who make that vocation their own, there will be circumstances that oblige them to violate the dictates of an ethic of ultimate ends in order to exercise their political functions responsibly. To be sure, he did write movingly of rare "here I stand, I can do no other" moments when the two ethics converge. But this is the limiting case. For the most part, an ethic of responsibility will diverge from an ethic of ultimate ends. This is why Weber concluded that politicians' hands will always be at least somewhat dirty.

For Sartre, these were timely issues – thanks to the crucial role the French Communist Party played in the Resistance and thanks to the vicissitudes of world Communism in its pre- and then postwar moments of High Stalinism. Sartre's play did not initiate this "conversation," however. His play was

---

[11] Max Weber, "Politics as a Vocation," in *From Max Weber: Essays in Sociology*, ed. Hans Gerth and C. Wright Mills (New York: Routledge, 2007), 77–128.

intended, in part, to counter Albert Camus's brief for *moral* constraints on political action – a case Camus developed, also in theatrical form, in *The Just Assassins (Les justes)*. There were other notable interventions into this debate as well – Maurice Merleau-Ponty's *Humanism and Terror*, for example.[12] Two decades later, New Left politics in the United States and elsewhere rekindled an interest in these problems, though the discussion never advanced much beyond where Sartre and the others had left it. In recent decades, as the specter of revolution, real or imaginary, has faded from the scene, so has interest in the problem Sartre and the others investigated. However, questions about the nature and extent of constraints on means in political contexts remain unresolved. If and when politics again takes an extraparliamentary turn, one can expect that the discussion will resume.

What this has to do with ethical traditions is just that in the Stalin era, the position Sartre investigated came to be identified with Marxism. There were two relatively independent reasons for this: one having to do with Marxism itself or, more precisely, with its theory of history; the other with the Bolshevik turn many Marxists took in the aftermath of the October Revolution. From at least the time of the Second International, historical materialism had become foundational for the Marxist worldview. As it happened, it was, in large part, by examining that theory – reconstructing it and defending it (at least at first) according to rigorous disciplinary (and therefore academic) standards – that analytical Marxism came into being.[13] What the scrutiny lavished on historical materialism eventually made plain is that historical materialism is not a theory of historical inevitability, after all.[14] But this was not the understanding in Marxism's golden age or in its postrevolutionary successor stage. In the orthodox view, shared by (classical) Social Democrats and Communists alike, communism is the inevitable outcome of History's course – and the sooner that end comes the better for everyone. For some within the working-class movement, this conviction inspired quietism or, more often, what Leninists called "economism" (essentially, trade unionism): Marxists went about their private or reformist business with the assurance that, at some future time, the revolution will set everything right. For others, the thought of history's inevitable end spurred a radical (and voluntarist) commitment to revolutionary political styles. For these impatient historical materialists, the question was

[12] Maurice Merleau-Ponty, *Humanism and Terror: The Communist Problem*, trans. John O'Neil (Edison, NJ: Transaction, 2000).
[13] See G. A. Cohen, *Karl Marx's Theory of History: A Defence* (Oxford: Oxford University Press; and Princeton, NJ: Princeton University Press, 1978). For further discussion of Cohen's seminal reconstruction of historical materialism, see Erik Olin Wright, Andrew Levine, and Elliott Sober, *Reconstructing Marxism* (London: Verso, 1992), chaps. 2–5. See also my *Engaging Political Philosophy*, chap. 6.
[14] See G. A. Cohen, "Historical Inevitability," in Cohen, *History, Labour and Freedom: Themes from Marx* (Oxford: Oxford University Press, 1988), 51–82, and Wright, Levine, and Sober, *Reconstructing Marxism*.

how best to hasten the onset of humanity's inevitable future. Although Lenin famously proclaimed patience (along with irony) the virtues of a Bolshevik, he was the most distinguished leader of the impatient, nonquietistic camp.

In the end, though, the differences were less momentous than might appear because, for both the patient and impatient alike, faith in the revolution's inevitability gave rise to what G. A. Cohen has called an obstetric conception of politics.[15] Just as a midwife or obstetrician helps along the inexorable biological process of birth, socialist reformers and revolutionaries help an inevitable historical process to unfold. Helping can be more or less interventionist. Bolshevism was strongly interventionist, with important consequences for its "ethic." Lenin and his followers took seriously the injunction that the revolutionary's first (and only?) duty is to make the revolution. As remarked, other Marxist currents lapsed into more conventional political styles.

It bears repeating that historical materialism, properly understood (or revised), is not really a theory of historical inevitability at all. It does identify reasons why "forces of production" (technology, broadly construed) will develop continuously, barring exogenous interferences; and it identifies a process inherent in technological development that leads "social relations of production" (real, as distinct from juridical, property relations) to change discontinuously, in order to accommodate to ever higher levels of development. This process leads, ultimately, to communism. But, as with any other endogenous process, the historical materialist dynamic would determine the outcome only in the absence of countervailing factors. But this is a subtle point: an unreflective but natural inference from historical materialism to "economistic" or Bolshevik politics is therefore hard to resist.

This is why, throughout the twentieth century, Marxists and quasi Marxists of all stamps, reformers and revolutionaries alike, thought differently. Oddly, in some ways, this was a fortunate turn of events. Had the Bolsheviks been less determined obstetricians and, I would add, less vigilant pediatricians after the revolution's "birth" – in other words, had they intervened less to help History along – they might never have seized power, and then, having seized it, held on to it for as long as they did. Thus, their political style, and the "ethic" associated with it, changed history. But history changed their ethic, in turn. As everyone knows, the world (or at least the European) revolution that was supposed to follow immediately from the collapse of imperialism's "weakest link" never quite materialized. For the Bolsheviks, therefore, the first priority came to be support for the world's only workers' state, awaiting the time when revolutionary upheavals would again erupt – the next time with more successful outcomes. As this hope failed to materialize too, the need to build "socialism in one country" came to be a Bolshevik (or, by then, a

---

[15] G. A. Cohen, *If You're an Egalitarian, How Come You're So Rich?* (Cambridge, MA: Harvard University Press, 2000), chap. 4.

Stalinist) tenet. This caused Bolshevik ethics to turn into something it plainly had not been before 1917.

On the theory, such as it was, of this transformation, Z.A. Jordan's account remains unsurpassed.[16] Jordan reconstructs the twisted rationale(s) that transformed putative proletarian revolutionaries into agents of the Soviet state – allegedly, but not exclusively, thanks to historical exigencies that no Marxist before the Russian Revolution had imagined. Jordan's genealogical account is a fitting counterpart to Sartre's play, which remains perhaps the best dramatization of the facts on the ground – conditioned, three decades after Soviet power was established, by a Soviet leadership bent on subordinating everything, entire generations even, to the interests of a self-described workers' state encircled by imperialist powers intent on destroying it.

We could argue endlessly about whether the Stalinist version of Bolshevism constitutes a Marxist ethic or whether Trotsky's "correction" of its crude "deformations" does. We could argue endlessly too about what a "classical" Leninist position might be on these matters, and on whether Lenin "revised" Marxist positions on politics and ethics, as Jordan argued, or only adapted them to historical circumstances. The fact remains that none of this amounts to an ethical tradition – first because it represents only a small, though politically important, component of the many varieties of theory and practice that have identified with Marx and Marxism, but also because, to the extent that there is a tradition involved, it is the tradition of revolutionary politics, not of Marxism per se. In its ethical dimensions, Bolshevism owes more to Jacobinism or even to Puritanism than to the main currents of nineteenth- or early twentieth-century Marxism. This is a point that many Bolsheviks – and their Stalinist, Trotskyist, and Maoist successors – would accept. They saw themselves as the latest actors in an age of revolution that began, along with the modern state and modern capitalism, in the Netherlands and England in the seventeenth century and that, eventually, came to shape the political terrain of the entire planet.

Marx was indeed a revolutionary, and so were most classical Marxists. But the ethic Sartre dramatized hardly resonated within the Marxist camp before the Bolshevik Revolution. It did not become dominant, even in postrevolutionary Russia, until Stalin determined that the world proletariat's first task was to build socialism in that one country. Rather than identifying this ethic with Marxism, it would therefore be more apt to say that a centuries-old strain of revolutionary theory and practice, distinguished by its disregard of moral constraints, came to take on a Marxist coloration. That this occurred is of great historical and political interest, but of little philosophical or ethical significance. The ethic Sartre brought literally to center stage is too extreme to raise serious moral philosophical concerns. Its distinguishing feature is that

---

[16] Z. A. Jordan, *The Evolution of Dialectical Materialism* (New York: St. Martin's Press, 1967), chap. 12: "Historical Materialism as a Guide to Action."

it ignores moral complexity. It is, as it were, an ethic of responsibility severed entirely from any ethic of ultimate ends. By now, the bankruptcy of this way of thinking has become clear to everyone. Even if the Age of Revolution has not yet run its course, the political style associated with Robespierre and Saint-Just has everywhere lost its appeal.

Such an ethic has little to say, even by implication, about poverty. Its position would just be that the poor matter insofar as they can be put to use for advancing or retarding revolutionary objectives. It is worth noting, however, that nearly all self-identified Marxists, including Bolsheviks, were wary of the poor, disparaging lumpen elements as useless at best, and potentially counterrevolutionary. This is not, and never has been, a distinctively Marxist *insight*. Throughout the nineteenth and twentieth centuries, "bourgeois" investigators of revolutionary movements advanced similar views. Indeed, it has become almost a truism that the agents of revolutionary change are never the most desperate and oppressed members of society. Those who fall under that description are usually too incapacitated to change the world, too bereft of the requisite organizational abilities and vision. They are, in other words, too oppressed to take up the revolutionary mantle or even to agitate seriously for far-reaching reforms. In the view of most Marxists, if the poorest of the poor can be brought along, fine. But, in most likely circumstances, time and effort are better spent neutralizing rather than recruiting them. Needless to say, under socialism, poverty will disappear; but the poor themselves will not be the ones mainly responsible for bringing about that welcome result.

Poverty

Marx and Marxists often spoke of the poor and therefore of poverty, the state of being (materially) poor, but the concept is not integral to any distinctively Marxist theory. When Marxists use the word, they use it in its colloquial sense. In nineteenth-century Europe, poverty was ubiquitous. In the twentieth century, it receded significantly in the more developed capitalist countries, while becoming ubiquitous throughout much of the less developed world, largely in consequence of the integration of large swathes of Africa, Asia, Latin America, and Oceana into the capitalist world system. Poverty was nearly eliminated in much of Northern Europe in the middle and late twentieth century, thanks to strong labor unions and social democratic governments. In the United States, it became increasingly sequestered in decaying urban areas where African Americans and Latinos constitute the majority of the poor, and in some rural areas where poverty and "race" are less closely correlated. In the United States as a whole, the majority of the poor are still white, as was the case in Marx's own environs and in the countries where most nineteenth- and early twentieth-century Marxists lived. In its colloquial (and therefore also Marxist) sense, the term connotes an *insufficiency*, not necessarily an *inequality*. Thus, one could imagine a society in which income and wealth are distributed unequally, but in which no one is poor. This was the situation approximated in Northern Europe. The rest of the world is still far from that point; and, with the ascendance of neoliberal economic policies and so-called free trade, many of the gains that have been won, in Europe and elsewhere, have been put increasingly in jeopardy.

Because the term poverty has no strict technical meaning within Marxism, Marxists, like anyone else, can use it to designate abnormally insufficient asset or income levels. When they do, they usually relativize what counts as "normal" and "abnormal" to prevailing economic and social circumstances. But they can also take these words to refer to a more absolute standard, determined by what counts as sufficient for meeting basic human needs. I would conjecture that in the nineteenth century, the latter understanding predominated, and that now the former understanding does. This change reflects conditions in developed societies. It has no particular theoretical significance. In developed countries, though inequality is rife, and lately on the rise, few people are so desperately poor that their most basic needs go unmet; thus hardly anyone would count as poor by nineteenth-century (or contemporary Third World) standards. This is true even in the most inegalitarian "First World" countries. In the United States, for example, the "ill fed," "ill housed," and "ill clothed" have largely receded into memory, along with the Great Depression that, for a while, brought these descriptions into public consciousness. To be sure, there are disturbingly many people who are ill housed or not housed at all, but abject poverty is usually not the reason why. Inadequate mental health care is, along with out-of-control housing costs. There are many who are ill fed too, but hardly anyone anymore dies of starvation or suffers from severe (involuntary) malnutrition. Americans suffer instead from fast food and other profit-maximizing innovations of the food-processing industry. Finally, the poor in the United States seldom dress in rags; indeed, they are famously not ill- but well-clothed. Thus, today's poor are less poor than were the poor of the past. That this is so is well understood throughout our political culture. Marxists have adapted their uses of the term to this prevailing understanding. In this sense, they do believe that conceptions of poverty must be adjusted to diverse and changing levels of socioeconomic development. But there is nothing distinctively Marxist in this conviction; it is part of the political culture.

However, Marxists have added a wrinkle to the prevailing understanding. It is implicit in a recent innovation in Marxist theory: the concept of "late capitalism." All Marxists believe that capitalism's historical mission is, as Marx and Engels wrote in *The Communist Manifesto*, rapidly and massively to augment the level of development of productive forces, bringing into being a degree of abundance sufficient for establishing and sustaining socialism and eventually communism. The view of everyone who defended the Bolshevik Revolution, and of many who did not, was that this mission had been generally completed by the time Russia broke away from the world capitalist system. In earlier times, humanity's compelling drive to develop productive forces in order to meet urgent needs and diminish burdensome toil drove history along. But for almost a century now, our long-standing interest in development has coexisted with competing, equally compelling interests, involving the deployment of productive forces for more refined "needs" – for meaningful work, productive leisure, and spontaneous enjoyment of life. Thus, the notion of "late capitalism" came into being. The term designates the forms capitalist societies take after the capitalist mode of production has become, so to speak, overripe (and increasingly rotten). For earlier generations of Marxists, it should never have come to this: capitalist development was supposed to cause capitalism to break down long before it could rot. But as it became increasingly apparent that this prediction had failed, the case against capitalism had to be rethought.

This exigency led to a (largely implicit) rehabilitation of the "utopian socialism" Marx and his followers had always inveighed against. Utopian socialists faulted capitalism and defended socialism on normative (usually moral) grounds. In contrast, "scientific socialism," which Marx and his followers defended, based its case against capitalism on the (inevitable) unfolding of the "laws of motion" of the capitalist mode of production itself. Because scientific socialists believed that normative standards, along with other forms of consciousness, are, like legal and political superstructures, relative to the modes of production they help to reproduce, they thought that they have no independent, transhistorical critical force. Thus, scientific socialism did not just differ from utopian socialism; it outright repudiated its claims. It took decades before Marxists attached to orthodox positions conceded that the utopian socialists had been proved right.[17] However, for as long as scientific socialism was upheld as the correct view, most Marxists acknowledged utopian socialism's claims only implicitly and unwittingly. They were, so to speak, utopian socialists without knowing it.

As such, Marxists have long faulted capitalist societies for the injustices they sustain or, at least, for those injustices that capitalism causes or encourages. They did so on moral – utopian socialist – grounds, but also because, like nearly everyone else, they wanted to rid the world of humanly caused and therefore humanly rectifiable miseries. Like many liberals, most Marxists believed that poverty falls under this description. They therefore believed that contemporary poverty – certainly in economically developed countries, but perhaps also in less developed parts of the world – has more to do with resource maldistributions than with genuine resource deficits. If anything, recent Marxism is more wedded to this conviction than mainstream liberal egalitarianism is. It is implicit, after all, in the concept of late capitalism, the idea that capitalism long ago developed productive forces to the point that socialism became materially possible.

[17] See, for example, Cohen, *If You're an Egalitarian.*

Poverty, Race, and Gender

Living in a racially homogeneous society, where class struggles were becoming increasingly salient, Marx had little to say about race – though he did venture opinions about New World slavery, British rule in India, and other pertinent topics. What Marx wrote was antiracist and insightful. But it was put forward in the spirit (and context) of journalistic reportage, not sustained theoretical inquiry. As issues of race became more pertinent to the working-class movement, Marx's successors continued along similar lines. In the United States, Marxist historians or historians influenced by Marx were in the forefront of efforts to pay scholarly attention to race relations. Nevertheless, as Marxists, they tended to see the phenomena they investigated through the prism of class struggle, and to accord little, if any, explanatory autonomy to racial concepts in their own right. For Marxists, class analysis has always been the key to understanding the social world. Post–World War II anticolonial struggles, black power movements, and New Left theorists (black and white) faulted Marxism on this account – sometimes expressly, sometimes only implicitly. They won the day. This is why nowadays even those who still identify with Marxism hold that class and race are, to some degree, independent forms of oppression, calling for independent (though not incompatible) explanations and remedies. Although self-identified Marxists have professed this view in recent years, it is at odds with the spirit that animated Marxism throughout its history. Any Marxist political practice that takes this thought on board is therefore, so to speak, less Marxist than past Marxisms were. Its scope, at least with regard to racial politics, is less comprehensive than was once assumed.

At a theoretical level, it is possible to embrace this diminution of Marxism's political role and, in so doing, to avoid any threat of inconsistency by maintaining that the explanatory scope of Marxist theory is correspondingly less than used to be imagined – class analysis explains only some, not all, of what is of interest to those engaged in emancipatory struggles with racial dimensions. This is a consistent position, and it reflects real world political conditions in much the way that a nearly exclusive focus on class struggles reflected the political realities of classical Marxism's time and place.

Similar considerations apply to gender-based oppression. Marxists were among the pioneers of feminist theory and practice. Engels's *Origins of the Family, Private, Property and the State*, perhaps the first sustained theoretical account of female oppression, is a key text of the Marxist theoretical tradition. Engels was not alone in moving feminist concerns into the political consciousness of Marxist militants. The Marxists of the Second International and, at first, their Bolshevik successors were second to none in making women's equality a concern. Nevertheless, in this case too, as one would expect, the issue was relegated to a secondary status – as a facet of class-centered explanatory theories and practices. Second-wave feminism brought this fact to everyone's attention, reproaching Marxism on this account. Coming at a time when Marxist orthodoxy was beginning to enter into a protracted crisis, culminating in its apparent demise (or long-lasting eclipse), there were not many feminists who tried to reconcile their theory and practice with Marxism. Marxists who were also feminists usually described themselves as "socialist feminist," a broader category than "Marxist feminist." But socialist feminism, Marxist or otherwise, was never a majority current within what was once called the women's liberation movement. This was the case even in the late 1960s and early 1970s, when second-wave feminism was still new on the scene and when Marxism was still a vital presence in the milieus in which it arose. Marxism and feminism parted ways more clearly later on, as Marxist concerns came to be of less importance in the ambient political culture.

There is a similar, though less honorable, story to tell about oppressions based on sexuality. Decades before mainstream political opinion began to contemplate equal rights for homosexuals, Marxist thinkers associated with the Second International did advocate equality, notwithstanding the fact that what we would now call homophobia was rife in the working class, as throughout most sectors of society. However, this was a flash in the pan. Marxist political formations were heroic in their determination to overcome working-class racism, but they were largely silent on homophobia. It was not until homosexuals themselves, inspired by liberation movements of Marxist provenance, took up the cause that Marxists joined the struggle unambivalently. Until that time and subsequently, Marxists were probably better, and certainly no worse, than proponents of other progressive political currents. But this had more to do with the generous and solidaristic dispositions that led people to identify with Marxism than with Marxist theory itself.

The current fixation on "gender, race, and class" in academic circles and within the political groupings that constitute large sectors of today's enfeebled Left is a bastard offspring of classical Marxism's concern with working-class emancipation. Note that, according to this postmodern shibboleth, "class" comes last, almost as an afterthought. This is understandable, given how history has unfolded; but it is also unfortunate. A powerful explanatory program has been set aside, only to be replaced by well-meaning professions of opposition to the oppression of nearly everyone (except middle- and upper-class white men). Marxism systematically unified a theory of history, an account of human emancipation, and a concern with the wretched of the earth. For postmodern opponents of ostensibly coequal and independent oppressions, only the latter concern still resonates. For them, all that is left is a largely sentimental attachment to victimhood. The consequences are anything but salutary, even for – indeed, especially for – the victims of racial and gender-based oppressions.

Perhaps it could not have been otherwise. Even so, the fact that Marxists relegated issues of race and gender to the margins of their concerns is lamentable. Nevertheless, Marxism was plainly not a contributing factor to either the racialization or feminization of poverty. Quite the contrary. In capitalist societies, Marxists have always been at the forefront of struggles on behalf of oppressed racial groups and women. Even the version of Marxism that became official doctrine in Communist countries had, for the most part, an ameliorative effect on racial and gender oppression and therefore on the poor among disempowered racial groups and women. Marxist theory by itself may not provide militants with all the theoretical means they need for waging anti-racist or antisexist struggles. But Marxists' hearts have always been in the right place. For as long as Marxism has existed, Marxists have fought the good fight.

Relieving Poverty

Marxists deny that people are poor by choice or in consequence of more subtle defects of character or will. For them, as for proponents of most other social theories, the causes of poverty are structural, not individual. This is not to deny that, for every person who is poor, a story can be told about why this is so that makes no reference to social facts. Marxists are sensible metaphysicians; they believe that collective entities are decomposable into individuals without remainder, just as individuals are decomposable into chemicals, and chemicals into atoms and atoms into the basic units of matter. Accounts of what happens can be put forward at any of these or other intermediate levels, but lower-level accounts seldom explain what happens at higher levels; even when lower-level explanations are conjoined. Thus, a complete molecular account of, say, everything implicated in World War I would not explain the causes of that war or anything else about its history. Or, to take a more pertinent example: if a class of 100 students is graded on a curve, so that only 10 percent get As, there is an individual-level explanation for why each A student got the A he or she did. But the conjunction of these explanations would not explain the social fact that 10 percent of the students got As, and that 90 percent did not. The structure of the grading system, a social fact in its own right, explains that. The point is quite general: social facts, like the nature and extent of poverty in particular societies, call for social explanations. The reason why some percentage of a population is poor will seldom be as easily discernible as the reason why 10 percent of the students graded on a curve got As. But, if we assume genuine resource deficits are not the cause of their poverty, the explanation will be just as irreducibly social.

As I have said, Marxists are not concerned with poverty as such. I have also tried to make it plain that when "Marxism" is used to designate a body of thought, rather than a historically identifiable political tendency, it is a mistake to think of it as an overarching comprehensive doctrine rather than as a constellation of related theories. In none of these is poverty a theoretically pertinent social fact, except insofar as it correlates with class membership. Class membership, class structure, and class struggle are explanatory concepts and also objects of explanation. Poverty is not.

I must qualify this observation, however. Marx forged his economic theory within a conceptual framework shaped by classical (especially Ricardian) political economy. The classical economists held that labor (or, in Marx's analytical scheme, "labor power") is compensated at its value, where the value of labor power is equivalent to the value of the goods and services necessary for reproducing it. Fluctuations in supply and demand will cause wages to rise or fall, but in principle workers' wages hover at a subsistence level. Marx's still useful concept of "a reserve army of (industrial) labor" – of a pool of dispossessed workers looking for jobs, depressing wage levels by insuring that the supply of ready labor always exceeds the demand – was a contribution to the classical account; it helped explain why wages tend to approach subsistence levels. But, as the working-class movement gained strength, wages rose – thanks mainly to collective bargaining and other forms of collective action. Thus, the classical view came to be increasingly confounded by circumstances. Accordingly, vestiges of Ferdinand Lasalle's Iron Law of Wages, which claimed that the workers' share of the wealth labor produces can never rise substantially above a subsistence level, dropped out of Marxist economic theory. But Marx's economic theory never quite outgrew its origins. Thus, for Marx and Marxists, the most exploited people, proletarians, are also normally among the poorest, though they are seldom as desperately poor as their lumpen cousins, many of whom constitute the industrial reserve army. Paradoxically, lumpen elements suffer from poverty even more than workers do precisely because they are *not* exploited by capital.

Thus, what Marxist theory has to say about class structure and about the structural position of the proletariat is also indirectly a claim about the poor or, rather, about some of the expressly social factors that cause two (somewhat) distinct categories of poor people to become and remain poor. To this extent, Marxism does explain *some* poverty after all. Some of it is a by-product of the exploitation of labor; some of it is a consequence of the way capitalism immiserates those whom it excludes from the ranks of the exploited.[18]

For Marxists who are Kantians, the alleviation of poverty could be construed as a moral imperative. Much the same can be said for Marxists who have imbibed the moral intuitions of the ambient culture. The former description designates a handful of (nonorthodox) theoreticians in the twentieth century – the latter, the vast majority of individuals who identified with Marxism throughout its history. Of course, for orthodox Marxists and for Marx himself, moral imperatives, requirements of justice, and notions of superogation are ideological constructs, at best. They therefore have no proper role in Marxist or, more precisely, scientific socialist thinking. However, as I have

---

[18]   For a more precise account of the connections between income and wealth, on the one hand, and class position, on the other, see John Roemer, *A General Theory of Exploitation and Class* (Cambridge, MA: Harvard University Press, 1982).

several times remarked, this conviction was honored more by its frequent and conspicuous breach than by its observance.

Marxists believe that, in moving toward communism, poverty will disappear. They also believe that under communism poverty will be only a distant memory. They therefore recognize no tension between relieving poverty or, insofar as it is different, removing the effects of poverty and promoting other human goods – specifically, those that will come increasingly within our reach as we move forward toward a communist future. But, again, in this endeavor, the end of poverty is essentially a by-product, not a deliberate objective.

As political strategists, some Marxists may from time to time have thought that things would have to get worse before they could get better. That this thought was a temptation to which many Marxists succumbed is debatable. Marxists, including official Communists with a reformist streak, seem to have had something of a guilty conscience where their own revolutionary militancy, or lack of it, was concerned. They were therefore the ones most inclined to claim that those who were more revolutionary than they subscribed to this view. It was as if the ruthlessness of the revolutionaries absolved the reformers of their pusillanimity.

Allowing that there is nevertheless some truth in the claim, it is worth pointing out that there is nothing distinctively Marxist about wanting situations to worsen so that they can ultimately improve. From time immemorial, physicians and other healers have deployed therapies that they know will make their patients worse off in the short run; so have political leaders of all stamps. Marxists do subscribe to a theory of history that maintains that the leap into the realm of freedom requires a revolutionary transformation. If there were a clear connection between revolutionary agency and poverty, then, arguably, it would be reasonable for revolutionary Marxists to want to worsen the condition of the poor. But, as we know, the poor, especially the desperately poor, are not the most revolutionary strata of society. In the right conditions, they can be mobilized to fight for revolutionary changes but, in the classical Marxist view, the principal agent of social revolution is the industrial proletariat, not poor people per se. Leninists and later Maoists ascribed a revolutionary role also to the peasantry of the still largely agrarian societies in which they struggled against colonial and semicolonial powers and against their national bourgeoisies. Most of the peasants they mobilized were poor by any standard, but it was their class position, not their poverty, that made them, along with workers, agents of revolutionary change in Leninist and Maoist theory. Equally impoverished lumpen elements in the city and countryside were regarded as they always had been in Marxist circles. It is therefore fair to say that Marxist revolutionaries have nothing to gain by making poverty worse or by being indifferent to its scourges. If not moral scrupulousness, then theoretically grounded strategic thinking leads to this conclusion.

For the same reason, claims that efforts to relieve poverty have counter-revolutionary consequences are also wrongheaded from a Marxist point of view. The worst that a Marxist is likely to say about poor relief is that it is unlikely to be efficacious, except in superficial ways (that can nevertheless be important, even life-saving, for some beneficiaries); and that it can deflect energies away from the larger struggle against the causes of poverty and other humanly rectifiable evils. These can be reasons not to enthuse about private charity work or welfare state measures (most of which have nothing directly to do with alleviating poverty anyway) or to be critical of them, but they seldom, if ever, rise to the level of reasons to oppose efforts to relieve poverty or its effects. To the best of my knowledge, Marxists have never thought otherwise. They certainly reject the religious and philosophical convictions that typically motivate charity work. Most Marxists also regard welfare state institutions as meretricious palliatives that impede the development of the revolutionary consciousness necessary for putting an end to the misfortunes capitalism causes. But Marxists would never actively oppose attempts at ameliorating the condition of the destitute. In Communist countries, identification with Marxism, or rather with the version of Marxism that had become official dogma, was often a prerequisite for success in many professions; therefore, careerists and other opportunists joined dedicated revolutionaries under the Marxist tent. But people who became Marxists in Western and Third World countries generally did so for estimable and selfless reasons. They were hardly moral beasts by nature. Neither were they led to moral bestiality by their theoretical convictions. Because these convictions do not directly speak to issues of poverty as such, their views about poverty effectively lapsed into the default position dictated by ordinary human decency. Thus, they wholeheartedly favored its relief.

Remedies

The "remedy" for poverty is also the remedy for the societal ills that Marxism aims directly to rectify. That remedy consists in overcoming capitalism by instituting an economic order based on social ownership and forms of economic coordination that avoid the deleterious consequences of market arrangements or, at least, of markets "as we know them." There is no single Marxist view of what, if anything, constrains the implementation of this remedy. As remarked, Bolshevism, in its most extreme forms, recognized few, if any constraints on revolutionary political activity. But there are Bolshevik positions that are more nuanced, and there are Marxist positions – the majority, in fact – that are not Bolshevik at all.

In any case, what is morally imperative, in the Marxist view, is not so much the alleviation of capitalism's evils, poverty included, but the struggle against their underlying causes – the struggle against capitalism and for socialism. To that end, Marxists have always been internationalists – in solidarity with anticapitalist, anti-imperialist, prosocialist movements everywhere. But, like charity, the class struggle begins at home. Thus, Marxists were the first "to think globally and act locally." Moreover, Marxist political formations – (pre-Bolshevik) Social Democratic, Communist, Trotskyist, and Maoist – have always been organized at local and regional levels and controlled, as far as possible, at a national level. There have been four international confederations of Marxist political organizations – the first, second (Social Democratic), third (Communist), and fourth (Trotskyist) Internationals. Of these, the Communist International was, by far, the most controlling – but, even so, it seldom "micromanaged" national, much less regional or local, party activities. Its de facto executive committee, the Comintern, was interested, in the main, in assuring that the policies of national parties accorded with its frequently changing "general line." Thus, there is a sense in which, for politically engaged Marxists, fellow citizens do matter more than distant strangers. But this is a strategic exigency, necessitated by the national organization of the capitalist system, not a moral requirement. In principle, the workers and oppressed peoples of all countries matter as much as the workers and oppressed peoples of one's own.

Marxists therefore have no reason not to support global campaigns to end hunger or to prevent preventable diseases, except insofar as they are wary of charity work. I would venture that most Marxists would agree that charity can be mildly ameliorative. But they would also be inclined to fault it as a salve for guilty consciences and as a snare that leads well-meaning people away from more useful revolutionary or reformist political work. It is not just skepticism about the efficacy of charitable endeavors or hostility toward do-gooders that underlies this attitude. It is the conviction that humanly rectifiable causes of human misery call for political solutions – and that, in the final analysis, "the only solution is revolution."

Similarly, Marxists have nothing against perpetrators of good deeds, whether they be government entities or private philanthropic organizations. But they would be more inclined than liberals to question their motives. In the Marxist view, these efforts too are largely irrelevant – because the problems they address can be resolved only through the radical transformation of fundamental economic, political, and social structures. All Marxists agree that that kind of transformation requires focused social struggles conducted by organized workers – or workers and peasants – and their allies. This is why most Marxists would look favorably, say, on poor peoples' campaigns (organizations of the poor themselves).

But on the general question of who should do what in the struggle to change the world, the Marxist position is clear at a level of generality that hovers above the point where "the narcissism of small differences" creates dissension. This side of communism, the class struggle is inexorable, and everyone must take sides – because not taking sides is tantamount to siding with the prevailing system of exploitation and oppression. There are many "intermediate class positions," of course, and also lumpen elements, and, in some parts of the world, influential remnants of feudal class structures. Nevertheless, in the final analysis (as Engels would say), the class struggle of our time has two main class actors: the proletariat and the bourgeoisie. It is natural, as it were, for workers to militate as proletarians and for capitalists to militate on the other side. But Marxists of all stripes have always believed that anyone can side with the proletariat regardless of their class position at birth. Indeed, almost all the great Marxist leaders, including Marx and Engels and Lenin, joined the working-class movement from the outside, as intellectuals.

The fact that, throughout Marxism's history, many nonworkers (and non-peasants) have sided with the proletariat is difficult to reconcile with the principled amoralism of scientific socialism. So too is the stance of revolutionary workers (and peasants) who, *The Communist Manifesto* notwithstanding, have long had more "to lose [than] their chains." Could it just be that they want to be on the side they think will eventually win? I don't think so. After all, even if victory is inevitable, which everyone must long ago have realized at some level it is not, it is plainly far off; and life is short. This is why I think it fair to say that many, perhaps most, Marxists have always been motivated by moral concerns to some extent, even if they are loath to admit it. This fact hardly speaks to the existence of a Marxist ethical tradition, however. Rather, it bears witness to the moral rectitude of people who are drawn to anticapitalist, prosocialist causes.

Thus, I would conclude as I began by insisting that however insightful and important Marxist positions on poverty may be, poverty is not and cannot be a topic on which a Marxist ethical tradition has anything to say: not just because poverty is an issue for Marxists only indirectly but, more importantly, because there is no ethical tradition that is distinctively Marxist.

13

Poverty and Natural Law

Stephen J. Pope

Natural law ethics as developed by Thomas Aquinas (1225–74 CE) and his heirs constitutes a vital intellectual tradition. The interpretation of this ethic has gone through many stages and variations over the course of the past eight hundred years. Just as the nature of poverty changed significantly from the medieval to the modern and contemporary periods, so also has natural law reflection on poverty.[1] This chapter begins with an exposition of the basic lines of Thomas Aquinas's natural law ethic, particularly as it was applied to poverty; provides a brief explication of one of this tradition's most important early modern advocates, Bartolomé de Las Casas, O.P., the sixteenth-century "Defender of the Indians"; and examines the work of John Finnis, one of the founders of the "new natural law theory," and the use of his theory by a development economist, Sabina Alkire. Finally, these three descriptive sections are followed by an account of the relevance of natural law ethics for the issue of poverty today.

It should be understood that a single chapter can only briefly treat authors who deserve much more extensive examination than is possible here. This chapter attempts to show that the natural law tradition provides significant grounds for promoting justice for the poor as a matter of human rights and the common good, and that justice at its core aims at empowering the poor to act as agents of their own lives.

Thomas Aquinas

Thomas Aquinas's interpretation of natural law drew from an amalgam of various ancient pagan and early Christian courses, including Aristotle, the Stoics, Cicero, Saint Paul, the church fathers, and Augustine.[2] It also adopted

---

[1] See Bronislaw Geremek, *Poverty: A History*, trans. Agnieszka Kolakowska (Cambridge, MA: Blackwell, 1994).

[2] See Michael Bertram Crowe, *The Changing Profile of the Natural Law* (The Hague: Martinus Nijhoff, 1977). The philosophical roots are carefully examined in Yves

insights from medieval civil and canon law, particularly the account given by the twelfth-century canon lawyer Gratian and those who commented on his *Decretum*, and the early scholastic theologians.[3] Thomas regarded religious sources of wisdom as primary but also affirmed the capacity of the human mind to come to moral insight. Every person at least knows the "common principles" of practical reason.[4]

While Thomas and his heirs worked within a Christian framework, it is possible to employ essential components of his account of the natural law in nontheological ways. The phrase "natural law" refers most basically to an ethic based on an account of the human good as it can be identified by reason. This is perhaps why Yves Simon insists that "the question of natural law is itself philosophical."[5] Both "nature" and "law" have many meanings within Thomas's own corpus and, even more so, in the history of natural law ethics. "Nature" refers primarily to the formal and final causes that mark human nature, "an interior, an immanent law of operation,"[6] and a thing's "nature" is that which makes it what it is as a certain kind of thing. A "law" is most generally a rule and measure of human action.[7] The rule of human action is reason, and the reasonable ordering of human conduct leads to human well-being or the human good. The natural law, then, is the intelligent ordering of human actions to the human good.[8]

Natural law reflects the nature we share as the particular kind of "rational animals" that we are. As animals, we have bodily needs and desires that make life possible and physically comfortable. As social, we live in groups, establish and maintain bonds of reciprocity, and build relationships through multiple forms of direct and indirect cooperation. As rational, our behavior is guided by understanding, reasoning, planning, and other cognitive operations. Human emotions and affections are of course important in their own right, but their functioning too is shaped if not dominated by our cognitive

---

R. Simon, *The Tradition of Natural Law: A Philosopher's Reflections*, ed. Vukan Kuic (New York: Fordham University Press, 1965, 1992). See also Stephen Pope, "Natural Law and Christian Ethics," in *The Cambridge Companion to Christian Ethics*, ed. Robin Gill (Cambridge: Cambridge University Press, 2001), 77–95.

3 Several recent works have emphasized the religious roots of the theory, most importantly, Jean Porter, *Divine and Natural Law: Reclaiming the Tradition for Christian Ethics* (Grand Rapids, MI, and Cambridge: Novalis and Eerdmans, 1999), and Servais Pinckaers, *The Sources of Christian Ethics*, trans. Sister Mary Thomas Noble, O.P. (Washington, DC: Catholic University of America Press, 1995).

4 Thomas Aquinas, *Summa Theologiae* (Rome: Marietti, 1947), I-II, 93, 2. This chapter focuses on natural law as "reason based" and so prescinds from its religious interpretations.

5 Simon, *The Tradition of Natural Law* (1992), 63.

6 Ibid., 121.

7 *ST* I-II, 90, 1.

8 See entry for "Reason and Natural Law," in *The Oxford Handbook of Theological Ethics*, ed. Gilbert Meilaender and William Werpehowski (New York: Oxford University Press, 2005), 148–67.

powers. Practical rationality in the broad sense allows us to make choices among alternatives, to plan for future events, and to take responsibility for being the authors of our acts. Ethics is both made possible and required by the fact that we have significant degrees of self-mastery over our own lives.

Our intellectual powers give us a significant basis for understanding the moral requirements of life in community. Natural law ethics presumes that a reasonable human being can understand the moral wrongfulness of stealing, lying, and the like and that we are accountable to one another for acting accordingly. General moral principles have traditionally been articulated in particular religious moral codes, but natural law ethicists maintain that any reasonable person, whatever his or her religious affiliation, is capable of recognizing their normative force.

Thomas followed Aristotle in holding that every human being, knowingly or not, wisely or not, seeks a state of well-being, happiness, or flourishing (*beatitudo, eudaimonia*). To seek to flourish is to seek the human good. Thomas takes as the "first principle of practical reason" that we ought to seek good and avoid evil.[9] The most basic moral implication of seeking good and avoiding evil is to will the good for ourselves and every other human being. While conditions of finitude make it impossible for us to do concrete good for every human being whom we encounter, the duty of benevolence requires that we refuse to do unjust harm to anyone – at the very least we are to be committed to a policy of nonmaleficence toward others.

What Thomas called the "order of love" holds that we ought to be most concerned either for those people who are related to us through ties of family or friendship or for those (including the poor) who are in the greatest need of assistance.[10] In particular cases, the prudent person makes judgments based on a careful weighing of degrees of need and connection[11] and in terms of an order of good that recognizes both the greater excellence of spiritual goods and, at times, the greater urgency of corporeal needs.[12]

The primary precepts of the natural law are known by all reflective people as they reflect on what it means to do good and avoid evil. Thomas believed that everyone can recognize the rightness of giving people what we owe them, being consistent in our actions, and treating other people as we think we ought to be treated (the golden rule). The "secondary precepts" of the natural law that we find in various moral traditions are attempts by human reason to identify the implications of the basic moral drive to do good and avoid evil. The task of working out these implications is exercised by practical reason and formulated in positive laws and moral conventions. The more precise applications of principles to concrete policies can be difficult to discern and elicit

---

[9] See *ST* I-II, 94, 2.
[10] See *ST* II-II, 26.
[11] *ST* II-II, 31, 3 ad 1; and ad 3.
[12] *ST* II-II, 32, 3.

agreement upon. It is one thing, for example, to argue that the working poor should be paid a just wage and another to determine precisely what amount of money constitutes a just wage at a given time and place.

A particular moral code can be understood as the accumulated wisdom of a community regarding the meaning of doing good and avoiding evil under its own contingent human circumstances. Thomas attributed moral variations across cultures to three causes – intellectual confusion caused by disordered passions;[13] inadequate development of culture, education, and civilization;[14] and varying historical circumstances whose contingencies require moral adaptation.[15] Communities can over time develop greater moral understanding. For example, Thomas notes that the polygamy of the biblical patriarchs was gradually replaced by monogamy,[16] and we can note that we have gone from condoning to condemning slavery. But communities can also persist in mistaken moral prejudices and misunderstandings, Again, Thomas cited German tribes that approved of stealing from outsiders,[17] and we can note the persistence of racial bias in our own society. Thomas held that the natural law provides overarching criteria for assessing the moral legitimacy of human acts and policies. Civil law is morally legitimate only if it accords with the moral requirements identified by practical reason. In the twentieth century, Martin Luther King Jr. invoked natural law in claiming that segregation laws in the South were immoral.[18]

Benevolence has as its primary obligation the fulfillment of the duties of justice – giving to each what is his or her due. A central consideration of justice concerns property, the prohibition of theft and the significance of property for the common good. Thomas held that nature as such does not incline to a distinction of possessions but that the institution of private property was devised by reason for the benefit of human life. He largely adopted Aristotle's defense of the legitimacy of property as facilitating care, social order, and wise management of resources.[19] What is lower exists for the sake of what is higher, he reasoned, and property exists for the sake of human beings. He thus regarded property as an addition to the natural law[20] and part of the "right of nations" (*ius gentium*).[21]

---

[13] See *ST* I-II, 99, 2 ad 2.
[14] See *ST* I-II, 94, 6.
[15] See *ST* II-II, 57, 2.
[16] See Thomas Aquinas, *Summa Contra Gentiles* III, 124.1, and *Summa Theologiae*, Suppl. 65, 1.
[17] See *ST* I-II, 94, 4.
[18] See "Letter from a Birmingham City Jail," in *Testament of Hope: The Essential Writings of Martin Luther King, Jr.*, ed. James Washington Jr. (San Francisco: Harper and Row, 1986), 298–303.
[19] See *ST* II-II, 66, 1, citing *Politics* I, and 66, 2 echoes *Politics* II.5, 1263a25–30.
[20] See *ST* I-II, 91, 3, and esp. I-II, 94, 5.
[21] *ST* I-II, 95, 4; also I-II, 57, 3.

Property owners have a moral responsibility to use their property in a morally legitimate manner. Wealth is instrumentally valuable for the material and social conditions of the good life, but its possession can lead to ambition, greed, and other vices. Property owners have a responsibility to care for their own dependents and to use what is excess to meet the needs of the poor.[22] There is a natural law support for the channeling of resources and energies that is analogous to what is found in various general Jewish, Christian, and Islamic casuistic instructions regarding justice and mercy.[23]

This ethic is concerned not only with minimal physical survival but also with the goods that allow for human flourishing in a comprehensive sense. Thomas regarded "necessity" as including not only the bare minimum of goods required to sustain life but also the other goods that make possible a good life within one's social context. Concern for the poor must not issue in acts that humiliate the poor. Thomas recognized the suffering not only of the destitute but also of the "shamefaced poor," members of the nobility who had come on hard times. He held that what is necessary for one person's decent life might not suffice for another's and, conversely, that what is rightly regarded as a "necessity" for one person might be "superfluity" for another – that is, beyond what a person and his or her dependents need to maintain their social status.[24] Everyone must give superfluous goods to those who are unable to provide for themselves. No one is required to give of his or her necessities to the needy, unless he or she encounters a person in extremis, on the verge of death without any other possibility of immediate assistance. In times of emergency, the person in desperate need may take from the rich without moral wrongdoing.[25]

Poverty is an evil to the extent that it denies people the goods that constitute a good or even minimally decent human life. As philosopher John D. Jones puts it, the evil in poverty for Thomas consisted in "a frustration of people's ability to acquire the goods and services – to engage in the *ars possessiva* – by which people can sustain themselves, assist others, and provide for other necessities of life."[26] Poverty in a broad sense is thus found when people are deprived of anything necessary for human flourishing, including, in their order of importance, goods of the soul, goods of the body, and external goods.[27] We possess certain inbuilt inclinations to all three kinds of human goods.[28] External goods are instrumentally valuable because they aid human

[22] See Stephen J. Pope, "Thomas Aquinas on Almsgiving, Justice, and Charity: An Interpretation and Assessment," *Heythrop Journal* 32 (1991): 167–91.
[23] See, in this volume, Chapters 4, 9, and 10 by Kent Van Til, Sohail H. Hashmi, and Noam Zohar, respectively.
[24] *ST* II-II, 32, 5, 6.
[25] *ST* II-II, 66, 7.
[26] John D. Jones, "Poverty as *Malum Simpliciter*: A Reading of Aquinas's *Summa contra gentiles* 3.133," *Philosophy & Theology* 13, no. 2 (1999): 232.
[27] See *ST* I-II, 2–4.
[28] See *ST* I-II, 1–5.

beings. Goods of the body are important for human well-being, but they are ultimately less valuable than goods of the mind. This hierarchy builds from the more elemental to the more rational and distinctively human, but all levels of good are part of human well-being.

Social observers in Thomas's day did not strive for scientific precision in their understanding of poverty. The pauper was typically a person of "small means" who had been forced into such a state by circumstances out of his or her control. Thomas recognized the suffering that comes with poverty into which people are thrust or kept outside their own control. Socioeconomic poverty involves an inability to obtain sufficiency of external goods, such as food, shelter, and clothing, which can and often does lead to deprivation of mind or body. Lack of healthy food, for example, can make one physically sick and in some cases inspire hatred for those who have access to healthy food. Thomas believed that there is a valuable role for voluntary renunciation of possessions for those seeking religious or moral growth, but he did not confuse this path with the involuntary one.

The greatest responsibility for the poor, Thomas maintained, was held by the political rulers because they bear the greatest responsibility for the common good. Political authorities are responsible for providing not every good but only the public good that is indispensable for the functioning of the political community. A good ruler seeks to preside over a society that is self-sufficient, that is, one able to "procure unto itself the necessities of life."[29] This goal leads political authorities to distribute emergency aid in cases of disasters, but most importantly it involves the ongoing task of securing justice, social order, and peace throughout the political community and in its relations with its neighbors.[30]

Any society has many forms of association, companionship, and community – families, schools, clubs, guilds, corporations – each of which makes its own distinctive contribution to the larger society. The "principle of subsidiarity" guards against excessive centralization of power and responsibility by assigning responsibility to the lowest competent social agency within the social order. Many individuals and groups have their own regional responsibilities for the poor – for example, the confraternities that focus on widows and orphans.

Thomas's view of the individual's personal response to the poor can be understood as operating on three levels: (1) everyone has a moral duty in justice to meet the immediate needs of the extreme poor whom he or she encounters (e.g., by buying a meal for a randomly encountered hungry homeless person; (2) everyone has a moral duty of charity to give his or her superflua to the poor (e.g., by donating a percentage of an unexpected financial windfall

---

[29] "On Kingship," in *The Political Ideas of St. Thomas Aquinas*, ed. Dino Bigongiari (New York: Macmillan, 1953), 178.

[30] *ST* I-II, 98, 1.

to a charity); and (3) someone may choose to care for the poor in ways that go beyond what is morally required and engage in supererogatory work (e.g., by volunteering to work at a soup kitchen on a regular basis). Category (1) concerns particular individuals who have a claim of justice (though perhaps not legal justice), category (2) does not direct us to specific individuals ("objects of charity") but does bind us to meet some charitable need in virtue of our excess property (perhaps something akin to Kant's imperfect duties),[31] and category (3) is praiseworthy but not morally mandatory. Whereas refusing to fulfill the demands of the first or second category is blameworthy, failure to meet the third is not.

Thomas seemed to assume the permanence of poverty as a range of conditions that run from the relative deprivation and dependence to the more intense suffering caused by catastrophes. He did not of course have access to anything like a modern theory of the causes of poverty. He recognized that poverty is caused sometimes by natural forces, such as bad weather that leads to drought and famine, disease, and so forth, and sometimes by unjust conduct, such as theft and robbery, unjust business practices, and unjust decisions by civil authorities. Civil authorities provide the prime protection for the poor in the legal domains. Poverty that is traceable to the wrongdoing of individuals must be identified as such, and culprits held accountable and made to pay appropriate restitution.[32]

Natural law for Thomas constituted a basic framework for understanding the general morality of poverty, but it did not yield a detailed set of policy prescriptions. The best way to avoid human-generated poverty, Thomas suggested, is to inculcate virtue in citizens and future rulers. Those who exercise authority as civil rulers must learn prudently to apply justice to contingent circumstances. Citizens are trained to do what is right through proper education and upbringing and by learning to obey just laws. The alleviation of poverty takes place through the exercise of charity and justice by all parties.

German historian Ernst Troeltsch regarded natural law as essentially a legitimating ideology for stratified medieval societies.[33] At least seen from our perspective, Thomas's ethic lacks a call for significant socioeconomic structural reform to address the systemic causes of poverty. Thomas did not present a comprehensive economic theory of the empirical interrelations of productivity, consumption, and investment. Nor did he propose a political-economic system of income transfer via taxation and distribution by government bureaucracy. He assumed with other medieval theologians that we live in a "zero sum" economic world with a fixed amount of material goods. He

---

[31] Kant, *Foundations of the Metaphysics of Morals*, trans. Lewis White Beck (Indianapolis: Bobbs-Merrill, 1959), Second Part, 39–42.

[32] *ST* II-II, 66, 5.

[33] See *The Social Teachings of the Christian Churches*, trans. Olive Wyon, 2 vols. (New York: Harper and Row, 1960), 1:257–72.

thus gave much more attention to commutative justice, the justice between parties, than to distributive justice, and people in his age did not even use the later term, "social justice."

Bartolomé de las Casas

Thomas observed that human reason is able to advance gradually from less to more knowledge as it reflects changing contingent circumstances on the practical relevance of the general principles of the natural law.[34] The natural law treatment of poverty did, in fact, undergo considerable development through the modern and contemporary periods.

Sixteenth-century Spanish Dominicans revitalized Thomistic natural law when called upon to consider its relevance to the recent discovery, conquest, and governance of the New World. Francisco de Vitoria, O.P. (1483–1546), of the University of Salamanca used Thomistic natural law in his development of the just-war theory and the first theory of modern international law. He was also a pivotal figure in providing a scholastic defense from Spanish exploitation of the Native Americans of the New World.

Bartolomé de las Casas, O.P. (1474–1566), was a contemporary of Vitoria, who was profoundly shaped by his first-person experience of massive Spanish injustice in the Conquest.[35] Over the course of many years Las Casas underwent a gradual but profound conversion from slave-owning plantation owner to relentless and outspoken advocate for the indigenous people of the Americas. The fact that millions of people were either murdered or left in conditions that would inevitably lead to their death seemed of little or no concern to those who profited from their destruction. The fact that the cause of death was often "germs" adds the moral guilt of negligence to Spanish responsibility for the horrors they perpetrated by the use of "guns and steel."[36] The process of moral awakening led Las Casas to use his talent to defend the indigenous people by means of prophetic homilies, theological treatises, impassioned letters, and juridical briefs to the Spanish court.[37] Las Casas's tracts describing the terror inflicted on Indians had significant influence on the 1542 New Laws of the Indies, which one scholar describes as "the only body of laws in western

[34] See *ST* I-II, 91, 3 ad 1; I-II, 94, 5.
[35] See Paul S. Vickery, *Bartolomé de Las Casas: Great Prophet of the Americas* (New York: Paulist Press, 2006).
[36] See J. Diamond, *Guns, Germs, and Steel: The Fates of Human Societies* (New York: W. W. Norton, 1997).
[37] See Bartolomé de las Casas, *Obras completas* (Madrid: Alianza Editorial, 1989–90). English translations of Las Casas include *The Only Way*, ed. Helen Rand Parish, trans. Francis Patrick Sullivan, S.J. (Mahwah, NJ: Paulist Press, 1992); *Indian Freedom: The Cause of Bartolomé de las Casas, 1484–1566: A Reader*, ed. Francis Patrick Sullivan, S.J. (Kansas City: Sheed and Ward, 1995); *A Short Account of the Destruction of the Indies*, trans. Nigel Griffin (New York: Penguin, 1992); and *In Defense of the Indians*, trans. Stafford Poole, C. M. (DeKalb: Northern Illinois University Press, 1992).

colonial history which had as its main content a declaration of rights and free-doms of indigenous peoples."[38]

Trained primarily as a canon lawyer, Las Casas had a rather eclectic manner of argumentation that invoked natural law on behalf of the natives. Against colonists who claimed a moral right to subjugate "inferior" peoples, he argued that the natives as human beings have a natural right to their free-dom. Las Casas started to view an equality of human dignity beneath social, cultural, and other differences that distinguish people. Las Casas was thus one of the first to argue that human rights are the proper expression of natu-ral law;[39] Thomas himself employed the language of "right" (*ius*) but he used it in a sense different from the modern notion of "human rights" or "natu-ral rights."[40] Writing of the natives, he insisted, "There is no power on earth sufficient to reduce their status as free men ... since liberty is the most pre-cious and supreme of all the goods of this temporal world and so loved by all creatures, both sensible and insensible, and even more by rational ones, and therefore is protected by natural law."[41] Rejecting the Aristotelian argument that some human beings are slaves by nature, Las Casas invoked natural law to provide a direct and powerful affirmation of a set of human rights pos-sessed by all human beings throughout the world. These include the right to life, the right not to be unjustly enslaved, the right not to be subjected to eco-nomic exploitation, a right to worship according to one's conscience, and the right to be immune from unjust attack. Las Casas also invoked natural law in the moral protection of communities from unjust attack. The people of every society, he argued, have a natural right to their own *dominium*, the legitimate ownership of their own liberty, possessions, and way of life.[42]

Apologists for the Conquest, the foremost of whom was the human-ist Ginés de Sepulveda, also invoked natural law in their attempt to jus-tify Spanish actions. The natives' "barbaric" culture was said to be proof of their inferior humanity and was judged to be a violation of natural law, which in turn led to a host of other violations of nature, including cannibal-ism, incest, and sodomy. Natural law, furthermore, demanded that these crimes be punished and their practitioners subjected to Spanish control for their own good. Only harsh training on the labor and land system known

---

[38] Roger Rushton, *Human Rights and the Image of God* (London: SCM, 2004), 137. Afraid of losing the colonies altogether to rebellious colonists, the king soon revoked key provisions of the law. Chief among these was the legal ban on the inheritance of *encomienda*.

[39] See Brian Tierney, *The Idea of Natural Rights* (Ithaca, NY: Cornell University Press, 1997): Jean Porter, *Nature as Reason* (Grand Rapids, MI: Eerdmans, 2005); and Rushton, *Human Rights and the Image of God.* The discontinuity thesis is proposed by Ernest Fortin, "On The Presumed Medieval Origin of Individual Rights," *Communio* 26 (1999): 55–79.

[40] See Tierney, *The Idea of Natural Rights.*

[41] From Las Casas's Letter of 1546, cited in Rushton, *Human Rights and the Image of God*, 135.

[42] Rushton calls *Apologética Historia* the "first great work of ethnography." Ibid. 124.

as *encomienda* could induce such corrupt people to embrace a modicum of moral decency.[43]

Apologists attempted to use what they regarded as the poverty of the natives as evidence of their laziness, dishonesty, and mental inferiority.[44] Las Casas, on the other hand, countered by amassing evidence of the natives' ingenuity, hard work, and practical intelligence. While they may not have had all the material abundance and technological advantages of European societies, the natives before the invasion were at least able to subsist in relative comfort. And it was in fact the gold, silver, and other natural riches of the land that triggered the "violent and blind and uncontrollable greed"[45] of the invaders. The natives were either murdered or plunged into abject poverty by their conquerors, who then claimed that the natives needed the superior guidance of the Spanish to avoid such debasement.

The subject of volition to which Las Casas applied his critique was clear. Responsibility for the impoverishment of the natives lay squarely at the feet of the leaders of the Spanish invasion, their soldiers, and their agents; responsibility also lay with the Spanish crown and the church. Las Casas argued that the natural law demands that the Spanish monarch, as responsible for the common good, fulfill his moral duty to acknowledge the full humanity of the Indians, that he recognize their natural right to political independence and self-governance, and that the Spanish conquistadores restore freedom and pay restitution to their victims. The just war doctrine did not justify an attack on indigenous people on the grounds that they are pagans or even because they practice offensive forms of worship, such as human sacrifice.[46] The natives therefore have a right to restitution as victims of an unjust war. He went even further than Vitoria in arguing not only that the king had no right to allow the conquest but also that the natives had a right to use lethal force if doing so constituted a necessary means of exercising their natural right of self-defense in the face of unjust aggression.[47]

Thomas knew that tyranny can lead to poverty, but Las Casas became acutely aware of the systematic nature of the exploitation that led to the impoverishment of communities and even whole societies. Decades of living with the oppressed allowed him not only to function more effectively as an advocate for the oppressed but also to grow in friendship with them. This experience

---

[43] See Las Casas, "Twenty Reasons against the Encomienda System," in Sullivan, *Indian Freedom*, 240–47; L. B. Simpson, *The Encomienda in New Spain: The Beginning of Spanish Mexico*, rev. ed. (Berkeley: University of California Press, 1966); Lewis Ulysses Hanke, *Aristotle and the American Indians* (Bloomington: Indiana University Press, 1970); and Anthony Pagden, *The Fall of Natural Man: The American Indian and the Origins of Comparative Ethnology* (Cambridge: Cambridge University Press, 1982).
[44] See Las Casas, *Life of Columbus*, in Sullivan, *Indian Freedom*, 49–52.
[45] Ibid., 50.
[46] See Sullivan, *Indian Freedom*, 299–303, and Rushton, *Human Rights*, 150.
[47] See "The Just War of the Indians," in Sullivan, *Indian Freedom*, 166–78.

led him to use natural law as a moral weapon to defend the poor in a way that Thomas never did. Whereas Thomistic justice reminded the rich of their duties to the poor, Las Casas encouraged the poor to affirm their own rights. His writings and homilies denounced the powerful and strove to empower the poor. Whereas the standard interpretation of the Thomistic "order of love" gave priority to members of one's own family, socioeconomic class, and country, Las Casas focused on the needy foreigner and the oppressed stranger.

Poverty is caused, Las Casas understood, not only by specific crimes of the powerful but also by unjust economic practices, institutions, and laws. The real barbarians, Las Casas argued, were not the natives but the Spanish, whose rapacious greed led them to lose all self-control in their ferocious campaign against innocent men, women, and children. He knew that avarice motivated unjust practices that were justified by pervasive prejudice against natives.

Las Casas applied natural law to his specific circumstances to argue that the Spanish monarchy must change the laws so that justice can be brought to the New World. While he did not call into question the legitimacy of social hierarchy, or inherited privilege, Las Casas insisted that the sovereign has a special responsibility to care for those in his charge who are least able to defend themselves against unscrupulous opportunists.

Natural law also supports retributive justice that condemns crimes against innocent people, punishes their perpetrators, and ensures that their victims receive just restitution. Though Las Casas was too much of a realist to believe that the legal authorities in either Spain or the Indies were likely to require a complete renunciation of Spanish power, he argued from natural law for the essential restoration to the Amerindians of their freedom and stolen property. Beneficiaries were to return stolen goods either to survivors or, if none could be found, to their villages or, if these have been destroyed, to other natives from the area.[48]

In summary, we can say that Las Casas, like Thomas, understood poverty to be the privation of the goods necessary for a decent human life. He saw in a way that most of his contemporaries did not that the native people in the New World were what we would call "high-risk groups." In fact, they were beyond the point of "risk," and some communities became nearly extinct. Las Casas insisted that responsibility be attributed to the Spanish conquistadores and those who cooperated with them. Bringing justice to the natives meant using all available means to protect them from Spanish predators. The remedy to this particular form of poverty lay in changing Spanish policy in the region, especially putting an end to slavery and abolishing the *encomienda* system. Las Casas believed that the imperative to bring justice to the natives was a broad-ranging and deep duty of everyone holding power in Spanish society and in the New World.

[48] See ibid., 284.

John Finnis

We turn now to a contemporary approach to natural law, the "new natural law theory" of John Finnis, Germain Grisez, Joseph Boyle, and their colleagues.[49] The founder of this theory is theologian Grisez, but this chapter attends to his close collaborator, philosopher and lawyer Finnis, because he has devoted considerable attention to issues of justice. Finnis, moreover, emphasizes that natural law is defended in terms of a theory of practical rationality that does not take as foundational any particular theological or metaphysical system.

The new natural law theory has had a significant impact in a variety of fields that make it the necessary reference point to any treatment of natural law today. Its authors have devoted their time and energy both to theoretical matters and to practical moral controversies concerning sexual and biomedical ethics. While they have given relatively little attention to issues of poverty, we can briefly examine how the theory has been applied in the work of development economist Sabina Alkire.

New natural law theory seeks to address a pluralistic audience in legal and ethical terms. It strives to provide a moral theory that accounts for the range of human goods and morality in ways that escape utilitarianism and Kantianism. The central moral imperative of the theory is stated as follows: "In all one's deliberating and acting, one *ought* to choose and in other ways will – and other persons, so far as satisfying their needs is dependent on one's choosing and willing, have a *right* that one choose and will – those and only those possibilities the willing of which is compatible with integral human fulfillment."[50] The key phrase "integral human fulfillment" concerns any and all human persons and in all relevant aspects of their lives. These aspects are identified in terms of "basic goods" that include human life (including health and procreation), knowledge and aesthetic appreciation, skilled performance, meaningful work and play, self-integration, practical reasonableness, justice and friendship, and religion.[51]

Finnis's major text, *Natural Law and Natural Rights*, describes the theory's three essential components: a set of basic practical principles that indicate the basic forms of human flourishing as goods to be pursued, a set of basic methodological requirements of practical reasonableness, and a set of general moral standards.[52] Actions that conform to the principles of practical

[49] See John Finnis, *Natural Law and Natural Rights* (Oxford: Clarendon Press, 1980); Germain Grisez, *The Way of the Lord Jesus*, vol. 1: *Christian Moral Principles* (Chicago: Franciscan Herald Press, 1983); and Robert P. George, ed., *Natural Law Theory: Contemporary Essays* (New York: Oxford University Press, 1994).

[50] John Finnis, "Commensuration and Public Reason," in *Immensurability, Incomparability, and Practical Reason*, ed. Ruth Chang (Cambridge, MA: Harvard University Press, 1997), 225.

[51] See Finnis, *Natural Law and Natural Rights*, 86–90; later publications offer variations on this list.

[52] See ibid., 23.

reasonableness are consistent with integral human flourishing. These principles are formulated, in abbreviated form, in the following imperatives: have a harmonious set of commitments, do not arbitrarily discount or exaggerate any of the basic goods, do not unfairly discriminate between people, do not identify any "particular project" with the overriding significance only due to a basic good, pursue general commitments with purpose and creativity, use efficient means to one's ends, do not ignore foreseeable negative consequences to one's acts, do not intentionally harm any dimension of human well-being, promote the common good, and do not violate one's conscience.[53]

The principles of practical reasonableness contain a variety of implications for poverty and its reduction. Poverty is an evil because it prevents integral human flourishing. Natural law objects to human behavior that unjustifiably causes poverty. It prohibits the kind of discrimination that often targets the poor; it generates a sense of duty to care for the poor; and it regards government, responsible for promoting the common good, as having a serious moral obligation to address the causes of poverty.

New natural law theorists recall some important themes from Thomistic natural law that are important for the question of poverty. Devoting considerable attention to issues of justice, Finnis's *Natural Law and Natural Rights* draws from Thomas's arguments to support the legitimacy of private property, the obligatory nature of distributive justice, and the priority of the common good to the private good of individuals (within the bounds of what is compatible with willing the integral human flourishing of all interested parties).[54]

Property carries an inherent moral responsibility. Businesses help the poor by providing employment and by charging just prices for goods and services and just interest rates on loans.[55] Government has a responsibility to ensure that the basic and social needs of citizens are met when they are unable to provide for themselves. Owners fulfill a major requirement of justice in paying taxes "imposed for redistributive purposes."[56] Thomas did not promote a radical utopian egalitarianism, but he did note the injustice of a world in which the super-rich coexist with those in extreme poverty. The economy need not be envisioned as a "zero-sum game" to recognize that "if some have a super-abundance ... then others must, in the real world, be going short of what they are entitled to."[57] Indeed, Finnis goes on to observe, again on natural law rather than religious grounds, that anyone who retains superfluous goods is not only depriving but even stealing from the poor.[58]

53 John Finnis, *The Fundamentals of Ethics* (New York: Oxford University Press, 1983), 17; see also *Natural Law and Natural Rights*, 108–26.
54 See John Finnis, *Aquinas: Moral, Political, and Legal Theory* (New York: Oxford University Press, 1998), 120–21.
55 Ibid., 207, where Finnis argues that Thomas's ethic can accommodate loans of money at market rates of interest.
56 Ibid., 195.
57 Ibid., 195–96.
58 Ibid., 196.

The new natural law theory provides grounds for criticizing racial and gender discrimination, the exploitation of workers at home and abroad, the unequal educational opportunity that leaves poor people at a significant competitive disadvantage to the middle class, and the exclusion of millions from medical care. Fairness and equity are key marks of justice that are violated by arbitrary preferences or exclusions based on irrelevant partiality. More generally, the new natural law provides grounds for objecting to harmful conditions that make it unreasonably difficult for individuals to pursue integral human flourishing, including the basic goods of health, the cultivation of aesthetic appreciation, and capacities for skilled performance. New natural law provides strong grounds for identifying and objecting to the existence of destructive social contexts within which poor people make decisions and act. One might wonder, though, if Finnis's strong concentration on individual acts and individual responsibility lends itself to a neoconservative tendency to reduce the cause of poverty to the bad behavior of poor people, for example, in terms of substance abuse and familial instability. Such a view of the poor can aggravate their oppression by contributing to their stigmatization and cultural marginalization.

Finnis often focuses on matters of personal morality. His exposition of Thomas examines the treatment of possessions in the *Summa Theologiae* as including goods needed for meeting the necessities of life as distinct from superfluous goods that must be made available to the poor.[59] Finnis's position accords with Thomas's comment that, "if I am aware of another person's extreme, evident, and urgent need, and there is no one else to give relief in time, I have a duty of strict justice (not merely 'charity') to relieve that need by handing over resources that I own even though they are not superflua but rather those needed … for fulfilling my proper responsibilities to myself and others."[60]

Interpreting "needs" to include the range of goods appropriate to one's "station in life" might be misused by those who would rationalize a materialistic lifestyle, Finnis notes, but "the true measure of one's needs is not the emotionally motivated expectations and patterns of consumption conventional among one's social class, nor exaggerated fears about possible future penury, but the bona fide judgment of a practical reasonableness which includes, as always, general justice and love of neighbor as oneself."[61] There are no formulas for distinguishing proper from improper use of one's wealth, and the final judgment about how to act is facilitated by the virtue of prudence.

Recognition of the fact that justice has not only domestic but global significance inspires a heightened sensitivity to the profound impact of the decisions, policies, and conduct of multinational actors, both governmental and

---

[59] Ibid., 191.
[60] Ibid., 192.
[61] Ibid., 194.

corporate, on the poor of the developing world. The radical expansion of natural law from the medieval village context to globalized world culture testifies to the staying power and adaptability of the tradition. Because responsibility is related to power, international agents who deeply influence social patterns in the developing world must be given incentives to support rather than undermine the socioeconomic rights of the needy. Those who wish to extend this line of analysis on behalf of the poor will want to develop an account of natural law that embraces both the cultural identities of particular societies and the universal human rights of the poor of every society. People around the world need not pursue justice for the poor in exactly the same way, but every society ought to strive to empower its citizens to become ever more effective agents of their own freedom and economic development. While the language of particular religious and moral or ethical traditions at times jar against one other, the human nature that we all share provides a basis of mutual understanding, cooperation, and commitment to develop policies that better enable the poor to pursue integral human flourishing.

Development economist Sabina Alkire, the director of the Policy and Human Development Initiative at Oxford University, works primarily from the perspective of Amartya Sen's "capabilities approach" to poverty.[62] Her *Valuing Freedoms: Sen's Capability Approach and Poverty Reduction* employs an interdisciplinary approach as the best way to acknowledge the multidimensional nature of the challenges presented by poverty.[63] She argues against the excessively narrow income- and need-centered approaches to poverty reduction and against purely economic theories of poverty reduction. The World Bank's *World Development Report, 2000/01* recognized, as Sakiko Fukuda-Parr notes in Chapter 2 on "Global Poverty and Unequal Development," that even "employment generating growth and expansion of social services are not enough to reduce poverty; people are poor because they are powerless and lack access to opportunities." As Fukuda-Parr explains, "material assets are not enough; people also need the political freedom to hold authorities to account and to have a say in decisions that affect their lives."

Alkire takes as her starting point Sen's goal of not simply increasing economic growth or real incomes of the poor but also expanding their capacities to enjoy "valuable beings and doings."[64] Sen, however, does not specify which capabilities ought to be considered, nor who determines which capabilities ought to be advanced, nor how various capabilities ought to be related to one another. Finnis accords with Sen in regarding social institutions in terms

---

[62] See, inter alia, Amartya Sen, *Development as Freedom* (New York: Anchor, 2000), and, for a contemporary discussion, see Sakiko Fukuda-Parr, "Global Poverty and Unequal Development," Chapter 2 in this volume.

[63] Sabina Alkire, *Valuing Freedoms: Sen's Capability Approach and Poverty Reduction* (New York: Oxford University Press, 2002).

[64] Ibid., 2, citing Sen, *Development as Freedom* (New York: Knopf Press, 1999), 75.

280 Stephen J. Pope

of their ability to enable people to flourish, but he provides a level of moral specificity missing from the capability theory.

Alkire identifies six attractive features of Finnis's account of natural law: it provides structure but also flexibility in adaptation to particular circumstances, is founded in practical reason alone rather than in a metaphysical account of the good, draws from available empirical information regarding plural human ends and moral principles, accords a central role to human freedom and self-determination, draws from the Aristotelian and Thomistic intellectual traditions, and treats normative issues and participatory procedures with analytical clarity.

The "capabilities approach" offers the most useful attempt to understand the impact of poverty on human lives, but, Alkire maintains, it can be further refined and developed into a tool that can be applied to microeconomic poverty reduction initiatives. Finnis's theory of basic goods supplies a way of specifying the basis from which people make value judgments and apply them in practical ways to concrete contexts. Alkire connects the theory to real-life particular projects of goat rearing, female literacy classes, and rose garland production within the developing world.[65] Most useful is Finnis's identification of the "basic goods," or what Alkire calls the "dimensions of human development"[66] that people pursue in every society. These are goods, not simply arbitrary preferences, and so they provide the "starting points for collective action."[67]

Poverty reduction concerns these dimensions, but particular communities must decide which of these dimensions are most important in their own particular situations. Alkire finds the account of these dimensions to be especially helpful as the basis for public dialogue and communal evaluation of the capabilities that are relevant to small-scale projects within poor communities. What Alkire calls Finnis's "principled pluralism" thus provides an account of plural human goods and plural principles of practical reason that can be brought to bear in attempts to enhance the capabilities of poor people and so reduce poverty. Finnis's account of moral agency and especially free choice coheres well with Sen's emphasis on participation and empowerment, capacity building, strengthening institutions, and mobilizing local communities to engage in collective action.[68] Alkire's work illustrates the basic direction in which one appropriation of natural law notions of human dignity, practical reason, subsidiarity, and the common good are able to inform systematic responses to poverty reduction. Taking personal and communal moral agency seriously implies that poverty is best addressed not simply as determined by the plans of outside "experts" but also through galvanizing the energies and intelligence of local communities.

[65] See Alkire, *Valuing Freedoms*, chap. 7.
[66] Ibid., 47.
[67] Ibid., 50.
[68] See ibid., 3.

Conclusion: Natural Law and Poverty

The historical development of natural law reflection on poverty displays significant continuity. Continuity lies in the central anthropological assumption that people have an inherent capacity to act and live together in community in a manner that is intelligent, free, and peaceful. Continuity also is found in its vision of morality rooted in the human good, the intrinsic worth of every person, and the duties of justice to assist those who are socially disadvantaged or otherwise victims of injustice. Contemporary natural law regards justice as working for the actualization of this potential in each society, local community, and person and promotes human well-being through the principles of the common good, subsidiarity, and human dignity. It thus agrees with the moral principle that there ought to be no "discounted humans, not of equal moral worth, simply by virtue of their gender"[69] or any other trait. The major development beyond Thomas's account of natural law concerns the evolution of human rights discourse as the primary mode of communicating the inherent dignity of the person.

Thomas's own normative response to poverty can be put in terms of virtues that fulfill the natural law and the vices that violate it. Poor individuals sometimes suffer from vices that lead to their suffering, but they can learn corrective virtues that allow them to overcome internal and external obstacles to living humanly decent lives. Affluent individuals are tempted to slide into vices like greed and excessive ambition, but they may be more capable of overcoming their own moral defects and assume their proportionate responsibility for the common good.

Las Casas's experience of the poor as victims of harsh oppression led him to focus on the freedom of the poor from the control of their tormentors, whom he understood to be not only vicious persons but also agents of a degrading and otherwise unjust political, economic, and legal system. Unlike Thomas, Las Casas spoke of the moral claims of these victims in terms of their natural rights to freedom, political self-governance, and cultural integrity. Las Casas regarded the proper goal of ethical responsibility as restoring the agency and freedom of the natives.

Contemporary natural law exemplified in Finnis builds on the medieval and early modern insights just noted. It views the human person as social, intelligent, and free. Like Las Casas, Finnis employs the discourse of human rights within the older Thomistic language of justice and the common good. He emphasizes the obligation of all human agents to act justly and to remedy injustice. Alkire adopts the new natural law because it provides language of the "dimensions of human development" that must be considered in local efforts at poverty reduction.

---

[69] Nancy J. Hirschmann, "Poverty and Morality: A Feminist Perspective," Chapter 7 in this volume.

None of our authors suggests that natural law generates an empirically based account of either the causes of or proper solutions to the problem of poverty, yet it does constitute a basic moral framework within which such accounts can be morally evaluated. This framework includes an uncompromising acknowledgment of the dignity of the person that grounds an ethic of human rights. The basic human rights of individuals cannot be sacrificed for perceived short- or long-term beneficial consequences for the poor. Natural law cannot countenance a trading of freedom for bread, as both components are necessary for human flourishing. The natural law tradition provides grounds for regarding negative rights or immunities, however, as properly coordinated with the fulfillment of socioeconomic rights or entitlements. Michael Walzer properly notes that the extent to which the latter can be fulfilled is of course relative to the character of particular political communities.[70]

There are, then, inherent limits to natural law, and to any ethical theory, as a perspective from which to consider poverty. Determining the best means for reducing poverty is a matter of prudential judgment rather than ethical theory (though, as noted, the means used to alleviate poverty have to be within the moral constraints that protect human dignity). Natural law ethics provides a morally useful but not sufficient perspective from which to consider poverty. Natural law ethics, in other words, underdetermines our grasp of and response to poverty. Understanding the complex and multidimensional reality of poverty demands that we take into account not only its ethical dimensions but also its economic, political, cultural, and other dimensions. Alkire's synthesis of Sen and Finnis presents one way of filling out our understanding of natural law in this regard, but not the only way. Natural law constitutes an ethical framework within which various other theories of society and the economy can operate in their own ways, and presumably it might also be fruitfully related to other approaches to development economics.

We can close with three general advantages provided by a natural law approach to poverty. First, as "reason based," the natural law tradition seeks to establish a basis for moral reasoning, reflection, and dialogue that is not tied to a particular religious authority. This aspect of natural law is particularly relevant to the moral dimension of public policy dialogue about poverty. Religiously based in-group bonding has at times been attended by strong out-group religiously supported animosity. Appeals to religious identity in pluralistic societies can create obstacles to dialogue about social morality, including the moral dimensions of poverty. When religion is fragmenting, natural law holds out the possibility of greater intellectual integration because it focuses on goods commonly sought by all people because they are human beings. Natural law holds that common humanity provides a perspective from which to criticize the tendency of group loyalties to become antagonistic and exclusive. This is not to say that particular religious loyalties ought to be replaced by an abstract moral universalism or that particular religious discourse ought to be replaced by natural law discourse, but only that the practical limitations of the former can to some extent be corrected by the latter.

Second, the natural law emphasis on moral agency has a number of important implications. Human volition obviously plays a variety of roles in creating and maintaining conditions that lead to poverty and to overcoming those conditions. Poverty is influenced by a vast range of factors that run from decisions of policy makers, politicians, and powerful economic agents to the choices of consumers about how to spend their money and of citizens about how to vote. The direct injustice of those who consciously choose to exploit the poor in sweatshops and brothels is aggravated by the "passive injustice" of those who are indifferent or apathetic.[71] Poverty is, of course, sometimes due to forces beyond any human control (disease, earthquakes, hurricanes, etc.), yet the massive negative effects of major natural disasters on human well-being are all too often magnified by either human agency or apathy. The natural law attentiveness to moral agency resists abdication of proper degrees of responsibility.

Natural law's emphasis on the possibilities of human goodwill and positive action resists the temptation of the poor to lapse into fatalistic acceptance of their lot. Its awareness of the social context of human agency provides an ethical basis for rejecting any attempt to reduce the causes of poverty to the bad decisions or moral vices of the poor. It also calls us to be alert to the impact of systematic injustices on the economic prospects of the poor. The central emphasis on agency regards emergency assistance to the poor as necessary but not a proper substitute for long-term programs that promote empowerment, grass-roots community organizations, and civic participation. The best programs for the alleviation of poverty strive to actualize the natural human capacities to act intelligently, productively, and self-responsibly. Natural law ethics thus seeks to avoid the extremes of both radically autonomous individualism and domineering paternalism.

Third, natural law carries a number of fundamental considerations regarding moral responsibility for poverty reduction. The fundamental duty of benevolence for one another is exercised under conditions of finitude. We are to be concerned about the poor, yet this concern does not take precedence over all other responsibilities. The writings of Thomas Aquinas, Las Casas, and Finnis recognize a gradation of moral responsibilities that form a series of concentric circles, beginning with the near and extending to the most distant.[72] Practical reason pursues an ordered love of family and friends, community and country. At the same time, the most urgent needs of the poor also claim a primacy of place for the use of social resources.

---

[71] See Judith N. Shklar, *The Faces of Injustice* (New Haven: Yale University Press, 1990).
[72] See *ST* II-II, 26. See also Stephen J. Pope, *The Evolution of Altruism and the Ordering of Love* (Washington, DC: Georgetown University Press, 1994).

Natural law approaches responsibility for domestic poverty in terms of three principles: the principle of solidarity holds that those who have the greatest basic need or who suffer from the greatest deprivation should be given priority of moral concern; the principle of subsidiarity holds that the solution to social problems should be pursued by the most efficient agency at the lowest level of responsibility; and the principle of the common good regards the state as ultimately responsible for promoting the public good when other agencies fail to do so. The state is responsible to stimulate economic development, to promote a robust civil society, and to promote the opening of opportunities for the enhancement of the capabilities of the poor. Philanthropy has a valuable role to play in addressing the needs of the poor, but charity does not substitute for the more primary obligations of justice.

The principle of subsidiarity and the natural order of love suggest that we have, in general, the strongest obligation to the poor of our own communities and society. At the same time, the principle of solidarity identifies a responsibility on the part of governments, particularly of affluent countries, to address the "grotesque levels of poverty and inequality"[73] that mark global human society. The principle of solidarity does not countenance a view of the world as an aggregate of self-contained nation-states that bear no responsibility for the poor of other countries, no matter how desperate. The practical execution of global responsibilities is distributed among states, NGOs, and other international agencies. It is not possible for most people to become self-sufficient economic agents if they suffer from severe malnourishment or live in communities locked in violent conflict, so policies to eliminate poverty must first address the most immediate needs of those who are threatened with imminent death or other grievous forms of suffering such as extreme malnutrition.

Poverty relief must also address the long-term causes of persistent poverty, as Alkire, Sen, and many others note. Subsidiarity suggests that programs of poverty relief will aim to promote just governance (and less corruption), economic development, and the growth of robust civil society. In general, the relief of absolute poverty in one's own country takes precedence over the reduction of absolute poverty in another country and the reduction of relative poverty in one's own country takes priority over the reduction of relative poverty in another country. The more serious the level of domestic poverty, the stronger would seem to be its level of moral precedence relative to global poverty. Conversely, the less serious the relative domestic poverty, the more precedence must be given to absolute global poverty. These generalizations are, of course, matters of moral principle that have to be applied in the practical world according to the possibilities perceived by those who exercise the virtue of political prudence. Natural law provides a normative framework for morally evaluating projects and proposals, but the will to craft and execute them will not come from ethical theory alone.

[73] Fukuda-Parr, Chapter 2 in this volume.

14

Afterword

Michael Walzer

These are engaging and insightful essays, and it has been illuminating to watch them grow, from the first drafts circulated before the Ethikon conference in March 2008, to the conference discussions, to the revised and final versions. After reading the final versions, I went back and reread Michael Harrington's *The Other America*, still one of the best accounts of poverty in the United States, though much has changed since it was published in 1962. Harrington's perspective might best be called "social-democratic" – he is the advocate of a strong welfare state. As one of the participants in the Ethikon conference pointed out, this was a perspective missing among the essay writers. It is closely related to, but also different from, the arguments found in the essays on Marxism and egalitarian liberalism. Because my own views are social democratic in character, I will represent that perspective in this commentary on the collected essays. But I will try as best I can to do justice to the very different views described by our authors.

Poverty is a good topic through which to address the differences among religious and political-philosophical traditions because, as the Bible says, it is always with us – has always been and will always be with us, at least until the messianic age. Ethikon topics like "civil society" have been harder, especially for people writing out of the religious traditions, who can plausibly say that there was no such thing as civil society when their canonical texts were written. But poverty is a commonplace of religious as well as secular argument. And the terms of the argument are mostly common also. I am going to describe them as a series of polarities – voluntary-involuntary, deserving-undeserving, private-public, particular-universal, among others – even though I understand that polar oppositions often misrepresent the nuances and complexities of the contrasted arguments. I will point out some of the misrepresentations, but the polarities will give readers a useful overview of what is at stake in the ongoing discussion.

The crucial definitional polarity is between multidimensional and single-factor descriptions of the poor. The single factor is wealth or income; the many dimensions include misery, humiliation, domination, and loss of self-esteem (the different terms used in biblical Hebrew to describe the poor, discussed by Kent Van Til and Noam Zohar, nicely convey the idea of multidimensionality). It is easiest to understand poverty as the condition of not having enough money, and this understanding lends itself, obviously, to statistical documentation and analysis. But it does not get at the actual experience of *being poor* – or, at least, the common experience.

There is another polarity that may illuminate this one: between voluntary and involuntary poverty. In some of the religious traditions, great value is attached to the ascetic who chooses a life free from getting and spending, a life without money and with very few possessions. But this is not a choice that involves misery, humiliation, domination, and loss of self-esteem. Ascetics command respect from their fellow believers; their self-esteem, by all appearances, is secure; and while they may subject themselves to the strict rules of a monastic order, they are not at the bottom of the political heap. Multidimensional poverty is, so far as I can tell, never voluntary.

On the other hand, the multidimensionally poor, the miserable and the oppressed, the wretched of the earth, are often depicted in the religious traditions as God's most beloved children. So it might seem odd that pious men and women would not choose to be among the wretched in order to be among the most beloved. And, similarly, for secular Marxists, the members of the proletariat, the working (but not the lumpen) poor, "immiserated" by the capitalist system, are celebrated as the agents of revolutionary transformation. Some Marxist militants choose to live among the workers and share the hardships that produce working-class consciousness. But many do not; Marx himself did not. Lighting an expensive cigar, Big Bill Haywood of the Workers of the World (the Wobblies) famously said, "Nothing is too good for the proletariat." Hardship, by contrast, is not good, and the secular left never thought that it was. Nor do any of the religious traditions hold that wretchedness is good, even if the wretched are preferred by God. A life with little money and few possessions may be a religious vocation, but not a life of misery.

And yet, in most of the religious traditions, and among some secularists too, there are many conventional "goods," many beautiful commodities, many pleasures, many forms of self-indulgence, that are not thought to be good at all for men and women who aim to be good. The simple life is, again and again, said to be the best life. Not asceticism, but moderation: among Muslims, writes Sohail Hashmi, "The ideal is the median, the life of self-sufficiency, *closer to the poor than to the rich*" (my emphasis). David Loy's strong dislike for "consumerism" derives, he tells us, from the Buddhist tradition. Certainly, there are many religious depictions of the rich in negative terms, sometimes simply because of the luxuries they enjoy – as if these enjoyments were bad in themselves. But more often the rich are denounced because their wealth has been stolen from the poor: "For ye have eaten up the vineyard," says the Israelite prophet Amos, "the spoil of the poor is in your houses." For

Marxists, rich capitalists exploit the workers, seizing the surplus value they create. But this value, properly distributed, would not be bad at all, even if it was used, as it would be, to purchase consumer goods. In the social democratic tradition, the aim of union organization and welfare state agitation is to make consumer goods of all sorts – refrigerators and washing machines, television sets and computers – universally available as well as to make working men and women politically effective citizens. The good life is not "closer to the poor" but as close to the rich as it is possible to get in a just society – and here I am talking, multidimensionally, of a life that is not only economically prosperous but also not-miserable, not-humiliated, and not-dominated.

The common religious dislike of materialism makes this a complicated issue, but I think that this version of the good life, replete with consumer goods, would still be "good" for most Jews, Christians, Hindus, and Confucians – and probably for Muslims and Buddhists, too. Indeed, the critique of materialism, though common to all the religious traditions, has never been very effective in any of them.

If it is not a good thing to be poor, then it follows that the poor should be helped to escape, if not from their poverty, then at least from their misery. All the religious traditions stress the importance of helping the poor: this is the great object of charitable giving. But there is another crucial polarity, well established in Christendom but recognizable in other traditions too (though Noam Zohar denies that it appears in Jewish writing), between the deserving and the undeserving poor. The first group deserves our help; the second does not. This is not a distinction available in Hindu thought, where all the poor presumably "deserve" their poverty because of wrongs they committed in a previous existence. As Arvind Sharma explains, however, that does not mean that they do not also deserve our assistance – assisting the poor is a religious duty, whose fulfillment may earn us a better life in some future incarnation.

The undeserving poor are, according to the standard doctrine, voluntarily poor, but not because they have chosen poverty as a religious vocation. Rather, in the eyes of their critics (and some would say that the undeserving poor exist only in the eyes of their critics), their poverty is the result of self-indulgence: they are drunkards, vagabonds, "welfare queens." They are lazy, indolent, shiftless, parasitical on the rest of us (virtuous citizens). The lumpen proletariat belongs in this category too, though its members are condemned more because of their uselessness in the revolutionary struggle than because of their unwillingness to accept the discipline of steady work. I should not say "condemned": no doubt, they too are victims of the capitalist system, but not victims that Marxist militants have any time for. In England in the early modern period, the undeserving poor were sent to workhouses; something similar would probably happen to the lumpen proletariat after the revolution.

Women often appear among the undeserving poor: the right-wing attack on "welfare queens" has historical precedents. Requiring single mothers to work is also, as Nancy Hirschmann tells us, not a modern invention (though we do not send them to the workhouse these days). Beggars are of both sexes (and all ages), but the begging woman, often with a little child in hand, is a standard trope of religious iconography. Most religions would enjoin almsgiving, but the impulse to get the woman off the streets and into some disciplinary setting is strong in Protestant Christianity and perhaps in other religions as well. Classical liberals and libertarians, because they (unlike Locke) do not believe in state discipline, would presumably offer the begging women a charitable gift – but not so large a gift as to free her from the discipline of the labor market. She should be working. Joseph Priestly, a Dissenting preacher and early defender of the French Revolution, argued that the charity should be minimal: "The greater the provision that is made for the poor, the more poor there will be to avail themselves of it: as, in general, men will not submit to labor if they can live without it."

The deserving poor, by contrast (on this view), do not want charity; they prize their dignity and want to work if they possibly can, and so they do not need to be forced but only to be helped. They are the victims of famine or flood; men and women out of work because of an economic collapse; people disabled or in ill health; the objects of racial, religious, or gender discrimination. Here too women are disproportionately represented, but the trope is masculine: the male head of a family, desperately looking for work. His obvious need is not for a few coins or a loaf of bread but for a job – a boost into the working world. The natural law tradition, says Stephen Pope, aims at providing just this kind of help, by "empowering the poor to act as agents of their own lives." This is also the view of Maimonides, who argues in his summation of Jewish philanthropic doctrine, that the highest form of *tzedakah* is a gift, a loan, a partnership, or a job that "strengthens the hand" of the poor man, "so that he has no need to beg from other people." The argument for agency and independence is, I think, common to all the traditions discussed in this book, though the simple injunction to give alms is probably more frequently expressed, at least in religious literature.

Here we come to another polarity – between the relief of poverty and its abolition (which may require the radical transformation of the society we live in). If the poor will always be with us, then relief will always be necessary. But we might aim at a kind of relief that would make everyday relief unnecessary. Imagine a society (or a world) where all the people who can be independent have been helped to achieve independence and where all the permanently dependent have been guaranteed the assistance they need. Then no one will be begging, and the standard form of relief – almsgiving or one-to-one charity – will be unnecessary. I would think that the revolutionary future suggested by the Marxist maxim "From each according to his ability, to each according to his need" matches this picture, though the revolution won't be driven, as Andrew Levine makes clear, by a kindly concern for the poor. In the nearer run, abolition without revolution is the aim of the social democratic welfare state with its array of benefits: old-age pensions, unemployment insurance, universal health care, and so on. Egalitarian liberals would also endorse the welfare state, even if it does not meet their model of an entirely just society – which might well require a social revolution. From the standpoint of equality, the welfare state is at least a step in the right direction.

But is abolition a peculiarly secular – perhaps also a statist vision? There does seem to be some resistance to it in the religious traditions. Thus, Noam Zohar quotes a rabbinic midrash:

David proclaimed before the Holy One: ... Master of the Universe, render your world level, making rich and poor equal! He responded: ... If they will all be rich, or all poor, who will be capable of giving in kindness?

Sohail Hashmi cites a similar teaching from the Qur'an: "He has raised you in ranks, some above others, so that He may try you in the gifts that He has given you." And the same view can be found among Christians: "Nothing graces the Christian soul so much as mercy," says Ambrose, "mercy as shown chiefly towards the poor." How would the pious Christian show his mercifulness if mercy had no object – if no one was poor? The image that lies behind all these texts is of the pious individual handing a gift to the orphan child or the begging woman, or bringing soup to the homebound sick, or contributing some small amount, regularly, to the local church's charity fund.

But this kind of charity depends on what might be called the "nearness" of the poor: they live among the people who are enjoined to help them. They are a visible presence in everybody's everyday social life. But their visibility may be radically reduced in modern economies. Michael Harrington's main point about "the other America" is its radical otherness: the poor live apart; they are mostly out of sight and, as a result, often out of mind. Living in isolated rural pockets or in segregated zones of sprawling cities, they are almost a separate nation (as Disraeli first argued in his novel about "the two nations"). Helping the members of this nation can't be the work of charitable individuals. It requires assistance on a much larger scale and, though some religious organizations are able to work on this scale, state action is almost certainly necessary.

A common critique of both charity and state action is that it makes for dependency; the poor become the permanent clients of well-to-do patrons, or religious organizations, or the welfare state. What we should aim at instead is empowerment and, again, independence – which sometimes requires, as libertarians might say, the "tough love" that pushes the poor into the labor market. Of course, the poor can also be helped into the labor market by counseling, schooling, job training, and daycare for their children. Programs of this sort aim to turn the welfare state away from clientage, to make it an agent of economic independence. By contrast, the pious helpers and comforters of the poor require – so their critics say – the ongoing dependency of the people they comfort and help.

The Marxist claim is that only a revolution will abolish poverty, and that seems to be the view of some of the Catholic liberation theologians – who come very close, it might be said, to making Marxism their preferred theology. The argument here is about the causes of poverty, and the relevant polarity is between a structural account, which emphasizes the "system," usually the capitalist system, and what might be called a natural account, which emphasizes human failings and nature's disasters (famine, earthquake, tsunami, and so on). Marxism is obviously a structuralist account; it predicts the overthrow of the system, and looks on any ameliorating measures, charitable or welfarist, with suspicion: they will only delay the end. In fact, however, a structuralist account is perfectly compatible with amelioration; social systems can be changed gradually in ways that benefit their most vulnerable and miserable members. That, indeed, is the social democratic project.

What I have called the "natural" account would hold that individual and familial impoverishment will be a feature of any social system, given human aggression, greed, indifference, laziness, and so on – and given the certain-to-come calamities of the natural world. This is probably the common religious view; it need not lead only to an emphasis on almsgiving; it too is consistent with practices that aim at independence for as many of the poor as possible. But it does undercut, as the Marxists say, any commitment to large-scale social change, and it probably does not help much with efforts of the poor to empower themselves, to organize unions or movements that aim at social change – and whose activists and militants must insist that social change will make a difference. I do not know if Gandhi's movement for village cooperatives and a sustainable poverty is an exception to this statement or a demonstration of it. Might the movement have changed India or did it only delay the kind of change that India needed? In any case, the view that the poor are always with us tends to go along with the view that the world (as it is) is always with us.

Whether the focus is on relief or abolition, the question of agency is crucial: who is to do the necessary work – individual men and women, religious organizations, social movements, or state officials? The key polarity here is private-public. Relief is first of all the work of generous individuals, and it may well be, as David Loy says it is in the case of Buddhism, "even more beneficial to the donor than to the recipient." The poor are the occasion for the spiritual progress of the well-to-do. But because this progress takes the form of increasing generosity, it brings real benefits to the poor. Kindness grows as it is exercised, but it is nonetheless unable to deal with poverty as a widespread social condition: "Individual *dana* [gifts of money and other valuables] will not provide a solution to global poverty." Indeed, it cannot provide sufficient relief and comfort for the most vulnerable groups in a single country or a single city. Hence, most of the religious traditions aim at some form of collective provision: a charity fund, a soup kitchen, a shelter for the homeless. The Catholic doctrine of subsidiarity suggests that this sort of help is best provided at the most local level, in the neighborhood, in the parish, by a confraternity or a holy society of volunteers who know the men and women they are helping.

But public relief on a much larger scale is necessary today, given the character of mass society, the mobility of populations, the impersonality of urban life, and the increasing invisibility of the poor. Now the state is the critical agent, and once the state is engaged with its extensive resources and power, the idea of relief is transformed into one or another version of abolition: the state is at "war" with poverty. It is, no doubt, a long war, but the goal is victory. Social movements and leftist political parties are part of the same war; they aim to influence state policy; they do not commonly engage in charitable activity themselves. I have described this as a modern phenomena, but the state or, better, the emperor, is a central agent in Confucian thought (in Hindu writings too) – and has been from the beginning. The extended family and the state are the arenas of poverty relief, reduction, and abolition in this tradition, and the head of state is judged by his success in sustaining or improving the material life of his subjects. He is the responsible agent, though if he fails to bring prosperity, he is himself subject only to "the mandate of heaven." His personal kindness is important, I suppose, but his intelligence and prudence are more important, for they enable him to fulfill the duties of his office. Intelligence and prudence count for a lot in the social democratic welfare state too, but now the responsibility of public officials is enforced by the political process with its periodic elections. Heaven's mandate has expired.

But does the work of the welfare state make religiously inspired kindness and generosity unnecessary? Clearly, it does not. In most welfare states, religious charities supplement public provision and greatly improve the quality of care available to the poor. When there is a company of volunteers alongside the company of civil servants, the welfare state is a much better place, and most of the volunteers in modern democratic welfare states are religiously motivated. The motivation is strong, because all the religious traditions hold that charitable gifts (of time and energy as well as money) are obligatory. They are not superogatory acts of kindness, but dutiful acts. Or, perhaps better, because I am not sure I understand how the different religions deal with this question, mercy and kindness are indeed voluntary, but somehow not entirely voluntary. Think about how "volunteering" often is not entirely voluntary in the army.

Once we know the agents of poverty relief and abolition, we need to ask whose agents they are: for whom do they act? Here we come to a standard polarity, familiar from discussions of many different issues, between particularism and universalism or between a local focus and a global focus. Are the poor whom we must help our brothers and sisters, our neighbors, our fellow believers, our fellow citizens (the plural possessive pronoun is crucial here) – or are they the distant others, the strangers, the poorest citizens of the poorest countries in the world? It is clear from these chapters that the local focus, with its crucial pronoun, is dominant almost everywhere. International distributive justice has received almost no attention at all from Muslim scholars, according to Sohail Hashmi. Arvind Sharma claims that some Hindu texts "could be adduced" in support of a global campaign against poverty, but he does not indicate that any texts have been so adduced. Peter Nosco argues, "The inward-looking tendencies of both Confucianism and Chinese civilization generally make it difficult to imagine circumstances under which Confucians would be exercised by poverty in alien lands." The case is the same for Judaism, according to Noam Zohar's report: "The idea of ... *tzedakah* duties toward faraway persons is, I believe, not encountered in traditional sources."

Marxism is obviously an internationalist doctrine, but its protagonists are not interested in poverty relief or abolition apart from the revolutionary project. Feminists are commonly universalists, seeking a global solidarity of women and a global empowerment, which would certainly address poverty issues among many others. Liberals of both sorts, egalitarian and libertarian, are committed to doctrines that have universal reach; both justice and property rights are supposed, if fully realized, to bring about the end of poverty everywhere. Libertarians are more interested in the economics of wealth production than in the politics of poverty reduction (the second of these, on their view, only gets in the way of the first). Egalitarian liberals are not, so far as I can tell, directly engaged in the politics of poverty reduction, and their political arguments are not driven primarily by the fact of poverty. To be sure, anger at injustice is often anger at the extent of the human suffering produced by poverty, but it is also, and among egalitarian writers more importantly, anger at inequality and exploitation. Their indignation is focused on the fact that some people live in mansions while others live in hovels, and that the fantastic wealth of the first group is produced at the expense of the second. Egalitarians, and feminists too, support state action both at home and abroad, though they do not have much to say about its possible forms. Libertarians, by contrast, trust in the global market (so long as it is free).

Christianity seems to be the only religious tradition that is explicitly committed to a universal concern for the poor (and, among natural law theorists, for social justice generally). The passages from Calvin quoted by Kent Van Til are telling, and I expect that similar quotations could be brought from many other writers. The Christian answer to the question "Who is my neighbor?" is radically universalist: any human being who needs my help. Still, Christians also believe that charity begins at home, and the Catholic doctrine of subsidiarity stands in tension with any effort to help distant strangers – though not, perhaps, with efforts to help them help themselves. Missionary work is one way of expressing this universal concern; it is also an almost paradigmatic example of relief rather than abolition. When pious Christians work in someone else's country, without access to political power (even when they are protected by a colonial regime), the work they can do is severely limited.

Enabling the distant poor to help themselves probably means enabling them to create a welfare state of their own. At least, that is the social-democratic argument I would defend. The state is the necessary agent of collective self-help. Only its officials can mobilize resources, assist in economic development, regulate the market, organize public education, and provide health care and social security. Global subsidiarity must focus on the state. Because states can also be predators, however, it is critical to aim at something like (as close as possible to) a democratic state – a state in the hands of its own citizens. I do not think that any of the religious traditions pay sufficient attention to the democratic state. Confucianism is, in a sense, a statist but also an authoritarian doctrine, and the Confucian emperor was never, in fact, an effective agent of poverty relief – for there was no branch of government, no countervailing social force, that could press him to take effective action. The revival of Confucianism in China today is certainly an improvement over communist totalitarianism – both for the poorest citizens and for everyone else. But descriptions of workers in the export factories of southern China sound very much like Engels's account of Manchester in 1844, which is not a sign of imperial or Central Committee solicitude. In any case, the record of modern despots is abysmal; they are more likely to intensify misery than to relieve it. Democracy is by far the best political foundation for poverty relief and abolition.

The politics of poverty figures hardly at all in the traditions, even the secular traditions, represented here. Marxists are interested in political agency but only for revolution, not for any of the more ordinary, day-in, day-out efforts to help the poor. Liberal egalitarians are concerned with the design of a just society but have little to say about its achievement. Libertarians do not believe in politics, except at the margins. Feminists are advocates of organization and empowerment, but their focus is narrow; it does not extend to the general abolition of poverty but aims to address only the special vulnerability of women and children. Only! In fact, this is an enormous project, and its realization would require a coalition that extended across gender lines – and class and ethnic and religious lines, too. The old labor movement is a model, undervalued and rarely considered among secular theorists today. Religious writers often gesture toward the role of public officials in the relief of poverty but have nothing to say about the political pressure necessary to make sure that the role is responsibly enacted. Here is the starkest version of the private-public polarity. Public action on behalf of the poor requires political enforcement; private action requires only moral education. And moral education is what all the religions' traditions aim at: the making of pious men and women, who will act out of loving kindness, individually and communally, to help the poor. This is not the educational purpose of the modern state, where schooling has different ends in view. Nor is it a sufficient guarantee that the state will do the work it must do if the poor are to get the help they need. At the end, poverty demands a political response.

Select Bibliography

World Poverty

Chambers, Robert. *Whose Reality Counts? Putting the First Last.* London: Intermediate Technology Publications, 1997.

Moser, Caroline. *Reducing Global Poverty: A Case for Asset Accumulation.* Washington, DC: Brookings Institution, 2007.

Narayan, Deepa, and B. Patel. *Voices of the Poor: Can Anyone Hear Us?* New York: Oxford University Press, 2000.

Sen, Amartya. *Development as Freedom.* New York: Oxford University Press, 1999.

Stewart, Frances, Ruhi Saith, and Barbara Harriss-White. *Defining Poverty in the Developing World.* New York: Palgrave Macmillan, 2007.

Buddhism

Bond, George D. *Buddhism at Work.* Sterling, VA: Kumarian Press, 2003.

Chambers, Robert. *Whose Reality Counts?* London: Intermediate Technology, 1997.

Loy, David. *The Great Awakening: A Buddhist Social Theory.* Boston: Wisdom Publications, 2003.

Macy, Joana R. *Dharma and Development: Religion as Resource in the Sarvodaya Self-Help Movement.* Sterling, VA: Kumarian Press, 1991.

Sizemore, Russell F., and Donald K. Swearer, eds. *Ethics, Wealth and Salvation: A Study in Buddhist Social Ethics.* Columbia: University of South Carolina Press, 1990.

Christianity

Groody, Daniel, ed. *The Option for the Poor in Christian Theology.* Notre Dame, IN: Notre Dame Press, 2007.

Hoppe, Leslie J. *There Shall Be No More Poor among You: Poverty in the Bible.* Nashville, TN: Abingdon Press, 2004.

Pattison, Bonnie L. *Poverty in the Theology of John Calvin*. Eugene, OR: Pickwick Publications, 2006.
Pixley, Jorge. *The Bible, the Church and the Poor*. Maryknoll, NY: Orbis, 1989.
Van Til, Kent. *Less Than $2.00 a Day: A Christian View of Global Poverty and the Free Market*. Grand Rapids, MI: Eerdmans, 2007.

Classical Liberalism

Ashton, T. S. *The Industrial Revolution*. New York: Oxford University Press, 1997.
Bastiat, Frederic. *Selected Essays on Political Economy*. Ed. George B. de Huszar. Irvington-on-Hudson: Foundation for Economic Education, 1995. See esp. "What Is Seen and What Is Not Seen," "The Law," and "The State."
Bauer, Peter. *From Subsistence to Exchange*. Princeton, NJ: Princeton University Press, 2000.
Beito, David. *From Mutual Aid to the Welfare State: Fraternal Societies and Social Services, 1890–1967*. Chapel Hill: University of North Carolina Press, 2000.
Green, David. *Working Class Patients and the Medical Establishment*. New York: St. Martin's Press, 1985.

Confucianism

Bell, Daniel A., and Hahm Chaibong, eds. *Confucianism for the Modern World*. Cambridge: Cambridge University Press, 2003.
Fan, Ruiping. "Reconstructionist Confucianism and Health Care: An Asian Moral Account of Healthcare Resource Allocation." *Journal of Medical Philosophy* 27, no. 6 (2002): 675–82.
Hansen, Chad. "Freedom and Moral Responsibility in Confucian Ethics." *Philosophy East and West* 22, no. 2 (1972): 169–86.
Lee, Seung-hwan. "Was There a Concept of Rights in Confucian Virtue-Based Morality." *Journal of Chinese Philosophy* 19 (1992): 241–61.
Rosemont, Henry, Jr. "Why Take Rights Seriously? A Confucian Critique." In *Human Rights and World Religions*, ed. Leroy S. Rouner, 167–82. Notre Dame, IN: University of Notre Dame Press, 1988.

Feminism

Chant, Sylvia. *Gender, Generation and Poverty: Exploring the "Feminisation of Poverty" in Africa, Asia and Latin America*. Northampton, MA: Edward Elgar, 2007.
Fuchs, Rachel. *Gender and Poverty in Nineteenth-Century Europe*. Cambridge: Cambridge University Press, 2005.
Hirschmann, Nancy J. *The Subject of Liberty: Toward a Feminist Theory of Freedom*. Princeton, NJ: Princeton University Press, 2003.
Hirschmann, Nancy J., and Ulrike Liebert, eds. *Women and Welfare: Theory and Practice in the United States and Europe*. New Brunswick, NJ: Rutgers University Press, 2001.
Nussbaum, Martha. *Women and Human Development: The Capabilities Approach*. Cambridge: Cambridge University Press, 2000.

Hinduism

Das, Gurcharan. *India Unbound*. New York: A. A. Knopf, 2001.
Misra, Vikas. *Hinduism and Economic Growth*. Bombay: Oxford University Press, 1962.
Rudolph, Lloyd I. *In Pursuit of Laksmi: The Political Economy of the Indian State*. Chicago: University of Chicago Press, 1987.
Sharma, Arvind. *The Hindu Scriptural Value System and the Economic Development of India*. New Delhi: Heritage, 1980.
"The Purusarthas: An Axiological Exploration of Hinduism." *Journal of Religious Ethics* 27, no. 2 (Summer 1999): 223–53.

Islam

Bonner, Michael, Mine Ener, and Amy Singer, eds. *Poverty and Charity in Middle Eastern Contexts*. Albany: State University of New York Press, 2003.
Iqbal, Munawar, ed. *Islamic Economic Institutions and the Elimination of Poverty*. Leicester, UK: Islamic Foundation, 2002.
Kuran, Timur. *Islam and Mammon: The Economic Predicaments of Islamism*. Princeton, NJ: Princeton University Press, 2004.
al-Qardawi, Yusuf. *Fiqh az-Zakat: A Comparative Study*. Trans. Monzer Kahf. London: Dar al-Taqwa, 1999.
ur-Rahman, Afzal. *Economic Doctrines of Islam*. Lahore: Islamic Publications, 1995.

Judaism

Flusser, David. "Blessed are the Poor in Spirit...." *Israel Exploration Journal* 10 (1960): 1–13.
Jacobs, Jill. *There Shall Be No Needy: Pursuing Social Justice through Jewish Law and Tradition*. Woodstock, VT: Jewish Lights, 2009.
Levine, Aaron. *Economic Public Policy and Jewish Law*. Hoboken: Ktav; New York: Yeshiva University Press, 1993.
Maimonides, Moses. "Laws of Gifts to the Poor." In *The Code of Maimonides [Mishneh Torah], Book 7: Agriculture*, (Part X), trans. Isaac Klein, chap. 7. New Haven: Yale University Press, 1979.
Walzer, Michael, Menachem Lorberbaum, Noam Zohar, et al., eds. " Taxation " and "Welfare." In *The Jewish Political Tradition, vol. 3: Community*. New Haven: Yale University Press, forthcoming.

Liberal Egalitarianism

Beitz, Charles R. *Political Theory and International Relations*. Princeton, NJ: Princeton University Press, 1979.
Dworkin, Ronald. *Sovereign Virtue*. Cambridge, MA: Harvard University Press, 2000.
Pogge, Thomas. *World Poverty and Human Rights*. London: Polity Press, 2002.
Rawls, John. *A Theory of Justice*. Cambridge, MA: Harvard University Press, 1971; rev. ed., 1999.

Sen, Amartya. *Inequality Reexamined*. Cambridge, MA: Harvard University Press, 1992.

Marxism

Cohen, G. A. *Karl Marx's Theory of History: A Defence*. Princeton, NJ: Princeton University Press, 2000.

Elster, Jon. *An Introduction to Karl Marx*. Cambridge: Cambridge University Press, 2008.

Levine, Andrew. *A Future for Marxism?* London: Pluto Press, 2003.

Lukes, Steven. *Marxism and Morality*. New York: Oxford University Press, 1987.

Marx, Karl. *Selected Writings*. Ed. David McClellan. 2nd ed. New York: Oxford University Press, 2000.

Natural Law

Cunningham, Lawrence S. *Intractable Disputes about the Natural Law: Alasdair MacIntyre and Critics*. Notre Dame, IN: University of Notre Dame Press, 2009.

Finnis, John. *Natural Laws and Natural Rights*. Oxford: Clarendon Press, 1980.

Porter, Jean. *Nature as Reason*. Grand Rapids, MI: Eerdmans, 2005.

Rushton, Roger. *Human Rights and the Image of God*. London: SCM, 2004.

Simon, Yves. *The Tradition of Natural Law*. New York: Fordham University Press, 1992.

Index

direct relief, 12–13
Dirty Hands (Sartre), 249–50
distributive justice, 238–39
divorce
    Judaism and, 211
    women and, 145, 153–54
Dogen, 55
$1 a day, 20, 21, 23, 136–37, 229
dominium, 273
Dong Zhongshu, 116
dukkha (ill-being), 6–7, 45, 46–47, 56
Durkheim, Emile, 242–43
dvijas, 168
Dworkin, Ronald, 225, 239–40
    envy test and, 228
    luck egalitarianism and, 227–28
    talents and, 228

EAP. *See* East Asia and Pacific
Earned Income Tax Credit, 147–48
East Asia and Pacific (EAP), 29–30
    life expectancy in, 26
    literacy rate in, 25
    mortality rate in, 26
    PPP in, 23
    women in, 137–38
ebyon, 63
ECA. *See* Europe and Central Asia
Eden, Frederic, 103–4
education, 27
    inequality in, 37–38
    Locke and, 156–57
    marriage, 147–48
    women and, 137–38
Egalitarian Liberalism, 6–7
Egypt, 12, 29–30, 197
employment, 19
    character and, 154
    Christianity and, 74
    Islam and, 190
    Judaism and, 218
    PRWORA and, 148
    TANF and, 148
emptiness, 45, 53
encomienda, 273–74
End of Poverty (Sachs), 39–40
Engels, Friedrich, 257–58. See also
    Communist Manifesto, The

environmental exploitation, 40
envy test, 228
epistemological break, 245
equality, 18, 101. *See also* feminism
equalization of achievements, 227
equalization of the means to achieve-
    ments, 227
Essay on the Poor Law (Locke), 150
ethic of responsibility, 250
ethical theories, 243
ethics
    of Confucianism, 129
    feminism and, 134
    of Greeks, 243
    of public goods, 110
Ethics of Redistribution, The
    (Jouvenel), 107
Eucharist, 78
eudaimonia, 267
Europe and Central Asia (ECA)
    GDP history in, 86
    life expectancy in, 26
    literacy rate in, 25
    mortality rate in, 26
    PPP in, 23
European Union, 16–17
evyon, 209

fair equality of opportunity, 239–40
    Barry, B., and, 240
famine
    in China, 121
    in India, 162–63
Fan Zhongyan, 122
FDI. *See* foreign direct investment
feminism, 7–8, 134–59, 292
    classical liberalism and, 155–59
    ethics and, 134
    Islam and, 194
    Marxism and, 257–58
    violence and, 10
feng shui, 116
filial piety, 117
Finnis, John, 265, 276–80
    property and, 277
First Treatise of Government (Locke),
    105
Five Classics, of Confucianism, 115

usury and, 199–201
women and, 140, 192–94, 197–98
Islam, Tazul, 137–38
Islamic Economics, 13
Islamic Society of North America,
     202–3
Israel, 205, 210, 211
issa (envy), 46
ius gentium (right of nations), 268
ius utendi, 64
Iyer, Balasubramania, 177

Jacobinism, 253
Jainism, 160
James (Jesus's brother), 65
jātis, 167–68, 169
Jesus, 63, 67, 79–80
  as Messiah, 73
  Sermon on the Mount by, 63–64
Jim Crow laws, 103–4
Johannesburg Conference on
     Sustainable Development, 38–39
John XXIII (Pope), 66
Jones, John D., 269–70
Jordan, Z. A., 253
Joseph of Arimathea, 80
Jouvenel, Bertrand de, 107
Judaism, 2, 204–19
  divorce and, 211
  employment and, 218
  marriage and, 210–11
  property in, 64–65
  women and, 210
Judgment Day, 73–74
Julian (Roman emperor), 76
junzi (gentleman), 115
Just Assassins, The (Sartre), 250–51
Just War, 10, 274

kāma, 165–66, 177
Kane, P. V., 178
Kant, Emmanuel, 243, 245–46
  Weber and, 250
Kantianism, 224, 248
  Marxism and, 260–61
  natural law and, 276
Kapp, K. W., 161–62
karma, 7–8, 44–61, 172

bhikkhu and, 51–52
  rebirth and, 52–53
  women and, 50
Kenya, 27
ketubah (marriage contract), 210–11
khalifa, 183
Khuankaew, Ouyporn, 50
kibbutz, 213
Kicking Away the Ladder (Ha-Joon
     Chang), 40
King, Martin Luther, Jr., 268
Kingdom of God, 73
Kittay, Eva, 143–44
Knights of Pythias, 105
Knights of Tabor, 103–4
Kok-Chor tan, 238–39
Korea, income in, 20–21
Kṣatriyas, 167–68

LAC. *See* Latin America and
     Caribbean
Lactantius, 76–77
laissez faire, 111
Lal, Deepak, 161–62
land
  Confucianism and, 121
  women and, 139
las Casas, Bartolomé de, 10, 265,
     272–75
  Aristotle and, 273
Lasalle, Ferdinand, 260
Last Supper, 78
late capitalism, 255–56
Latin America and Caribbean (LAC),
     30
  life expectancy in, 26
  literacy rate in, 25
  mortality rate in, 26
  PPP in, 23
laws of fellowship, 103
laws of motion, capitalism and, 256
LDCs. *See* Least Developed Countries
Least Developed Countries (LDCs),
     20–21
Lectures on Jurisprudence, The (Smith,
     A.), 84
Lenin, Vladimir, 251–52
Leo XIII (Pope), 66

Printed in the USA
CPSIA information can be obtained
at www.ICGtesting.com
LVHW040504310723
753816LV00001B/40